BIRDS

OF EUROPE, NORTH AFRICA, AND THE MIDDLE EAST

A PHOTOGRAPHIC GUIDE

Copyright © 2017 by Princeton University Press

Published by Princeton University Press, 41 William Street, Princeton, New Jersey 08540
In the United Kingdom: Princeton University Press, 6 Oxford Street, Woodstock, Oxfordshire OX20 1TR

Originally published in French as *Tous les oiseaux d'Europe* © Delachaux et Niestlé, Paris 2015

All rights reserved

ISBN (pbk) 978-0-691-17243-9

Library of Congress Control Number: 2016945500

British Library Cataloging-in-Publication Data is available

This book has been composed in Minion and ITC Franklin Gothic

Printed on acid-free paper. ∞

English edition typeset by D & N Publishing, Baydon, Wiltshire, UK

Printed in France

10 9 8 7 6 5 4 3 2 1

BIRDS

OF EUROPE, NORTH AFRICA, AND THE MIDDLE EAST
A PHOTOGRAPHIC GUIDE

FRÉDÉRIC JIGUET &
AURÉLIEN AUDEVARD
TRANSLATED BY TONY WILLIAMS

Princeton University Press

Princeton and Oxford

Contents

Introduction

Birds are present in all environments, from mountaintops to city centres, and some seabirds even spend most of their lives in the open ocean, far from land. Most common species are easy to see and may be spotted by anyone, be it pigeons in town squares, gulls at the seaside or ducks on a park lake. In fact, three species of pigeons occur in our towns, at least four species of gulls are common enough to be seen on all our beaches, and there are more than ten species of ducks that regularly occur on inland lakes. Everyone knows the Cuckoo's song, but few know what it really looks like and even fewer that the plumage of male, female and young are different. It is therefore tempting to want to get to know the birds that occur around us.

There are some ten thousand species of birds worldwide, around 860 of which have been observed in Europe. This complete guide includes all the European species, illustrated with photos and notes that allow the main identification characteristics to be seen at a glance. A few lines about each family or genus help to identify these convenient groupings rapidly. Then, each species is presented with a short account, giving essential information on specific identification, voice, habitat and distribution. The **Identification** section includes average size (length), or wingspan for birds of prey and certain seabirds. Distinctive features of the different plumages are noted, as well as any characteristic behaviour. Differences between well-marked races/subspecies (ssp.) are noted where relevant.

The **Voice** section gives a brief description of the male's song, when it is a useful way of finding the species, and/or the species' normal call, usually its contact call. Putting into words the sounds emitted by a bird is fraught with difficulty, but the suggested transcriptions should help the reader to imagine the sounds concerned.

Black-winged Stilt trying to catch an insect.

The **Habitat** section details the main habitats used by a species, stating differences between summer and winter habitats when relevant, as some species have different preferences according to the season. Finally, the distribution maps distinguish between areas frequented whilst breeding (red), wintering (pale blue) or throughout the year (purple). Species without a map are those that occur as vagrants or have been introduced locally.

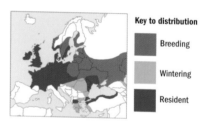

Key to distribution

Breeding

Wintering

Resident

Taxonomy and species names have seen much change recently. There are a number of authoritative lists of both English and scientific names, none of which exactly matches each other. Here, species are presented in a modern taxonomic order as far as possible. The English names are those most frequently used and a few alternative names are given where relevant. The prefixes in brackets indicate international names (the shorter name without the prefix is the one usually used in Europe). Scientific names are those that are most widely accepted.

Identifying a bird

In order to identify a species in view, certain criteria may be useful. Some species are quite easy to identify, from one or two distinctive features not shared by other species. Others can only be determined by using a combination of features. Important criteria are often: overall size, structure and silhouette, behaviour, voice and, of course, plumage colour and that of the bare parts.

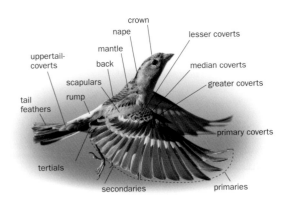

STRUCTURE AND SILHOUETTE

The general appearance of a bird depends on its shape, its structure, including length and shape of bill, legs, wings and tail, and the bird's body form and perceived centre of gravity. Wings may be short or long, pointed or round, longer than the tail when the bird is at rest, or shorter. The distance between the tip of the primaries and that of the tertials (the 'primary projection') is often very useful in separating similar species such as reed warblers or leaf warblers.

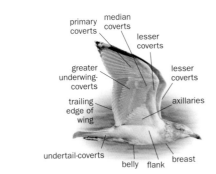

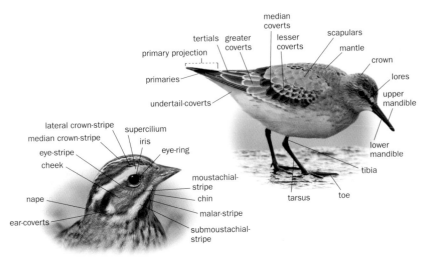

In certain raptor species, females are bigger than males. In the larger gulls it is the male that is bigger with a more massive silhouette, but it may be difficult to differentiate between the smallest males and the biggest females; thus it is often possible to determine the sex of two members of a pair when they are side by side, especially if typical of the sex. However, the majority cannot be sexed simply by size.

PLUMAGE AND BARE PARTS

Identifying birds often necessitates knowing the name and location of the different types of feathers that cover the body. Forehead, crown, nape, mantle, back, rump, uppertail-coverts and tail feathers succeed each other from the bill to the tail. On the wing, lesser, median and greater coverts protect the base of the secondaries on the arm. The innermost secondaries, shorter than the others but covering them on the closed wing, are called tertials. The four annotated photographs on the previous page name the main body parts and principal feather tracts. The bare parts are all those areas of horn or skin not covered with feathers: bill, legs, claws, iris and sometimes the eye-ring. Bill size and shape are often important in identifying a species but may vary according to age, sex or even between individuals. In the larger gulls, the colour of the bill, legs and iris change according to age, the fully adult colours only being acquired after 4 or 5 years. In many waders, the female's bill is longer than the male's. Iris colour can help in determining a bird's age or sex. In harriers, adult males have a pale eye and young males in their first autumn already have a very pale iris compared to that of females, although their plumages are identical. In reed and Sylvia warblers the iris is reddish-brown in adults but grey-brown in first-year birds.

The Marsh Harrier's iris is yellow in the adult male, pale brown in the female and black in immatures.

VOICE

A feature of birds is that most are very vocal. Vocalisations are often quite varied as they differ according to their use: defending territory, begging for food, distracting an intruder, contact call, alarm call, distress call – the list is long. Young birds often have a different call from that of the adult. Many species have local dialects with variations in the phrases of their songs, but tonality is

A snipe pushes its bill deep into the mud, searching out worms with the tip of its bill.

A heron captures its prey (often fish, here a newt) by stabbing it with its bill.

A flamingo often sleeps on one leg.

A spoonbill filters water by sweeping the surface with the tip of its bill.

normally unchanged. Quite a few species also mimic and include the songs of other species; the sounds copied obviously depend on what that individual has heard before.

BEHAVIOUR

The way in which a bird stands, flies, walks or feeds is often characteristic. The flamingo sleeps on one leg; the heron captures its prey by stabbing it with its bill; the spoonbill filters water with sweeping movements of the bill on the water surface; the snipe pushes its bill deep into the mud, searching for worms by touch; the crossbill uses its crossed bill to extract seeds from conifer cones. Typical examples of behaviour are as numerous as the species themselves, but what is important to remember is the visible behaviour of a species when it is observed.

LIGHT AND WEATHER

A bird's silhouette and activity vary according to prevailing conditions. The grey tone of a gull's back won't appear the same if the bird is seen in full sunlight, under an overcast sky, or against the light. It is always a good idea to compare colours with nearby birds. When it's cold, birds puff up their plumage to trap air that serves as thermal insulation. The body thus appears big and round, and the entire silhouette is different. When it's windy, a bird on the ground will tend to face towards the wind, its feathers pressed against its body; it then appears slimmer and longer. It is important to keep these possibilities of a different perception of silhouette and structure in mind, as in many cases identification depends on comparison with similar species that have, for example, a darker or duller colour, or a plumper or longer body. Wet feathers often appear darker, and a damp forehead will be flatter with the bill appearing longer.

MOULT

Birds' feathers wear, abrade and are regularly renewed. Most small birds renew their body feathers twice a year, the larger wing and tail feathers once a year. It takes more than two years for a big bird of prey to change all its flight feathers. The moult of flight and tail feathers often occurs in late summer, or on arriving at African wintering grounds for long distance migrants (e.g. reed warblers). During moult, some feathers are short as they are still growing. When moult is complete, the new feathers are longer and often more colourful than those they have just replaced.

The silhouette of the same bird can change according to its position and its attitude, as seen here in a juvenile Dotterel.

On the wing of a large eagle, all the flight feathers are the same length during the bird's first year and the trailing edge of the wing is more or less straight; during the second year those feathers that have been moulted will be longer and the trailing edge of the wing will appear irregular, with a ragged edge.

Many species have different plumages in summer and winter. In the breeding season, males are generally looking their best and most colourful, in order to seduce a female. These brighter feathers are moulted at the end of the summer, often for a duller winter plumage, which is less visible to predators. During moult the visible structure of a bird may change. A typical example is wing length and shape. Different species of plover can be identified in part by the relative lengths of tail, wing-tips and tertials. If the longest primaries are in growth, or if the tertials are in growth, the perception of the bird's structure is altered.

The basic principles of birdwatching briefly presented here should help to understand the possible variations in the identification criteria for each species that are given in the species texts. This will allow not only the naming of a species but also sometimes to go further and try to ascertain the age and sex of the observed bird. You can now discover all of Europe's bird species and understand the criteria used in their identification

The Bar-tailed Godwit's dull winter plumage and colourful breeding plumage.

SWANS Large waterfowl with white plumage (except rare, introduced Black Swan); young greyish.
All species fly with extended neck. Note variation in bill size, shape and colour. Inhabit waterbodies.

Mute Swan *Cygnus olor*

Juvenile

grey plumage

extended
neck in flight

dark bill

arched wings
during display

orange bill
with black
knob

Adult

Immature

dull bill

IDENTIFICATION
150 cm. Large,
thick neck,
round head,
black triangular
mask in front of
eye. Black knob at base of bill, larger in
male. Adult with bright orange bill,
juvenile's is grey. Displaying male swims
forward with wings lifted and feathers
spread. Often aggressive near the nest;
gregarious in winter. **VOICE** Loud whistle
from wings in flight. Call when annoyed is
a whistled, varying grunt. **HABITAT** Lakes,
fishponds, canals, even in urban areas.

Black Swan *Cygnus atratus*

Adult

frosted black
plumage

bright red
bill with
pale band

130 cm. Very elegant, with slim neck,
frosted black plumage, bright red bill
with pale vertical band. An escape (of
Australasian origin); a few pairs breed at
scattered sites, where they winter.

Tundra Swan *Cygnus columbianus*

IDENTIFICATION
120 cm. Very similar to Whooper Swan but smaller, thicker neck, shorter bill is black with basal yellow patch with rounded edge (ssp. *bewickii*). Less yellow than in Whooper Swan, not reaching nostril; variable extent of yellow, sometimes reduced to small spot in front of eye, particularly in the Nearctic race *columbianus* (which has been observed in Europe) – beware, bills covered in mud may appear black. Young grey with dull bill. **VOICE** Call is a honk, given once or twice. **HABITAT** Large quiet waterbodies surrounded by crops or meadows.

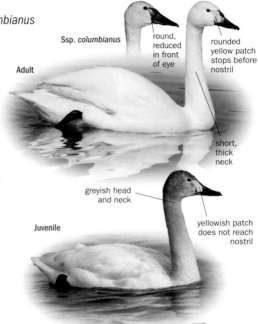

Ssp. *columbianus*

round, reduced in front of eye

rounded yellow patch stops before nostril

Adult

short, thick neck

greyish head and neck

Juvenile

yellowish patch does not reach nostril

Whooper Swan *Cygnus cygnus*

IDENTIFICATION
150 cm. As large as Mute Swan (p. 12), but slimmer. Pure white plumage. Very long neck often held vertically, long conical, bright yellow bill with black tip; the yellow comes to a point under the nostril. Juvenile greyish with dull bill. **VOICE** Loud, bugling calls, often 3 or 4 at a time. Faint whistling from wings in flight. **HABITAT** Winters on quiet waterbodies, also feeding in nearby fields.

long slim neck

Adult

yellow patch comes to a point under the nostril

greyish plumage

whitish base to bill reaching nostril

Juvenile

GREY GEESE Several species of varying size, all of which are very gregarious; one breeds in Britain, the others are winter visitors. Note size and shape, bill and foot colour, and also characteristics of forehead, neck and belly. Adults have a pale bill tip (nail), which is black in juveniles. In winter, immature birds have mantle feathers of mixed age; adults have completed their moult with feathers of the same age.

(Greater) White-fronted Goose
Anser albifrons

wide white border

brown forehead

Adult
ssp. *albifrons*

dark grey

Juvenile
ssp. *flavirostris*

forehead and
base of bill white

orange
bill

short,
pale pink
bill

uniform
belly

Adult
ssp. *albifrons*

dark bars on
belly

IDENTIFICATION
71 cm. Small
goose with a
short, conical,
pale pink bill
(ssp. *albifrons*),
white forehead with vertical edge (brown in young in early winter), large irregular black bars on the belly (sometimes absent in first-winter birds). Underparts very dark in flight, black tail with white border. The *flavirostris* race (breeds in Greenland) has an orange bill, and dark head with a non-contrasting eye. **VOICE** High-pitched call, more musical and less nasal than that of Greylag, *kiou-iou*. **HABITAT** Breeds in Arctic tundra, winters near extensive, quiet waterbodies with surrounding crops.

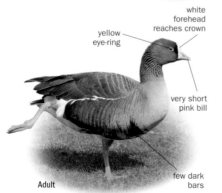

white
forehead
reaches crown

yellow
eye-ring

very short
pink bill

Adult

few dark
bars

Lesser White-fronted Goose
Anser erythropus

IDENTIFICATION 61 cm. Rare, most coming from reintroduced populations in Scandinavia, wintering in the Netherlands. Very similar to White-fronted Goose but smaller, more compact, with short neck, small round head, very short, pale pink bill and narrow yellow eye-ring; the white front goes further back over forehead than in White-fronted. Few black bars on the belly. Very similar to White-fronted Goose in flight. **VOICE** Like White-fronted Goose but higher-pitched.

Greylag Goose *Anser anser*

IDENTIFICATION
80 cm. Large
goose, the most
massive, with
thick neck, large
bill, pink feet
and pale belly. In flight, pale ash-grey
wing-coverts contrast with mantle. Rump
paler than mantle; pale tail with broad
white edge. Bill orange (ssp. *anser*,
breeds W Europe), bright pink in ssp.
rubirostris (E Europe and Siberia); need
good light for certain racial identification.
VOICE Call is nasal, loud *kia-ga-ga, ang-
ang.* **HABITAT** Waterbodies, meadows and
crops; feeds on grass and tubers.

broad white edge

ash-grey
bands

Adult
ssp. *anser*

greyer
mantle

bright
pink bill

large
orange bill

Adult ssp. *rubirostris*

Adult
ssp. *anser*

thick
neck

pale
belly

pink
feet

Pink-footed Goose *Anser brachyrhynchus*

IDENTIFICATION
70 cm. Very
similar to Bean
Goose (p.16),
small, compact,
short bill with
pink subterminal patch. Very dark head
and neck, mantle frosted ash-grey, grey
tail with large white border; bright pink
feet. **VOICE** Call similar to that of Bean
Goose but a little higher-pitched.
HABITAT As other geese
in winter.

tail mainly
white

wings
ash-grey

very pink
bill

2 generations
of feathers
(moult)

thick
neck

frosted mantle,
feathers identical

short bill
with pink
bar

Juvenile

bright
pink feet

Adult

BEAN GOOSE The two forms of Bean Goose are sometimes considered to be two different species. They are presented separately here.

'Tundra' Bean Goose *Anser fabalis rossicus*

dark mantle and head

short bill, black with small orange band

Adult

orange feet

very dark wings

thin white border

IDENTIFICATION
75 cm. Smaller and less slender than 'Taiga' Bean Goose, neck thicker. Dark brown mantle, neck and head darker, black tail with indistinct white border. Orange feet. Black bill with more or less vertical, narrow, subterminal orange band. Bill shorter, thicker and less orange than that of 'Taiga' Bean Goose. Some young have largely pale orange bill, with white margin around base of bill on forehead. In flight, wings dark with fine pale border. **VOICE** Call *ank-ank*, of variable tone. **HABITAT** In winter, meadows, crops, near large, quiet waterbodies.

'Taiga' Bean Goose *Anser fabalis fabalis*

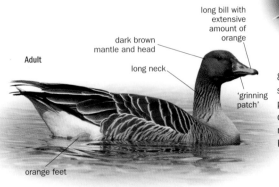

long bill with extensive amount of orange

dark brown mantle and head

Adult

long neck

'grinning patch'

no black bars

orange feet

85 cm. As 'Tundra' Bean Goose but more slender, longer neck. Bill longer with less prominent 'grinning patch', orange colour often more extensive, as high as the nostrils, but large amount of variation. Head and mantle slightly lighter.

VAGRANT OR ESCAPED GEESE Three rare species, two Nearctic and one Asian, individuals of which are sometimes seen in company of other geese. Only the Nearctic species are considered to have potentially arrived naturally.

Snow Goose *Anser caerulescens*

65–75 cm. Replaces Greylag Goose in North America. White plumage with black primaries, pink bill with visible black 'grinning patch'. The 'blue' morph has a blue-grey body, white vent, white neck with a dark line up the side. The wing pattern separates it from white domestic Greylags. Some feral populations have become established in Europe and escapes occur regularly; birds of wild origin are rare vagrants.

white plumage

black primaries

pink bill with visible black 'grinning patch'

Adult

Blue morph

Ross's Goose *Anser rossii*

55–65 cm. Very similar to Snow Goose, but clearly smaller, with small, blue-based pink bill. Very rare vagrant originating from Arctic Canada; escapes more likely.

Adult

black primaries

white plumage

short, blue-based pink bill

horizontal black bars

orange bill

Bar-headed Goose *Anser indicus*

73 cm. Resembles a Greylag Goose, but has ash-grey body and dark bar in front and at back of neck, rear of crown black with 2 black lines joining eye and cheek in adults; the rest of head white, bill and feet orange. Escapes; a few established birds breed.

white neck with dark brown border

mantle and belly ash-grey

Adult

BLACK GEESE Dark geese, mainly of Nearctic origin, with populations in Siberia, Svalbard and Greenland. Winter visitors, except for the introduced Canada Goose, which is now widespread.

Brent Goose *Branta bernicla*

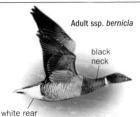

Adult ssp. *bernicla*

black neck

white rear

Juvenile ssp. *hrota*

small collar

short black bill

white half-collar

pale flanks

grey-brown flanks

Adult ssp. *bernicla*

collar almost invisible

white spots

Juvenile ssp. *bernicla*

very noticeable white collar

Adults and juvenile ssp. *nigricans*

grey-black back

blackish and white flanks

Adult ssp. *bernicla*

IDENTIFICATION 58 cm. Very dark small goose, head, neck and breast black, flank colour variable according to subspecies. Incomplete white collar on sides of neck. Young birds with white fringes on wing-coverts, absent or poorly marked collar. Pale-bellied Brent (ssp. *hrota*, breeds in Svalbard, Greenland and Arctic Canada): pale grey flanks extensively marked with white; belly between legs white. Dark-bellied Brent (ssp. *bernicla*, breeds in Siberia): dark grey flanks, fewer white marks less defined towards the rear, belly between legs frosted dark. Black Brant (ssp. *nigricans*, breeds in Pacific Arctic): greyish-black flanks, uniform and same colour as belly in front, extensively marked with white at the rear; grey-black back, darker than *bernicla*; black patch on belly between legs; noticeable white collar, often joined in front of neck; often with rounder head and shorter bill. **VOICE** Low, guttural *rrron-rrron...* **HABITAT** Extensive bays, mudflats, estuaries, rocky coastlines at low tide, where it feeds on seaweeds.

Barnacle Goose *Branta leucopsis*

IDENTIFICATION
64 cm. Recalls
Brent Goose,
but very pale
grey flanks, ash-
grey back
marked with black lines, and white face
with black lores contrasting with black
neck. All-black tail. In flight, underwings
quite uniform ash-grey. **VOICE** Call a
barked *ka*, a single syllable of varied
tone. **HABITAT** Meadows near the coast
and quiet waterbodies.

black lores

ash-grey back marked with
black lines

white cheeks
and forehead,
sometimes
yellowish

Adult

very pale grey
flanks

black
tail

pale belly

Red-breasted Goose *Branta ruficollis*

IDENTIFICATION 57 cm.
Breeds in eastern Siberia.
Small, dark goose with very
thick neck and very short
black bill; black mantle,
black flanks with large white
band along wing; brick-red front of neck and cheeks.
Two narrow white bars on wing-coverts in adult, less
well-marked bars in juvenile.

brick-red
neck

black
tail

black
belly

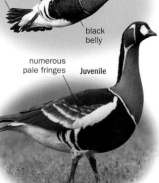

numerous
pale fringes   **Juvenile**

white bars

black mantle

Adult

small
black bill

brick-red
front of
neck and
cheeks

black-
and-white
flanks

Canada Goose *Branta canadensis*

Ssp. *parvipes*

meduim-length black neck

small straight bill

white band on chin

long black neck

white cheek

brown-grey flanks and mantle

Adult ssp. *interior/canadensis*

IDENTIFICATION 80–105 cm. Very large goose, long, black neck with white cheeks that join on the throat. Quite uniform mottled grey-brown plumage, black tail and white rump. Bill black. Body and bill size variable according to subspecies: *canadensis* and *interior* races are largest, long bodied and have long bill with straight upper edge; *parvipes* race is smallest, approaching size of Cackling Goose, but has longer bill with straight upper edge. **VOICE** Call is a loud, trumpeted *or-lu*. **HABITAT** Breeds on lakes, even in urban areas.

Cackling Goose *Branta hutchinsii*

Ssp. *hutchinsii*

short, thick neck

short, stout bill

pale breast

tiny bill

Ssp. *minima*

dark breast

IDENTIFICATION 60–70 cm. Sister to the Canada Goose, but smaller and more compact, with short neck, round head and steep forehead, shorter bill and peaked on top of upper mandible, with a prominent nail. The *hutchinsii* race (Atlantic northern Canada, possible wild origin of a few vagrant birds): large, but even so smaller than Canada Goose, from which it differs in the size and shape of bill; breast usually pale. The *minima* race (Pacific northern Canada, escapes from captivity): very small, dark breast, often with white collar and very small bill.

Common Shelduck *Tadorna tadorna*

IDENTIFICATION
60 cm. Large pied duck, white body, black neck and head (with bottle-green sheen), wide black collar, black band along centre of belly. Bright red bill, with basal knob (in male), pink legs. Juvenile duller with brown neck and white face. In flight, white wings with black primaries. Nests in burrows. **VOICE** Call a nasal *ga-ga-ga-ga...* a *slis-slis-slis* when displaying. **HABITAT** Marshes, mudflats, saltpans, large estuaries, along the coast.

Adult female

Male in flight

black bands

dull bill

green speculum

black-and-white wings

red knob

green sheen

pink legs

Adult male

reddish-brown band

Ruddy Shelduck *Tadorna ferruginea*

IDENTIFICATION
64 cm. Large reddish duck of arid habitats in North Africa and Middle East; introduced in Europe, scattered breeding populations. Bicoloured wings, black primaries with white wing-coverts. Male has a narrow black collar and pale beige head. Female without collar, with beige face. **VOICE** Call a nasal trumpeting. **HABITAT** Inland lakes, rivers, marshes, sometimes far from water.

without a collar

Female

pale head

black collar

reddish body

grey legs

black primaries

Male

Egyptian Goose *Alopochen aegyptiaca*

68 cm. Large duck resembling a dull Ruddy Shelduck but with black-bordered pink bill, grey head with reddish mask around eye, beige breast with central black spot, bright pink legs. Originates in Africa, including the Nile valley. Escape from captivity, established.

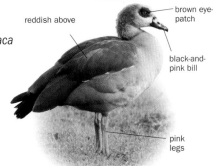

brown eye-patch

reddish above

black-and-pink bill

pink legs

DABBLING DUCKS Several species in which the females are very similar, but silhouette, bill and speculum (coloured wing panel in ducks) colour allows for them all to be identified.
In summer males are in 'eclipse' plumage resembling that of the female but more uniform; bill colour remains typical of the male.

Mallard *Anas platyrhynchos*

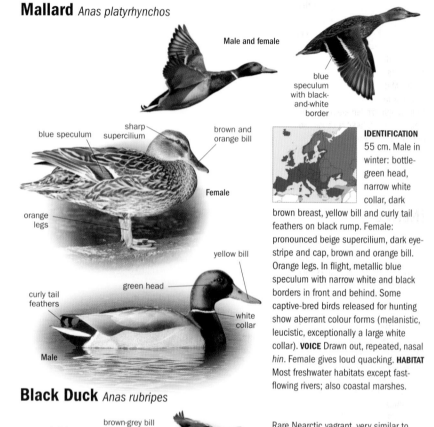

Male and female

blue speculum with black-and-white border

blue speculum

sharp supercilium

brown and orange bill

Female

orange legs

curly tail feathers

green head

Male

white collar

yellow bill

IDENTIFICATION
55 cm. Male in winter: bottle-green head, narrow white collar, dark brown breast, yellow bill and curly tail feathers on black rump. Female: pronounced beige supercilium, dark eye-stripe and cap, brown and orange bill. Orange legs. In flight, metallic blue speculum with narrow white and black borders in front and behind. Some captive-bred birds released for hunting show aberrant colour forms (melanistic, leucistic, exceptionally a large white collar). **VOICE** Drawn out, repeated, nasal *hin*. Female gives loud quacking. **HABITAT** Most freshwater habitats except fast-flowing rivers; also coastal marshes.

Black Duck *Anas rubripes*

dark brown plumage

brown-grey bill

Female

white underwings

uniform blackish-brown body

greenish-yellow bill

Male

Rare Nearctic vagrant, very similar to Mallard but entirely blackish-brown plumage, metallic blue speculum with black border without any white. Bill yellow (male) or brown (female). Hybrids with Mallard possible: paler plumage with a narrow white border in speculum and males with curled tail feathers.

Gadwall *Anas strepera*

IDENTIFICATION
51 cm. Male grey with black rear and white speculum, inner secondaries white, median secondaries black and outer ones grey. Female resembles female Mallard. Black bill in male, orange with black ridge in female. **VOICE** Male: rough *rrrr*, female quacks like female Mallard. **HABITAT** Larger, well-vegetated freshwater bodies.

white speculum

rusty band

Male in flight

all grey with black rear

white speculum

Male

black bill

white speculum often visible

uniform brown-grey head

Female

orange bill with black ridge

(Northern) Pintail *Anas acuta*

IDENTIFICATION
56 cm (plus 10 cm of long thin tail in male). Slender duck, grey, long neck, long tail. Male: dark brown head with white line along side of neck, bicoloured bill, grey with black ridge; long tail streamers. Female slim and long, dark grey bill, uniform brown-grey face without a supercilium. Metallic green speculum with wide white trailing edge. **VOICE** Male: short, rapid, smooth whistle in 2 phrases, *tii-lii*. **HABITAT** Breeds on lakes and tundra pools in N Europe, winters further south; in Europe on well-vegetated lakes and estuaries.

grey wings

long neck

green speculum framed rufous and white

bluish bill

Male in flight, eclipse plumage

uniform brown face

long black bill

Female

bluish-grey legs

long streamers

brown head and long white neck

grey and black bill

Male

vermiculated flanks

(Northern) Shoveler *Anas clypeata*

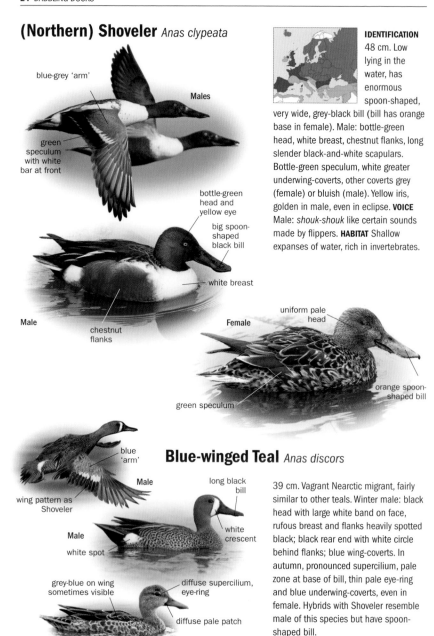

blue-grey 'arm'

Males

green
speculum
with white
bar at front

bottle-green
head and
yellow eye

big spoon-
shaped
black bill

white breast

Male

chestnut
flanks

Female

uniform pale
head

orange spoon-
shaped bill

green speculum

IDENTIFICATION
48 cm. Low
lying in the
water, has
enormous
spoon-shaped,
very wide, grey-black bill (bill has orange
base in female). Male: bottle-green
head, white breast, chestnut flanks, long
slender black-and-white scapulars.
Bottle-green speculum, white greater
underwing-coverts, other coverts grey
(female) or bluish (male). Yellow iris,
golden in male, even in eclipse. **VOICE**
Male: *shouk-shouk* like certain sounds
made by flippers. **HABITAT** Shallow
expanses of water, rich in invertebrates.

blue
'arm'

Male

wing pattern as
Shoveler

Male

white spot

grey-blue on wing
sometimes visible

Blue-winged Teal *Anas discors*

long black
bill

white
crescent

diffuse supercilium,
eye-ring

diffuse pale patch

Female and juvenile

39 cm. Vagrant Nearctic migrant, fairly
similar to other teals. Winter male: black
head with large white band on face,
rufous breast and flanks heavily spotted
black; black rear end with white circle
behind flanks; blue wing-coverts. In
autumn, pronounced supercilium, pale
zone at base of bill, thin pale eye-ring
and blue underwing-coverts, even in
female. Hybrids with Shoveler resemble
male of this species but have spoon-
shaped bill.

Eurasian Wigeon *Anas penelope*

IDENTIFICATION
46 cm. Smallish duck. Male: round rufous head, golden-yellow peaked forehead, pinkish breast, mouse-grey flanks and upperparts, black rear. In flight, metallic green speculum with large black edges, white bar in centre of wing, greyish lesser coverts. Female: brown-grey head, darker mask on eye, reddish-brown flanks. Grey bill with black tip and edges. Greyish axillaries, sometimes barred, can appear whitish. **VOICE** Male: rising then descending loud whistle *vou viiiiiii-u*. **HABITAT** Any expanse of water, grazes on banks or in meadows.

white wing-bar

grey axillaries

Female and male

barred axillaries

Male

rufous head with yellow blaze

black-and-white rear

bluish bill with black tip

pink breast

round brown head

dark mask

bluish-grey bill with black tip

Female

brown flanks

American Wigeon *Anas americana*

52 cm. Nearctic vagrant, similar to Eurasian Wigeon, usually occurs singly in winter and then in company with Eurasian Wigeon. Male: pinkish-grey head, bottle-green mask behind eye, cream forehead continues far onto crown, grey bill with vertical black edge at head; greyish-pink flanks. In flight, white axillaries. Female: very difficult to distinguish from Eurasian Wigeon, greyer head, redder flanks, white axillaries.

pronounced mask

white axillaries

Male

Male

black-and-white rear

pinkish-brown flanks

grey head with long pale blaze

bluish-grey bill with black tip

dark greyish head with pronounced mask

Female

reddish flanks

Garganey *Anas querquedula*

blue-grey 'arm'

Male in flight

double supercilium

Female

dark bill

long white supercilium

long slim scapulars

grey flanks

Male

IDENTIFICATION
39 cm. Male: dark brown head and breast, long white supercilium from eye backwards; grey flanks, elongated black-and-white scapulars. Green speculum with white borders in front and behind, male has pale bluish-grey underwing-coverts, brown-grey in female. Female has pronounced cream supercilium underlined with dark eye-stripe; pale patch at base of bill bordered with second brown line on the cheek. Grey legs. **VOICE** Male has very rapid, dry, rough rattle *krrrrrr*. **HABITAT** Well-vegetated lakes, with algal vegetation and reedbeds. Winters in the Sahel.

Eurasian Teal *Anas crecca*

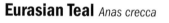

vague supercilium

green speculum often visible

black-and-green speculum with white bar in front

orange-based bill

Female

Female

clear patch on undertail-coverts

reddish head, green mask with pale edges

horizontal black-and-white line

Male

black bill

yellow triangle

IDENTIFICATION
36 cm. Small compact duck. Male: grey body with horizontal white line above flanks bordered below with black, rufous head with broad bottle-green mask outlined with yellow, beige breast spotted black; yellow rear with black edges, black bill. Green and black speculum with white line above. Female: ill-defined supercilium behind eye, bill has orange base. **VOICE** Male: sharp, whistled tingle *pliii*. **HABITAT** Extensive wetlands, marshes, large estuaries.

Cinnamon Teal *Anas cyanoptera*

43 cm. A Nearctic species; records from
France and Britain are probably escapes.
Similar to Blue-winged Teal but bigger more
spoon-shaped bill, similar to that of
Shoveler. Male: reddish body, blue coverts on
arm of wing, green speculum, red iris and
yellow legs. Female: uniform face and large
bill. Beware of Blue-winged Teal × Shoveler
hybrids, particularly females.

uniform face

spoon-shaped bill

Female

uniform face

blue coverts

reddish

Male

orange legs

Green-winged Teal *Anas carolinensis*

36 cm. Nearctic equivalent of Eurasian Teal, rare vagrant to
Europe observed each winter. Male: no white line along flanks
but vertical white line on side of breast; less marked pale
border to green mask; finer black spots on breast. Female: very
similar to Eurasian but has rufous band at top of speculum and
bill often darker without orange base.

rufous band

dark-based bill

Female

green mask hardly edged

horizontal black line

Male

vertical white stripe

wings white below, grey above

Marbled Teal *Marmaronetta angustirostris*

41 cm. A dabbling duck of desert
habitats around the Mediterranean,
including S Spain. Sexes similar. Grey
and beige plumage covered in pale
spots with darker mantle, dark mask
through eye, dark grey bill with pale
base in female. In flight, grey wings with very pale secondaries.
Very rare away from breeding areas, on well-vegetated lakes
and marshes; escapes from captivity possible.

brown plumage with large white spots

dark mask

Red-crested Pochard
Netta rufina

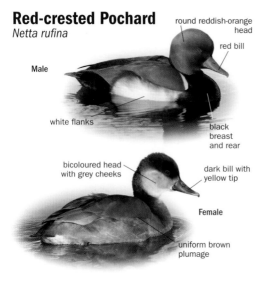

round reddish-orange head

red bill

Male

white flanks

black breast and rear

bicoloured head with grey cheeks

dark bill with yellow tip

Female

uniform brown plumage

IDENTIFICATION
55 cm. Large diving duck. Male: black breast and rear, brown back, white flanks, big round red and orange head with bright red bill. Female: bicoloured head, dark brown crown and pale cheek, dark bill with pale tip. Grey wings with large white wing-bar. Eclipse male: like female but bright red bill. **VOICE** Generally silent. **HABITAT** When breeding, discreet on well-vegetated lakes. On large inland waters in winter.

black-and-white head

black bill

reddish neck

black belly

black rear

White-faced Whistling Duck
Dendrocygna viduata

48 cm. Of sub-Saharan African and South American origin (like Fulvous Whistling Duck). Those that are seen in Europe are probably escapes. Distinctive silhouette with long neck and long grey legs. Black head with extensive white face, reddish neck, black belly and finely barred black-and-white flanks. Black bill.

Fulvous Whistling Duck *Dendrocygna bicolor*

49 cm. Distinctive, long legs extend beyond tail in flight, upright stance on ground, long neck when on water. Pronounced white streaks on flanks, black back with reddish bars, rufous body, grey bill. The few records from Spain and France may concern escapes or may be wild birds accompanying Pintail from their wintering sites in the Sahel.

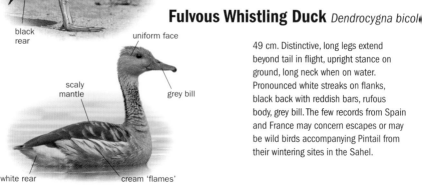

uniform face

grey bill

scaly mantle

white rear

cream 'flames'

DIVING DUCKS Smallish, quite compact ducks, legs situated far back on the body. They feed by diving underwater. Localised breeders, they spend the winter in large flocks on undisturbed inland lakes and reservoirs with plentiful molluscs, invertebrates and aquatic vegetation. Sea ducks (eiders, scoters, goldeneyes and sawbills; pp. 34–42) also dive, but most species are more associated with the sea. Stifftails (p. 41) are restricted to freshwater lakes.

Common Pochard *Aythya ferina*

IDENTIFICATION
46 cm. Male: black breast and rear, reddish head with flat forehead, grey body, uniformly-coloured back and flanks, conical black bill with grey subterminal band; red eye. Female: beige-grey with brown breast, pale zone before eye and darker crown. Dark grey wings with ash-grey central wing-bar.
VOICE Generally silent. **HABITAT** Breeds on quiet waterbodies with vegetated banks. Gregarious in winter, on extensive inland waters.

Male

grey wing-bar

red head — red iris

Male

bluish-grey and black bill

dark grey bill with pale band

grey back and flanks

pale brown head

Female

grey flanks

Tufted Duck *Aythya fuligula*

IDENTIFICATION
44 cm. Small diving duck with round head and a crest. Male: long floppy crest, black-and-white plumage, grey bill with black tip, slightly spoon-shaped. Female: brown, often with white patch on forehead and sometimes white undertail-coverts. Adults have golden-yellow eye, juveniles brown. White wing-bar on black wings. Immature male has brown feathers on flanks, becoming white during first winter. **VOICE** Occasional grunts. **HABITAT** As Common Pochard.

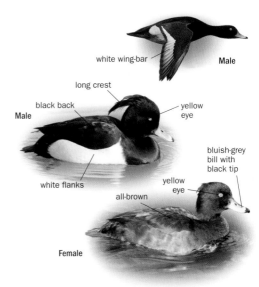

white wing-bar

Male

long crest

black back

Male

yellow eye

bluish-grey bill with black tip

white flanks

yellow eye

all-brown

Female

(Greater) Scaup *Aythya marila*

bottle-green head without crest

grey body

yellow eye

Male

white bar on primaries

Female

grey bill with large black nail

white wing-bar on secondaries

yellow eye

white zone around bill

Female

brown body, grey flanks

black nail

IDENTIFICATION
47 cm. Large, tricoloured diving duck, with very round head, without a crest. Male has breast and rear black, black head with green sheen, finely barred back and white flanks; yellow iris, black bill with large black nail. Female is brown with a large white patch on forehead and at base of bill, often a pale patch at back of cheek; flanks greyer and paler than brown breast. Immature male brown with black head and grey showing on the back. In flight, large white wing-bar. **VOICE** Silent. **HABITAT** Marine coasts, ports, large inland lakes.

Lesser Scaup *Aythya affinis*

Male

grey bar on primaries

white wing-bar on secondaries

mantle with crude stripes

black head

rudimentary crest

Male

blue-grey bill with very small black nail

42 cm. Nearctic diving duck, annual vagrant, similar to Greater Scaup but smaller, head not as round, with a slightly peaked hindcrown. Males have mantle crudely vermiculated with black, bill with very small, round black nail. Female has a large white blaze around base of bill. In flight, white wing-bar only on secondaries, grey on the primaries (wing-bar entirely white in Greater Scaup and Tufted Duck).

white blaze around bill

very reduced black nail

Female

Ferruginous Duck *Aythya nyroca*

Male in flight

IDENTIFICATION
40 cm. Small reddish-brown diving duck with white rear end, uniformly coloured breast and flanks, white wing-bar and white belly visible in flight. Male chestnut-red, mantle and rear brown-black, grey-black bill with pale and black tip, white iris. Female more brown on the head, dark iris, more uniform bill. **HABITAT** Well-vegetated lakes.

long white wing-bar

white iris

white undertail-coverts

grey bill with black nail

Male

bronze-chestnut

dark iris

white undertail-coverts

Female

dull reddish-brown

Ring-necked Duck *Aythya collaris*

42 cm. Nearctic diving duck, annual vagrant, resembling Tufted Duck. Head less rounded, peaked crown, rear of flanks coming high up on the back, long tail. Male black, grey flanks with a white vertical band before the breast; yellow iris, dark grey bill with black tip, neat white subterminal band and fine white line at its base. Female has similar bill, pale area in front of eye, pale eye-ring extending backwards as a fine eye-stripe. Grey wing-bar in flight.

peaked head without a crest

Male

characteristic tricoloured bill

grey flanks with white area at shoulder

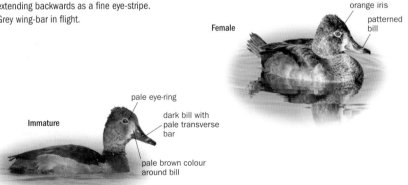

orange iris

patterned bill

Female

pale eye-ring

Immature

dark bill with pale transverse bar

pale brown colour around bill

Canvasback *Aythya valisineria*

reddish head with flat forehead

red iris

tertials darker

Male

long, unmarked, black conical bill

52 cm. Very rare Nearctic vagrant in Europe; some birds are escapes. Large diving duck very similar to Common Pochard, but bigger and longer, longer neck, longer bill entirely dark; male with paler grey flanks and mantle; female with characteristic long bill.

characteristic head and bill shape

Female

long, unmarked, black bill

Redhead *Aythya americana*

round head

orange iris

dark grey

Male

tricoloured bill

47 cm. Very rare Nearctic vagrant, mainly to Iceland and Britain. Very similar to Common Pochard but head rounder, bill more spoon-shaped with black tip and pale subterminal band. Male has a yellow iris, darker rear of back, finely vermiculated. Female: resembles Common Pochard with different head shape, tricoloured bill, no contrast between breast and flanks.

very uniform plumage

Female

grey bill with large black tip

Hybrid diving ducks

It is not rare to see hybrid diving ducks presenting characteristics intermediate between 2 species. The close observation of a group of diving ducks resting on a large lake will often reveal the odd hybrid that can vary even if they have the same parent species. Male Tufted Duck × Common Pochard have black heads, grey flanks and lack a dark grey back, resembling a Tufted Duck or Greater Scaup. Male Common Pochard × Ferruginous Ducks resemble the latter but show a contrast between a dark red or black breast and paler flanks, and between the flanks and darker back; the bill often shows a pale band behind the black tip.

peaked head with violet sheen

reddish-yellow iris

black at bill base

finely vermiculated dark grey back

Male Tufted Duck × Common Pochard

white blaze

vermiculated

Female Tufted Duck × Common Pochard

crest

black back

white iris

Male Tufted Duck × Ferruginous Duck

very short crest

orange iris

white rear

Male Tufted Duck × Common Pochard

slightly crested

Male Tufted Duck × Ferruginous Duck

yellow iris

dark iris

pale patch on cheek

Female Tufted Duck × Common Pochard

white area at base of bill

reddish breast

beige flanks

reddish round head

Male Tufted Duck × Ferruginous Duck

whitish-orange iris

pale iris

darker grey mantle

brown-black breast

white undertail-coverts

grey flanks

dark reddish breast

black undertail-coverts **Male Tufted Duck × Ferruginous Duck**

Common Eider *Somateria mollissima*

large head

uniform plumage

Female in flight

Female

uniform front

conical, pointed, long bill

barred flanks

triangular head with black

characteristic greenish-yellow bill

white breast

Male

black flanks and belly

IDENTIFICATION
65 cm. Very large, with large rounded head, conical bill with whitish tip and pointed lateral plate reaching the forehead. Male black and white: black, greenish nape, white back, flanks and rear black; in flight white wings with black primaries and greater coverts. Female grey to reddish-brown finely barred black; dark in flight. Dives to feed.
HABITAT Rocky maritime coasts with plentiful shellfish, estuaries, large inland lakes, still rivers.

First-winter male

Brown head and neck

yellow bill

white breast

Male in flight

black belly

Ssp. *borealis* (Iceland)

white 'sails'

bright yellow bill, large frontal plate

Ssp. *dresseri* (North America)

white 'sails'

very rounded frontal plate

King Eider *Somateria spectabilis*

59 cm. Occurs in winter, Arctic origin. Smaller than Common Eider, female very similar but head rounder, short, dark bill including nail. Male: black back, white breast, black flanks with white bar at rear; bill red with large, yellow bordered black, laterally flattened frontal plate, smaller in young males; in flight wings black with a white oval.

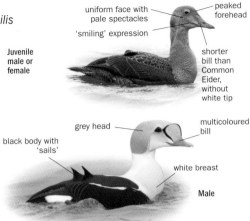

uniform face with pale spectacles

'smiling' expression

peaked forehead

Juvenile male or female

shorter bill than Common Eider, without white tip

grey head

multicoloured bill

black body with 'sails'

white breast

black body with 'sails'

Male

Steller's Eider *Polysticta stelleri*

50 cm. Breeds in the Siberian Arctic, winters in N Europe, vagrant to rest of Europe. Small eider, male black and white with peaked crown and black spectacles, orange-tinted breast and flanks. Female dark brown, speculum reminiscent of that of Mallard.

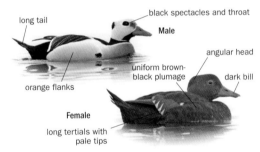

long tail

black spectacles and throat

Male

angular head

uniform brown-black plumage

dark bill

orange flanks

Female

long tertials with pale tips

Spectacled Eider *Somateria fischeri*

55 cm. Originating from Canadian and Siberian Arctic, a few occur in Norway; winters in holes in the pack ice in the N Pacific. A little smaller than Common Eider with large black-bordered, white oval around the eye and skin covering the base of the bill. Male has black flanks and breast, white spectacles on a green face, orange bill. Female rufous with beige spectacles.

black spectacles

white wings

Male

black belly

uniform pale face

skin on grey bill

Female

Common Scoter *Melanitta nigra*

Males and female

black secondaries

IDENTIFICATION
49 cm. Sea duck with entirely dark plumage, round head. Male entirely black, short bill with reduced knob at base, which has a yellow-orange zone above and between the nostrils, not touching the forehead. Female dark brown with dark cap and pale cheeks, dark grey bill. In flight, wings totally black, whitish belly in first-winter birds. A little jump precedes the dive. **HABITAT** Sea coasts with rocky bottom and plentiful shellfish.

Male

round head

small black knob

orange patch

black bill, sometimes with yellow at nostrils

all black

bicoloured head with pale cheek

Female

Velvet Scoter *Melanitta fusca*

white secondaries

Male

brown plumage

angular head

Female

pale patches

black nostrils only slightly bulging

white speculum sometimes visible

white iris

white crescent

yellow bill

Male

IDENTIFICATION
55 cm. Larger than Common Scoter with more elongated head, longer bill, white secondaries visible in flight, sometimes when swimming. Male black with small white crescent under the white eye, bill yellow on sides and nail without a knob. Female dark brown, grey-black bill, pale zone between bill and eye, and another round pale zone on rear cheek. First-winter birds have pale belly. White wing-bar characteristic in flight. Dives without a bounce but spreads its wings. **HABITAT** Winters on sea coasts and extensive lakes.

Black Scoter *Melanitta americana*

49 cm. Nearctic counterpart of Common Scoter. Very similar, but male's bill has larger knob with orange-yellow base. Female identical to that of Common Scoter, bill sometimes shorter, thicker at base with extensive yellow reaching nostrils. Very rare in winter, in flocks of Common Scoters.

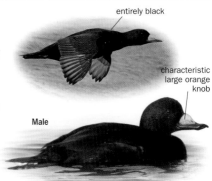

entirely black

characteristic large orange knob

Male

Surf Scoter *Melanitta perspicillata*

50 cm. Vagrant Nearctic scoter, size of Common Scoter with bigger, more massive head and large conical bill. Male: black with white patch on nape (all ages) and on forehead (adult only); bill white encircling black disc at base with red tip; white iris. At a distance, silhouette and white markings are characteristic. Female: dark cap, pale patch in front of bill and behind eye, thick-based grey-black bill. Dives after a small jump with spread wings.

angular head

double pale patches on face and cheek

dark large bill

white forehead

large colourful bill

Female

white nape

Male

black circle

White-winged Scoter *Melanitta deglandi*

54 cm. Very similar to Velvet Scoter, which it replaces in N America (*deglandi* race) and in Siberia (*stejnegeri* race). Nearctic males: small square black knob at base of bill with reddish nail, otherwise with yellow sides bordered black, larger white crescent under eye and brownish flanks. Siberian males: prominent, pointed knob at base of bill, which has wide reddish sides underlined with yellow, as far as the nail; the white crescent is even more evident, rising behind the eye.

very long white crescent

pointed knob

red sides underlined with yellow

Male ssp. *stejnegeri*

long white crescent

knob

sides orange bordered with black

Male ssp. *deglandi*

brown flanks

Long-tailed Duck *Clangula hyemalis*

wings black above and below

cheek spot

dark cap

Female winter

Male

large black circle

long streamers

Male winter

black flanks

brown cheeks

white spectacles

Female summer

small, thick grey bill

black head with white mask

white flanks

reddish scapulars

Male summer

short, black-and-pink bill

IDENTIFICATION

43 cm (plus 12 cm of tail in male). Small bicoloured diving duck, looking black and white, male with a long thin tail. In winter, male has dark belly, white neck with black spot on the cheek; the female has a black cap, grey bill and brown back, the elegant male a white cap, greyish face and vertical pink band on bill, and long, thin pale grey scapulars. Immature males resemble females in early winter, then have adult-type scapulars. In flight wings entirely black, sides of rump white, reminiscent of a small wader. **VOICE** Silent in winter. **HABITAT** Breeds on pools and marshes in the Arctic tundra; winters at sea, very rare inland.

Smew *Mergellus albellus*

black mask

short crest

short grey bill

Male

reddish-brown cap

short grey bill

Female

white throat

grey body

IDENTIFICATION

41 cm. Small, bicoloured diving duck. Black-and-white male has small black mask in front of eye, black back, dark rear, grey flanks. Female has a reddish-brown head, often shows an angular forehead, and extensive white throat; grey body. Short, grey bill. Young male similar to female with a black mask and forehead becoming white during the winter. **VOICE** Silent in winter. **HABITAT** Lakes, undisturbed waterbodies.

Red-breasted Merganser *Mergus serrator*

IDENTIFICATION
55 cm. Elongated body, long, thin red bill, double slender crest on nape giving the bird a shaggy, perplexed expression. Male: black head with bottle-green sheen, white collar, beige breast streaked black, grey flanks, white wings and black back; breast and flank colour allow for separation from Goosander at a distance. Female: reddish-brown colour of head grading into grey on neck, slightly paler throat, grey back and forewing. In flight, large white speculum separated in two by black line (uniform in Goosander). **VOICE** Silent in winter. **HABITAT** Usually maritime, along coasts, sometimes on extensive inland waters.

slender crest — thin, slightly upturned red bill

Male

grey flanks

dark breast

upturned red bill

shaggy crest

Female

ill-defined brown/grey demarcation

Goosander *Mergus merganser*

IDENTIFICATION
63 cm. Larger and stockier than Red-breasted Merganser, thicker bill-base, larger triangular head with a thick, low crest on nape. Male: black head with bottle-green sheen, white breast and flanks, black back. Female: reddish-brown head with sharply defined white throat and grey neck. In flight, male has white wings with extensive black tips, the female's are tricoloured: black outer wing, large white speculum, grey secondary-coverts. Immature males are similar to females but have more white on wings. **VOICE** Male emits a muffled cooing, the female a hard croaking. **HABITAT** Undisturbed waterbodies with fish, rivers and mountain lakes.

compact crest — thin red bill

Male

white breast and flanks

thin, straight red bill

long double crest

Female

sharp demarcation

white breast

Common Goldeneye *Bucephala clangula*

Male

Female

white inner wing

black outer wing

grey front of wing

green sheen

yellow iris

black-and-white body

thick black bill

Male

white circle

white iris

brown head

Female

black bill with yellow band

IDENTIFICATION
44 cm. Diving duck reminiscent of 'sawbills' (see previous page) but short, conical grey bill. Male: bottle-green head with round white spot in front of yellow eye; white neck, breast and flanks, black rear and mantle. Female: grey body with white secondaries that are visible on closed wing, round brown head. In flight, blackish underwings. Immature male: dark brown head with diffuse pale patch in front of eye, which is not necessarily round. **HABITAT** Gregarious, forming small groups on undisturbed large inland waters.

Barrow's Goldeneye *Bucephala islandica*

violet sheen

very peaked forehead

Male

white crescent

more peaked forehead

Female

very short bill

IDENTIFICATION
47 cm. Breeds in Iceland and Canada. A few rare observations from northern coasts; may be escapes. Very similar to Common Goldeneye, a little larger, bill shorter but thicker base, different head shape with high, peaked crown, peaking in front of eye (less conical head). Male has a white crescent in front of eye, head with purple rather than green sheen. The female is distinguished especially by head and bill shape, the latter often with more orange.

Ruddy Duck *Oxyura jamaicensis*

IDENTIFICATION 39 cm. Introduced Nearctic diving duck with long pointed tail. Male with reddish-brown body, bicoloured black-and-white head, blue bill (grey in winter); extensive white on cheeks in male. Female's plumage less red than male's, cheeks beige crossed by diffuse horizontal brown line. In flight, compact with all-dark wings. **HABITAT** Undisturbed inland waterbodies, lakes surrounded by vegetation. Breeds in Britain and France, where it is being culled.

black cap and white cheek

flat blue bill

Male

red body

dark bill with no swelling

dark straight bar

Female

White-headed Duck *Oxyura leucocephala*

IDENTIFICATION 45 cm. A little larger than Ruddy Duck, breeding in Central Asia, N Africa and Spain; a few vagrants recorded in W Europe each year; once bred in Corsica. Male: white head with small black cap that does not reach the eye, blue bill (grey in winter) with basal swelling. Female: grey bill with basal swelling, white line below cap. Sometimes in the company of Ruddy Duck, with which it can hybridise. **HABITAT** Well-vegetated eutrophic lakes.

long tail

white face

swollen blue bill

reddish-brown plumage

Male

large dark zigzag bar

swelling

Female

Bufflehead *Bucephala albeola*

white cheeks and nape

bicoloured

bottle-green sheen

Male

pink legs

36 cm. Nearctic vagrant, rare but annual in Europe; some are escapes. Small, compact with short grey bill. Male: black head with extensive white cheeks joining on the nape, green and violet sheen; white flanks, black back. Female has dark brown head and small white cheek patch; grey breast and flanks. Pink legs. Dives like a Common Pochard.

white patch on cheek

dark brown head

Female

Hooded Merganser *Lophodytes cucullatus*

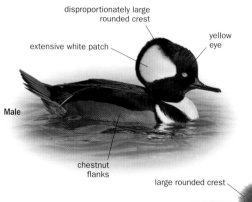

disproportionately large rounded crest

yellow eye

extensive white patch

Male

chestnut flanks

46 cm. Small Nearctic sawbill; very rare vagrant to W Europe, most are probably escapes. Male with long white crest bordered black behind the head; female's crest is rufous, erected when birds feel threatened or during display. Bill shorter than that of Goosander and Red-breasted Merganser, yellow with black upper edge.

large rounded crest

brown head

Female

short yellow-based bill

Mandarin Duck *Aix galericulata*

45 cm. Asian duck; many escapes have established viable nesting populations, particularly in W Europe. Male unmistakable with 'sails', immense orange cheeks and long white supercilium; red bill with white tip. Female: numerous pale spots on breast and flanks, thin white eye-ring, bill with nail like male. Inhabits undisturbed lakes and rivers with willows and reedbeds; nests in a tree hole.

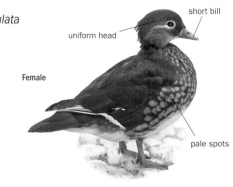

short bill

uniform head

Female

pale spots

white mask

orange 'sails'

short red bill

Male

2 white bars

Wood Duck *Aix sponsa*

47 cm. Nearctic duck; many escapes, a few genuine wild vagrants in the Azores. Male very colourful with red eye-ring and base to bill, green floppy crest. Female very similar to Mandarin but large white patch around eye, black nail on bill and less spotted flanks.

striped head

bill terminates in a point

Female

fine pale lines

bottle-green head

multicoloured bill

Male

single white line

Harlequin Duck *Histrionicus histrionicus*

reddish flanks

mottled round head

Male

white circle

white spots

white band, bordered black

short bill

Female

IDENTIFICATION
41 cm. Arctic diving duck, breeding in Iceland and Canada. Rare vagrant to the rest of N Europe, on sea coasts in winter. Very round head, short bill with pale tip. Male has characteristic white, blue-grey and black pattern, brick-coloured flanks. The female resembles a scoter, with diffuse pale face and white spot at rear of cheek.

Baikal Teal *Anas formosa*

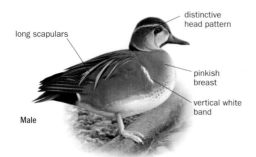

distinctive head pattern

long scapulars

pinkish breast

vertical white band

Male

41 cm. Small Siberian teal, migratory, rare vagrant in Europe, often with Eurasian Teal. Male: yellow face with long black tears, peaked crown, pink breast separated from grey flanks by vertical white line (as in Green-winged Teal); long thin black-and-white scapulars. Female as female Eurasian Teal except for dark border around white circle at bill base.

Falcated Teal *Anas falcata*

low crest

very uniform head

Female

whitish-yellow triangle

long slender tertials

bottle-green head with brown crest

Male

50 cm. Siberian dabbling duck; migratory, vagrant to Europe often in company of Wigeon. At a distance, male grey with a dark head; conical head with green mask, white throat and thin black-and-white collar. Long, overhanging black-and-white tertials, whitish-yellow patch on the rear flanks as in Eurasian Teal.

GAMEBIRDS Sedentary species closely related to the domestic chicken, comprising grouse, partridges, quails and pheasants. Terrestrial, ground nesting, short rounded wings. Often in groups: families with a female and several young, or groups of unattached males.

Hazel Grouse *Tetrastes bonasia*

IDENTIFICATION
37 cm. Small compact forest grouse, with a large head and short crest; cryptic plumage, underparts very scaly, pale line on scapulars and black terminal tail-band characteristic in flight. Black throat (male) or grey with white spotting (female). Discreet, moves on the ground or along horizontal branches. **VOICE** Song: short high-pitched phrases, a pronounced first note followed by chirping. **HABITAT** Cool mountain conifer or mixed forests, with dense undergrowth.

red wattle
black throat
short tail
Male
short crest
brown throat
Female
spotted whitish flanks

Rock Ptarmigan *Lagopus muta*

IDENTIFICATION
33 cm. Small grouse, plumage varying according to season; throughout the year white wings and black tail. In winter, plumage is spotless white, black lores and red wattle of male very visible; female has just a prominent black eye. In summer, the belly remains white, the rest of the body is finely vermiculated brown and black. White, feathered legs. Very confident in its camouflage, it allows a close approach.
VOICE Hoarse call similar to that of Garganey.
HABITAT High mountain rock scree and meadows, typically above 2,000 m, close to permanent snow; but near the coast in northern latitudes.

black lores
red wattle
pale lores
Female summer
Male summer
black border to tail
white wings
small red wattle
entirely white
Female winter
feathered legs

Willow Grouse (Willow Ptarmigan) *Lagopus lagopus*

reddish head

white wings

Female

very black
feathers

Male

white wings

white lores

Winter

IDENTIFICATION
39 cm.
Resembles Rock
Ptarmigan but
bigger bill,
heavier body
and clearly more reddish plumage. The
male lacks a black line in front of eye,
and has a dark reddish plumage with
white wings and belly. Female redder
than Rock Ptarmigan, with small red
wattle and conspicuous black barring.
Entirely white in winter. **VOICE** Male:
accelerating loud cackles, finishing with
a trill *coc-coc-corr*. Female: nasal *niac*.
HABITAT Heather moors, bushy tundra,
boreal forest.

Red Grouse *Lagopus lagopus scotica*

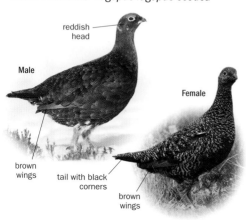

reddish
head

Male

Female

brown
wings

tail with black
corners

brown
wings

IDENTIFICATION
36 cm. A British
endemic, similar
to Willow Grouse
but with brown
belly and wings
including primaries; only the legs are
white. Male's body is dark reddish-brown,
female with black barring. **VOICE** As
Willow Grouse. **HABITAT** Heather moors,
poorly vegetated hillsides.

Black Grouse *Tetrao tetrix*

IDENTIFICATION
50–58 cm.
Male: black bill, red wattles, all-black plumage except for white undertail-coverts, long downcurved tail feathers; in flight, central white wing-bar. Female brown finely vermiculated with black and beige as female Capercaillie, but slimmer, small bill, no pale braces and short and finely barred tail; no orange on breast. Males display at sunrise on traditional sites (leks) that females visit to mate. **VOICE** While displaying, long cooing and aggressive hissing. **HABITAT** Upper limit and clearings of conifer forests.

small red wattle

First-summer male

feathers vermiculated with brown

short tail

Female

brown body

red wattle

black with blue sheen

brown-grey breast

long forked tail

lyre-shaped tail feathers

Male

(Western) Capercaillie

Tetrao urogallus

IDENTIFICATION
75–90 cm. Very large and stocky. Male with a large head, pale bill, red wattles, shaggy goatee, brown back and white spot at bend of wing; long rounded tail; uniform dark wings in flight. Female large, vermiculated with scaly flanks, orange more uniform breast, heavily barred tail. Males display on traditional sites without forming groups, spreading their tail into a fan, calling with neck stretched upwards. **VOICE** While displaying, in early morning, accelerating guttural notes and a sound like a popping cork, followed by high-pitched rapid chirps. **HABITAT** Ancient, open conifer forests, clearings, often quite flat ground.

round tail

white undertail-coverts

red wattle

brown wings

Male

bottle-green breast

small grey bill

orange breast

long rounded tail

Female

Red-legged Partridge *Alectoris rufa*

grey-brown above

white throat surrounded with black

striped bib

barred flanks

red legs

IDENTIFICATION 34 cm. Grey-brown above, chestnut and black-barred flanks. Round white throat, large bib of black stripes on breast, pronounced white supercilium. Red bill, eye-ring and legs. Tail feathers reddish forming a triangle on either side of tail in flight. Flight consists of a series of rapid wingbeats followed by a descending glide. **VOICE** Song: rhythmic, jerky *touc touc touc...tchuc-tchucar*. **HABITAT** Drier, open, cultivated spaces, crops, open maquis, vineyards, also meadows and cultivated areas. Mediterranean, introduced further north.

Rock Partridge *Alectoris graeca*

black at base of bill

white throat

large, well-defined dark line

grey breast

black at base of bill

brown spot

vinous mantle

collar narrow in front

grey rump

Ssp. *whitakeri*

IDENTIFICATION 35 cm. Very similar to Red-legged Partridge but extensive white bib extending to a point on the neck, bordered with a black line, no black streaks on breast, narrow pale supercilium. **VOICE** Song is higher-pitched than that of Red-legged Partridge, guttural and not as loud. **HABITAT** Open alpine areas above the treeline; grassy scree on sunny slopes at altitude, sometimes with scrub. Sicilian Rock Partridge: The *whitakeri* subspecies is endemic to Sicily, occurring from sea level to slopes on Mount Etna. Irregular, thinner black collar, often incomplete at lowest point, pale patch behind the eye, body more colourful with vinous-green back contrasting with grey rump, redder undertail-coverts.

Chukar *Alectoris chukar*

IDENTIFICATION
34 cm. Similar
to Rock
Partridge but bib
cream (not
white) and point
at base of neck underlined with a well-
defined black V. Brown ear-spot, white at
base of upper mandible (black in Rock
Partridge). **VOICE** A rhythmic series of low
indistinct notes, interrupted with muffled
series of *ga-ga-ga*... **HABITAT** Cultivated
areas, maquis and garrigue, rocky
slopes. Replaces Rock Partridge in
E Europe; introductions for hunting
elsewhere in Europe.

white at base
of bill

cream
throat

grey
breast

Barbary Partridge *Alectoris barbara*

IDENTIFICATION
35 cm. Large
brown collar
with white spots,
grey head with
dark brown cap
and beige eye-mask. Grey breast, flanks
with more white barring than brown.
VOICE Song is long series of repeated
complex sounds, with prolonged series
of muffled *trai trai trai* notes. **HABITAT**
Any open habitat, garrigue, maquis,
clearings. Replaces Red-legged Partridge
in N Africa, Sardinia and Canary Islands.
Introduced to Gibraltar and Madeira.

grey
face

white-spotted
brown collar

ashy-grey
breast

brown
crown-stripe

Male

grey-brown plumage

orange face

flanks barred with chestnut

reddish-brown breast patch

duller face

Female

indistinct breast patch

Grey Partridge *Perdix perdix*

IDENTIFICATION 30 cm. Quite uniform plumage. Male has orange throat, chestnut bars on flanks and large, inverted dark red U mark on lower breast. Female has drabber plumage. Young are pale brown striped black and beige. In flight, round tail with reddish sides. Gregarious, found in pairs or groups (coveys). **VOICE** Song is a repeated, long, trailing and grating *kerrrrree*. **HABITAT** Agricultural plains, crops and meadows, with or without hedgerows.

Common Quail *Coturnix coturnix*

Male

dark throat (black, brown or reddish)

pink legs

golden streaks

Female

pale throat

IDENTIFICATION 17 cm. Small and round with a small head and no tail. Light brown plumage with black-and-beige streaks, very noticeable on flanks. Male has dark throat (reddish to black), female has pale throat. Very discreet, rarely seen as it stays hidden in vegetation; most often located by song. **VOICE** Song is 3 high-pitched notes sounding like falling drops of water, *pit pit pit* (often interpreted as *wet-my-lips*), followed by a soft grunt, *arrra*, only audible when close. **HABITAT** Extensive open grassy areas; meadows, cereal crops, steppe.

Small Buttonquail *Turnix sylvaticus*

white eye

large black spots

uniform orange belly

IDENTIFICATION 16 cm. Very discreet, reminiscent of Common Quail but flight feathers black and wing-coverts pale. Female more colourful than male, reddish-orange belly, large black spots on flanks, white iris. **VOICE** Song: female gives a soft incessantly repeated *hou*, a sound like that of blowing into a bottle. **HABITAT** Scrub, cultivated fields (pumpkins), dry meadows, near the coast, in Morocco and Algeria; almost extinct in Spain.

Common Pheasant *Phasianus colchicus*

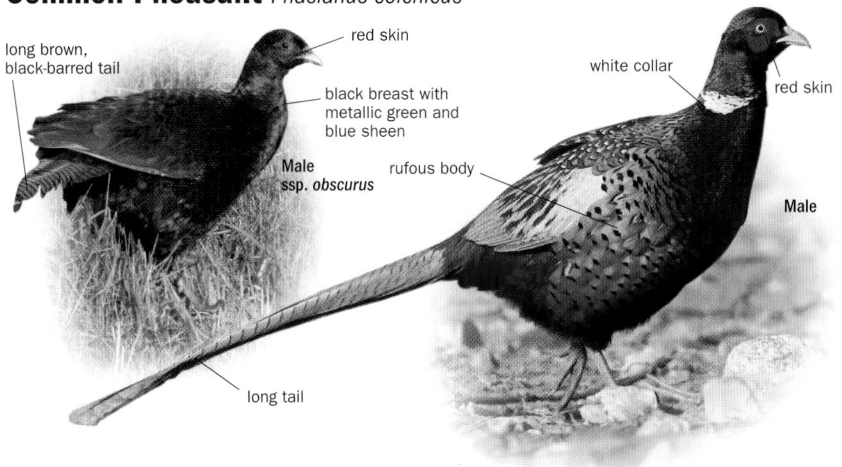

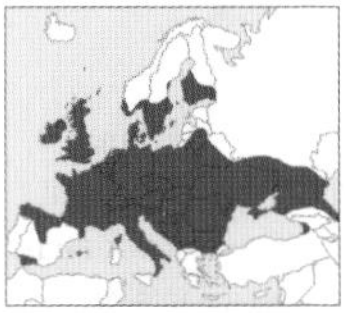

long brown,
black-barred tail

red skin

white collar

red skin

black breast with
metallic green and
blue sheen

rufous body

**Male
ssp. *obscurus***

Male

long tail

IDENTIFICATION
80 cm. Male:
long, slender,
black-barred
bronze tail;
overall a rufous
colour with beige and black markings,
variable according to variety; extensive
bare red skin on cheek surrounding eye;
some have a white collar, cap white or
bottle-green. Certain individuals are
totally black with bottle-green sheen,
'Green Pheasant'. Female beige with
black markings, uniform face and spotted
flanks. Feeds on the ground and roosts in
trees. **VOICE** Song: loud double shouted
note that carries far, *koooorkok*,
associated with whirring the wings whilst
on the ground. **HABITAT** Deciduous and
mixed forests, farmland with hedgerows
and forest edges. Very many reared birds
of various strains are released for hunting.

barred throat

Female

long tail

uniform beige belly

sometimes has
white crown

variable collar
size

Male

long tail

Golden Pheasant *Chrysolophus pictus*

Male 100 cm (of which 65 cm is the disproportionately long tail), female 70 cm (half is tail). Male has yellow cap and rump, bright reddish underparts, golden cape barred with black, and black-barred bottle-green mantle. Female more brown than rufous, barred belly, yellowish legs. Introduced into Great Britain, found at scattered sites in extensive forests with thick undergrowth.

Female

yellow face

yellow-brown legs

black-barred golden cape

Male

red breast and belly

black face

black-barred white cape

Lady Amherst's Pheasant *Chrysolophus amherstiae*

white breast

Male

Female

reddish colouring

grey legs

Same size as Golden Pheasant, male has even longer white-barred black tail. Male has black cap with red at rear and black bib, black-barred white cape, yellow rump and white belly. Female more rufous than brown, unbarred belly, grey legs. A relict population of introduced origin subsists in the south of England, now probably near to extinction.

Reeves's Pheasant *Syrmaticus reevesii*

Female

long tail

uniform orange face

barred breast

IDENTIFICATION 60–80 cm plus 100 cm tail in male. A disproportionately long tail, white with narrow black bars. Male: a reddish-brown and orange with large white spots on the wings, white head with a black mask with white spot below the eye and black collar. Female: similar to female Common Pheasant but uniform reddish-beige head and neck, dark brown cheek and cap and beige crescent under eye. Often hidden within bushes. **VOICE** Alarm, a repeated liquid *pyit*. **HABITAT** Dense forest with well developed undergrowth. Introduced to France from China.

black-and-white head

bronze-yellow neck

Male

very long tail

California Quail *Callipepla californica*

26 cm. Small American quail, introduced. Round body, male with blue-grey breast, scalloped belly, black throat bordered with white and long downcurving feathers like a lamp above the forehead. Female is drab. Gregarious, it lives hidden in thick vegetation. Song is a loud, musical, repeated *ka-kwin-ko*. Inhabits farmland with bushes and dry scrub, vineyards, open garrigue. Feral in the Aléria plain in Corsica.

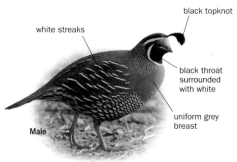

black topknot

white streaks

black throat surrounded with white

uniform grey breast

Male

Northern Bobwhite *Colinus virginianus*

white supercilium

white throat

25 cm. Nearctic species introduced in Italy in dry agricultural areas around Milan; a few relict populations formed from hunting releases in central France. Small and round, large white throat edged with black, long white supercilium, breast and flanks reddish spotted with black and white. Song is a loud repeated *toui tveit*.

Black Francolin *Francolinus francolinus*

white on cheek

black head

Male

uniform buff head

very scalloped wings

reddish undertail-coverts

Female

IDENTIFICATION 35 cm. Very discreet, usually detected from call. Round body, short black tail, often stands very upright. Male has black head, white cheek, dark rufous collar and black body with white V-shaped spots. Female has buff face and reddish nape. **VOICE** Song a phrase of 7 rhythmic, detached syllables. **HABITAT** Fields, scrub and wasteland. In Europe, only in Cyprus.

Erckel's Francolin *Francolinus erckelii*

reddish cap

yellow legs

40 cm. Occurs naturally in Eritrea, Ethiopia and Sudan, introduced in Italy on Zannone island (between Rome and Naples). Reddish cap bordered with black, white cheek, grey body spangled black and rufous, bright yellow legs. Heavy-bodied with a short tail, it often stands very upright.

DIVERS (LOONS) Diving birds that winter not only on the sea, but also inland. Breed on lakes in the taiga and Arctic tundra. Fly with outstretched neck, legs extending beyond the tail; underwings uniformly dark, the contrary in grebes. Distinguished from cormorants by their pointed bill, short tail and they glide smoothly under the surface when diving, without a prior jump.

Red-throated Diver *Gavia stellata*

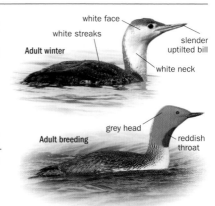

white face
white streaks
Adult winter
slender uptilted bill
white neck

grey head
Adult breeding
reddish throat

IDENTIFICATION 61 cm. Small diver, the slimmest, with slender uptilted bill and flat forehead. Adult: in winter very white neck, ashy-grey crown and band at back of neck, white above the eye. In summer, grey neck with brick-coloured throat patch, uniform grey-brown back. Immature: grey neck, only slightly chequered back. In flight, immature's grey or adult's white neck characteristically held lowered.

Black-throated Diver *Gavia arctica*

chequered black and white
Adult breeding
black throat
black-and-white lines

eye within dark feathering
uniform mantle
Adult winter

white oval
scaly mantle
white patch
Immature winter
medium bill

IDENTIFICATION 69 cm. Only a little larger than Red-throated Diver, with straight stouter bill, forehead less flat, curved neck, bicoloured with grey rear half; diagnostic white patch at rear of flanks. Dark cap descends to eye, no pale eye-ring. Immature has scaly back, the adult's is uniform. In spring, neck ashy-grey behind and black in front, with a lateral band of fine black-and-white vertical lines; back chequered black and white, the white patch at rear of flank still present.

CONFUSION SPECIES

Great Crested Grebe (p. 58)

Cormorant (p. 81)

Great Northern Diver *Gavia immer*

black head

heavy black bill

collar and throat with white stripes

Adult breeding

pointed forehead

heavy blue-grey bill

scaly mantle

Immature winter

dark face

black flanks

IDENTIFICATION
80 cm. Large diver with stout bill, angular pointed crown and thick neck.
Grey bill with upper edge black in winter, totally black in summer. In winter, back of neck blackish, with dark square patch on side of neck at its base; grey cheek with pale zone around eye. Mantle in immatures marked with pale scales, uniform in adults. In spring, black head with black-and-white striped thin line on throat and lateral band on neck; mantle marked with a black-and-white grid pattern.

White-billed Diver *Gavia adamsii*

pale face

Immature winter

clearly marked scaly mantle

thick upturned ivory bill

ivory bill

Adult breeding

black-and-white grill

IDENTIFICATION
84 cm. Arctic species, very rare in S Scandinavia and N Britain.
Very similar to Great Northern Diver but bill thicker and pale, becoming ivory-yellow at the tip; appears very upturned. Silhouette and plumage like that of Great Northern but first-winter birds have very pale face, diffuse pale sides of neck, and clear scaly pattern above.

Pacific Diver *Gavia pacifica*

IDENTIFICATION Closely related to Black-throated Diver, it has been observed in Britain and Spain. Similar to that species but without the white patch at rear of flanks, often a fine dark line on the throat, and pronounced black band on belly between legs. Often the head looks rounder and the neck thicker.

Adult winter

entirely black flanks

black chinstrap

First-winter

chinstrap sometimes absent

scaly back

black rear to flanks

angular grey nape

Adult breeding

violet sheen on throat

black rear to flanks

DIVERS AND GREBES IN FLIGHT

Great Northern Diver

black collar

thick bill

pale neck (adult) or more uniform grey (immature)

Red-throated Diver (see p. 56)

white continues behind the wing

brown

Red-necked Grebe (see p. 58)

Black-throated Diver (see p. 56)

dark side to neck

Great Crested Grebe (see p. 58)

white

GREBES Small fish-eating birds with lobed feet and thin, pointed bill; they breed on quiet freshwater areas, building a floating nest supported by aquatic vegetation. Chicks have black-and-white-striped heads and are often carried on their parents' backs. Gregarious in winter. In flight, white bar on rear edge of wing and sometimes on front edge, varies according to species.

Great Crested Grebe *Podiceps cristatus*

black cap

black-and-rufous head plumes

Breeding

long white neck

reduced black crest

pink bill

Winter

long neck

IDENTIFICATION 49 cm. Large grebe with long neck, white face, black cap and lores, front of neck largely white; thin bill, pink in winter, black in summer. Breeding: black-crested crown and long head plumes with rufous cheeks; pairs display face-to-face running across the water and offering each other waterweeds. Juvenile: black stripes on face. In flight, white scapulars linking white secondaries and leading edge to wing. **VOICE** Guttural cawing when displaying. **HABITAT** Lakes and reservoirs, and the sea in winter, sometimes in loose flocks.

Red-necked Grebe *Podiceps grisegena*

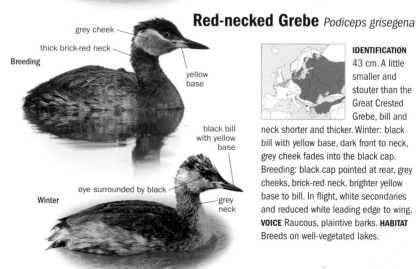

grey cheek

thick brick-red neck

Breeding

yellow base

black bill with yellow base

eye surrounded by black

Winter

grey neck

IDENTIFICATION 43 cm. A little smaller and stouter than the Great Crested Grebe, bill and neck shorter and thicker. Winter: black bill with yellow base, dark front to neck, grey cheek fades into the black cap. Breeding: black cap pointed at rear, grey cheeks, brick-red neck, brighter yellow base to bill. In flight, white secondaries and reduced white leading edge to wing. **VOICE** Raucous, plaintive barks. **HABITAT** Breeds on well-vegetated lakes.

Black-necked Grebe *Podiceps nigricollis*

IDENTIFICATION
31 cm. More rounded silhouette than that of Slavonian Grebe, more tousled rear and more peaked forehead. Thin, black, pointed bill, slightly upturned; bright red eye. Breeding: rufous flanks, black back, neck and head with a tuft of golden feathers on the cheek. Winter: dark grey front of neck, white mark at rear of dark cheek. In flight, broad white wing-bar on secondaries and inner primaries. **VOICE** Silent in winter. In display, rapid and vibrant trill. Territorial call, characteristic loud repeated double note, *ii-tiic*. **HABITAT** Lakes and reservoirs with vegetation, shallow waters in summer; gregarious in winter, on undisturbed lakes and other waterbodies.

red eye

golden cheek

rufous flanks

black neck

Breeding

peaked forehead

black cheek

upturned bill

Winter

dark front to neck

Slavonian Grebe *Podiceps auritus*

IDENTIFICATION
35 cm. Often confused with Black-necked Grebe, but also resembles small Great Crested Grebe with a short bill; quite flat forehead, totally white cheeks, pale front of neck. Well-defined black cap in winter, bright red eye, black bill with white tip. Breeding: rufous flanks and front of neck, golden-yellow lateral crests and drooping, long black neck collar. In flight, reduced white wing-bar on secondaries and white leading edge to inner wing in adult (black in immature). **VOICE** Silent in winter. On breeding grounds commonest call is a low but easily audible trill; display is a drawn-out pulsating, descending laugh. **HABITAT** Expanses of freshwater, sometimes on the sea.

yellow crest

straight bill

extensive black cheek

Breeding

reddish breast

straight white-tipped bill

neat, flat black

white cheek

Winter

white front of neck

Little Grebe *Tachybaptus ruficollis*

Breeding

chestnut cheek

yellow patch

very dark body

shaggy white rear end

brown cap and buff cheek

quite slim yellow-orange bill

Winter

IDENTIFICATION 26 cm. The smallest of our grebes, like a small ball with a shaggy round rear end; short bill. In winter, buff with brown cap and back, small yellowish bill. In summer, black bill with yellow skin at gape, chestnut neck, black cap, breast and back; dark flanks but white rear end. **VOICE** Male's song is characteristic high-pitched long trill, *bibibibibibi...* **HABITAT** Freshwater lakes and ponds, rarely brackish areas.

Pied-billed Grebe *Podilymbus podiceps*

Breeding

grey cheek

white spectacles

black bar on bill

black throat

spectacles

pale thick bill

uniform head

Winter

35 cm. Rare Nearctic vagrant, very similar to Little Grebe but bigger, large angular head, thick ivory-coloured bill, head more uniformly dark. Breeding: vertical black band on bill, black chin and white eye-ring. In winter, dark wings with pale edge on tips of secondaries. A few records in winter; in spring occasional birds display.

SHEARWATERS AND PETRELS Shearwaters and petrels are marine birds that only come to land in order to breed in a burrow or rocky scree. They feed out at sea, sometimes near the coast, and only visit their breeding colonies at night. Silent at sea, they fly mainly by gliding on the wind, often just above the waves. The nostrils on the bill form a tube that evacuates salt filtered from the sea water that they drink. They sometimes settle on the sea in large flocks, termed rafts.

Cory's Shearwater *Calonectris borealis*

very white underwing

IDENTIFICATION 52 cm. Large shearwater with dark upperparts and white underparts, with thin whitish line across uppertail-coverts; yellow bill with dark tip. Grey-brown head appears dark at distance; brown-grey upperwings with paler transverse band, white underwings but primaries black below, including at their base, forming a dark wing-tip. Flies with slow wingbeats, glides low over water with bowed wings. **VOICE** Silent at sea, but noisy at colonies after dark. **HABITAT** Breeds on Atlantic islands.

larger, thicker bill than Scopoli's Shearwater

underside of base of primaries dark

Scopoli's Shearwater *Calonectris diomedea*

grey head

tube-shaped nostrils

yellow hooked bill with dark tip

IDENTIFICATION 50 cm. Until recently considered conspecific with Cory's Shearwater. Very similar to Cory's Shearwater but the wing-tip of underwing is different: pale base of primaries forms a continuation of white onto the wing-tip. Other differences are hardly perceptible in the field: slightly smaller, bill a little more slender, slightly different calls. **VOICE** Similar to Cory's Shearwater. **HABITAT** Breeds on Mediterranean islands: a few colonies on nearby Atlantic coast.

head and neck grey

white base to flight feathers from underneath

Cape Verde Shearwater *Calonectris edwardsii*

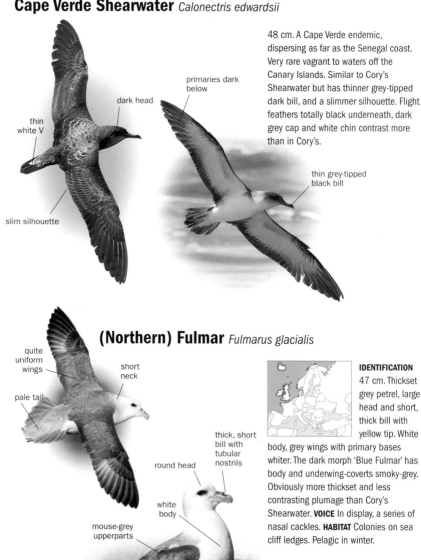

48 cm. A Cape Verde endemic, dispersing as far as the Senegal coast. Very rare vagrant to waters off the Canary Islands. Similar to Cory's Shearwater but has thinner grey-tipped dark bill, and a slimmer silhouette. Flight feathers totally black underneath, dark grey cap and white chin contrast more than in Cory's.

primaries dark below

dark head

thin white V

thin grey-tipped black bill

slim silhouette

(Northern) Fulmar *Fulmarus glacialis*

quite uniform wings

short neck

pale tail

thick, short bill with tubular nostrils

round head

white body

mouse-grey upperparts

IDENTIFICATION
47 cm. Thickset grey petrel, large head and short, thick bill with yellow tip. White body, grey wings with primary bases whiter. The dark morph 'Blue Fulmar' has body and underwing-coverts smoky-grey. Obviously more thickset and less contrasting plumage than Cory's Shearwater. **VOICE** In display, a series of nasal cackles. **HABITAT** Colonies on sea cliff ledges. Pelagic in winter.

Great Shearwater *Puffinus gravis*

47 cm. Smaller and more slender than Cory's Shearwater, black cap and white collar (isolated black 'beret'), clearly defined white band on uppertail-coverts, dark undertail-coverts and dark mark on belly. Elegant flight, wings less arched than in Cory's, fewer wing flaps. Rare migrant along Atlantic coast in summer, mainly at sea; breeds in S Atlantic during the austral summer.

dark undertail-coverts

black cap

narrow white rump

narrow white collar

dark belly patch

black tail

black cap

black bill

white throat

Sooty Shearwater *Puffinus griseus*

plumage entirely sooty-brown

long black bill

long slim wings

small white panel on underwing

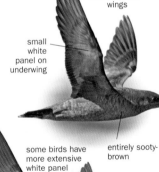

45 cm. Slimly-built large shearwater with almost entire plumage sooty-black. Long slim wings, with central white panel on underwing. Dark underparts, unlike the darkest Balearic Shearwater. Elegant flight, flaps wings rarely; long looping glides, often high above the sea, brings underside into view. Uncommon summer migrant along the Atlantic coast, originating from the S Atlantic, where it is very common.

some birds have more extensive white panel

entirely sooty-brown

belly always brown

Manx Shearwater *Puffinus puffinus*

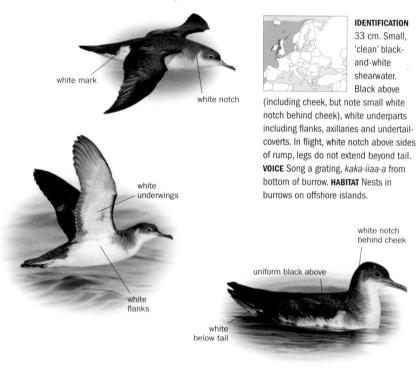

white mark

white notch

IDENTIFICATION
33 cm. Small, 'clean' black-and-white shearwater.
Black above (including cheek, but note small white notch behind cheek), white underparts including flanks, axillaries and undertail-coverts. In flight, white notch above sides of rump, legs do not extend beyond tail. **VOICE** Song a grating, *kaka-iiaa-a* from bottom of burrow. **HABITAT** Nests in burrows on offshore islands.

white underwings

white flanks

white below tail

white notch behind cheek

uniform black above

Macaronesian Shearwater *Puffinus baroli*

Ssp. *baroli*

white undertail-coverts

whiter face

eye within greyish face

short bluish bill

underwings very white

black undertail-coverts

Ssp. *boydi*

27 cm. Breeds and winters in the Canary Islands, Azores and Madeira. Smaller and more compact than Manx Shearwater, white face surrounding eye, white underwings including primary bases, secondaries paler from below. Blue bill with black tip. In flight, rapid wingbeats and short, direct glides. Ssp. *baroli* (Canaries and Madeira): white undertail-coverts; ssp. *boydi* (Cape Verde): black undertail-coverts.

Yelkouan Shearwater *Puffinus yelkouan*

IDENTIFICATION
33 cm. Very similar to Manx Shearwater but brown-black above, dark behind cheek, black tips to the axillaries forming dark bar, and dark marks on undertail-coverts. In flight, feet protrude beyond tail. Obviously bicoloured and less 'dirty' than the palest Balearic Shearwater. **VOICE** Sings in the burrow: long nasal inhaling followed by higher-pitched exhaling. **HABITAT** Widespread in the Mediterranean.

brown spots on axillaries and flanks

no white mark

white underparts

blackish-brown above

blackish-brown below tail

Balearic Shearwater *Puffinus mauretanicus*

IDENTIFICATION
36 cm. Very similar to Yelkouan Shearwater but browner plumage, especially underparts; these are darker with smoky colour on neck, lower belly and flanks; dark axillaries and brown undertail-coverts. Darkest individuals show only trace of a pale band in centre of belly. Distinguished from Sooty Shearwater by less slim silhouette and flapping flight lower over the sea. **VOICE** Silent at sea. **HABITAT** Breeding restricted to Balearic Islands; wanders to Bay of Biscay and Britain after breeding.

dark underwings

often very little white but always some

paler belly (uniform in Sooty Shearwater)

grey-brown above

grey belly

European Storm-petrel *Hydrobates pelagicus*

white band on underwing

little white on sides

white rump

square tail

short wings with uniform undersides

very short black bill with nasal tubes

white rump

black delicate feet

IDENTIFICATION
15 cm. Small black petrel with square white rump and wide white band in centre of underwing. Short tail, not forked, white rump extending onto the flanks. Upperwing uniform, wings angled with flapping flight; sometimes paddles on water to feed. Ssp. *melitensis* in the Mediterranean is larger with different habits. **VOICE** In the burrow, purring and rumbling calls. **HABITAT** Breeds on rocky islets in N Atlantic and W Mediterranean.

Leach's Storm-petrel *Oceanodroma leucorhoa*

pale band on wing

'dirty' V-shaped white rump

forked tail

broad wings

uniform underwings

white extending only slightly on the sides

IDENTIFICATION
20 cm. Large storm-petrel with forked tail, V-shaped white rump hardly extending to flanks, long wings with grey wing-bar along secondary coverts, often has pale face. Black underwings. Hesitant flight on angled wings, very different from the smaller European Storm-petrel; more direct and rapid flight in strong winds. **VOICE** Silent at sea, complex calls from breeding burrow, a rattling mixed with other notes. **HABITAT** Breeds on islets and coasts of N Atlantic.

RARE PETRELS AND ALBATROSSES A few species of seabirds that breed elsewhere are rare visitors to our seas. Originating from the North and South Atlantic, even the Antarctic, they disperse over the oceans during the austral winter. They vary in size from the diminutive storm-petrels that are not much larger than a swallow to the gigantic Wandering Albatross with a 3 m wingspan.

Madeiran Storm-petrel *Oceanodroma castro*

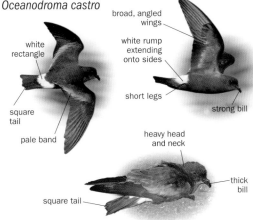

20 cm. Breeds on oceanic islands to the west of Portugal, the Azores, Madeira and the Canaries; a few have been seen in the Bay of Biscay. Resembles Leach's Storm-petrel but with a wide, square white rump extending onto belly; square tail, broad wings with shorter pale band not reaching the leading edge of wing. More direct, less hesitant flight with glides on arched wings, like shearwaters.

broad, angled wings

white rectangle

white rump extending onto sides

short legs

strong bill

square tail

pale band

heavy head and neck

thick bill

square tail

Monteiro's Storm-petrel *Oceanodroma monteiroi*

Sister species with Madeiran Storm-petrel, only officially separated in 2008. Endemic to the Azores where it breeds during the summer; as yet it has not been recorded in European waters. Slightly forked tail and different moult cycle.

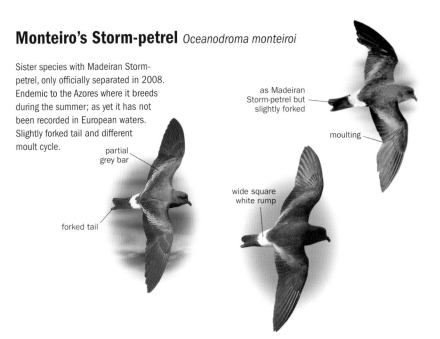

as Madeiran Storm-petrel but slightly forked

moulting

partial grey bar

wide square white rump

forked tail

Wilson's Storm-petrel *Oceanites oceanicus*

square
tail

wide pale
band

yellow
webs

in moult in summer
in Europe

straight trailing edge to wings
very wide white rump
reaching far down sides

long feet extend
beyond tail

16–18 cm. Annual migrant from the Antarctic and subantarctic. A little bigger than European Storm-petrel, trailing edges of wings straight, underwings black, broad white rump extending onto flanks, rounded tail, legs extend beyond tail, and yellow webs of feet that are difficult to see. More direct flight than Storm Petrel: paddles on water to feed with dangling legs. Individuals often in active primary moult in summer in Europe.

Black-bellied Storm-petrel *Fregetta tropica*

white coverts

black rear

central black
stripe
sometimes
absent

20 cm. Very rare vagrant to the Atlantic coast. Broad wings with straight trailing edges, feet reach beyond tail, grey band on the outer wing, wide white rump, square tail. Black breast and white belly with wide black median bar, sometimes narrow or absent; white greater and median underwing-coverts, lesser coverts black. Black on undertail-coverts as far as between legs (not in White-bellied Storm-petrel *F. grallaria*, with white belly and darker above). Flight similar to that of Wilson's Storm-petrel, bouncing on the waves.

White-faced Storm-petrel *Pelagodroma marina*

white
supercilium

pale
rump

white
below

dangling legs

rounded wings

20 cm. Large, elegant, slim storm-petrel, grey and white, long wings are large and rounded at tip, long dangling legs with yellow webs. Paddles on surface of sea. White underparts, grey rump, white face and black cheeks, long bill. Square black tail, rounded when fanned. Breeds on Madeira and Canaries, could disperse into Bay of Biscay.

Swinhoe's Storm-petrel *Oceanodroma monorhis*

20 cm. Breeds in the Pacific with vagrant individuals recorded in N Atlantic. Identical silhouette and flight to Leach's Storm-petrel but dark rump and white quills to outer primaries. Pale band across inner wing.

no white on rump

forked tail

pale band

entirely black below

long wings

short bill

dark rump

forked tail

Bulwer's Petrel *Bulweria bulwerii*

27 cm. Breeds on Canaries, Madeira and Azores. Entirely brownish-black small petrel with pale band across base of wing; slender silhouette with long neck and round head, long wedge-shape tail appears pointed, very long slender wings. Thicker bill than that of storm-petrels, with large nail. Flies low over the water with slow elastic wingbeats, and arced glides.

long graduated tail

black bill

entirely dark below

pale band on wing

entirely brownish-black

Jouanin's Petrel *Bulweria fallax*

31 cm. Larger and stouter than Bulwer's Petrel with clearly heavier bill. Can recall a dark *Pterodroma* petrel but long pointed tail and uniform dark underwings. Breeds in the Indian Ocean off the Arabian Peninsula. One European record: 3 birds (1 of which was collected) near Trévise in Italy, 2 November 1953.

broad wings

long graduated tail

thick bill

Fea's Petrel *Pterodroma feae*

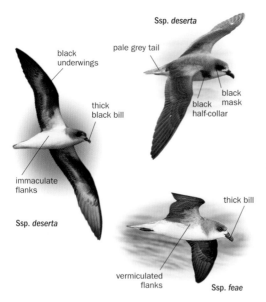

Ssp. *deserta*

black
underwings

pale grey tail

black
mask

thick
black bill

black
half-collar

immaculate
flanks

Ssp. *deserta*

thick bill

vermiculated
flanks

Ssp. *feae*

35 cm. Breeds on Madeira (ssp. *deserta*) and Cape Verdes (ssp. *feae*), wintering at sea in northern Atlantic. Reminiscent of a shearwater but has a big head, narrower angled wings and thick short black bill. Brownish-grey above, with paler grey rump and tail; grey head with dark mask through eye, dark half-collar on upper breast. White underparts but dark underwings (in good light, pale primary bases). Effortless flight, with long high-reaching glides, describing big vertical arcs. Ssp. *feae* is very similar to ssp. *deserta*, but darker uppertail-coverts, flanks mottled with dark and vermiculated axillaries. Recently considered to be a separate species.

Zino's Petrel *Pterodroma madeira*

quite uniform
dark head

grey rump
and tail

vermiculated
flanks

thinner
black bill

thinner bill

very white
underwings

pale individual

33 cm. Breeds on Madeira. Closely related to Fea's Petrel but much rarer, shorter thinner bill; very difficult to separate at sea.

Bermuda Petrel *Pterodroma cahow*

35 cm. A Bermudan endemic, dispersing into the Atlantic for winter. Very rare vagrant; an individual occupied a burrow in the Azores in 2002 and again the following year. Size, silhouette and bill as in Fea's Petrel, uniform grey above from back to cap, black mask and white forehead. Undersides of wings white with black leading edges, black spots on outer greater coverts and secondaries. Narrow white V on rump.

Black-capped Petrel
Pterodroma hasitata

40 cm. Breeds in the West Indies; very rare pelagic vagrant off N Atlantic coasts. Big and slim, black cap and white forehead, large white collar sometimes thin, large white rump. Very thick bill. Variable head pattern, some individuals are very white with small black cap hardly reaching eye, others reminiscent of Bermuda Petrel with grey nape; distinguished from below by large white collar separating black cheek from black pectoral patches. Black underwings, underparts as in Bermuda Petrel.

small amount of white on rump

black M

variegated underwings

grey half-collar

thin white collar

white rump

black cap

Dark form

thin black line

no collar

large white collar

reduced black cap

black bar

half-collar

black greater coverts

dark collar absent

Pale form

Pale form

white underwings

Soft-plumaged Petrel *Pterodroma mollis*

35 cm. Breeds in the S Atlantic and Indian Oceans. Very similar to Fea's Petrel (formerly considered conspecific with Fea's and Zino's), but rump and tail same as the mantle, and has more marked grey collar, sometimes complete; thick bill. An individual was photographed at Varanger in Norway, 6 June 2009.

often complete collar

dark underwings

Trindade Petrel *Pterodroma arminjoniana*

Dark morph

blackish-brown

mottled

central white band

Intermediate form

a little pale

white belly

underwings sometimes with a little white

Pale morph

entirely dark above

Dark morph

37 cm. Breeds in the S Atlantic, very rare vagrant to Azores. Quite compact silhouette with short tail, bill as in Zino's Petrel, variable plumage. Dark underwings with grey bases to flight feathers and greater coverts. Dark morph: entirely blackish-brown. Pale morph: brown above, dark head and breast and white belly with paler throat. Intermediate forms have pale spots on belly and more pale areas on underwing.

Black-browed Albatross *Thalassarche melanophris*

Wingspan 200–235 cm. Common breeder in S Atlantic (Falklands, S Georgia), rare vagrant in N Atlantic. Very large, long winged; black mantle, upperwings and tail, contrasting with white rump and neck. Massive bill without tube on upper ridge, grey with black tip (immature), yellow with red tip (adult). Underwings white with broad black border on leading and trailing edges; wing centre greyish in immatures. In wind, gliding flight with high arcs, without flapping.

Adult

entirely black wings

grey tail

yellow bill with red tip

broad black border

black 'eyebrow'

Adult

dark underwings

Immature

grey collar

black bill

Yellow-nosed Albatross *Thalassarche chlororhynchos*

Wingspan 180–205 cm. Smaller and slimmer than Black-browed Albatross. Breeds in S Atlantic, rare vagrant in to N Atlantic; an immature during June and July 2007 in Britain and Norway. Underwings with narrower black leading edge, black bill with yellow line on upper edge and red tip (adult), or all black (immature). White head with black triangle under eye (immature), pale grey head (adult). Typical albatross flight.

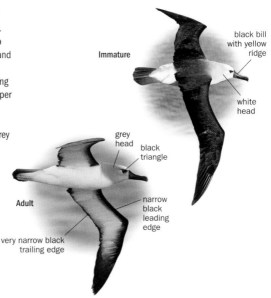

Immature

black bill with yellow ridge

white head

grey head

black triangle

Adult

narrow black leading edge

very narrow black trailing edge

Wandering Albatross *Diomedea exulans*

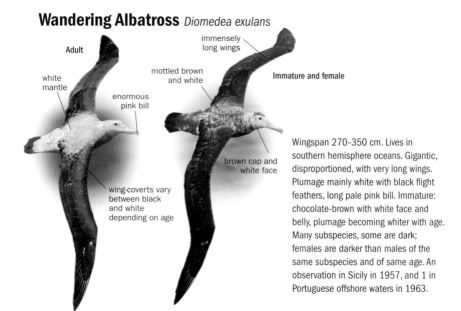

Adult

immensely long wings

white mantle

mottled brown and white

Immature and female

enormous pink bill

brown cap and white face

wing-coverts vary between black and white depending on age

Wingspan 270–350 cm. Lives in southern hemisphere oceans. Gigantic, disproportioned, with very long wings. Plumage mainly white with black flight feathers, long pale pink bill. Immature: chocolate-brown with white face and belly, plumage becoming whiter with age. Many subspecies, some are dark; females are darker than males of the same subspecies and of same age. An observation in Sicily in 1957, and 1 in Portuguese offshore waters in 1963.

Southern/Northern Giant Petrel *Macronectes giganteus/M. halli*

uniform upperparts

Northern Giant Petrel

Southern Giant Petrel

pale face and dark cap

bill with dark tip

underwings dark and uniform

pale head and neck grading into dark

nostrils in long tubes

yellowish bill with greenish tip

Wingspan 180–200 cm. Reminiscent of an enormous Fulmar, size of a Gannet, but with grey plumage (adult) or black (immature); massive yellowish bill with nostril tubes. Dark tip to bill in Northern Giant Petrel (subantarctic), adult variable but often has pale head with dark cap and nape (like a helmet). Southern Giant Petrel (Antarctic and subantarctic) has more uniform bill (with greenish tip), a uniformly coloured head but possibly with a pale face; white phase has a few black feathers here and there. One observation of an unidentified (as to species) Giant Petrel in Brittany, France in 1967.

Magnificent Frigatebird *Fregata magnificens*

Wingspan 215–245 cm. Tropical marine species, very rare vagrant in Europe. Very big, disproportionately long and slender wings often held in W shape, very long forked tail held tightly closed in flight (appears pointed). Long, thin hooked bill. Male: all black with red skin on throat. Female: white belly and black head. Immature: white head, breast and belly, a black half-collar on the breast. Often glides high above the sea; descends to fish from the water surface, very slow flaps, wings arched.

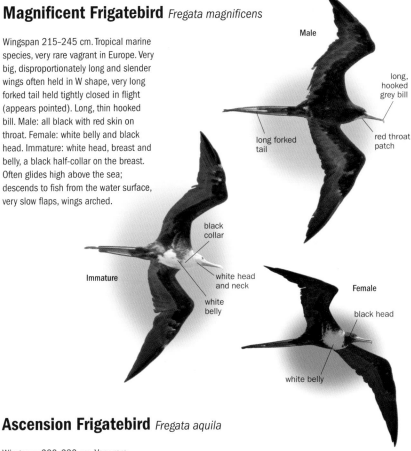

Male

long, hooked grey bill

long forked tail

red throat patch

black collar

Immature

white head and neck

white belly

Female

black head

white belly

Ascension Frigatebird *Fregata aquila*

Wingspan 200–230 cm. Very rare vagrant to Europe, 2 British records. Breeds on Ascension, in middle of the South Atlantic. A little smaller than Magnificent Frigatebird, with slimmer bill. Immature with complete black collar on the neck, white head, white on belly extends onto axillaries. Male has only violet sheen (never green) on upperparts.

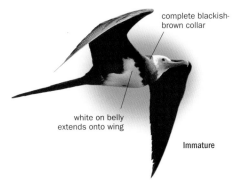

complete blackish-brown collar

white on belly extends onto wing

Immature

Red-billed Tropicbird *Phaethon aethereus*

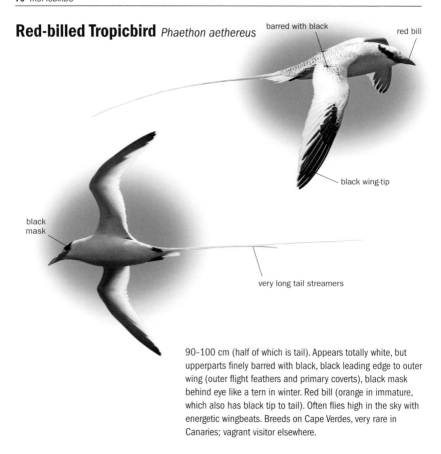

barred with black

red bill

black wing-tip

black mask

very long tail streamers

90–100 cm (half of which is tail). Appears totally white, but upperparts finely barred with black, black leading edge to outer wing (outer flight feathers and primary coverts), black mask behind eye like a tern in winter. Red bill (orange in immature, which also has black tip to tail). Often flies high in the sky with energetic wingbeats. Breeds on Cape Verdes, very rare in Canaries; vagrant visitor elsewhere.

White-tailed Tropicbird *Phaethon lepturus*

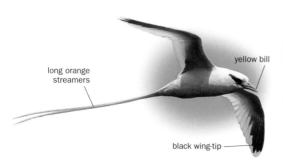

yellow bill

long orange streamers

black wing-tip

70–80 cm (half of which is tail), very rare vagrant in N Atlantic (principally Azores), breeds in West Atlantic. Very similar to Red-billed Tropicbird but has yellow bill and upperwing pattern is different: white primary coverts, black bar on inner wing, white areas without black barring. Tail streamers orange in adult.

GANNETS AND BOOBIES Large seabirds with long necks, long pointed bill, elongated wedge-shaped tail. They dive vertically when feeding, with wings folded into a W. They readily rest on water. One species breeds in Europe, the others are very rare vagrants.

Northern Gannet *Morus bassanus*

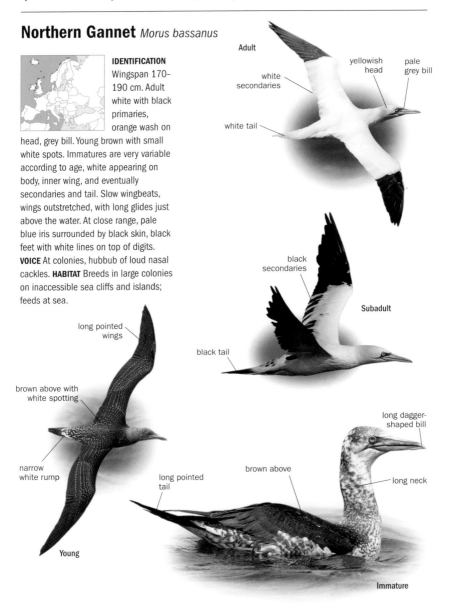

IDENTIFICATION
Wingspan 170–190 cm. Adult white with black primaries, orange wash on head, grey bill. Young brown with small white spots. Immatures are very variable according to age, white appearing on body, inner wing, and eventually secondaries and tail. Slow wingbeats, wings outstretched, with long glides just above the water. At close range, pale blue iris surrounded by black skin, black feet with white lines on top of digits.
VOICE At colonies, hubbub of loud nasal cackles. **HABITAT** Breeds in large colonies on inaccessible sea cliffs and islands; feeds at sea.

Adult

white secondaries

yellowish head

pale grey bill

white tail

black secondaries

Subadult

black tail

long pointed wings

brown above with white spotting

narrow white rump

long pointed tail

Young

brown above

long dagger-shaped bill

long neck

Immature

Brown Booby *Sula leucogaster*

white central band

brown head

bluish face

long pointed tail

pale bill

white belly

Adult male

Wingspan 130–150 cm. Breeds in the Red Sea, Cape Verdes; very rare vagrant on the European Atlantic coast. Small bicoloured, dark brown-and-white booby, with well-defined separation on the breast, pale bill and face, yellow legs. White undertail-coverts and axillaries. Immature has brown wash on belly. Upperparts uniform dark brown, no white on nape or rump.

pale underwings

brown head

brown belly

Immature

all brown above

Immature

dark iris

yellow face

pink bill

Adult female

Red-footed Booby *Sula sula*

Wingspan 120–140 cm. Small booby from the tropics with bright red feet; vagrant to France and Spain. Adult white morph: white body with black flight feathers and primary coverts, white tail, yellow-washed head, pale blue base to bill with black tip; brown morph: body and wing-coverts pale brown. Slim silhouette, longer tail than Gannet. Black iris.

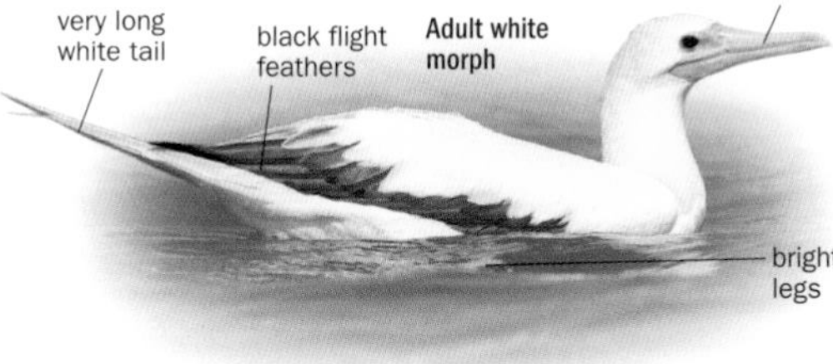

black flight feathers

Adult

speckled above

pink bill with black tip

long white tail

Immature

very long white tail

black flight feathers

Adult white morph

blue bill

bright red legs

Masked Booby *Sula dactylatra*

brown head

Adult

Immature in flight

black tail

yellowish bill

white underwings

black flight feathers

white iris

dark face

ivory-yellow bill

Adult

Wingspan 165–185 cm. Tropical booby; very rare vagrant to Europe, recorded off France and Spain. Adult white with black flight feathers and tail, black face with pale yellow bill. Immature: brown neck, white breast and belly, white nape and underwings (which look 'dirty' in Gannet). At close range, yellow iris and black legs.

black flight feathers

black legs

PELICANS Very large gliding birds, long bill with extendable pouch used when feeding. Large wings reminiscent of storks, allowing for gliding flight whilst migrating.

White Pelican *Pelecanus onocrotalus*

Adult

flight feathers black above and below

pink legs

yellow pouch

triangle of pink skin

black eye

Adult

Wingspan 245–295 cm. Black-and-white plumage. Pink skin on face surrounding eye, bill with grey mandibles and yellow pouch, small drooping crest. Flight feathers black above and below. In flight, large wings with fingered black flight feathers and white coverts reminiscent of White Stork, but shorter feet and enormous bill. Immatures washed brown. Rare breeder in E Europe; escaped birds of captive origin seen in winter or make prolonged stays.

Dalmatian Pelican *Pelecanus crispus*

grey legs

Immature

dark underparts

white eye

grey bill with orange pouch

shaggy neck

flight feathers greyish-white below

Adult

Wingspan 245–295 cm. Slightly greyish-white plumage, flight feathers black above but white below, easily visible in flight. Grey bill with orange pouch, pale eye surrounded by a little yellow skin, dark grey legs, shaggy crest. Immature has brown streaking on wing-coverts. Very rare vagrant to Europe away from a few small colonies in extreme SE; escapes or free-flying birds regularly seen in other parts.

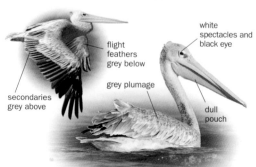

white spectacles and black eye

flight feathers grey below

grey plumage

secondaries grey above

dull pouch

Pink-backed Pelican
Pelecanus rufescens

Wingspan 225–260 cm. Small pelican of African origin. Escapes and free-flying birds in S France. Greyish plumage with flight feathers dark grey, not black, above and below. White swelling around eye, black spot in front of eye, tousled crest.

CORMORANTS Fish-eating birds with dark plumage, slightly hooked long bill, immatures with pale bellies. They sit low in water and dive to fish. May be seen standing with wings outstretched to dry them after swimming. Groups in flight form Vs. Species separated by size, silhouette and bill and chin skin colour. Three species breed in Europe.

(Great) Cormorant *Phalacrocorax carbo*

totally black above

outstretched neck in flight

Immature

yellow skin

white belly

hooked bill

white throat

long tail

white spot

Breeding adult

IDENTIFICATION
85 cm. Large size, black plumage, dark grey bill. Yellow skin in front of eye and on chin, surrounded with white on throat. Breeding: filamentous white feathers behind cheek and round white patch on thigh; more white on head in 'continental' *sinensis* race. The yellow chin skin ends in an upturned point in the 'Atlantic' *carbo* race. Immatures brown with pale underparts, sometimes white breast and belly. Dive preceded by small jump. In flight, energetic wingbeats, outstretched but curved neck. **VOICE** Silent away from colonies. **HABITAT** Lakes, ponds, rivers and sea coasts, even in deep water.

(European) Shag *Phalacrocorax aristotelis*

all black

Adult

slim lowered neck

yellow gape

tousled crest

green iris

Adult

black-and-yellow bill

brown upperparts

scaly coverts

Immature

white belly

pale legs

IDENTIFICATION
73 cm. Smaller and more slender than Great Cormorant, yellow-and-black bill, all-dark head with peaked crown and short crest when breeding. Adult: green sheen and green eye, bill black with yellow gape in summer, just a yellow base in winter. Immature: quite uniform brown, with paler underparts, yellowish base to bill. In flight, straight slim neck. **VOICE** Silent away from colonies. **HABITAT** Sea coasts, nests on sea cliffs or small islands.

'Mediterranean' Shag *Phalocrocorax aristotelis desmarestii*

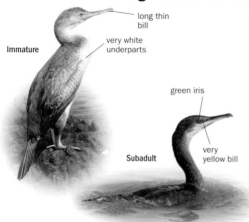

Immature

long thin bill

very white underparts

green iris

Subadult

very yellow bill

73 cm. Mediterranean form of European Shag. Breeds (as early as February) in Catalonia, Corsica and farther east. Visible from Mediterranean coasts in winter and early summer. Adult: yellow bill with dark upper edge. Immature: white underparts and very pale edges to upperwing-coverts.

Pygmy Cormorant *Phalacrocorax pygmaeus*

brown sheen

very short bill

long tail

Adult

50 cm. Small cormorant breeding in the Po delta (Italy) eastwards to Central Asia. Small angular head with peaked crown and very short black bill with barely visible yellow bare parts; very long wedge-shaped tail. When breeding, plumage with brown tint on head and neck. Immature: paler belly.

Double-crested Cormorant *Phalacrocorx auritus*

orange lores

bill partly orange-yellow

orange gular pouch

Immature

80 cm. Nearctic cormorant similar to Great Cormorant but a little smaller and slimmer. In winter, gular pouch has straight edge and is orange-yellow, including around the eye. Very rare vagrant; a few records from Britain, Ireland and France; annual in the Azores.

HERONS, BITTERNS AND EGRETS Long-legged birds inhabiting wetlands, feeding on small vertebrates (fish, frogs, voles) and both aquatic and terrestrial invertebrates, according to their habits. Territorial (bitterns) or colonial nesters; tree-nesting herons and egrets are often in mixed colonies. Other long-legged wetland species are in different families: storks (p. 93), spoonbills and ibises (p. 94) and flamingos (p. 97).

(Eurasian) Bittern *Botaurus stellaris*

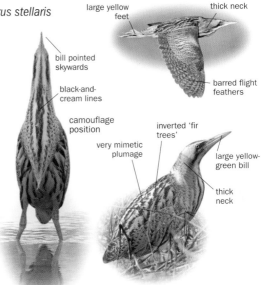

large yellow feet

thick neck

bill pointed skywards

black-and-cream lines

barred flight feathers

camouflage position

very mimetic plumage

inverted 'fir trees'

large yellow-green bill

thick neck

IDENTIFICATION
75 cm A massive heron with thick neck and brown plumage with fine black streaks; black crown and thin moustache; yellow bill and green legs. In flight, compacted neck and long feet extend beyond tail. Often stays immobile in reeds; to hide it lifts its neck skywards and sways like reeds in the wind. **VOICE** Song: very characteristic muffled *oump*, like the sound when blowing into a bottle. **HABITAT** Extensive, quiet reedbeds; avoids winter freezes.

Little Bittern *Ixobrychus minutus*

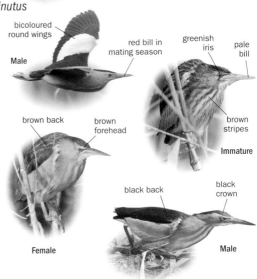

bicoloured round wings

Male

red bill in mating season

greenish iris

pale bill

brown back

brown forehead

brown stripes

Immature

black back

black crown

Female

Male

IDENTIFICATION
36 cm. Very small black-and-beige heron, resembles a miniature Eurasian Bittern. Male: black back, flight feathers and crown; buff underparts, neck and wing-coverts. Female: black back feathers with brown margins and browner neck, duller less contrasting plumage. Immature more striped. Yellow bill with black tip and green legs. In flight, black wings with large round buff patch in centre; elastic wingbeats. **VOICE** Song: a muffled, raucous far-carrying *ruuu*, repeated every 2 seconds. **HABITAT** Reedbeds, well-vegetated lakes, flooded ditches.

Black-crowned Night Heron *Nycticorax nycticorax*

uniform grey upperwings

feet extend only slightly beyond tail

Adult

large orange eye

brown with white spots

thick neck

large red eye

white plumes

black

black back

Immature

yellow legs

Adult

IDENTIFICATION
62 cm. Small, stocky heron with large head, short thick neck and yellow legs.
Adult: black cap and back, white forehead, 2 long white plumes on nape, uniform pale grey wings, black bill and large red eye. Immature: entirely brown streaked with buff, drop-shaped spots on back and wing-coverts, brown bill with dark tip, orange iris. Nocturnal habits, leaves colony at dusk while calling; slow wingbeats. **VOICE** Various croaks, particularly a morbid *kwak* in flight. **HABITAT** Marshes, lakes, rivers; roosts in trees.

Squacco Heron *Ardeola ralloides*

Breeding adult in flight

striped crown

brown scapulars with beige streaks

black-and-yellow bill

striped neck

all-white wings

yellow legs

long slender plumes

blue-based bill

tan back

Winter

Breeding adult

IDENTIFICATION
45 cm. Small heron with brown back and white wings. In summer, tan-coloured back, scapulars washed with yellow, white neck, crown striped with black, with long white plumes bordered with black. Blue-based bill with black tip. Reddish feet at height of courtship. Winter and immature: pale brown back, scapulars streaked brown, beige neck marked with vertical brownish-black lines. Often hunts in the open in shallow water. **VOICE** Raucous croaks similar to call of female Mallard. **HABITAT** Marshes, wet meadows, shallow lakes with bushes and a few trees.

Cattle Egret *Bubulcus ibis*

IDENTIFICATION
48 cm. Small
white heron with
black legs and
short yellow bill
(base red during
courtship). Adults have orange-washed
crown, breast and shoulders. Similar to
Little Egret but slightly smaller, stockier,
with black feet and shorter yellow bill.
Young birds are all white with a dark bill
on fledging, the bill quickly turning
yellow. **VOICE** Raucous *krat* in flight.
HABITAT Marshes, wet grazed meadows;
often hunts insects near farm animals.

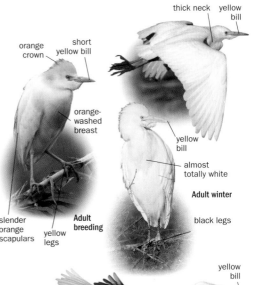

thick neck   yellow bill

orange crown   short yellow bill

orange-washed breast

yellow bill

almost totally white

Adult winter

slender orange scapulars   yellow legs   **Adult breeding**

black legs

Great Egret *Casmerodius albus*

IDENTIFICATION
93 cm. Large,
size of Grey
Heron but totally
white with black
legs (black feet,
pale base to tibia; legs red at height of
courtship period), yellow bill in winter,
black in summer (green skin in front of
eye). Unlike Little Egret, no elongated
nape feathers, but long slender plumes
on back and lower neck during courtship
period. In flight, angular neck held
folded; very long legs and slow
wingbeats. Longer neck than Little Egret.
The Nearctic race *egretta* has completely
black tibia and heavier bill (observed
annually in the Azores). **VOICE** Long
croaking calls at colonies and when
excited or disturbed. **HABITAT** Lakes,
marshes, reedbeds with bushes.

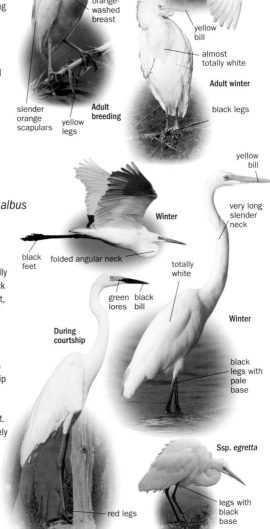

yellow bill

very long slender neck

Winter

black feet   folded angular neck

totally white

green black
lores   bill

During courtship

Winter

black legs with pale base

Ssp. *egretta*

legs with black base

red legs

Little Egret *Egretta garzetta*

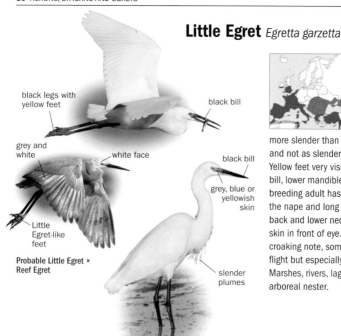

black legs with yellow feet

black bill

grey and white

white face

black bill

grey, blue or yellowish skin

Little Egret-like feet

Probable Little Egret × Reef Egret

slender plumes

IDENTIFICATION 60 cm. All-white small heron with black bill and legs, and yellow feet. Larger and more slender than Cattle Egret, smaller and not as slender as Great Egret. Yellow feet very visible in flight. Black bill, lower mandible grey in immatures; breeding adult has 2 long plumes on the nape and long slender feathers on back and lower neck. Grey or pale yellow skin in front of eye. **VOICE** Rough croaking note, sometimes when taking flight but especially at colonies. **HABITAT** Marshes, rivers, lagoons; a colonial, arboreal nester.

Western Reef Egret *Egretta gularis*

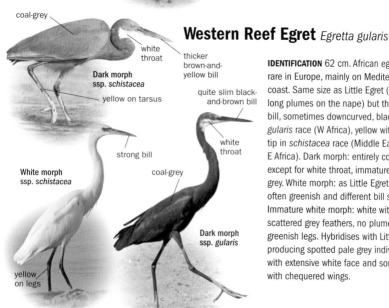

coal-grey

white throat

thicker brown-and-yellow bill

Dark morph ssp. schistacea

yellow on tarsus

quite slim black-and-brown bill

white throat

strong bill

coal-grey

White morph ssp. schistacea

Dark morph ssp. gularis

yellow on legs

IDENTIFICATION 62 cm. African egret, very rare in Europe, mainly on Mediterranean coast. Same size as Little Egret (with 2 long plumes on the nape) but thicker bill, sometimes downcurved, black in *gularis* race (W Africa), yellow with black tip in *schistacea* race (Middle East and E Africa). Dark morph: entirely coal-grey except for white throat, immatures ashy-grey. White morph: as Little Egret but feet often greenish and different bill shape. Immature white morph: white with scattered grey feathers, no plumes and greenish legs. Hybridises with Little Egret producing spotted pale grey individuals with extensive white face and sometimes with chequered wings.

Grey Heron *Ardea cinerea*

IDENTIFICATION
93 cm. Large, all grey, adult with black band behind eye continuing as black plumes on nape. Adult: white head including forehead, greyish-white neck with black stripes on front, long black line along flank. Immature: dark grey crown, darker neck and breast. In flight the neck is bent in a relatively non-angular S-shape, grey-black flight feathers and slightly contrasting dark grey wing-coverts. **VOICE** Rough, loud *fraank* slightly lifting, sometimes disyllabic. **HABITAT** Watercourses, lakes, fishponds, lagoons, the coast and even agricultural land where it hunts voles. Colonial breeder, usually in trees.

dark grey crown
bicoloured bill
wings bicoloured above
Immature
Adult
grey neck striped in front
folded neck
black mask
dark grey above
large orange bill
Adult

Purple Heron *Ardea purpurea*

IDENTIFICATION
80 cm. Very similar to Grey Heron but slightly smaller, slimmer, with different coloration. Long neck, rufous behind with long black-and-white stripes in front. Lead-grey back, reddish scapulars and shoulders, dark red belly with reddish 'trousers'. Immature: pale rufous above with pale feather edgings, striped below, pale neck lightly striped with pale brown. In flight, slender neck folded in an angular S-shape. **VOICE** *kreek*, shorter than call of Grey Heron. **HABITAT** Extensive reedbeds, marshes, shallow waters in major wetlands.

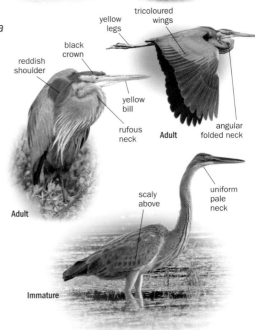

tricoloured wings
yellow legs
black crown
reddish shoulder
yellow bill
rufous neck
Adult
angular folded neck
Adult
scaly above
uniform pale neck
Immature

RARE HERONS, BITTERNS AND EGRETS Various species of Nearctic or African origin recorded in Europe.

reddish shoulder patch

strong bill

Adult

thin black stripes

reddish 'trousers'

Great Blue Heron *Ardea herodias*

95 cm. Nearctic migrant, very rare vagrant in Europe; annual in the Azores in autumn. Very similar to Grey Heron but appears more thickset with heavier, thicker bill, longer more angular neck; adults have reddish shoulders and 'trousers'. Often wine-red colour on neck. Immature: narrower black lines on front of neck than Grey Heron.

black head

short grey bill

white throat

faintly striped neck

Black-headed Heron
Ardea melanocephala

85 cm. African migrant heron. Very rare vagrant to Europe, 1 record from the Camargue in November 1971. Very similar to Grey Heron but a little smaller, white underwing-coverts, thus obviously showing tricoloured wings from below. Adult: black head and neck with extensive white throat and striped front of neck; black replaced by dark-grey in immature, which lacks the long thin plumes on the nape.

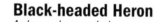

yellow lore

long slim bill

slate-coloured neck

Tricoloured Heron *Egretta tricolor*

Immature

greenish legs

65 cm. Very rare Nearctic vagrant to the Azores and Canaries. Very slim, long neck and bill. Yellow base to bill, yellowish legs, blue-grey above, front of neck mottled with black and white, white belly. Reddish neck, coverts and mantle with black barring in immature; coal-blue neck in adult, same colour as head.

Little Blue Heron *Egretta caerulea*

68 cm. Very rare Nearctic vagrant to the Azores and Ireland. Heavier than Little Egret, less so than Cattle Egret (longer bill); bill with thick base, greenish legs and feet. Immature has white plumage with grey bill, adult is dark blue-grey with grey, black-tipped bill.

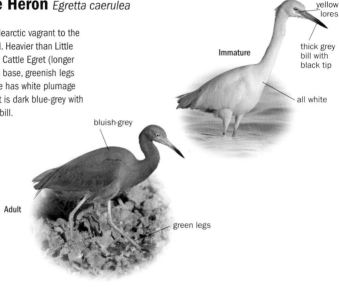

pale yellow lores

Immature

thick grey bill with black tip

all white

bluish-grey

Adult

green legs

Snowy Egret *Egretta thula*

60 cm. Nearctic equivalent of Little Egret; very rare vagrant to Britain, Iceland and the Azores. Yellow skin in front of eye, black legs with yellow band along their rear edge, and yellow feet. Adult has a shaggy crest of feathers, not long plumes.

bright yellow lores

bicoloured legs

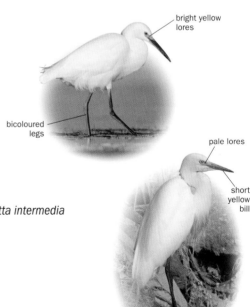

pale lores

short yellow bill

Intermediate Egret *Egretta intermedia*

66 cm. Very rare vagrant from Asia or sub-Saharan Africa, recorded in Italy. Only a little larger than Little Egret but shorter yellow bill with black tip, no nape plumes and entirely black legs reminiscent of Great Egret. Gape-line extends to just below eye (extends beyond eye in Great Egret).

blackish legs

American Bittern *Botaurus lentiginosus*

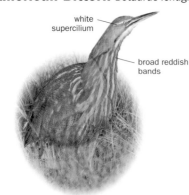

white supercilium

broad reddish bands

uniform flight feathers

uniform and obviously reddish

65 cm. Nearctic equivalent of Eurasian Bittern, very rare vagrant to W Europe and the Azores. More uniform above, fewer black markings, longer, thinner bill with black culmen, large black-bordered reddish streaks on front of neck, brown crown and pale supercilium. In flight, unbarred flight feathers and buff trailing edge to wings.

very dark lores

Adult

wide stripes

maroon nape

Immature

beige head

rufous head

slate-grey nape

Adult

Indian Pond Heron *Ardeola grayii*

45 cm. The W Asian equivalent of Squacco Heron, rare in winter in Kuwait and Oman; a Belgian record may have involved an escape. In winter, like Squacco Heron but neck with wider stripes and darker back (however, some Squaccos can be very dark), and dark lores.

Chinese Pond Heron
Ardeola bacchus

45 cm. The E Asian equivalent of Squacco Heron; a few records of adults in Europe (Hungary, Norway and Britain) of possible escapes. In winter looks like Indian Pond Heron but more reddish, the neck a more contrasting white and dark brown, with dark spots along each side; lores less obviously dark. Breeding: slate-coloured mantle, dark rufous head and neck, yellow bill with black tip.

Green Heron *Butorides virescens*

44 cm. Small Nearctic migratory heron; very rare vagrant. Similar to Little Bittern but bigger, with black crown, vinous cheeks, neck and breast, white streaks on throat and front of neck, slaty back, blackish-grey wings. Immature has white spots on flight feathers and greater coverts. Discreet, hunts in shallow waters, often hidden in vegetation and along watercourses lined with trees.

white spots on coverts

black cap

reddish neck

yellow legs

Immature

Striated Heron *Butorides striatus*

44cm. Small heron, resident in Africa, Asia and S America; inhabits lakes, mangroves and undisturbed coasts. A juvenile was recorded in Cyprus in October 2014. As Green Heron, but immature grey-brown with small white spots on wing-coverts, no rufous on neck. Adult mouse-grey with black crown and yellow legs.

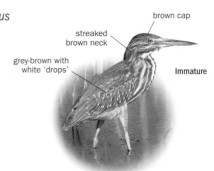

brown cap

streaked brown neck

grey-brown with white 'drops'

Immature

Yellow-crowned Night Heron
Nyctanassa violacea

58 cm. Nearctic heron, very rare vagrant to the Azores and Madeira. Recalls Black-crowned Night Heron but shorter, thicker bill, oval head. Adult has grey back, black head, white cheek and crest, pale fringes to wing-coverts. Immature is brown and covered with small white spots above, with a very heavy grey bill. Call is a loud *kyok* or *kouak*, higher-pitched and more nasal than that of Black-crowned Night Heron.

very heavy bill

big head

Immature

cream spotting

big head

white cheek

grey bill

plumes

Adult

Least Bittern *Ixobrychus exilis*

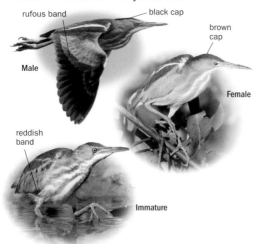

rufous band

black cap

brown cap

Male

Female

reddish band

Immature

32 cm. Nearctic bittern; very rare vagrant to Britain, Iceland and the Azores. Smaller than Little Bittern with distinctive wing pattern, tricoloured with black flight feathers, reddish greater coverts and buff coverts. Male has black back and rufous back of neck; immature very reddish, with black marks on scapulars.

Schrenck's Bittern *Ixobrychus eurhythmus*

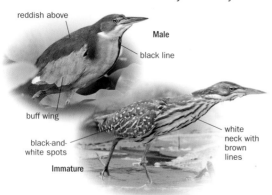

reddish above

Male

black line

buff wing

black-and-white spots

white neck with brown lines

Immature

35 cm. Rare Asian vagrant; 1 record from Italy in 1912. Male has black mantle, reddish cheeks contrasting with white throat, long dark mark down front of neck, grey flight feathers, tan coloured wing-coverts, and reddish scapulars. Immature with characteristic rufous, black-and-white mottled mantle, large reddish stripes on neck; female has wing-coverts like mantle, male as in adult.

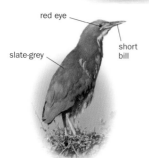

red eye

short bill

slate-grey

Dwarf Bittern *Ixobrychus sturmii*

29 cm. Very small sub-Saharan bittern, recorded once in the Canaries. Slate-grey above, uniform grey head, cheek, and side of neck; tan front of neck strongly striped brown (immature) or black (adult). Yellow bill with a black culmen, yellow legs with long toes. Immature has white-spotted wing-coverts.

White Stork *Ciconia ciconia*

IDENTIFICATION 105 cm. Large, slender, white with black flight feathers, red legs and bill. Flies with slow wingbeats, glides on thermals. Immatures have black tertials. Often migrates in flocks. **VOICE** Displays with bill-clapping on the nest whilst throwing head back. **HABITAT** Open fields with hedgerows, marshes, wet meadows, and rubbish tips. Nest is a big platform of sticks on a tree, roof, pylon or specially constructed nest-poles.

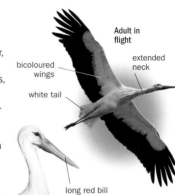

Adult in flight

extended neck

bicoloured wings

white tail

long red bill

black flight feathers

Adult

red legs

Black Stork *Ciconia nigra*

red spectacles

red bill

black neck

Adult

black neck

black underwings

Adult in flight

red legs

orange bill

Immature

brown neck

IDENTIFICATION 100 cm. Similar to White Stork but black neck and wings; white belly and axillaries. Red bill and legs; red skin around eye. Immature: duller neck and coverts with pale margins, grey bill and legs. In flight, silhouette as White Stork except that most of underwing black. **VOICE** Generally silent. **HABITAT** Mature undisturbed forests supplied with numerous watercourses feeding the area, and large trees for nesting. Migrant, winters in the Sahel.

Eurasian Spoonbill *Platalea leucorodia*

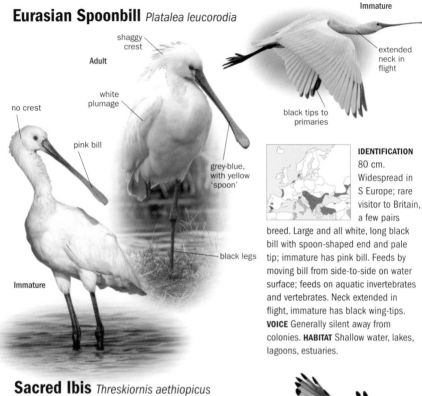

Immature

Adult

shaggy crest

white plumage

no crest

pink bill

extended neck in flight

black tips to primaries

grey-blue, with yellow 'spoon'

black legs

Immature

IDENTIFICATION
80 cm. Widespread in S Europe; rare visitor to Britain, a few pairs breed. Large and all white, long black bill with spoon-shaped end and pale tip; immature has pink bill. Feeds by moving bill from side-to-side on water surface; feeds on aquatic invertebrates and vertebrates. Neck extended in flight, immature has black wing-tips. **VOICE** Generally silent away from colonies. **HABITAT** Shallow water, lakes, lagoons, estuaries.

Sacred Ibis *Threskiornis aethiopicus*

fluffy black on rump

black head

white throat

thick downcurved black bill

Immature

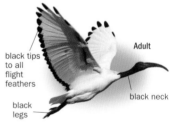

black tips to all flight feathers

Adult

black neck

black legs

72 cm. White plumage with black neck and fluffed-up tertials, downcurved black bill with thick base. In flight, black tips to flight feathers. Introduced feral populations in France and Italy, with individuals occurring elsewhere. Feeds on aquatic invertebrates, fish and amphibians.

Glossy Ibis *Plegadis falcinellus*

extended neck in flight

Adult

blue base to bill with fine white lines

IDENTIFICATION 60 cm. Widespread in S Europe; rare visitor to Britain. Medium-sized, dark plumage, long downturned bill. Adult: dark reddish body, wings with green sheen; fine white line above and below the lores. In winter, white specks on head and neck. In flight, neck extended and legs extend well beyond tail. **VOICE** Silent away from colonies. **HABITAT** Marshes, wet meadows, extensive wetlands with shallow water.

Adult

long downcurved bill

wine-red neck

green wings

Immature

white-spotted head

pale bill

Bald Ibis *Geronticus eremita*

75 cm. Very rare and threatened ibis, now existing only in Morocco and Syria; extinct in Turkey. Reintroduction programmes in Andalusia and Austria. Until the Middle Ages it bred quite widely in Europe. Short legs, thickset, long downcurved red bill, bare head apart from scraggy crest on nape in adult. Immature has grey head with no crest. Black plumage with green-and-purple sheen; pink legs do not extend beyond tail in flight. **VOICE** Silent away from colonies. **HABITAT** Breeds on remote cliffs. Feeds on the ground in dry open habitats.

shaggy crest

bald head

short stout red legs

African Spoonbill *Platalea alba*

red face

spoon-shaped
pink-edged bill

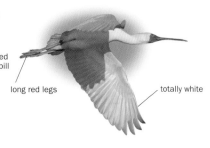

long red legs

totally white

90 cm. African species; a few European records of birds of dubious origin, has nested in France. All white but with grey bill and large area of bare red facial skin, white iris, pink legs. Immature has a pinkish-grey bare face and yellowish bill.

Yellow-billed Stork *Mycteria ibis*

black coverts

red face

scaly rose tint

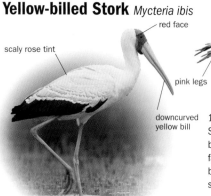

pink legs

black flight
feathers

downcurved
yellow bill

100 cm. Vagrant from tropical Africa; records from Spain and the Canaries. Reminiscent of White Stork but long thick-based yellow downcurved bill, bare red face, wing-coverts tinged with pink, pink legs and black tail. Immature has brown neck, mantle and scaly brown wing-coverts.

bare head

black upperparts

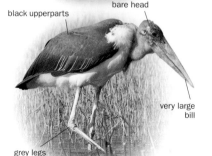

Marabou Stork
Leptoptilos crumenifer

150 cm. Very large African stork with a few records from France and Spain, probably escapes. Enormous bill, long grey legs, bald head and neck with dirty blackish face. Black above, greater coverts on the upperwing with white margins, white underparts. Often glides, slow wingbeats. Scavenger and predator.

very large
bill

grey legs

Greater Flamingo *Phoenicopterus roseus*

black flight feathers

Adult

pink underwing-coverts

extended neck

downcurved pink bill with black tip

long neck

Adult

pink legs

blue-grey base to bill

white neck

brownish-grey mantle

Juvenile

grey legs

IDENTIFICATION 120–145 cm. Male larger than female. Pinkish-white plumage with dark pink areas on wing, and black flight feathers. Pale pink downturned bill with triangular black tip. Immature: greyish plumage, black stripes on wings and back, and dark grey legs. Legs and neck extended in flight. Gregarious, moves slowly with neck in an S-shape; sleeps on 1 leg. **VOICE** Call: nasal *a-ha* or *ka-a*. **HABITAT** Saltpans, shallow saline lakes rich in micro-invertebrates, filters food using specialised bill with lamellae.

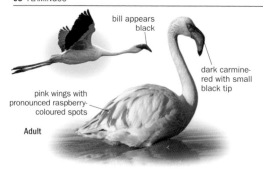

bill appears black

dark carmine-red with small black tip

pink wings with pronounced raspberry-coloured spots

Adult

Lesser Flamingo
Phoeniconaias minor

80–95 cm. Colourful small African flamingo. Dark bill with dark red base, appearing all black at a distance. Dark pink plumage, red feathers on the wings, very pink neck. Escapes or vagrants occasionally seen, particularly in the Camargue and in Spain.

Chilean Flamingo *Phoenicopterus chilensis*

Adult

bicoloured dull pale pink-and-black downcurved bill

grey to yellow legs with pink knees

100–120 cm. South American species, slightly smaller than Greater Flamingo, grey legs, pink knees and digits, black tip covers more than half the bill, pale plumage with some more colourful orange-red feathers. A few individuals occur, all escapes.

American Flamingo *Phoenicopterus ruber*

pronounced dark orange-pink colour

Adult

long bill with extensive black tip, pink lower mandible

pinkish-grey legs

125–145 cm. North American species, once considered conspecific with Greater Flamingo. More colourful plumage, reddish-pink, larger amount of black on bill; pinkish-grey legs. Regularly encountered as escapes.

RAPTORS Diurnal birds of prey, hooked bill covered at its base by skin termed the cere; their feet have very long hooked claws. Most species have a more or less specialised diet. This diverse family is here divided into several well-recognised groups.

European Honey-buzzard *Pernis apivorus*

IDENTIFICATION
Wingspan 115–135 cm. Size and silhouette recall Common Buzzard but has more outstretched head, longer tail, wings larger at base and narrower and more pointed at tip. Large dark bar on trailing edge of wing, tail with 1 terminal band and 2 intermediate bars. Variable plumage, white to dark brown with broad bars on belly. Underwing often darker with black carpal patch. Uniform upperparts apart from tail bars; head ash-grey (male) or brown (female), yellow iris, grey cere. Juvenile has white, reddish or dark brown morphs, very variable, with barred flight feathers, dark iris and yellow cere. **VOICE** Long plaintive ascending or descending whistle.
HABITAT Forests with clearings, areas with hedgerows and copses, feeds on wild bee and wasp nests.

dark carpal patch

wide dark band

diffusely dark flight feathers

grey head

close bands

brown head

Adult male pale morph

Adult female

3 bars on tail

brown head

Female dark morph

large black bars

diffuse dark tips

dark eye and yellow cere

Juvenile dark morph

Adult

tips of flight feathers clearly dark

tail bars not pronounced

grey head

black underwings

broad dark bars

Male dark morph

dark bill and round head

yellow eye

brown barred 'trousers'

Crested Honey-buzzard *Pernis ptilorhynchus*

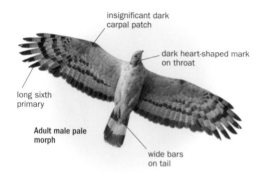

insignificant dark carpal patch

dark heart-shaped mark on throat

long sixth primary

Adult male pale morph

wide bars on tail

Wingspan 130–155 cm. Asian cousin of European Honey-buzzard, very rare migrant in Middle East, 1 record in Italy in May 2011. Larger with no dark carpal patch on underwing; often with black-margined white throat; squarer wing than European (very emarginated sixth primary). Male: black tail with wide central grey band. Female: similar to female European Honey-buzzard. Juvenile: same wing structure as adult, no dark carpal patch, flight feathers with undulating dark bars.

Female pale morph

pale carpal

diffuse tail bars

Juvenile dark morph

brown carpal patch

fingered sixth primary

quite long sixth primary

pale carpal

black collar

heavy bill

Female perched

white throat

Adult female

narrow bars

Common Buzzard *Buteo buteo*

IDENTIFICATION
Wingspan 110–130 cm. Brown plumage with white crescent on breast; underparts with horizontal barring (adult: dark iris) or vertical barring (juvenile: pale iris). Very variable plumage: white morphs (often with wide dark moustache, dark carpal patches, orange wash on tail), dark morphs (white crescent hardly visible), some individuals washed reddish. Tail with regular narrow bars (juvenile) or larger terminal band (adult). Upperparts uniform brown; no pale zone at base of primaries, tail rarely paler at base. **VOICE** Short descending *miaw*, more monotone and more frequently repeated by juveniles.
HABITAT All habitats with trees or copses.

Pale morph

insignificant black carpal

dark underwings

no well-defined band on tail

dark secondaries

Classic adult

dark underwings

Rufous adult

prominent bars on secondaries

bar on tail

streaked breast

diffuse black band

Pale juvenile

thin barring

well-defined black border

black carpal

dark iris

yellow cere

brown barring

pale head

pale iris

Pale adult

barred flanks

brown body and head

striped breast

Brown adult

Pale juvenile

Rough-legged Buzzard
Buteo lagopus

Male

Juvenile

dark pectoral patches

dark belly

only slightly barred

dark carpal patch

broad and narrow bands

pale primaries

dark secondaries

white base to tail

Juvenile

wide bar

dark head and breast

white belly

clear black band

Adult male

Juvenile

black belly

diffuse band

ill-defined band on trailing edge

pale iris

dark streaks on white

uniformly dark

unbarred tail

Juvenile

IDENTIFICATION
Wingspan 125–150 cm. Larger than Common Buzzard, white tail with black terminal band, underwing with black carpal square and dark brown 'trousers'. Feathered tarsi. Pale (juvenile) or dark iris (adult). Pale primary bases form a pale patch on upperwing. Head often white and plumage pale in juveniles, dark tail-band less well-defined. Adult more similar to Common Buzzard but dark 'trousers' and tail with distinct wide band; more than half the females and a third of males have thin bars. More inclined to hover when hunting. **VOICE** Call more descending than that of Common Buzzard, but normally silent in winter. **HABITAT** Open agricultural plains, polders, meadows, forest margins.

Steppe Buzzard *Buteo buteo vulpinus*

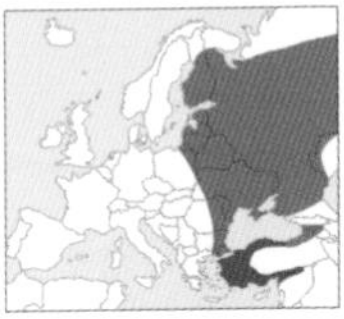

Wingspan 100–125 cm. Eastern subspecies of Common Buzzard, often with reddish plumage. Smaller and slimmer with whiter primaries that have pale bases above and more fingered outer primaries; very prominent black border on trailing edge of wing in adults; often with darker carpals. The brownish-grey morph is very similar to Common Buzzard; reddish morph recalls Long-legged Buzzard, but slimmer and shorter-winged, underparts more uniform without darker 'trousers', less evident dark carpal patch. It can be confused with Common Buzzards with reddish tail or of rufous plumage; structure and overall colour allows for separation. Intermediate individuals breed in Finland. Highly migratory, passing through the Middle East to winter in central Africa.

non-barred primaries

carpal patch

reddish underwings

rusty with dark terminal band

Adult pale rufous morph

Adult rufous morph

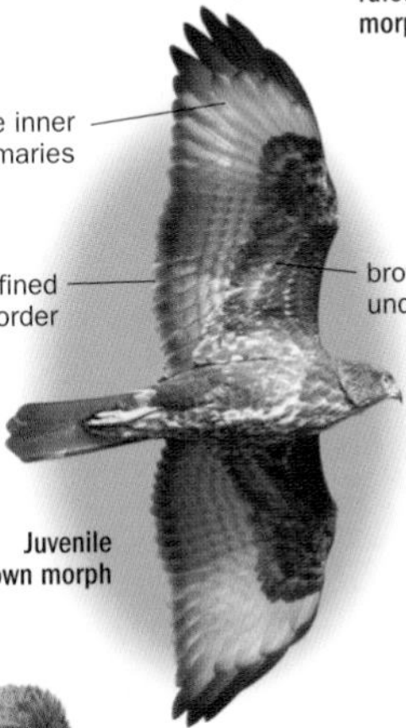

white inner primaries

ill-defined border

brown underwings

wide band

Adult dark morph

Juvenile brown morph

pale zone and dark eye-stripe

numerous dark bars

rounded 'hand'

Rufous morph

extensive rufous on flanks

rufous breast

rufous tail with dark band

Rufous morph

Long-legged Buzzard
Buteo rufinus

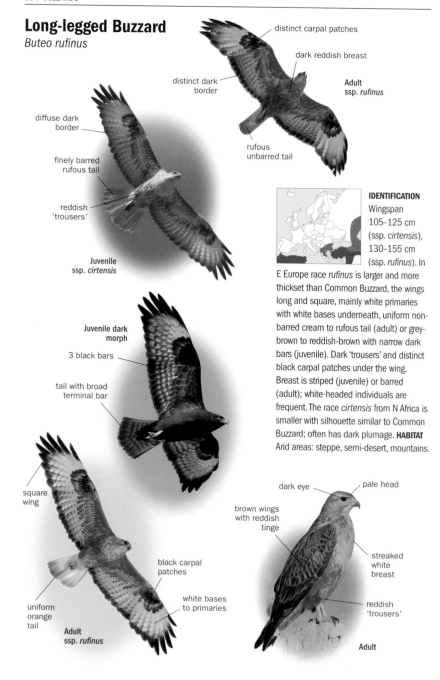

distinct carpal patches

dark reddish breast

distinct dark border

Adult ssp. *rufinus*

diffuse dark border

finely barred rufous tail

reddish 'trousers'

rufous unbarred tail

Juvenile ssp. *cirtensis*

Juvenile dark morph

3 black bars

tail with broad terminal bar

square wing

black carpal patches

uniform orange tail

white bases to primaries

Adult ssp. *rufinus*

dark eye

pale head

brown wings with reddish tinge

streaked white breast

reddish 'trousers'

Adult

IDENTIFICATION
Wingspan 105–125 cm (ssp. *cirtensis*), 130–155 cm (ssp. *rufinus*). In E Europe race *rufinus* is larger and more thickset than Common Buzzard, the wings long and square, mainly white primaries with white bases underneath, uniform non-barred cream to rufous tail (adult) or grey-brown to reddish-brown with narrow dark bars (juvenile). Dark 'trousers' and distinct black carpal patches under the wing. Breast is striped (juvenile) or barred (adult); white-headed individuals are frequent. The race *cirtensis* from N Africa is smaller with silhouette similar to Common Buzzard; often has dark plumage. **HABITAT** Arid areas: steppe, semi-desert, mountains.

Short-toed Eagle *Circaetus gallicus*

IDENTIFICATION
Wingspan
160–180 cm.
Larger than a
buzzard, longer
squarer wings.
Three clear dark bars on tail, underwings
with dark uniform mottling without dark
carpal patch. Underparts very white, with
sparse dark brown markings. Certain
individuals have very white underparts.
Brown above; yellow iris. Hovers with
slow flaps to locate prey. **VOICE** Vocal in
summer, short *kiou* or long plaintive call.
HABITAT Feeds on reptiles (snakes and
lizards) in areas of short vegetation,
sunny hillsides, scrub, steppe and
garrigue. Builds its nest within woodland,
often in a pine on the side of steep
ground. Spends the winter in sub-
Saharan Africa.

dark 'bib'

underwings white
mottled with
brown

Adult

white
underwings

broad
wings

pale
throat

3 bands on
tail

Pale morph

often hovers

band on tail

big head

yellow eyes

dark 'bib'

trailing legs

white belly with
brown bars

pale bar
on wing

Adult

KITES Scavenging raptors with long forked tails, used as a stabiliser in flight, square-winged with 'fingered' primaries. Often seen gliding over hay meadows being cut, looking for disturbed insects and voles.

Black Kite *Milvus migrans*

Juvenile

dark wing-tips

reddish-brown underwings

Adult

striped body

forked tail

grey tail

slightly forked tail

greyish head

black mask

dark brown body

Adult

black flight feathers

very pale body

Juvenile ssp. *lineatus*

black mask

grey cere

yellow legs

Juvenile ssp. *lineatus*

CONFUSION SPECIES

Marsh Harrier (p. 113)

Common Buzzard (p. 101)

IDENTIFICATION
Wingspan 130–155 cm. Dark brown plumage, paler head with fine black streaks; forked tail. Underwing with paler area at base of inner primaries. Squarer wings with more pronounced 'fingers' than Common Buzzard. Pale transverse band on upperwing. Juvenile with pale streaks on body. The Asian race *lineatus*, a very rare vagrant, is very pale with a dark mask through eye. **VOICE** Bleating, whistled trill. **HABITAT** Agricultural lowlands with trees for nesting, breeds in loose colonies; often at rubbish tips. Winters in Africa, returning in March.

Red Kite *Milvus milvus*

IDENTIFICATION Wingspan 140–165 cm. Widespread in W Europe; now common in many parts of Britain. Very similar to Black Kite but redder plumage, pale grey head with fine streaks, white primaries with black tips, deeply forked reddish tail with dark corners. More distinct pale band on upperwings than Black Kite, with more contrasting plumage. Juvenile with less forked tail and spotted body. **VOICE** Meowing followed by more whistled notes. **HABITAT** Wooded hillsides, forests; hunts in open areas with hedgerows and fields; visits rubbish-tips in winter.

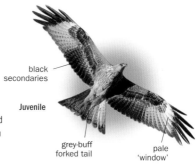

black secondaries

Juvenile

grey-buff forked tail

pale 'window'

bicoloured underwings

Adult

very forked reddish tail

reddish wings mottled with brown

greyish head

Juvenile

yellow legs

Swallow-tailed Kite *Elanoides forficatus*

Wingspan 110–135 cm. Nearctic migrant; a very rare vagrant with possibly 2 records: 1 from the Canaries and 1 from France. Small, bicoloured, resembles a slim Black-shouldered Kite (p. 126) with a long forked tail. Appears black above, white head, underparts and underwing-coverts.

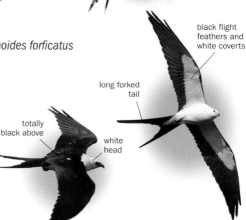

black flight feathers and white coverts

long forked tail

totally black above

white head

VULTURES Large birds of prey, scavengers, silent except at a carcass where there is a real pecking-order of species and within a species – dominant birds feed first. Often bald on parts of the face and neck in order to go deep into a carcass without getting too messy. Searches for food in flight, sometimes from very high, the Griffon Vultures in a group. Inhabits mountains and high plateaus with cliffs for nesting and large numbers of domestic sheep or wild ungulates.

Lammergeier (Bearded Vulture) *Gypaetus barbatus*

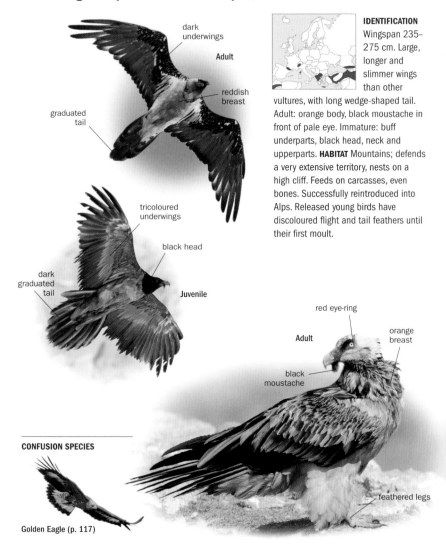

dark underwings

Adult

reddish breast

graduated tail

IDENTIFICATION
Wingspan 235–275 cm. Large, longer and slimmer wings than other vultures, with long wedge-shaped tail. Adult: orange body, black moustache in front of pale eye. Immature: buff underparts, black head, neck and upperparts. **HABITAT** Mountains; defends a very extensive territory, nests on a high cliff. Feeds on carcasses, even bones. Successfully reintroduced into Alps. Released young birds have discoloured flight and tail feathers until their first moult.

tricoloured underwings

black head

dark graduated tail

Juvenile

red eye-ring

orange breast

Adult

black moustache

feathered legs

CONFUSION SPECIES

Golden Eagle (p. 117)

Egyptian Vulture *Neophron percnopterus*

IDENTIFICATION Wingspan 155–170 cm. Adult is black and white, recalling White Stork. Long white wedge-shaped tail; black flight feathers, secondaries greyish above. Juvenile has dark brown plumage, paler on wing-coverts; immature becomes paler with age. Bare yellow face, long slim hooked bill, scraggy neck. **HABITAT** Rugged gorges and mountains in warm climates.

Adult

yellow head

graduated tail

black flight feathers

black, striped underwings

pale head

Juvenile

graduated tail

yellow bill with black tip

reddish-tinted white body

dark flight feathers with grey band

Adult

CONFUSION SPECIES

White Stork (p. 93)   White Pelican (p. 80)   Black Vulture (p. 111)

dark bill and iris

rufous ruff

white line

Immature

white head and ruff

brown mantle

Adult

black flight feathers

stocky grey legs

Griffon Vulture *Gyps fulvus*

IDENTIFICATION
Wingspan 230–265 cm. Very large with broad fingered wings. White head and neck, stocky grey legs. Black flight feathers and brown wing-coverts, the greater underwing-coverts mixed with white sometimes forming a bar. Adult has white bill and neck-ruff, immature has dark bill nail and brown ruff. **HABITAT** Nests in colonies on cliffs. Very gregarious. Can disperse far from breeding area. Several successful reintroduction programmes in S Europe, especially France.

Rüppell's Vulture *Gyps rueppellii*

white bill

light brown mantle

dark bill

wings with buff spots

black wings

Juvenile

Adult

mottled buff 'trousers'

Wingspan 220–255 cm. Recalls Griffon Vulture but slightly smaller, adult has buff spots on dark brown wing-coverts, body mottled with paler colour. Immature more uniform, dark brown. Very rare vagrant from sub-Saharan Africa, usually in vicinity of Griffon Vulture colonies, in Spain, Portugal or France.

(Eurasian) Black Vulture *Aegypius monachus*

Juvenile

small black head

dark underwing-coverts

greyish-black flight feathers

short black tail

IDENTIFICATION
Wingspan 250–285 cm. Huge, wings very square with deeply fingered primaries, graduated vertically and straight trailing edge. Adult has pale head, face and crown, dark in immature; large untidy ruff. Underwing-coverts darker than flight feathers. **HABITAT** Pairs are territorial, often nests in conifer on isolated scree. Successfully reintroduced in S Europe.

bluish bill with dark tip

Adult

Pale head

pale untidy ruff

Lappet-faced Vulture *Torgos tracheliotus*

Wingspan 250–280 cm. Very large African vulture similar to Black Vulture but heavier and more thickset, very broad wings, enormous bill, bare pink face. Very rare vagrant from sub-Saharan Africa or Arabia.

bare pink head

enormous bicoloured bill

pale brown mantle

Adult

uniform buff 'trousers'

buff thighs

wide rectangular wings

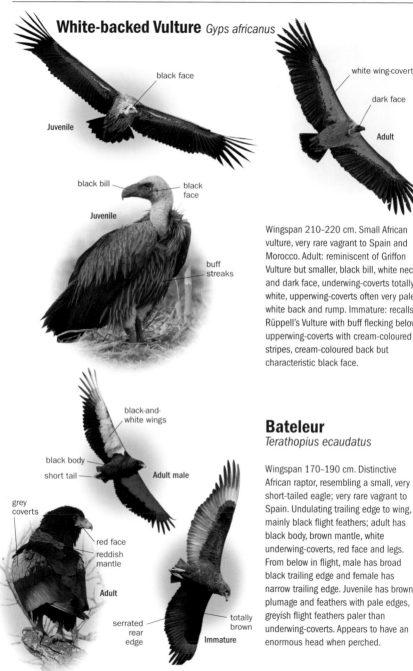

White-backed Vulture *Gyps africanus*

Juvenile

black face

white wing-coverts

dark face

Adult

black bill

black face

Juvenile

buff streaks

Wingspan 210–220 cm. Small African vulture, very rare vagrant to Spain and Morocco. Adult: reminiscent of Griffon Vulture but smaller, black bill, white neck and dark face, underwing-coverts totally white, upperwing-coverts often very pale, white back and rump. Immature: recalls Rüppell's Vulture with buff flecking below, upperwing-coverts with cream-coloured stripes, cream-coloured back but characteristic black face.

black-and-white wings

black body

short tail

Adult male

grey coverts

red face

reddish mantle

Adult

serrated rear edge

totally brown

Immature

Bateleur
Terathopius ecaudatus

Wingspan 170–190 cm. Distinctive African raptor, resembling a small, very short-tailed eagle; very rare vagrant to Spain. Undulating trailing edge to wing, mainly black flight feathers; adult has black body, brown mantle, white underwing-coverts, red face and legs. From below in flight, male has broad black trailing edge and female has narrow trailing edge. Juvenile has brown plumage and feathers with pale edges, greyish flight feathers paler than underwing-coverts. Appears to have an enormous head when perched.

HARRIERS Medium-sized raptors with long wings and tail; they hunt in low gliding flight with wings held upwards in shallow V, aided by a few flexible wingbeats. Nest on the ground in crops, coppice or reedbeds. In 'grey' harriers, immature and female with markedly barred tail and white rump. One-year-old males have plumage intermediate between that of immature and adult. Males have pale irises as soon as their first autumn.

Marsh Harrier *Circus aeruginosus*

IDENTIFICATION
Wingspan 115–140 cm. Large, dark brown harrier. Male tricoloured: straw-coloured head, brown body, grey tail with large grey band on wing including secondaries, entirely black primaries, yellow iris. Female uniform brown with diffuse pale crown, throat and shoulders. Juvenile as female except that crown and throat have orange tint and well-defined borders; dark wing-coverts. Reminiscent of Black Kite but unforked tail. Male has very variable plumage; some adult males are dark, resembling females. **VOICE** A rapid trill *kvey-ek-ek-ek...* **HABITAT** Marshes, reedbeds, wetlands as well as small numbers in cultivated land.

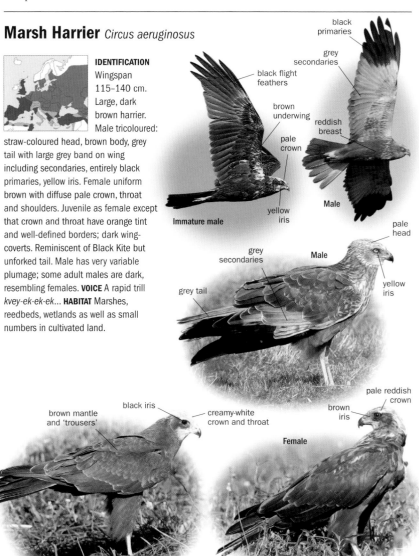

black primaries

grey secondaries

black flight feathers

brown underwing

reddish breast

pale crown

Male

yellow iris

Immature male

grey secondaries

Male

pale head

grey tail

yellow iris

black iris

brown mantle and 'trousers'

creamy-white crown and throat

Female

pale reddish crown

brown iris

Juvenile

Montagu's Harrier *Circus pygargus*

IDENTIFICATION
Wingspan 95–115 cm. Slim, narrow pointed wings, 4 distinct primaries at wing-tip. Male: smoky-grey; black primaries, grey secondaries with central black bar visible above and below, underwing-coverts and axillaries barred with rufous, 'trousers' with reddish streaks. Female: greater underwing-coverts and axillaries obviously striped, secondaries with large pale band, broad white eye-ring, black spot on underside of primaries. Juvenile: uniform rufous below, no pale collar or 'scarf', flight feathers with black tips. Rare melanistic form is entirely dark brown or black.
VOICE Silent away from nest. **HABITAT** Cultivated plains, cereal crops and meadows, steppe, moors.

Labels on illustration:

dark secondaries — dark tips — Adult male — brick-coloured body and underwings — black bars — Juvenile — dark head without obvious collar — rufous spotted axillaries — barred tail — pointed wing — pale-barred flight feathers — wide pale band — chestnut barring — dark head, breast and underwings — Melanistic female — Female — yellow iris — Male — white spectacles — dark patch — Female — black flight feathers — 'trousers' with rufous streaks — brow spot

CONFUSION SPECIES

Black Kite (p. 106)

Common Buzzard (p. 101)

Hen Harrier (p. 115)

Hen Harrier *Circus cyaneus*

IDENTIFICATION
Wingspan
100–120 cm.
Broader wings
than Montagu's
Harrier, 5
obvious primaries at wing-tip. Pale grey
male has black outer primaries, dark
trailing edge to wing, grey head, white
breast and white rump. Female striped,
can be identified by silhouette, broad
wings, white rump. Juvenile: buff
underparts with stripes. **VOICE** Silent
away from nest. **HABITAT** Forest clearings,
moors, woodland edge, countryside with
hedgerows, agricultural plains;
sometimes forms communal roosts in
winter. Typically nests in forested areas,
now also breeds in crops.

5 fingered primaries

dark
secondaries

small collar

Juvenile

reddish streaks
on body and
underwing

5 fingered
primaries

dark but spotted
secondaries

dark spot and
sharply-defined collar

Female

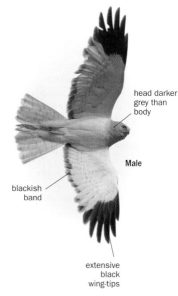

head darker
grey than
body

Male

blackish
band

extensive
black
wing-tips

grey body

black flight
feathers

uniform white
'trousers'

Male

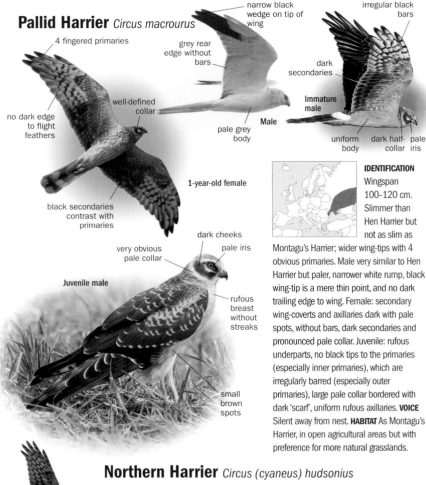

Pallid Harrier *Circus macrourus*

4 fingered primaries

narrow black wedge on tip of wing

grey rear edge without bars

irregular black bars

dark secondaries

no dark edge to flight feathers

well-defined collar

pale grey body

Male

Immature male

uniform body

dark half-collar

pale iris

black secondaries contrast with primaries

1-year-old female

IDENTIFICATION
Wingspan 100–120 cm. Slimmer than Hen Harrier but not as slim as Montagu's Harrier; wider wing-tips with 4 obvious primaries. Male very similar to Hen Harrier but paler, narrower white rump, black wing-tip is a mere thin point, and no dark trailing edge to wing. Female: secondary wing-coverts and axillaries dark with pale spots, without bars, dark secondaries and pronounced pale collar. Juvenile: rufous underparts, no black tips to the primaries (especially inner primaries), which are irregularly barred (especially outer primaries), large pale collar bordered with dark 'scarf', uniform rufous axillaries. **VOICE** Silent away from nest. **HABITAT** As Montagu's Harrier, in open agricultural areas but with preference for more natural grasslands.

very obvious pale collar

dark cheeks
pale iris

Juvenile male

rufous breast without streaks

small brown spots

Northern Harrier *Circus (cyaneus) hudsonius*

dark collar

black marks on wing and scapulars

Juvenile

slightly streaked

Male

rufous markings on underparts

Nearctic ssp. of Hen Harrier, often considered a full species; rare vagrant, which has occurred in Ireland, Britain and the Azores. Male: grey upper breast, brownish-red spotting on breast and flanks, large black trailing edge to wing, finely barred flight feathers. Juvenile: characteristic uniform dark brown head and neck, tan-coloured stripes on flank, sometimes on breast, 4 or 5 bars on short outer primary.

EAGLES Large to very large raptors with long square wings, talons with strong claws, and strong bill. Often glide in circles to gain altitude. Some species are migratory. Adult plumage acquired after several years.

Golden Eagle *Aquila chrysaetos*

IDENTIFICATION Wingspan 190–225 cm. Long wings and tail for an eagle. Adult: dark brown with golden crown, pale transverse band on underwing. Juvenile: white base to flight and tail feathers, broad black terminal band on tail. Immature: remnants of white in the wing. **VOICE** Whistled *klu* near nest. **HABITAT** Mountains and alpine meadows. Nests on cliff-face or isolated tree. Hunts small mammals, also scavenges in winter.

Adult

underwing darker than flight feathers

pale head

white band

Juvenile

yellowish crown

grey flight feathers

Adult

barred base

white base

brown head

white base to tail

Juvenile

dark body

Adult

long wings and tail

broken bars on tail

Pallas's Fish Eagle *Haliaeetus leucoryphus*

Wingspan 180–220 cm. Asian eagle; very rare vagrant with records from Scandinavia and Poland; formerly bred in the northern Caspian region. Long tail and long neck for a sea eagle. Adult has pale head and wide white bar in middle of tail. Immature is blackish with buff median coverts, white base to inner primaries, and cream-coloured rump.

pale inner primaries

long neck

Juvenile

white band

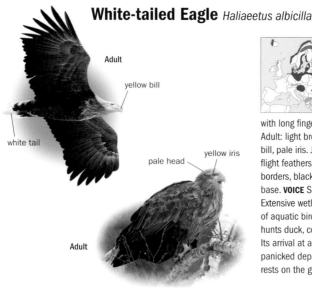

White-tailed Eagle *Haliaeetus albicilla*

Adult

yellow bill

white tail

pale head

yellow iris

Adult

IDENTIFICATION
Wingspan 190–240 cm. Characteristic silhouette, very broad wings with long fingers, short tail, heavy bill. Adult: light brown with white tail, yellow bill, pale iris. Juvenile: dark plumage, flight feathers with pale centres and dark borders, black bill with a small yellow base. **VOICE** Silent in winter. **HABITAT** Extensive wetlands with concentrations of aquatic birds and where it can fish; hunts duck, coots, and finds carcasses. Its arrival at a lake is announced by the panicked departure of all ducks. Readily rests on the ground when feeding.

dark head

dark iris

dark heavy bill

Juvenile

whitish-brown tail

brown head

pale iris

Subadult

often mottled

Bald Eagle *Haliaeetus leucocephalus*

enormous bill

Juvenile

blackish

white base to tail

Immature

Wingspan 180–240 cm. Nearctic sea eagle; an exhausted individual found in Ireland December 1987. As White-tailed Eagle but with more massive bill; adult has white head; juvenile often with very white underwing-coverts; immature with cream-coloured head, dark band behind eye, spotted whitish body, white tail with diffuse dark terminal band.

Bonelli's Eagle *Aquila fasciata*

IDENTIFICATION
Wingspan 145–
165 cm. Slender
eagle with long
tail. Adult: tail
with broad black
terminal band, uniform brown above,
small whitish 'saddle', streaked white
underparts, black carpal and transverse
band on underwing. Immature:
underwing bar and rufous streaked
underparts. Juvenile: uniform pale
reddish underparts as far as carpal, very
similar to Booted Eagle, but larger, more
rounded outer edge to tail in flight. **VOICE**
Generally silent. **HABITAT** Nests on cliffs,
hunts over undisturbed open areas,
garrigue and cultivated plains, where
there are pigeons and rabbits.

black tip

Juvenile

uniform tan

Adult

grey tail

dark underwing

white belly

regular narrow bars

white back

wide terminal bar

Adult

black carpal and bar

Adult

finely streaked breast

rusty head and neck

rufous 'trousers'

whitish 'saddle'

Adult

grey tail with dark terminal band

long feathered legs

finely barred grey tail

Juvenile

Booted Eagle *Aquila pennata*

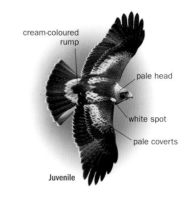

cream-coloured rump

pale head

white spot

pale coverts

Juvenile

white underwing

black flight feathers

dark head

Adult

Pale morph

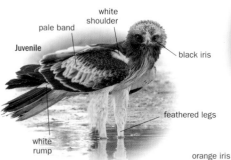

white shoulder

pale band

Juvenile

black iris

feathered legs

white rump

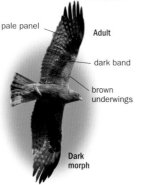

pale panel

Adult

dark band

brown underwings

Dark morph

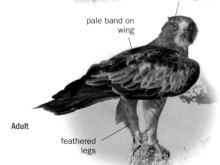

orange iris

pale band on wing

Adult

feathered legs

IDENTIFICATION
Wingspan 110–135 cm. Small eagle with short wings and variable plumage, tricoloured underwings with black primaries (pale inner primaries), brown coverts with pale transverse bar, and small white spots on shoulder ('landing lights'); it thus resembles Black Kite but has square not forked tail, narrow white rump, and upperparts more or less reddish-brown (dark morph with black greater coverts). Tail uniform brown below. **VOICE** When breeding a *kli-kli-kli*.... **HABITAT** Extensive deciduous forests, often on hillsides or in foothills, with clearings and extensive edges. Hunts small vertebrates.

CONFUSION SPECIES

Common Buzzard (p. 101)

Black Kite (p. 106)

Greater Spotted Eagle *Aquila clanga*

Wingspan 155–175 cm. Dark brown thickset eagle with very square wings (long 7th primary), long fingered primaries, flight feathers without barring. Very short tail, especially in juvenile. Generally wing-coverts and flight feathers same colour in adult. Juvenile variable, with large white patches at the tips of upperwing-coverts, white rump. Pale form (var. *fulvescens*) has buff to rufous body and wing-coverts, also with unbarred flight feathers. Intermediate forms with more or less buff from the 'trousers' up to the breast and on underwing-coverts. Rare in W Europe with a few individuals wintering at traditional sites each year. Hybrids with Lesser Spotted Eagle are becoming more frequent, and are very difficult to identify; look especially at structure and barring on flight feathers.

Juvenile var. *fulvescens*

orange-coloured coverts

underwing-coverts darker than flight feathers

Juvenile

dark flight feathers

white half-moon

7 unbarred fingered primaries

short tail

7 fingered primaries

Intermediate juvenile

7 fingered primaries

reddish breast

short tail

white spot

white rump

general colour dark brown

Adult and subadult

uniform brown mantle

heavy bill

gape stops level with eye

pale zone on primaries hardly visible

Adult

Juvenile

general colour dark brown

white spots

short tail

Lesser Spotted Eagle *Aquila pomarina*

Wingspan 145–170 cm. Small dull pale brown eagle, flight feathers darker than body. Smaller and more thickset than Greater Spotted Eagle, less-fingered flight feathers (short 7th primary) and less massive bill. Adult: 2 pale commas at carpal on underwing distinctive, often with pale underwing-coverts. Juvenile: white 'droplets' at least on greater coverts; distinguished from Spotted Eagle by structure, smaller bill, reddish nape, less feathered and more uniform 'trousers'.

pale brown coverts

white rump

Juvenile

small pale spots

6 moderately fingered primaries

Juvenile

uniform brown underwing-coverts

white border to trailing edge

pale brown upperwing-coverts

pale rump

white spot

Adult

6 moderately fingered primaries

smallish bill

underwing-coverts paler than flight feathers

pale brown body

double pale comma

Adult

Adult

dark brown flight feathers

Steppe Eagle *Aquila nipalensis*

Wingspan 165–190 cm. Thickset brown eagle with square wings, white rump and white base to primaries on underwing, wing-coverts paler than flight feathers; barred flight and tail feathers. Gape extends behind level of eye. White band on greater underwing-coverts in immature, forming well-marked line in juvenile. From Central Asia, winters in E Africa.

Subadult

white band punctuated with dark

barred flight feathers

white band

broad fingered wings

barred flight feathers

Immature

entirely brown

barred flight and tail feathers

brown underwing-coverts

Adult

barred flight feathers

rufous nape

long gape

Adult

dark brown

large cream-coloured bands

pale brown

white edge

white band

pale tip to tail

Juvenile

Juvenile

Eastern Imperial Eagle *Aquila heliaca*

white on shoulder

pale nape

Adult

pale 'window'

Juvenile

tan-coloured head

dark leading edge

white rump

white bands

broad black band

Adult

Juvenile

streaked breast and underwing-coverts

pale 'window'

Adult

white

pale nape

dark 'trousers'

Wingspan 175–205 cm. Large and thickset, broad square wings, strong heavy bill. Adult: dark underwing-coverts, long tail with broad black terminal band, golden crown, white bar on each shoulder. Juvenile: buff body streaked with brown below; upperwing-coverts spotted with white. Compared to juvenile Spotted Eagle var. *fulvescens*, white rump and back, longer tail and pale patch on inner primaries.

broad wings with fingered primaries

Juvenile

strong bill

streaked

uniform tan 'trousers'

Spanish Imperial Eagle
Aquila adalberti

Wingspan 180–210 cm. Like Eastern Imperial Eagle but juvenile with reddish-brown almost unstreaked plumage, quickly becoming paler. Adult: white leading edge to wing as well as band on shoulder.

Second-year

grey tail

Subadult

pale shoulder

pale wrist

Juvenile

uniform reddish-brown

small streaked bib

white leading edge

pale nape

broad black band

Adult

pale 'window'

pale nape

white leading edge

Adult

uniform grey base

dark bar

rufous head

uniform reddish-brown back

Juvenile

Osprey *Pandion haliaetus*

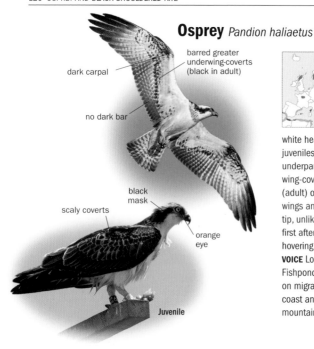

dark carpal

barred greater underwing-coverts (black in adult)

no dark bar

black mask

scaly coverts

orange eye

Juvenile

IDENTIFICATION Wingspan 155–175 cm. Black-and-white fishing raptor. Black mask on white head, yellow eye (orange in juveniles). Above entirely blackish-brown, underparts with black wrists and white wing-coverts, the largest with black tips (adult) or barred (juvenile). In flight, wings angled and slimmer towards the tip, unlike eagles. Fishes by diving feet first after having sighted prey whilst hovering; transports fish in its talons. **VOICE** Loud ringing whistling. **HABITAT** Fishponds or large rivers whilst nesting; on migration follows watercourses, the coast and may even be seen over mountain passes.

Black-shouldered Kite *Elanus caeruleus*

pointed wings

Adult

mantle with pale edges

orange-brown eye

Juvenile

forked tail

black primaries

blue-grey plumage

black shoulder

red eye

Adult

IDENTIFICATION Wingspan 76–88 cm. Size of Eurasian Hobby, ashy-grey above with black shoulders and dark grey primaries, underparts white with black primaries; slightly forked grey tail, shorter than wings when perched. White head with black 'mascara' and red eye. Juvenile: scaly back, brown wash on crown. Adept at hovering; voluntarily perches on wires and glides with upheld wings. **VOICE** Generally silent; call a feeble *gri-ek*. **HABITAT** Open countryside with hedgerows, cultivated plains with large trees and copses, forest edges. Has several broods per year.

Eurasian Sparrowhawk
Accipiter nisus

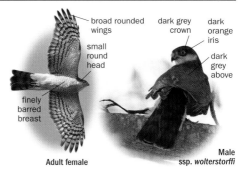

broad rounded wings · dark grey crown · dark orange iris · small round head · dark grey above · finely barred breast

Adult female

Male
ssp. *wolterstorffi*

IDENTIFICATION
Wingspan 60–80 cm. Size of a kestrel but rounded wings, angled in flight. Male: blue-grey above, finely barred with rufous below, grey head with reddish cheeks, orange iris. Female: grey above, barred with black below, narrow white supercilium, yellow iris. Juvenile: grey-brown, roughly barred reddish-brown below. Flight direct, brushing bush tops when hunting; turns quickly in flight, with wings and tail spread. The ssp. *wolterstorffi* of Corsica is smaller and darker; male is dark grey above, dark iris, underparts with broad rufous barring. **VOICE** Call a rapid *kikikiki...* or *kiukiukiukiu...* **HABITAT** Forest, hedgerows, wooded parks. Attacks small birds by surprise in flight, even at bird tables in winter.

brown fringes to wings and mantle · white supercilium · uniform blue-grey above · orange eye · yellow eye · barred tail · **Adult male** · reddish cheeks · **Juvenile** · roughly barred breast

Northern Goshawk *Accipiter gentilis*

IDENTIFICATION
Wingspan 90–120 cm. Resembles Eurasian Sparrowhawk but larger and more thickset, almost like a buzzard but weaker bill and legs; female much larger than male. Ash-grey above, finely barred below, crown and cheeks darker grey with pronounced white supercilium. Juvenile brown above, yellowish with streaks below and heart-shaped markings on flanks. In flight, wings less angled than Eurasian Sparrowhawk's. The rare Corsican subspecies *arigonii* is smaller and darker. **VOICE** Deeper and louder than Eurasian Sparrowhawk. **HABITAT** Extensive undisturbed forests for breeding, more open country in winter. Hunts birds up to the size of Wood Pigeon.

Juvenile · yellow eye · scaly upperparts · **Adult** · finely barred breast · barred brown tail · finely streaked 'trousers' · **Adult** · broad white supercilium · orange eye · strong bill · finely barred breast

Levant Sparrowhawk *Accipiter brevipes*

black spots

Juvenile

black stripe

barred tips

black stripe

4 fingered primaries

Female   barred belly

Wingspan 65–75 cm. Small migrant sparrowhawk with pointed wings and 4 fingered primaries. Male with very pale underwings, characteristic black tips to flight feathers, dark iris, no supercilium, blue-grey upperparts with unbarred tail, fine rufous bars on breast. Female with dark iris, no supercilium, dark throat stripe, brown-barred underparts, finely barred tail. Juvenile has underparts marked with streaks and spots, and dark iris. Migrates in sizeable flocks.

black eye

Male

black tips

Male

uniform face

Shikra *Accipiter badius*

Adult

yellow eye

Adult

very long tail

throat stripe

5 fingered primaries

Wingspan 55–60 cm. Small slim sparrowhawk of Asia and Africa, very rare breeder in extreme SE Europe. 5–6 bars visible on undertail, dark throat stripe, 5 fingered primaries (6 in Eurasian Sparrowhawk). Juvenile has straw-coloured iris, male has orange iris.

FALCONS Small, generally slim raptors with long pointed wings and long tail; diet comprises rodents, insects and small birds, which are hunted by hovering, chasing or diving in flight. Short, hooked bill.

Common Kestrel *Falco tinnunculus*

IDENTIFICATION
Wingspan 68–78 cm. Long tail and slender wings. Male: grey head with short black moustache, tail uniform grey with broad black terminal band, reddish-brown upperparts spotted black, cream-coloured underparts streaked black. Female and juvenile: pale brown with black barring above, cream with black streaks below, tail finely barred with broader terminal band. Often hovers to hunt; freely perches on roadside poles or wires. **VOICE** Rapid rattled trill, *kie-kie-kie-kie...* **HABITAT** In urban areas as well as open countryside.

reddish mantle spotted with dark 'arrows'
grey head
spotted breast
blue-grey tail
Male
dark moustache
heavily barred reddish mantle
heavily spotted
Juvenile and female
black band on tail
black claws
Female

Lesser Kestrel *Falco naumanni*

IDENTIFICATION
Wingspan 63–72 cm. Very similar to Common Kestrel but smaller, longer wings (reaching terminal tail-band when perched), poorly marked moustache (male with uniform grey cheeks), pale claws (black in Common Kestrel). Adult male: uniform red-brown back (a few black spots in first-year males), grey bar across greater wing-coverts reaching tertials, underparts barely marked. **VOICE** More rapid trill than Common Kestrel. **HABITAT** Warm, open, dry environments with sparse vegetation and plentiful large insects.

insignificant moustache
Adult female
dark-spotted rufous coverts
greyish tail with fine dark barring
blue-grey head
white claws
uniform reddish mantle
Second-year male
uniform reddish mantle
grey band
very few round spots
Adult male
white claws

Red-footed Falcon *Falco vespertinus*

brown head

black mask
around eye

Juvenile

barred tail with 2
generations of feathers

reddish mantle
and fringes

**Immature
male**

coal-grey
mantle

bluish-grey
barred tail

orange eye-ring
and base of bill

dark
moustache and
around eye

coal-grey
head and
body

Juvenile

deep
rufous
'trousers'

coverts darker
than flight
feathers

dark edge

orange legs

Adult male

**Adult
male**

IDENTIFICATION

Wingspan 65–76 cm. Resembles a kestrel in silhouette and size but more compact, wings same length as tail when perched. Male: uniform dark grey (including underwings) with rufous 'trousers' and orange-red cere. Immature male: variable with remains of juvenile plumage; barred flight and tail feathers, streaked underwings or body. Female: coal-grey with black barring above, orange spotted with black below; orange crown, white cheeks, thin black mask and malar-stripe. Juvenile: barred brown above, streaked cream below, white forehead and small black mask. **VOICE** Quite vocal; sexes have similar calls, a *kekekeke* when excited and a Hobby-like flight call *kew kew kew*. **HABITAT** Open country.

orange head
and breast

dark
around eye

barred bluish-
grey mantle

Adult female

Amur Falcon *Falco amurensis*

paler cheek

pale grey

blackish
crown

red
cere

grey

**Adult
female**

black
stripes

white
underwings

Wingspan 63–70 cm. East Asian counterpart of Red-footed Falcon; long-distance migrant wintering in S Africa, very rare vagrant to Europe. Male as Red-footed Falcon but white underwing-coverts, body paler grey than wings, darker trace of moustache. Female: grey crown, white underparts with clear black bars and streaks. Juvenile very similar to Red-footed Falcon. In spring, moult progressively brings out the white underwing-coverts in first-year males.

Merlin *Falco columbarius*

IDENTIFICATION
Wingspan 55–69 cm. Small compact falcon, recalling a sparrowhawk, with short but pointed wings. Male: dark grey above, black primaries and terminal tail bar; buff underparts finely streaked black. Diffuse mark on cheek. Female: dark brown, tail barred black (bars with equal width). Rapid, flapping flight often close to ground. **VOICE** Silent in winter; alarm near nest, rapid accelerating *kikikikiki...* **HABITAT** Moors, agricultural plains, steppe, coastal flats. Breeds on moors and tundra. Hunts small birds in ground-hugging flight.

orange-tinted streaked breast

blue-grey mantle

heavily barred flight feathers and breast

white supercilium

Male

white supercilium

brown moustache

brown mantle

brown area

Female

3 broad bars on tail

Juvenile ssp. *columbarius*

(Eurasian) Hobby *Falco subbuteo*

IDENTIFICATION
Wingspan 70–85 cm. Only slightly larger than Common Kestrel with long pointed wings, long tail, rusty 'trousers' and underparts streaked with black; blackish above, black head with white cheek, which extends upwards as a comma behind the black hooked mask at back of cheek; fine white line above eye. When perched, wings extend beyond the tail. Juvenile: dark brown, scaly above, cream 'trousers'. **VOICE** Repeated *kiu-kiu-kiu...* **HABITAT** Deciduous forests and surrounding country, where it hunts birds and insects in flight.

long pointed wings

Adult

black hook on cheek

black hook on cheek

Juvenile

streaked breast

rusty 'trousers'

square white cheek

barred tail

buff undertail-coverts

white supercilium

white supercilium

streaked breast

grey-black above with pale fringes

rusty 'trousers'

Adult

Juvenile

Eleonora's Falcon *Falco eleonorae*

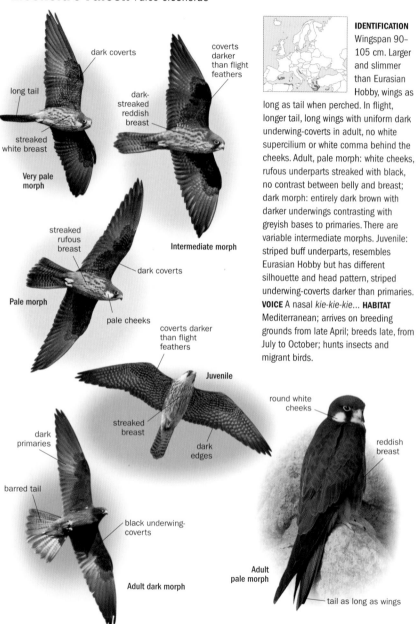

IDENTIFICATION
Wingspan 90–105 cm. Larger and slimmer than Eurasian Hobby, wings as long as tail when perched. In flight, longer tail, long wings with uniform dark underwing-coverts in adult, no white supercilium or white comma behind the cheeks. Adult, pale morph: white cheeks, rufous underparts streaked with black, no contrast between belly and breast; dark morph: entirely dark brown with darker underwings contrasting with greyish bases to primaries. There are variable intermediate morphs. Juvenile: striped buff underparts, resembles Eurasian Hobby but has different silhouette and head pattern, striped underwing-coverts darker than primaries.
VOICE A nasal *kie-kie-kie...* **HABITAT** Mediterranean; arrives on breeding grounds from late April; breeds late, from July to October; hunts insects and migrant birds.

dark coverts

coverts darker than flight feathers

long tail

dark-streaked reddish breast

streaked white breast

Very pale morph

streaked rufous breast

Intermediate morph

dark coverts

Pale morph

pale cheeks

coverts darker than flight feathers

Juvenile

streaked breast

round white cheeks

dark primaries

reddish breast

barred tail

dark edges

black underwing-coverts

Adult dark morph

Adult pale morph

tail as long as wings

Peregrine Falcon *Falco peregrinus*

IDENTIFICATION
Wingspan 90–115 cm. Large, thickset falcon, wings as long as wide tail when perched. Black crown and obvious moustache, white cheek and throat. Dark grey above with paler rump, tail with narrow black bars. Underparts white with narrow black bars, sometimes only on flanks. Juvenile dark brown, streaked below; variable head pattern, either uniform or with cream-coloured forehead and supercilium in larger northern birds (ssp. *calidus*). Adults of the Mediterranean race (ssp. *brookei*) are darker above, have an orangish wash to the breast, even broader moustaches, sometimes with rufous on nape. Immature *calidus* resemble Lanner Falcon but can be distinguished by narrow barred undertail-coverts, non-uniform central tail feathers, the white forehead without a dark band and paler greater underwing-coverts. **VOICE** Silent except near nest, when a *rek-rek-rek...* in series is given. **HABITAT** Open areas near nesting cliffs; and in towns and cities where it nests on high buildings and hunts pigeons. In winter, any open area with a concentration of prey. The *brookei* race is present in the Mediterranean; northern migrants of race *calidus* occur further south in winter.

Juvenile

cream-white supercilium

white forehead

greyish flight feathers with dull markings

pointed moustache

finely streaked undertail-coverts

Adult

yellow eye-ring and cere

Adult

dark precise markings on coverts

black mask

slate-grey back

Juvenile

broad moustache

longitudinal spots

bluish-grey tail

broad black moustache

white upper breast

Adult

lateral barring on flanks

barred tail with cream tip

CONFUSION SPECIES

Eurasian Hobby (p. 131)

Rare falcons (pp. 134–136)

RARE FALCONS Various species, most of which resemble Peregrine; distinguished by size, silhouette and colouring of head, undertail-coverts and bare parts. Beware of falconry escapes, often with jesses and may be of various hybrids.

Gyrfalcon *Falco rusticolus*

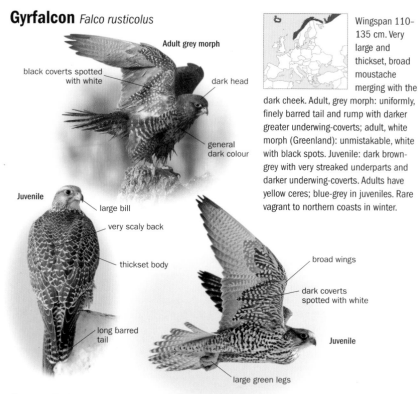

Adult grey morph

black coverts spotted with white

dark head

general dark colour

Juvenile

large bill

very scaly back

thickset body

broad wings

dark coverts spotted with white

Juvenile

long barred tail

large green legs

Wingspan 110–135 cm. Very large and thickset, broad moustache merging with the dark cheek. Adult, grey morph: uniformly, finely barred tail and rump with darker greater underwing-coverts; adult, white morph (Greenland): unmistakable, white with black spots. Juvenile: dark brown-grey with very streaked underparts and darker underwing-coverts. Adults have yellow ceres; blue-grey in juveniles. Rare vagrant to northern coasts in winter.

Sooty Falcon *Falco concolor*

yellow cere

Adult

uniform grey below

short tail

yellow cere

body entirely ashy-grey

yellow legs

Adult

Wingspan 78–90 cm. Adult entirely grey; slender silhouette, long wings (shorter tail than Eleonora's Falcon), yellow cere. Juvenile: as Eleonora's Falcon but terminal bar on tail wider than others and a black 'hook' to the mask behind the cheek as in Eurasian Hobby. Breeds in the Middle East; very rare vagrant to Europe.

Saker Falcon *Falco cherrug*

Wingspan 105–130 cm. Very large, thickset. Dark brown upperparts, underparts with heavy dark streaks except for uniform undertail-coverts. Whitish crown more or less streaked brown, inconspicuous short moustache. Juvenile with grey cere and eye-ring, dark underwing-coverts. Buff oval marks on each side of tail.

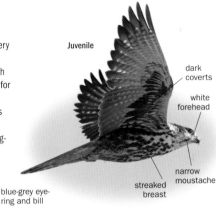

Juvenile

dark coverts

white forehead

streaked breast

narrow moustache

buff oval marks on tail

whitish crown

blue-grey eye-ring and bill

narrow moustache

brown above with new coverts

Lanner Falcon *Falco biarmicus*

Wingspan 95–105 cm. Slender, white forehead with black bar above and rufous crown. Blackish-grey above (spp. *feldeggii*, Italy and further east) or grey barred with black (ssp. *erlangeri*, N Africa). Pale below, sometimes only marks are black spots on flanks, or spotted breast and barred flanks. Juvenile easily confused with northern Peregrine, but forehead white with black bar above, very narrow pointed moustache, no streaks on undertail-coverts, uniform central tail feathers and dark brown greater underwing-coverts with a few spots.

pale supercilium

pale forehead

narrow moustache

zebra-striped coverts

rufous nape

spotted breast

rufous patch

Adult

narrow stripes

Juvenile ssp. *feldeggii*

narrow moustache

bluish-grey upperparts

white cheeks

pale crown

yellow cere and eye-ring

Adult ssp. *erlangeri*

narrow moustache

Immature

Barbary Falcon *Falco pelegrinoides*

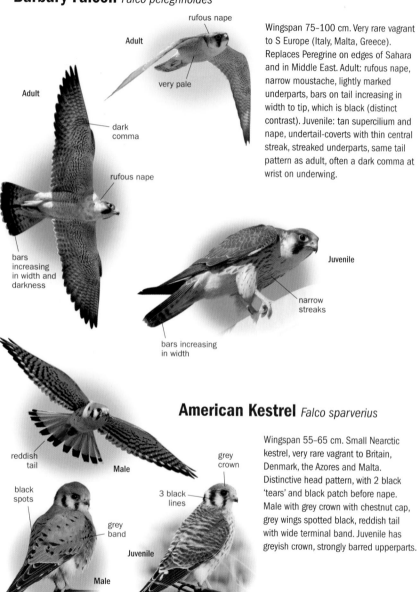

Wingspan 75–100 cm. Very rare vagrant to S Europe (Italy, Malta, Greece). Replaces Peregrine on edges of Sahara and in Middle East. Adult: rufous nape, narrow moustache, lightly marked underparts, bars on tail increasing in width to tip, which is black (distinct contrast). Juvenile: tan supercilium and nape, undertail-coverts with thin central streak, streaked underparts, same tail pattern as adult, often a dark comma at wrist on underwing.

rufous nape

Adult

very pale

Adult

dark comma

rufous nape

bars increasing in width and darkness

Juvenile

narrow streaks

bars increasing in width

American Kestrel *Falco sparverius*

Wingspan 55–65 cm. Small Nearctic kestrel, very rare vagrant to Britain, Denmark, the Azores and Malta. Distinctive head pattern, with 2 black 'tears' and black patch before nape. Male with grey crown with chestnut cap, grey wings spotted black, reddish tail with wide terminal band. Juvenile has greyish crown, strongly barred upperparts.

reddish tail

Male

grey crown

black spots

3 black lines

grey band

Juvenile

Male

RAILS, CRAKES AND GALLINULES Small to medium-sized and discreet, they rarely leave dense marsh or hay meadow vegetation. More easily detected from their calls in spring, or seen on migration feeding at the edge of a reedbed in the evening. Round body and rounded wings, long legs with very long toes.

Water Rail *Rallus aquaticus*

IDENTIFICATION
25 cm. Long slightly decurved bill, red at base. Brown striped with black above, ash-grey face and breast, black-and-white barred flanks, white undertail very visible when bird departs with tail raised. Juvenile: cream-coloured throat and neck, pronounced supercilium, but bill long and decurved. Short wings, tertials cover the primaries. Sometimes stands erect, pear-shaped; startled, it runs back into cover. **VOICE** Various calls, most characteristic is a descending raspy rattle, very loud and trailing away, *cruuii, cruuuii, cruuuiii...* **HABITAT** Reedbeds, marshes, canals, dense wet woodland floor, wet meadows or bramble patches.

Adult
red eye
long decurved red bill
grey face and underparts
black flanks barred with white
white undertail-coverts

brownish eye

brown upperparts with dark spots
Juvenile
'dirty' brown breast

Spotted Crake *Porzana porzana*

IDENTIFICATION
21 cm. Similar to Water Rail but short bill conical and straight, with broad red base. Upperparts brown with black streaks and a little white speckling, grey-brown breast spotted white, grey face with brown cheeks, finely brown, black-and-brown barred flanks. White-barred tertials, primaries hidden under tertials. **VOICE** Song: a loud whiplash-like *ouit*, repeated once per second. **HABITAT** Marshes with sedges and wet meadows, reedbeds on migration.

reddish-brown eye
uniform tan undertail-coverts
yellow bill with red base
Adult

white barring on wings
dull brown eye
yellowish-brown bill
delicate white spotting on breast
Juvenile

Little Crake *Porzana parva*

Male

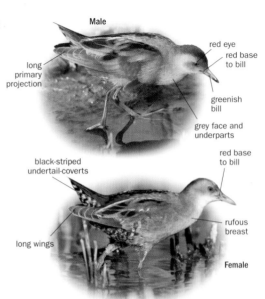

long primary projection

red eye
red base to bill

greenish bill

grey face and underparts

black-striped undertail-coverts

red base to bill

rufous breast

long wings

Female

IDENTIFICATION
18 cm. Smaller and slimmer than Spotted Crake, long wings with long primary projection, red base to bill, black-and-white barred undertail-coverts. Male: blue-grey underparts extend to legs, dull brown above with black braces, few white markings. Female: grey face, cream-coloured throat and neck, buff flanks, only the undertail-coverts are barred. **VOICE** Song: a single note *coua* repeated slowly then rapidly in sometimes never-ending phrases. **HABITAT** Ancient reedbeds with shallow water.

Baillon's Crake *Porzana pusilla*

barred flanks

greenish bill

short wing

Male

short primary projection

yellowish legs

brown patch on cheek

Female

bluish-grey face and underparts

brownish eye

short primary projection

clearly striped flanks and breast

Juvenile

IDENTIFICATION
17 cm. Smaller and more compact than Little Crake, short wings, short primary projection, barred flanks, and green bill without red base. Adult: blue-grey underparts, reddish-brown upperparts with black stripes and thin white streaks; black-and-white barred flanks from top of legs to undertail-coverts. Female is just a little duller, sometimes with pale throat and brown spot on cheek. Juvenile has greyish-brown underparts barred as far as the breast. **VOICE** Song a long repeated rattle reminiscent of Edible Frog, lasting a few seconds. **HABITAT** Wet flood meadows, with shallow water, sedge marshes; reedbeds on migration.

Sora *Porzana carolina*

20 cm. Nearctic vagrant. Very similar to Spotted Crake with cream undertail-coverts and short wings but buff neck and breast without spots, bill yellow with no red, uniform crown with single dark central stripe, no white marks on tertials.

no bars on wing

black eye and red eye-ring

black face

yellow bill

flanks marbled with white

Juvenile

Striped Crake *Porzana marginalis*

19 cm. Small sub-Saharan crake, rare vagrant to Italy and Malta. Uniform rusty undertail-coverts, juvenile has buff head and sides of breast, ash-grey in adult, spotted flanks, long white streaks on upperparts, green bill with dark culmen, green legs.

white spangling

small green bill

Juvenile

orangish rear

African Crake *Crex egregia*

22 cm. Sub-Saharan rail; a few records from the Canaries. Resembles Corncrake but has black-and-white barred flanks and undertail-coverts, grey face with red iris and very scaly upperparts; bill and legs longer.

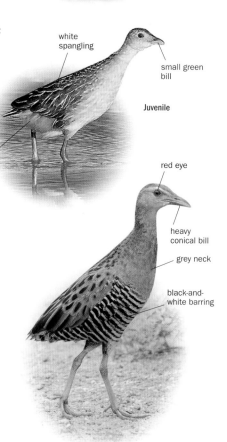

red eye

heavy conical bill

grey neck

black-and-white barring

grey head with rufous cheeks

greyish-brown eye

rufous flanks barred white

short thick bill

grey neck and breast

Juvenile

spotted black above

rufous shoulder

Adult male

Corncrake *Crex crex*

IDENTIFICATION 24 cm. Plump, wings as long as the short tail, pale grey face and neck, brown-and-white barred flanks, brown back with black streaks and buff scaly markings; thick-based short pink bill. In flight, round reddish wings and long buff legs that extend beyond the tail. **VOICE** Song: hoarse, guttural *kreet kreet* given at regular intervals, about 2 per second. **HABITAT** Hay meadows, often flood meadows or at altitude. Migrant, present from April to September.

(Common) Moorhen *Gallinula chloropus*

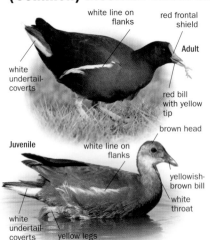

white line on flanks

red frontal shield

Adult

white undertail-coverts

red bill with yellow tip

brown head

Juvenile

white line on flanks

yellowish-brown bill

white throat

white undertail-coverts

yellow legs

IDENTIFICATION 29 cm. Slate-black underparts and brownish upperparts with broken white line along flanks, white undertail-coverts with black central line. Bill with red frontal shield and yellow tip. Green-yellow legs with long toes without lobes. Juvenile is grey-brown with pale throat, same white marks on flanks and undertail as adult, dark grey bill. Readily walks in the open, nervously jerking tail. **VOICE** Very vocal, various loud calls including a rolled *krrouou* and explosive *kikek*. **HABITAT** Marshes, lakes, canals and ponds, even in urban areas.

Lesser Moorhen *Gallinula angulata*

chestnut above

grey neck

big conical bill

23 cm. Sub-Saharan species, very rare vagrant to Spain. Similar to Common Moorhen with white stripes on flanks and white sides to tail, but very heavy yellow bill, strong and conical; culmen is red in adult and brown in juvenile; pinkish-yellow to yellowish-brown legs.

Eurasian Coot *Fulica atra*

IDENTIFICATION
39 cm.
Unmistakable,
entirely black
plumage,
pointed bill
with white frontal shield and dark red
iris. Thickset with large rear end and
rounded back; green-grey legs with long,
lobed toes. The junction of frontal shield
and bill forms a point at each side of
bill. Juvenile: dark grey above, whitish
throat and front of neck, frontal plate
yet to be formed. Runs a long distance
over water before take-off. **VOICE** Loud
trumpet-like calls, *couay, keuk.* **HABITAT**
Lakes, reservoirs. Builds its nest in
aquatic vegetation, sometimes in an
open position. Winters in large groups.
Eats aquatic plants or grazes on
waterside grasses.

black head darker
than body

white bill and
frontal shield

red eye

sharp
angle

Adult

dark cheeks and
crown

Juvenile

dark bill

white
neck and
breast

Red-knobbed Coot *Fulica cristata*

42 cm. Breeds
in Spain and
N Africa. Very
similar to
Eurasian Coot
but white frontal
shield topped with small red wattles in
breeding season, rounded junction of
frontal shield and bill, flatter back; in
flight, no white trailing edge to wing.
Adult has greyish tip to bill.

dark red wattles
on forehead

bluish hue to
white bill and
frontal shield

obtuse
angle

Adult

American Coot *Fulica americana*

35 cm. Nearctic equivalent of Eurasian Coot; very
rare vagrant to W Europe, in winter. Thick bill with dark
subterminal band, dark cusp to top of frontal shield,
white sides under tail.

dark tip
to bill

white sides
under tail

Purple Swamphen *Porphyrio porphyrio*

Adult

red bill and frontal shield

red bill and frontal shield

dark blue body

short tail

red legs

white undertail-coverts

red bill and frontal shield

Adult

Ssp. *madagascariensis*

IDENTIFICATION
48 cm. The largest and heaviest of the rail family in Europe, dark blue plumage with massive red bill topped with red frontal shield, pinkish-red legs, extensive white under tail. Juvenile with paler, greyer underparts. **VOICE** Very noisy; various calls, 1 similar to loud laughing, contact call a dry *tchuc*. **HABITAT** Marshes and ancient reedbeds. Discreet, rarely leaves dense vegetation where it eats young reed shoots. The African subspecies *madagascariensis* breeds along the Nile valley; rare records of this form in Europe probably concern escapes. As nominate subspecies but greenish back.

Allen's Gallinule *Porphyrio alleni*

green back

white to undertail

pinkish-brown legs

reddish bill

dark blue body

Adult

23 cm. Small African swamphen, slender, size of a Water Rail. Very rare vagrant to Europe. Adult: white sides to undertail, dark blue body and green back. Juvenile: brown legs, scaly upperparts, quite brown plumage.

turquoise

tricoloured bill

yellow legs

American Purple Gallinule
Porphyrio martinica

30–33 cm. Nearctic species, very rare vagrant to W Europe. Similar to Allen's Gallinule with green upperparts and blue body but has longer yellow legs, small blue frontal shield and yellow tip to bill; white undertail-coverts without black central bar.

CRANES Large long-legged birds, more closely related to bustards and rails than to herons. Grey plumage; fly with neck and legs extended, big groups on migration fly in V-shaped formation.

Common Crane *Grus grus*

IDENTIFICATION
Wingspan 180–220 cm. Large, ash-grey plumage, black flight feathers. Long slender grey legs, long neck, black in front and white behind, black face and white rear crown; pale, pointed short bill. Characteristic bushy ruff of feathers at rear. Rusty colour to back when breeding. Juvenile: pale brownish head, smaller tail ruff. **VOICE** Call is long, rolled *krrruuuu*. **HABITAT** Marshes, large lakes with islands for safe roosting, stubble in winter for feeding. Migrates at night.

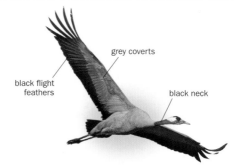

grey coverts

black flight feathers

black neck

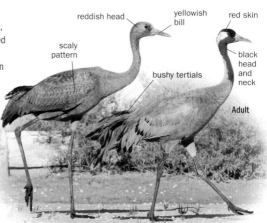

reddish head

yellowish bill

red skin

scaly pattern

bushy tertials

black head and neck

Adult

Juvenile

Demoiselle Crane *Grus virgo*

Wingspan 155–180 cm. Originates from Central Asia; occasional vagrants to Europe, often individuals in flocks of Common Crane, may concern escapes. Smaller and slimmer than Common Crane, thinner, shorter bill, black neck extends to breast, pale crown, white tuft behind eye, long thin black feathers at rear, not in a ruff. Juvenile has pale head with pattern similar to adult.

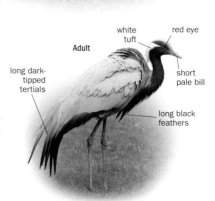

white tuft

red eye

Adult

long dark-tipped tertials

short pale bill

long black feathers

Sandhill Crane *Grus canadensis*

red forehead

grey

ruffled feathers

grey neck

Adult

grey wings with rusty spots

grey flight feathers

grey neck

Wingspan 155–180 cm. Very rare Nearctic vagrant. Smaller than Common Crane, plumage the same grey colour but neck also grey, grey bill, red forehead extends just behind the eye. Similar ruff of feathers at rear, often has rusty wash on back.

Siberian Crane *Grus leucogeranus*

black primaries

white secondaries

Juvenile

Wingspan 205–245 cm. Large white crane with black primaries; has become very rare in W Siberia, a few migrate via the Volga delta each year. Long bill, pink legs, adult with bare red face; juvenile has rusty wash to neck and upperwing-coverts, feathered face.

rusty neck

rusty mantle

Juvenile

pink legs

red face

white body

Adult

pink legs

BUSTARDS Inhabit wide open spaces, steppes and agricultural plains, nest on the ground. Males display on leks where the females come to mate; they then rear the young alone. Generally a dominant male mates with the majority of the females, as in Black Grouse.

Little Bustard *Tetrax tetrax*

IDENTIFICATION
43 cm. Male has distinctive black-and-white neck pattern in summer: grey throat, white V on black neck, white then black collar at base of neck; yellow-red iris. Female has black-and-brown spotting on breast with diffuse lower border. Male in winter: as female but finely vermiculated wings and clearer separation between breast and belly. In flight, primaries white with black tips, rapid wingbeats as in duck, male's 7th primary is short and stiff producing a whistling sound in flight. **VOICE** Song: very short repeated *prrrt*. **HABITAT** Meadows and alfalfa fields in agricultural plains, scrub and set-aside, steppe and abandoned vineyards in S Europe. Favours oilseed rape in autumn, especially in protected areas.

7th primary shorter and rigid giving a whistling sound in flight

black markings

white flight feathers

thick black neck with white band

Breeding male

long neck

short bill

tawny back with dark markings

Winter male

very finely vermiculated

white edge to wing

brown iris

Breeding male

finely vermiculated back

thick neck with black-and-white markings

Juvenile

long neck

uniform greater coverts with large black X-markings

Great Bustard *Otis tarda*

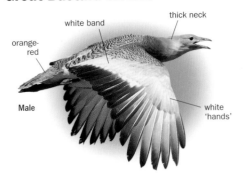

orange-red

white band

thick neck

Male

white 'hands'

IDENTIFICATION
45–65 cm. Large, long neck, heavy flight with slow wingbeats. Grey head, orange neck, reddish-buff upperparts with scaly black markings, white greater coverts. Male heavier, with slender white 'beard', thick neck with chestnut basal collar. Fluffs out neck, wings and tail in display. **VOICE** Song is a short, wet bark. **HABITAT** Open grassy plains and steppes. Recent attempted reintroduction in England.

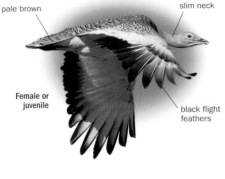

pale brown

slim neck

Female or juvenile

black flight feathers

reddish tail

Male

'beard'

Female or juvenile

round grey head with small bill

rufous mantle, scaled with black

long orange neck

white edge to wing

MacQueen's Bustard *Chlamydotis macqueenii*

60 cm. Very rare vagrant originating from
Central Asia; a migrant that winters in
the Arabian peninsula; a few old records
in Europe. Slim, uniform buff-grey neck
(juvenile) or with a thin lateral black line
(adult); long pale head with black-and-
white crest (without black in sister
species, Houbara Bustard, which is
sedentary in the Canaries and N Africa).
Buff upperparts strongly vermiculated
with black. Flies with slow wingbeats,
black flight feathers with white square at
base of primaries.

black on
crown

small pointed
bill

black line

buff upperparts with
dark spots

grey
neck

Houbara Bustard *Chlamydotis undulata*

50–60 cm. North African bustard, the ssp. *fuerteventurae*
breeds in the Canaries (small with much vermiculated dark
barring above); a few old records of the N African race *undulata*
from Spain (larger, less marked above). Very similar to
MacQueen's Bustard but more barring above (particularly on
wing-coverts) and male has completely white crown, without
black central feathers.

no white on
crown

white
'hand'

Ssp. *fuerteventurae*

heavily spotted

Ssp. *fuerteventurae*

dark plumage

no black on
crown

Male
ssp. *undulata*

vertical black
band

Ssp. *undulata*,
displaying male

moderately
spotted

WADERS Small or medium-sized birds, represented by several different families, most associated with wetlands. Many species have bill shape and length and leg length associated with their way of feeding. Many waders form large mixed flocks when not breeding.

(Eurasian) Oystercatcher *Haematopus ostralegus*

orange bill with dark tip

white dorsal patch

Adult

white base to tail

white collar

white wing-bar

flesh-coloured legs

Juvenile and winter

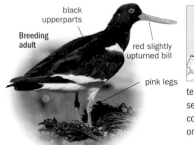

black upperparts

Breeding adult

red slightly upturned bill

pink legs

IDENTIFICATION 42 cm. Black-and-white plumage, long thick-based red bill with dark tip in juvenile. Entirely black above, white line on throat in winter. In flight, obvious white wing-bar on black wings, white rump and back and black terminal bar to tail. Thick pink legs. **VOICE** Rapid *kip-kip-kip…* in series and loud *klui* or *kic*. **HABITAT** Well-grazed meadows and coastal dunes when breeding, extensive coastal bays and rocky or sandy beaches in winter.

(Ruddy) Turnstone *Arenaria interpres*

bright rufous scapulars

white head with black markings

short, pointed black bill

Breeding adult

brown back with pale edges

orange legs

Winter

dark pectoral band

dull orange legs

IDENTIFICATION 23 cm. Small, short legs, dark plumage; in flight long white mark on back with white bases to flight feathers. Broad black bib throughout the year. Pointed black bill, orange legs. Dark face in winter, white with black markings in summer with rufous patches on the shoulders. Often in flocks feeding on the tide-line. **VOICE** A dry *kip* or rapid *tuca-tuc-tuc…* **HABITAT** Rocky coasts, pebble or sandy beaches with large amounts of sea wrack. Seen on wintering sites in Europe as early as late summer.

STILTS AND AVOCETS **149**

Black-winged Stilt *Himantopus himantopus*

IDENTIFICATION
35 cm. Elegant wader with black-and-white plumage, very slender, disproportionately long pink legs, long neck and needle-shaped bill. Black mantle and wings; white body, back and rump. Head often totally white; variable head markings, black crown and hindneck in some males; females have brown-black mantle. In flight, wings entirely black above and below, very long trailing legs behind tail. Juvenile: scaly upperparts. **VOICE** Very vocal, call repeated *kyuc-kyuc...*, or Black-headed Gull-like *craie*. **HABITAT** Lakes, bays and saltmarshes with shallow water, either saline or freshwater.

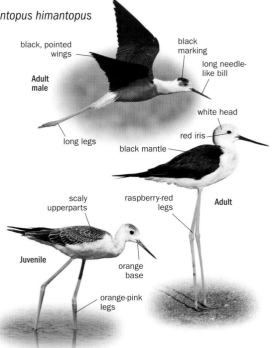

black, pointed wings

black marking

long needle-like bill

Adult male

white head

long legs

black mantle

red iris

black mantle

raspberry-red legs

Adult

scaly upperparts

Juvenile

orange base

orange-pink legs

Pied Avocet *Recurvirostra avosetta*

IDENTIFICATION
44 cm. Pied black and white, long upturned black bill; grey legs. Two black lines frame the white wing, black crown extends behind neck. In flight, black tips to wings, white tail. Juvenile: wing-coverts washed dirty-grey. Feeds by sweeping bill sideways in water. **VOICE** Call: fluty *klup-klup...* **HABITAT** Saltmarshes, saline or freshwater bays with shallow water. Colonial nester, gregarious in winter.

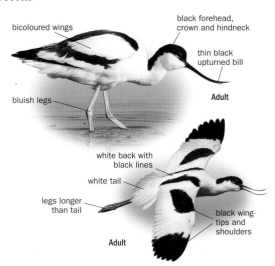

bicoloured wings

black forehead, crown and hindneck

thin black upturned bill

Adult

bluish legs

white back with black lines

white tail

legs longer than tail

black wing-tips and shoulders

Adult

Stone-curlew *Burhinus oedicnemus*

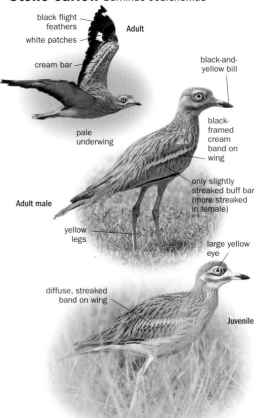

black flight feathers

white patches

cream bar

Adult

black-and-yellow bill

pale underwing

black-framed cream band on wing

only slightly streaked buff bar (more streaked in female)

Adult male

yellow legs

large yellow eye

diffuse, streaked band on wing

Juvenile

IDENTIFICATION
42 cm. Unobtrusive, easily recognised by big yellow eye with surrounding white crescents, thick yellow-based bill with black tip, yellow legs; rest of plumage buff with black markings, pale wing-bar with black upper and lower edges (less marked in juveniles), a quite uniform (in males) grey band below wing-bar is more streaked in females. In flight, wings look black with white markings. When approached crouches on ground or discreetly moves away, reluctant to fly. **VOICE** Vocal, especially in evening and at night; long whistled *cuurr-llliiiii* (hence the name Stone-curlew). **HABITAT** Steppe, short scrub, dry and stony grassland, ploughed land in cultivated areas.

Cream-coloured Courser *Cursorius cursor*

grey nape

white supercilium underlined with black

uniform sandy mantle

small downcurved black bill

Adult

whitish-grey legs

26 cm. A small wader of Middle Eastern and N African deserts; rare vagrant in Europe. Sandy plumage, white supercilium bordered below with black behind the eye, pale grey crown. Short black decurved bill, pale grey legs. Often holds itself upright, or runs rapidly leaning forwards, before stopping and becoming upright again. In flight, characteristic black wing-tips and totally black underwings. Flight call: soft *couit*.

Collared Pratincole *Glareola pratincola*

IDENTIFICATION
26 cm. A short-legged wader with long pointed wings and forked black tail with white edges resembling a giant swallow. Dull brown underparts, black flight feathers, white tips to secondaries form a band on trailing edge of wing. Rusty-red underwing-coverts visible in good light. Cream bib with black border, red base to bill, dark grey legs. When perched, tail as long as wings, or longer. Young: more uniform cream face and scaly above. **VOICE** Flight call: recalls that of terns, shrill *kit* or *kirit*. **HABITAT** Steppe, sparsely vegetated dry plains, saltmarsh, meadows with open ground, in the Mediterranean zone. Hunts insects in flight. Breeds colonially.

Adult

white band
rufous coverts
long forked tail with white sides
big black eye
olive-brown mantle and back
black bill with red base
Juvenile
small black bill with red base
uniform brown mantle
long wings
cream throat framed with black
Adult

Black-winged Pratincole *Glareola nordmanni*

26 cm. Very similar to Collared Pratincole but has black underwing-coverts and no white tips to secondaries in flight. Tail shorter than wings when perched, underparts darker, black lores and little red at base of bill. Longer legs.

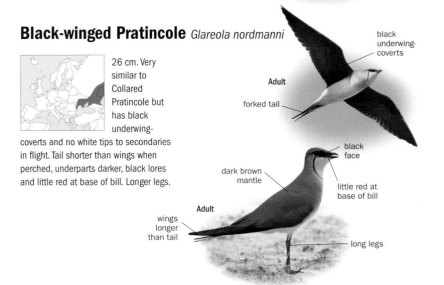

black underwing-coverts
Adult
forked tail
dark brown mantle
black face
little red at base of bill
Adult
wings longer than tail
long legs

Oriental Pratincole *Glareola maldivarum*

25 cm. Very rare Asian vagrant. Similar to Collared Pratincole with reddish underwing-coverts but has no trailing white edge to wing, shallowly-forked short tail (streamers shorter than wing-tips when perched), darker underwings, orange upper belly, blacker lores and less red on base of bill. Characteristic round nostril. Tail appears cut-off.

no white on trailing edge of wing

short tail without streamers

reddish underwing-coverts

Worn adult

dark lores

buff breast

short tail

round nostrils

fairly dark mantle

long legs

white supercilium

black-and-grey above

orange belly

Egyptian Plover *Pluvianus aegyptius*

20 cm. Very rare African vagrant; records from the Canaries, France and Spain may involve escapes. Unmistakable, often bobs body and tail. Blue-grey upperparts, characteristic black-and-white pattern of head, orange throat and belly, black pectoral band. In flight, has black band in middle of back and on wings; grey tail with white tip.

RINGED PLOVERS Small brown and white waders with short bills and black bands on face and breast; pattern different according to species.

Little Ringed Plover *Charadrius dubius*

IDENTIFICATION 17 cm. Small and slender, long body, tail longer than wings and tertials that cover primaries. Complete black collar on breast, white collar on nape; black eye-stripe, black line on forehead underlined with white. Narrow yellow eye-ring, flesh-pink to yellow legs, thin bill with dark base. Base to dark cheek angular on neck. No white wing-bar in flight. Juvenile: scaly above, less marked head pattern, very diffuse buff supercilium. **VOICE** Call is a descending short *piu*. **HABITAT** Freshwater environments: gravel pits, rivers with sand and gravel islands. Also saltmarshes on migration.

brown crown

black-and-white forehead

yellow eye-ring

very narrow wing-bar

pale legs

black mask

Adult

Adult

dark tip

black collar

yellow eye-ring

Juvenile

short, straight black bill

yellow legs

black patch on side

(Common) Ringed Plover *Charadrius hiaticula*

IDENTIFICATION 18 cm. Larger and more bulky than Little Ringed Plover, brighter orange legs, orange base to bill, no eye-ring. Large white forehead and supercilium, rounded base to dark cheek on neck. Broad black (breeding) or brown pectoral band formed by 2 half moons meeting. Juvenile: scaly above, duller legs, dark bill. **VOICE** Call: clearly rising disyllabic *tu-yp*. **HABITAT** Sand or shingle beaches, mudflats, coastline, saltmarshes, large estuaries.

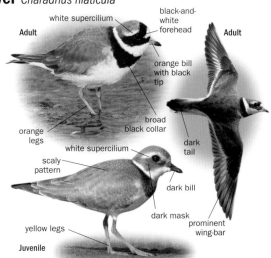

white supercilium

black-and-white forehead

Adult

Adult

orange bill with black tip

orange legs

broad black collar

dark tail

white supercilium

scaly pattern

dark bill

dark mask

yellow legs

prominent wing-bar

Juvenile

Kentish Plover *Charadrius alexandrinus*

rufous crown

black forehead

black bill

black mask

dark patches

Male

buff supercilium

black bill

sandy wings and mantle

Female with chicks

buff patches

IDENTIFICATION
16 cm. A ringed plover with white forehead, white collar continuing onto neck, narrow black or brown half-collar, black or grey legs, thin black bill. Male breeding: black band above the white forehead, large white supercilium, black eye-stripe and small black mask, chestnut nape. Female and winter birds: indistinct supercilium, dark lores, white collar on nape; juvenile: finely scaled above, greenish legs. White wing-bar in flight. **VOICE** Call: soft disyllabic *douit*; in flight, a soft *bip*. **HABITAT** Sandy beaches, dunes, estuaries and mudflats.

Dotterel *Charadrius morinellus*

black crown

Adult female breeding

white face and supercilium

white bar

rufous grading into black

yellowish-white supercilium

dark back with rufous-fringed scapulars

First-summer

indistinct white band

yellow legs

long white supercilium

black eye

small black bill

partially rufous belly

dark back with 2 generations of scapulars

Juvenile

IDENTIFICATION
22 cm. Smaller than Golden and Grey Plovers. Plump body, short yellow legs, dark crown and obvious white supercilium, narrow white pectoral band. Breeding: white throat, grey neck, brick-red breast and black belly, white behind the legs; rufous edges to scapulars. Female more colourful, better marked than male. Winter: greyish breast and flanks, completely white belly. Juvenile: dark marbled sides of breast and broad cream borders to black scapulars (dark grey with diffuse rufous border if autumn moult completed). In flight, entirely dark grey above without a wing-bar, white shaft to longest primary. Can be very confiding. **VOICE** Call: double *kvit*, soft *tiur* in flight. **HABITAT** Breeds on mountaintops and passes devoid of vegetation, and in tundra.

Grey Plover *Pluvialis squatarola*

IDENTIFICATION
28 cm. Grey, black and white plumage. Breeding: scaly black and grey above, uniform black below as far as legs, white lower belly and white collar continues above cheek. White rump and wing-bar and characteristic black axillaries visible in flight. Winter: mottled grey on neck and breast. Juvenile: buff wash to upperparts. Resembles Golden Plover but thicker bill, no yellow coloration. **VOICE** Call: whistled trisyllabic *tuuu-aa-uu*. **HABITAT** Estuaries, sandy and rocky coasts, saltmarshes.

Adult in flight

white wing-bar

black axillaries

white forehead, crown and nape

back studded with white

strong black bill

black breast, throat and mask

white undertail-coverts

Breeding

pale spotted back

strong bill

long greyish legs

wings longer than tail

Juvenile

(European) Golden Plover *Pluvialis apricaria*

IDENTIFICATION
27 cm. Quite thickset, wings only slightly longer than tail, tertials shorter than tail. In winter breast and flanks mottled grey and buff. Breeding: black underparts at far as legs, white undertail-coverts, thin white 'braces' extend to belly. Finely toothed tertials. White axillaries, rump as mantle and white wing-bars visible in flight. Gregarious, forming large flocks in winter, often with Northern Lapwings. **VOICE** Monosyllabic slightly descending melancholic call, *tuu*. **HABITAT** Breeds in Arctic tundra, winters in open areas, agricultural plains, ploughed land and short meadows.

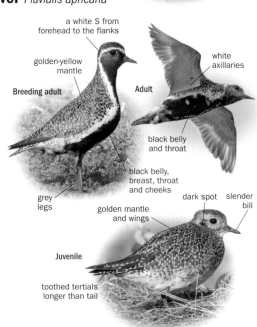

a white S from forehead to the flanks

golden-yellow mantle

Breeding adult

Adult

white axillaries

black belly and throat

black belly, breast, throat and cheeks

grey legs

golden mantle and wings

dark spot   slender bill

Juvenile

toothed tertials longer than tail

RARE PLOVERS Two species very similar to European Golden Plover, one from Asia the other Nearctic, are rare in summer (adults either in breeding plumage or moult) and autumn (juveniles). They can be differentiated by subtle differences in structure and colour, and have different calls. In flight, grey undersides to wings including axillaries are evident. Birds in breeding plumage often in moult in summer with white mixed in with black underparts.

white 'scarf' from forehead to shoulder — **Breeding adult** — **Juvenile**

coarse whitish spots on black back

long wings

grey axillaries

clear white supercilium

dark crown

dark spot

black undertail-coverts and belly

long wings

Juvenile

American Golden Plover
Pluvialis dominica

25 cm. Of Nearctic origin. More slender than European Golden Plover, longer legs, wings much longer than tail, tertials shorter than tail, long primary projection. Adult: entirely black below as far as undertail-coverts, but large white collar with wide round extremities on neck; coarsely spotted whitish on black back, little golden colour. Juvenile: dark crown, large white supercilium and grey mottling on underparts down to flanks, dull grey-and-white plumage with little or no golden colour. Call: *klu–i* with emphasis on first syllable, almost monosyllabic.

barely visible wing-bar

golden tints

Breeding adult

wings only slightly longer than tail

Adult

legs extend beyond tail

white S from forehead to flanks

golden tints

white supercilium

white on undertail-coverts

long bill

long tibiae

First-summer

Pacific Golden Plover
Pluvialis fulva

23 cm. Of Asian origin. Even more slender and longer with very long tibiae and legs extending beyond tail in flight; longer slimmer bill. Flight feathers only slightly longer than tail, tertials same length as tail. Breeding: as American Golden Plover but undertail-coverts black with white markings, white feathers along flanks, large markings on tertials, golden spots on mantle and wings. Juvenile: dark crown, characteristic structure of species, golden-yellow wash to plumage. Call: *soft tou-i*, similar to that of Spotted Redshank.

VAGRANT PLOVERS Three Asian, two Nearctic and one African species. Note breast and nape markings, leg colour, general structure and calls.

Lesser Sand Plover *Charadrius mongolus*

18 cm. Rare Asian vagrant. Very similar to Greater Sand Plover but more compact, often more upright with body not as long behind the legs, shorter thick bill. Dark legs do not extend beyond tail in flight. Breeding male: black mask, white throat, broad brick-red pectoral band. Female: trace of mask and orange breast. Winter: brown nape, white supercilium and throat, brown crescents on each side of breast. Two groups: *mongolus* (E Asia), flanks marbled with red-brick markings, white on forehead, often a black line at top of brick-red breast-band; *atrifrons* (Central Asia), black forehead with white spots and no spots on flanks. Call: rapid *tric*.

black forehead and white spots on lores

black mask

wing-bar

legs extend beyond tail

Adult

rufous breast

Male *atrifrons/pamirensis* group

white forehead with black above

rufous spots on flanks

thick, short bill

rufous pectoral band

white forehead

thick, short bill

rufous and grey sides to breast

shorter greenish-grey legs

Male *mongolus* group

greyish legs

Female *mongolus* group

Greater Sand Plover *Charadrius leschenaultii*

21 cm. Rare vagrant originating from Central Asia; a few W European records. Slimmer and longer than Lesser Sand Plover, stands with body more horizontal, long bill, long legs usually green and extend beyond tail in flight. Breeding male: white forehead, black mask, brick-red breast-band, often has some brick-red feathers on upperparts (ssp. *columbinus* from Turkey). Winter: pale supercilium in front of eye, brown nape, large brown crescent on each side of breast. Call: rolled *purr*, often repeated twice or more.

some rufous on scapulars

Male

black lores and mask

white forehead with black above

large, long bill

rufous collar

large, long dark bill

long pale legs

Juvenile

pale legs

Caspian Plover *Charadrius asiaticus*

Juvenile

wide supercilium

broad white supercilium

white lores

sandy coverts and scapulars with pale edges

rufous breast with black line below

long greyish-green legs

Breeding male

20 cm. Rare vagrant from Central Asian steppes. A little larger than Ringed Plover, slender, wings longer than tail. Green legs with long tibiae, long slender bill, pronounced white supercilium, extensive white throat surrounded with rufous; brown (winter) or brick-red (breeding male) breast-band. Brown hindneck, no white collar. Very narrow white wing-bar visible in flight. Contact call: rapid *tchup*.

Kittlitz's Plover *Charadrius pecuarius*

dark brown crown

black pattern on head

white nape-band

small pointed black bill

orange breast

Adult male

15 cm. Rare vagrant from Africa; very occasional record in W Europe. Long-legged, pale orange below, white supercilium continues to form large white patch on nape. Contrasting wing pattern in flight with black median upperwing-coverts, all others buff.

Semipalmated Plover *Charadrius semipalmatus*

narrow orange eye-ring

indistinct supercilium

white line above top of bill

Breeding adult

white line above top of bill

narrow black line

short bill

Juvenile

semipalmated toes

17 cm. Nearctic vagrant; rare in Europe, annual in the Azores. Very difficult to separate from Ringed Plover. Three diagnostic features: narrow white streak above gape, small web between inner 2 digits (both species have web between outer 2 digits), and rising *tchu-wi* call, hoarser, less whistled and less disyllabic than that of Ringed Plover. Also, has narrow yellow eye-ring, shorter bill with orange base to lower mandible, narrower breast-band, wing-coverts with more obvious pale fringes in juvenile.

Killdeer *Charadrius vociferus*

25 cm. Very rare Nearctic vagrant, occurring in Europe in autumn or winter. Large, elongated body with long tail, double black breast-band; rufous rump and prominent white wing-bar visible in flight. Long pointed black bill. Call: rising *kluii*.

long black bill

white supercilium

Adult

long neck

double black pectoral band separated by white

pale legs

Northern Lapwing *Vanellus vanellus*

IDENTIFICATION
30 cm. Large inland wader of black-and-white appearance, bottle-green
above with pink legs. Black breast-band, mask and crown with crest, longer in male than female. Rusty undertail-coverts. Female's bib spotted with white in summer. Juvenile has scaly upperparts. In flight, white tail with black subterminal band and rounded black wings with white tips, rolling wingbeats. Often runs on ground, stops, then bends forward to catch some prey. **VOICE** Vocal, musical whistled *tiouii*. Acrobatic roller-coaster display flights. **HABITAT** Wet meadows. Ploughed land and stubble in winter; often in sizeable flocks.

white tail with black subterminal band

white underwing-coverts

Adult

black crest, crown and forehead

pale edges on mantle and wings

First-winter

black collar

rounded wings

disproportionately long crest

white face with black markings

metallic sheen

Breeding adult

black breast

rufous undertail-coverts

Sociable Lapwing *Vanellus gregarius*

Breeding adult

black flight feathers

black band on tail

black crown

white supercilium and black eye-stripe

uniform beige back and breast

Breeding adult

dark lower belly

long black legs

brown crown

long supercilium joins on nape

pale edges to wing-coverts

First-winter

black edge to wing

28 cm. Rare vagrant from Central Asian steppes; occurs annually, individuals nearly always in Northern Lapwing flocks. Buff plumage, black legs, tricoloured wings with a black hand, the rest buff and white. Breeding: black crown and eye-stripe, white supercilium, black-and-rufous belly. Winter: broad white supercilium and uniform buff upperparts. Juvenile: pale edges to wing-coverts, brown crown. Call: rough *kretch*.

White-tailed Lapwing *Vanellus leucurus*

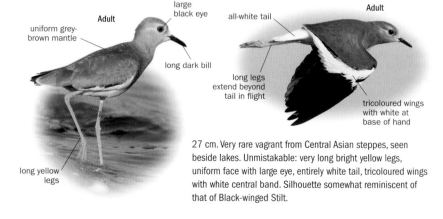

large black eye

Adult

uniform grey-brown mantle

long dark bill

all-white tail

Adult

long legs extend beyond tail in flight

tricoloured wings with white at base of hand

long yellow legs

27 cm. Very rare vagrant from Central Asian steppes, seen beside lakes. Unmistakable: very long bright yellow legs, uniform face with large eye, entirely white tail, tricoloured wings with white central band. Silhouette somewhat reminiscent of that of Black-winged Stilt.

Spur-winged Lapwing *Hoplopterus spinosus*

IDENTIFICATION
27 cm. Very rare vagrant (escapes?) to W Europe. Noisy tricoloured lapwing with black crown and bib, black belly, pale brown upperparts and wings with white band before black flight feathers. Black tail with white sides and white rump. Long black legs longer than tail in flight. Juvenile scaly above. **VOICE** Strident *puic*, recalling that of Black-winged Stilt. **HABITAT** Open environments, wasteland, often near water.

black tail

black

tricoloured wings

red eye

triangular white cheek

black belly

long legs

Oriental Plover *Charadrius veredus*

24 cm. Exceptional in Europe; a male was recorded in Finland in May 2003. Similar to Caspian Plover but larger and more slender. Male has white head, orange pectoral band bordered below with black, pinkish-yellow legs. Female has tan face and supercilium, and often a trace of the pectoral band; bill longer than that of Caspian Plover.

white face

rufous-and-black band

Male

pinkish legs

neat supercilium

long bill

Female

long legs

SANDPIPERS Small waders, gregarious in winter, dull grey-and-white plumage in winter, more colourful in summer. Length and shape of bill and legs helps in identification. Bill can be short or long and more or less curved. Legs usually black or greenish-yellow. White rump with or without central black band, white wing-bar visible in flight.

Dunlin *Calidris alpina*

Breeding adult ssp. *schinzii*
reddish-brown mantle
short bill
wing-bar
dark line in middle of rump
grey tail feathers
brown fringes to coverts and mantle
black belly
black legs

Juvenile
grey mantle

Winter adult
streaked breast

reddish head

Juvenile
streaked breast

brown fringes to coverts and mantle
bright rufous mantle
long bill
black belly
black streaks

Breeding adult ssp. *alpina*

First-winter ssp. *hudsonia*
very long bill
thin black streaks on flanks

IDENTIFICATION
19 cm. Black legs, quite long slightly downcurved bill, rump with central black band. Breeding: bright rufous on sides of back, streaked reddish-brown crown (Scandinavian race *alpina*), streaked breast, large uniform black patch on belly extending to legs. Birds breeding around the Baltic and in Scotland are duller, without bright rufous (ssp. *schinzii*). Winter: uniform grey above, uniform face without supercilium, totally white underparts, streaked sides of breast. Juvenile: yellowish-brown on head, dense black spots on breast and belly, diffuse pale 'braces'. The Nearctic race *hudsonia* may occur; look for fine streaks on flanks in winter, totally rufous-and-black mantle in summer, long bill. **VOICE** Flight call: rapid *prrru*. **HABITAT** Estuaries, coastal bays, mudflats, filter beds, coasts, even rocky coastline. Breeds on tundra. The commonest sandpiper.

Curlew Sandpiper *Calidris ferruginea*

IDENTIFICATION 20 cm. Longer-legged and longer more decurved bill than Dunlin. Black legs, white rump, well-defined white wing-bar. Breeding: dark brick-red body, black-and-silver scaled upperparts. Winter: uniformly grey above, finely streaked breast, white supercilium and black lores. Juvenile: regular scaly-patterned upperparts, no pale 'braces', orangey breast, white supercilium. **VOICE** Short loud *tiriit* in flight. **HABITAT** Marshes, coasts, estuaries, often in company of Dunlin.

clear white supercilium

Winter adult

wing-bar

scaly mantle and coverts

white rump

long curved bill

long wings

Juvenile

white supercilium

Winter adult

streaked breast and flanks

Breeding adults

dark-spangled rufous mantle

long downcurved bill

brick-red breast

long legs

Red Knot *Calidris canutus*

IDENTIFICATION 25 cm. Large thickset sandpiper, quite short bill, white rump finely barred with grey. Breeding: brick-red underparts, rufous, grey-and-black marbled upperparts (more colourful in ssp. *islandica*), uniform brick-red face with black eye, dark green-grey legs. Winter: grey above with fine black feather-shafts, pale supercilium, greyish bib and fine streaking on breast and flanks. Juvenile scaly above, orangey on breast. **VOICE** Flight call: double nasal *uait*. **HABITAT** Coastal bays, estuaries, mudflats, rocky coast. Migrants from Arctic Siberia (ssp. *canutus*) or Greenland/Canada (ssp. *islandica*, shorter bill and lighter rufous).

numerous brick-red spots

Adult ssp. *islandica*

short bill

white supercilium

grey mantle

brick-red head, breast and belly

streaked white breast and flanks

scaly mantle and coverts

Winter

streaked dark crown

orange spots

reddish streaked breast

Juvenile

black bill

brick-red breast

Adult ssp. *canutus*

thickset appearance

Sanderling *Calidris alba*

Winter — white rump with central dark line

grey tail feathers

Breeding adult

reddish head

rufous scapulars with black centres

wide wing-bar with dark edges

black leading edge

short broad bill

whitish breast

characteristic 3-lobed dark centres

wings slightly longer than tail

Juvenile

black legs

IDENTIFICATION
20 cm. Same size as Dunlin but more thickset, shortish bill quite thick, black legs. Breeding: rufous face and upper breast barred with black and white, black-and-rufous mantle extensively barred white. Winter: pale grey above, obvious black shoulder on wing, no streaked upper breast. Pale face with slight supercilium. Young has black mantle spangled with white, black shoulders, tan wash on breast. In flight, white wing-bar and pale grey band along arm bordered with black. Often in flocks, running along beaches near the surf. **VOICE** Flight call is short, soft *plit*. **HABITAT** Sandy beaches, shingle and rocky coasts, along tidal wrack.

Little Stint *Calidris minuta*

dark-streaked crown

rufous back with dark markings

rufous head

Breeding adult

short thin black bill

diffuse dark centres

black legs

Winter

narrow supercilium

streaked upper breast

rufous on scapulars

white supercilium

white 'braces'

scaly coverts

Juvenile

IDENTIFICATION
14 cm. Small, black legs, short relatively straight bill, short tail.
Breeding: rufous face and breast with fine black streaking, streaked rufous and black below, male the more colourful. Winter: grey mantle and scapulars with diffuse black centres to feathers, streaked upper breast, narrow supercilium. Juvenile: white 'braces' on back, rufous on scapulars, scaly wing-coverts. In flight, grey tail with central black band on rump. **VOICE** Flight call is rapid *tit*. **HABITAT** Beaches, estuaries, coastal bays, mudflats, muddy expanses inland.

Temminck's Stint *Calidris temminckii*

IDENTIFICATION
14 cm. Small, short greenish-yellow legs, elongated body with long wings gives a unique silhouette. Slightly decurved short bill with pale base. Breeding: quite uniform but black scapulars with contrasting white indentations. Winter: uniform face without supercilium, large greyish bib, relatively uniform grey above. Juvenile is uniformly grey-brown; scaly upperparts without white 'braces'. In flight, white tail and rump with central black band. **VOICE** Flight call: clear, rolling *tirr-tirr-tirr*. **HABITAT** Beaches, marshes, wet meadows, saltpans.

dark scapulars

pale-edged tertials

short dark bill with pale base

dark breast

Breeding adult

white eye-ring

grey head

grey mantle and wings

Winter adult

dark bill with yellowish base

yellow legs

Purple Sandpiper *Calidris maritima*

IDENTIFICATION
21 cm. Size of Dunlin, unmistakable with very dark plumage, orange legs, medium-length bill with orange base. Breast and flanks heavily streaked with dark grey, only slightly scaly dark grey above, blackish lores. Juvenile: white edges to wing-coverts. In flight, looks very dark with narrow wing-bar, white sides to rump. **VOICE** Rapid *kvitt*, mono- or disyllabic. **HABITAT** Rocky coasts, rocks on the surf-line.

yellowish base to bill

dark head

pale-fringed coverts

First-winter

dark grey mantle

dark bill with orange base

Winter adult

streaked flanks

spotted head and breast

rufous on scapulars

orange legs

Breeding adult

Broad-billed Sandpiper *Calidris falcinellus*

Breeding adult

dark crown with double white supercilium

dark lores

long black bill with bent tip

arrow-shaped spots

2 generations of feathers

Transitional plumage (juvenile to first-winter)

dark bill with pale base and bent tip

white 'braces'

greenish-grey legs

black crown with double white supercilium

wing-bar

white rump with central dark line

white fringes to coverts

streaked breast

Juvenile

IDENTIFICATION
17 cm. Smaller than Dunlin, darker, paler legs, longish downcurved bill looking slimmer and bent at tip. Black crown, double supercilium. Adult: black arrow-marks on breast and flanks, dark back with pale 'braces' in worn plumage. Juvenile: streaked breast, narrow white 'braces'. White rump with central black bar visible in flight. **VOICE** Call a rising sharp trill, *criiiic*. **HABITAT** Coastal sites, marshes, fishponds.

Buff-breasted Sandpiper *Tryngites subruficollis*

First-summer

dark-centred rufous scapulars without fringes

finely streaked rufous crown

scaly mantle

uniform face

bright yellow legs

black spots

pale-fringed rufous wing-coverts

Juvenile

yellowish legs

19 cm. Rare Nearctic vagrant; occurs in Europe annually, usually on short grass near the coast. Resembles a Ruff but obviously smaller with shorter, almost straight bill, yellow legs. Adult: scapulars with black centres and broad diffuse buff fringes. No white on rump nor wing-bar in flight. Juvenile: black back feathers with pronounced cream-coloured edges creating a very regular, bicoloured scaly pattern. Uniform buff face, small black spots on sides of breast.

Ruff *Calidris pugnax*

IDENTIFICATION
22–32 cm.
Wader with short
and only slightly
decurved bill
and orange legs.
Male much bigger than female with very
variable breeding plumage, with a big
ruff of rufous, white or black feathers,
barred, marbled or uniform. Winter:
black bill with orange base, large diffuse
dark centres to mantle feathers and
scapulars, giving very scaly appearance;
quite uniform greyish breast. Juvenile:
buff face, unstreaked buff breast, short
primary projection, yellowish legs. White
ovals each side of rump and white wing-
bar visible in flight. **VOICE** Silent. **HABITAT**
Wet meadows, marshes, filter beds.
Spectacular displays on leks when males
spar together.

'Red'
breeding
adult male

pink
bill

reddish
face and
breast

orange
legs

white
wing-bar

white sides
to rump

pinkish
bill

reddish ruff
spangled
with black

big black
spots

'Brown-red'
breeding adult
male

orange
legs

white
head,
neck and
breast

pink bill
with black
tip

grey-and-white
vermiculated mantle

'White' breeding
adult male

white
eye-ring

long tan tertials
spotted
with black

dark bill

rufous-and-
black ruff

'Black'
breeding adult
male

black-spotted
belly

white eye-
ring

long grey tertials
spotted black
and brown

Breeding female

long
black bill

short primary
projection

Juvenile

unstreaked
buff breast

greenish-
grey legs

indistinctly
marked
crown and
scaly superscilium

long
bill

Juvenile

long
black bill

yellow
legs

Stilt Sandpiper *Calidris himantopus*

dark arrow-shaped marks with white edges

no wing-bar

dark streaks

barred white rump

long brownish legs

Juvenile

rufous crown and cheeks

grey tail

Adults

3-lobed dark centres

long downcurved bill

long yellow legs

barred breast

Breeding adult

21 cm. Rare Nearctic vagrant; a few records of adults in summer or juveniles in autumn. Resembles Curlew Sandpiper but more slender, long legs, whitish rump. Green legs, downcurved bill is thin at tip. Breeding: reddish crown and cheeks, heavily black-barred underparts. Winter: quite uniform grey above, streaked flanks. Juvenile: finely streaked buff breast, streaked flanks, greenish legs. Call similar to that of Curlew Sandpiper.

Pectoral Sandpiper *Calidris melanotos*

white supercilium

scapulars with pale edges

Juvenile

clear edge to spotted breast

dark bill with brown base

reddish crown and cheek

greenish-yellow legs

brownish wings with darker feather centres

Adult

21 cm. Rare migrant from the Nearctic and Siberia, annual in small numbers on coasts or extensive wetlands, mainly in autumn. Medium-sized sandpiper with larger more thickset body than Dunlin, bill shorter, green legs. Large bib of dense black streaks at all ages, with clear-cut lower edge. Adult: less contrasting scapulars with diffuse fringes. Juvenile: white-and-rufous fringes to scapulars, pronounced white 'braces', ill-defined supercilium and reddish crown, finely streaked. Call: reeled *krrt* similar to that of Curlew Sandpiper.

Sharp-tailed Sandpiper *Calidris acuminata*

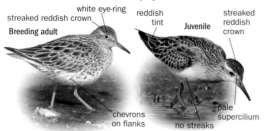

white eye-ring

streaked reddish crown

Breeding adult

reddish tint

Juvenile

streaked reddish crown

chevrons on flanks

pale supercilium

no streaks

19 cm. Rare Asian vagrant, in summer or in autumn, principally at extensive coastal wetlands. Like Pectoral Sandpiper but juvenile has streaked reddish crown, pronounced white supercilium, buff breast without central streaks. Breeding adult: dark crown, dark chevrons on flanks and undertail-coverts. Call: soft *uip*.

White-rumped Sandpiper *Calidris fuscicollis*

17 cm. Rare but annual Nearctic vagrant, often on coasts. Small, slender sandpiper, wings much longer than tail, long primary projection, black legs, short slightly downcurved bill. Winter: grey face and breast with narrow white supercilium, grey streaking on breast continues far along flanks, to tail. Juvenile: rufous-and-white fringes to scapulars, pronounced white supercilium, streaks on buff breast and along flanks. Call: squeaky high *tsii*.

Juvenile

white supercilium

long wings

white-and-rufous fringes to scapulars

streaked flanks

black bill with brown base

white supercilium

dark lores

streaked flanks and breast

black legs

Winter adult

Baird's Sandpiper *Calidris bairdii*

16 cm. Rare but annual Nearctic vagrant, usually on coasts but sometimes inland. Like White-rumped Sandpiper in structure with very long wings and primary projection but with straighter bill. Ill-defined supercilium, pale patch in front of eye. Breeding adult: finely streaked large grey bib and black scapulars with cream fringes, recalling Temminck's Stint. Juvenile: uniformly and markedly scaly above. Call: buzzing *priit*.

white spot in front of eye

white fringes

Juvenile

long wings

black spots on scapulars

small pointed bill

streaked breast

Breeding adult

Red-necked Stint *Calidris ruficollis*

14 cm. Very rare Asian vagrant, mainly breeding-plumaged adults in summer (the easiest to identify). Very similar to Little Stint but obviously longer in silhouette, less compact body, short bill. Breeding: uniform unstreaked reddish face and throat, bordered below with a band of delicate black spots and streaks; uniform grey wing-coverts, black-and-rufous markings on scapulars. Juvenile: as Little Stint but slimmer, ill-defined white 'braces' and relatively uniform greyish wing-coverts.

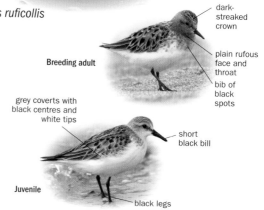

Breeding adult

dark-streaked crown

plain rufous face and throat

bib of black spots

short black bill

grey coverts with black centres and white tips

short black bill

Juvenile

black legs

Semipalmated Sandpiper *Calidris pusilla*

dark anchor-shaped centres

no 'braces'

black bill

Juvenile

grey coverts with pale tips

greenish-black legs

semipalmated toes

black bill

short wings

grey scapulars with large black centres

black streaks

Adult

14 cm. Rare Nearctic vagrant, annual on western coasts. Very similar to Little Stint but black bill often darker than legs; notably, has small webs between toes. Breeding adult: bib of black streaks on breast, grey scapulars with black centres contrast with wings and mantle. Juvenile scaly above, dull coloured, without well-defined white 'braces', more uniformly grey wing-coverts. Call: short buzzing *tchrrp*.

Western Sandpiper *Calidris mauri*

reddish cheeks

striped rufous crown

rufous scapulars with black centres

Breeding adult

streaked breast

arrow-shaped spots

reddish tint to scapulars

finely streaked

large supercilium in front of eye

grey-brown mantle

Winter adult

prominent supercilium in front of eye

long black bill

pectoral streaks

Juvenile

semipalmated toes

15 cm. Very rare Nearctic vagrant. Very similar to Semipalmated Sandpiper, bill often longer and narrower at tip, black legs and slightly webbed toes. Breeding adult: black chevrons on breast and flanks, reddish colouring on cheeks and scapulars. Juvenile very similar to Semipalmated, but rufous on scapulars, better defined streaking on neck, supercilium wide in front of eye, lighter coloured cheeks. Appears slimmer, recalls a miniature Curlew Sandpiper. Call: shrill *tchitt*.

Least Sandpiper *Calidris minutilla*

14 cm. Rare Nearctic vagrant occurring in late summer and autumn. Resembles Temminck's Stint with greenish-yellow legs, short downcurved bill, but more compact body, pronounced supercilium reaches base of bill. Winter adult: greyish scapulars with large diffuse dark centres, bib of diffuse streaking. Juvenile: mantle like that of Little Stint with black-and-rufous feather fringes. Call: soft rising *truuip*.

white supercilium

slim bill with brown base

Winter adult

coverts with dark centres

pectoral streaks

yellowish legs

rufous scapulars with black centres and white tips

white supercilium reaches bill

greenish-yellow legs

dark, short, downcurved bill

Juvenile

Long-toed Stint *Calidris subminuta*

15 cm. Very rare Asian vagrant. Very similar to Least Sandpiper with short bill and greenish-yellow legs but longer toes, at least as long as bill, dark forehead and kinked supercilium that does not reach forehead. Pale lower mandible, legs longer than tail in flight. Winter: even darker centres to wing-coverts and scapulars. Call: low *trrip*.

rufous scapulars with very dark centres

tertials with reddish-brown edges

Breeding adult

streaked breast

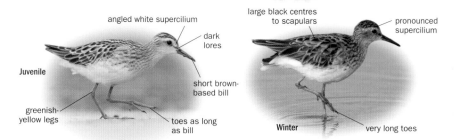

angled white supercilium

dark lores

Juvenile

greenish-yellow legs

short brown-based bill

toes as long as bill

large black centres to scapulars

pronounced supercilium

Winter

very long toes

Great Knot *Calidris tenuirostris*

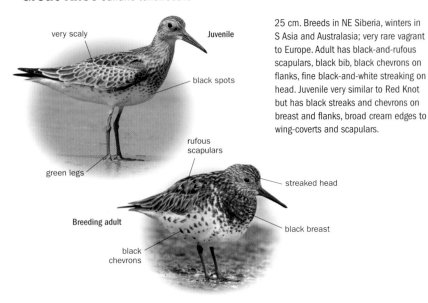

very scaly

Juvenile

black spots

rufous scapulars

green legs

Breeding adult

black chevrons

streaked head

black breast

25 cm. Breeds in NE Siberia, winters in S Asia and Australasia; very rare vagrant to Europe. Adult has black-and-rufous scapulars, black bib, black chevrons on flanks, fine black-and-white streaking on head. Juvenile very similar to Red Knot but has black streaks and chevrons on breast and flanks, broad cream edges to wing-coverts and scapulars.

Grey-tailed Tattler *Tringa brevipes*

mouse-grey

white supercilium

Juvenile

cream spots

yellow legs

Adult

black lores

barred flanks

27 cm. Very rare Asian vagrant, with records from Britain and Sweden. Uniform mouse-grey with white supercilium and dark eye-stripe. Resembles a Common Redshank with short yellow legs. Breeding adult has grey barring on breast and flanks. Juvenile has pale narrow borders and indentations on wing-coverts and tertials. Call: whistled *tui-di*.

WOODCOCKS AND SNIPES Very long-billed waders with cryptic brown-and-black plumage, yellowish 'braces'; snipes have striped heads. Rapid direct flight. Feed on worms found in the soil or in mud. Three species resident in Europe, one migrant and four vagrants.

(Eurasian) Woodcock *Scolopax rusticola*

IDENTIFICATION 36 cm. Large rotund terrestrial wader with cryptic brown plumage. Head appears pointed with a large black eye and transverse black barring on crown. Long bill with thick base, short pink legs. When disturbed, takes flight with a lot of clatter, showing rufous rump and rounded wings. **VOICE** The display flight over its territory, called 'roding', is accompanied with soft sounds of *ourt* regularly repeated, then very sharp *iiiist* notes. **HABITAT** Forests, woods and woodland edges, nearby fields and open areas for feeding at night.

cryptic brown, black and rufous upperparts

large black eye

pale bill with darker tip

streaked pale brown flanks

American Woodcock
Scolopax minor

28 cm. Nearctic vagrant. The only European record is of a juvenile in central France in October 2006. Smaller than Eurasian Woodcock, greyish plumage above and uniform orangey below.

reddish bill with dark tip

uniform buff flanks

pink legs

Jack Snipe *Lymnocryptes minimus*

IDENTIFICATION 19 cm. Small, large head, shortish bill thick at base. Mantle dark with yellow stripes, streaked breast, black centre to crown. When disturbed presses itself to the ground only flying at last minute. Bobs its body whilst feeding. **VOICE** Short non-explosive *yech* on taking flight. **HABITAT** Marshes, wet meadows, ponds.

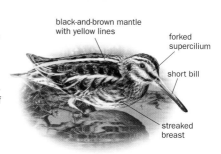

black-and-brown mantle with yellow lines

forked supercilium

short bill

streaked breast

Common Snipe *Gallinago gallinago*

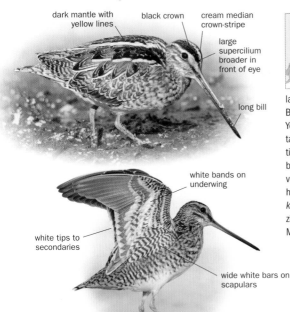

dark mantle with yellow lines

black crown

cream median crown-stripe

large supercilium broader in front of eye

long bill

white bands on underwing

white tips to secondaries

wide white bars on scapulars

IDENTIFICATION
26 cm. Black-and-cream striped crown with cream central stripe, large supercilium enlarged in front of eye. Barred buff-washed flanks, white belly. Yellow lines on dark back, reddish-brown tail with black barring and small white tips to feathers. Probes the mud with its bill to search for worms. Hides in vegetation, stops motionless at slightest hint of danger. **VOICE** Explosive grating *krrrretsh* on taking-off, followed by zigzagging escape flight. **HABITAT** Marshes, wet meadows, reedbed edges.

white lines

very rufous tail with white corners

large white tips to upperwing-coverts, forming 3 lines

rufous tail with big white corners

Great Snipe *Gallinago media*

medium-long bill

black barring on flanks and belly

28 cm. Migrant; in Europe from April/May to August/September. Breeds in Scandinavia and N Europe to Siberia, and winters in sub-Saharan Africa. Thickset snipe, medium-length bill, black barring on belly and flanks, large white spots on the upperwing-coverts form 3 white lines on wing. Reddish tail with large white corners, dark underwing. When taking flight, infrequently gives soft call; does not zigzag.

Wilson's Snipe *Gallinago delicata*

26 cm. Nearctic equivalent of Common Snipe; very rare vagrant, annual in the Azores. Very difficult to separate; narrower white trailing edge of wing, wide black bars (as broad as white bars) on underwing-coverts and axillaries, broad black bars on flanks, more contrasting back (black and golden), very rufous central tail feathers, outer ones with large white tips.

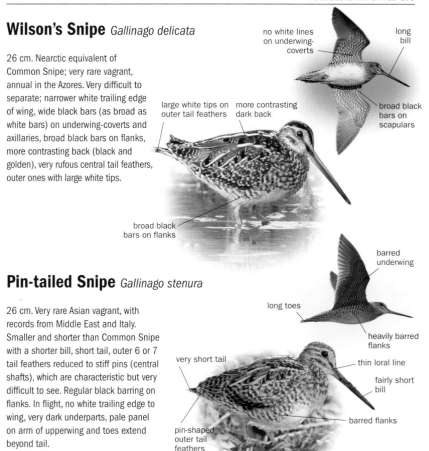

no white lines on underwing-coverts

long bill

large white tips on outer tail feathers

more contrasting dark back

broad black bars on scapulars

broad black bars on flanks

Pin-tailed Snipe *Gallinago stenura*

26 cm. Very rare Asian vagrant, with records from Middle East and Italy. Smaller and shorter than Common Snipe with a shorter bill, short tail, outer 6 or 7 tail feathers reduced to stiff pins (central shafts), which are characteristic but very difficult to see. Regular black barring on flanks. In flight, no white trailing edge to wing, very dark underparts, pale panel on arm of upperwing and toes extend beyond tail.

barred underwing

long toes

heavily barred flanks

very short tail

thin loral line

fairly short bill

barred flanks

pin-shaped outer tail feathers

Swinhoe's Snipe *Gallinago megala*

28 cm. Very rare vagrant from Siberian taiga; breeds in the Urals. Like Pin-tailed Snipe, 2–5 outer tail feathers are reduced but not pin-like. Differs from Common Snipe in having no white on secondary tips and shorter bill. Distinctive display song. Marbled buff tertials with black bars, pale wing-coverts.

short tail

very pale wing-coverts

narrow outer tail feathers

DOWITCHERS Vagrant Nearctic waders. The two species of Dowitcher are very similar; juveniles have a different pattern on the tertials; calls are diagnostic.

Long-billed Dowitcher *Limnodromus scolopaceus*

clear long cream
supercilium

Juvenile

dark lores

dark centres
to tertials

long bill with
wide greenish
base

streaked
flanks

greenish legs

grey mantle

finely barred
black-and-
white tail

Winter adult

28 cm. Rare Nearctic and Siberian vagrant, annual in W Europe on coastal marshes and estuaries. Silhouette of a large sandpiper with long straight bill of a snipe, eye placed far back on head. Greenish legs, pronounced off-white supercilium with dark crown and lores. In flight, has white trailing edge to wings, white 'cigar' stripe on back, black-and-white barring on rump and tail. Juvenile: tertials with uniform grey centres and narrow pale edges. In winter: grey mantle feathers with diffuse dark centres, grey breast, barred flanks. Call: brief monosyllabic *kyip*, sometimes double.

Short-billed Dowitcher *Limnodromus griseus*

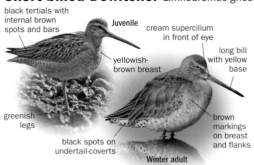

black tertials with
internal brown
spots and bars

Juvenile

cream supercilium
in front of eye

long bill
with yellow
base

yellowish-
brown breast

greenish
legs

brown
markings
on breast
and flanks

black spots on
undertail-coverts

Winter adult

27 cm. Very rare Nearctic vagrant; occurs in autumn or winter. Very similar to Long-billed Dowitcher but bill often shorter, tertials with pale central marks, sometimes just a discreet longitudinal line. In winter is best distinguished by call, a disyllabic whistled lower *tudlu*, recalling Turnstone's call.

Upland Sandpiper *Bartramia longicauda*

large black
eye

short straight
bill with
yellow base

long
tail

coarsely barred

yellow legs

30 cm. Very rare Nearctic vagrant, especially to the Atlantic coast. Reminiscent of a curlew with long tail and short, almost straight bill (like an elongated Stone-curlew). Yellow legs, tail far longer than the wings; often has upright posture. In flight, no white on rump and dark underwing. Call in flight: *kip-ip-ip-ip-ip...*

GODWITS Large waders with long legs, very long oversized bills, straight or slightly upturned, black legs. Brick-red underparts in breeding plumage, totally grey in winter. The two common species have different wing and tail patterns. See also vagrant Hudsonian Godwit on p. 179.

Black-tailed Godwit *Limosa limosa*

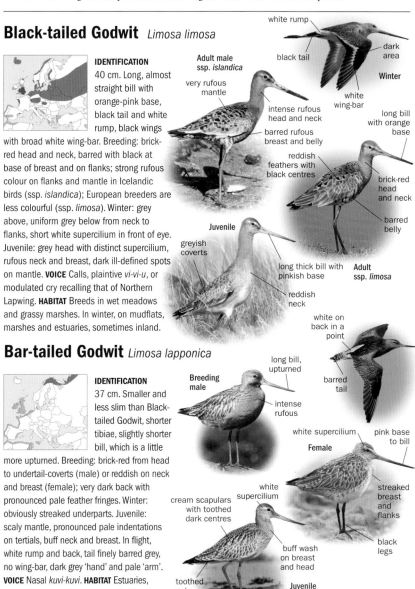

IDENTIFICATION
40 cm. Long, almost straight bill with orange-pink base, black tail and white rump, black wings with broad white wing-bar. Breeding: brick-red head and neck, barred with black at base of breast and on flanks; strong rufous colour on flanks and mantle in Icelandic birds (ssp. *islandica*); European breeders are less colourful (ssp. *limosa*). Winter: grey above, uniform grey below from neck to flanks, short white supercilium in front of eye. Juvenile: grey head with distinct supercilium, rufous neck and breast, dark ill-defined spots on mantle. **VOICE** Calls, plaintive *vi-vi-u*, or modulated cry recalling that of Northern Lapwing. **HABITAT** Breeds in wet meadows and grassy marshes. In winter, on mudflats, marshes and estuaries, sometimes inland.

white rump
dark area
black tail
Winter
Adult male ssp. islandica
very rufous mantle
white wing-bar
intense rufous head and neck
long bill with orange base
barred rufous breast and belly
reddish feathers with black centres
brick-red head and neck
barred belly
Juvenile
greyish coverts
long thick bill with pinkish base
Adult ssp. limosa
reddish neck

Bar-tailed Godwit *Limosa lapponica*

IDENTIFICATION
37 cm. Smaller and less slim than Black-tailed Godwit, shorter tibiae, slightly shorter bill, which is a little more upturned. Breeding: brick-red from head to undertail-coverts (male) or reddish on neck and breast (female); very dark back with pronounced pale feather fringes. Winter: obviously streaked underparts. Juvenile: scaly mantle, pronounced pale indentations on tertials, buff neck and breast. In flight, white rump and back, tail finely barred grey, no wing-bar, dark grey 'hand' and pale 'arm'. **VOICE** Nasal *kuvi-kuvi*. **HABITAT** Estuaries, coastal bays, mudflats; very rarely inland.

white on back in a point
long bill, upturned
barred tail
Breeding male
intense rufous
white supercilium
pink base to bill
Female
cream scapulars with toothed dark centres
white supercilium
streaked breast and flanks
buff wash on breast and head
black legs
toothed pale edges
Juvenile

CURLEWS Large, streaked brown waders with long decurved bills and white on back. Head pattern and call are important when identifying the two commoner species.

Eurasian Curlew *Numenius arquata*

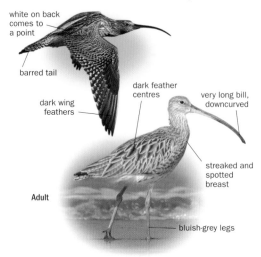

white on back comes to a point

barred tail

dark wing feathers

dark feather centres

very long bill, downcurved

streaked and spotted breast

Adult

bluish-grey legs

IDENTIFICATION
54 cm. Very long decurved bill, longer in female. Uniform face, diffuse supercilium, crown only slightly darker than face, pale eye-ring. White 'cigar' on back and rump in flight. Barred underwings, almost completely white in eastern birds (ssp. *orientalis*), which winter on the Mediterranean coast. **VOICE** Fluty loud call, *kour-liii*. **HABITAT** Breeds in wet meadows and on moors. Winters in coastal bays, estuaries and on mudflats.

Whimbrel *Numenius phaeopus*

white area on back

Adult ssp. *phaeopus*

barred tail

dark flight feathers

Adult ssp. *phaeopus*

lateral crown-stripe with black sides

long bill

streaked breast

barred flanks

bluish-grey legs

more contrast

brown and beige

Ssp. *hudsonicus*

brown rump

beige below

Ssp. *hudsonicus*

IDENTIFICATION
41 cm. Smaller, with shorter bill than Eurasian Curlew. Dark lines on head: eye-stripe and each side of crown, with pale median crown-stripe. White 'cigar' on back is very visible in flight but absent in Nearctic race (ssp. *hudsonicus*), which is a rare vagrant to Europe having a barred brown rump and back. **VOICE** Call: whistled *huhuhuhuhuhu*...given mainly in flight, very different from Eurasian Curlew's call. **HABITAT** Sandy or rocky coasts and marshes.

Slender-billed Curlew *Numenius tenuirostris*

Frequent migrant to European coasts in the 18th century, now considered possibly extinct; the last authentic sighting dates from the end of the 20th century. Small curlew with very slender bill, uniform face and round spots on flanks.

streaked neck

very slim bill

characteristic round spots on breast

Little Curlew *Numenius minutus*

30 cm. Small Asian curlew; very rare vagrant. Uniform face with pale lores, dark lateral stripes on crown. Dark rump, white belly and flanks, mottled buff neck. Resembles Upland Sandpiper but shorter tail, longer bill and unbarred flanks. Call: *cui-cui-cui*... softer than that of Whimbrel.

barred underwings

dark crown and clear supercilium

short bill

grey legs

Hudsonian Godwit *Limosa haemastica*

30 cm. Nearctic species; very rare vagrant to Europe, with records from the Azores, Britain and Norway. Smaller than Black-tailed Godwit with black underwing-coverts but similar pattern on wings and tail. Adult has very dark mantle, greyish face and rufous-barred black underparts. Upturned bill with orange base. Call: repeated nasal *ket*.

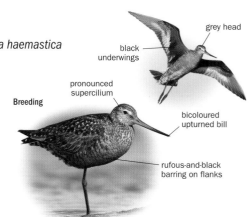

grey head

black underwings

pronounced supercilium

Breeding

bicoloured upturned bill

rufous-and-black barring on flanks

LARGER SANDPIPERS Waders with long legs and long straight or slightly upturned bills. Always near water. Leg colour and call are very useful in separating the species.

Common Redshank *Tringa totanus*

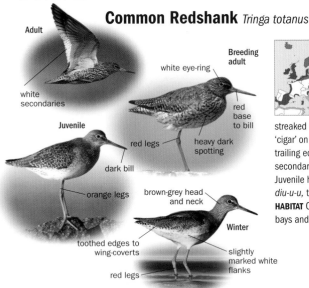

Adult

white secondaries

Juvenile

Breeding adult

white eye-ring

red legs

dark bill

red base to bill

heavy dark spotting

orange legs

brown-grey head and neck

toothed edges to wing-coverts

red legs

Winter

slightly marked white flanks

IDENTIFICATION
26 cm. Red legs, red-based straight thickish bill, streaked greyish breast, streaked white flanks. In flight a white 'cigar' on the back and white triangles on trailing edge of wing (white tips to secondaries and inner primaries). Juvenile has orange legs. **VOICE** Trisyllabic *diu-u-u*, the second 2 notes more muted. **HABITAT** Coastal marshes, wet meadows, bays and estuaries.

Spotted Redshank *Tringa erythropus*

clear white supercilium in front of eye

pale grey above

Winter adult

white 'cigar'

legs extend beyond tail

white flanks

red legs

uniform wings without wing-bar

Adult

uniformly barred breast and flanks

Juvenile

Breeding adult

slim black bill with red base

pale teeth on sides of tertials

orange legs

black plumage

black legs

IDENTIFICATION
31 cm. Larger and slimmer than Common Redshank, dark red legs with longer tibiae, slimmer and longer bill with red base to lower mandible. Breeding: black from head to belly. Winter: pale grey above, white below, prominent white supercilium and black lores, unmarked flanks. Juvenile has barred underparts as far as legs, no streaks. In flight, a white 'cigar' on the back but no white in the wing. **VOICE** Emphatic, disyllabic whistled *tchui-uit*. **HABITAT** Marshes, wet meadows, estuaries and mudflats.

Greenshank *Tringa nebularia*

white rump and back

Juvenile

pale feather edges on brown back

Adult

dark wings

heavily streaked white head

greenish-yellow legs

Breeding adult

greenish legs

slightly upturned long bill

dark spots on white flanks

IDENTIFICATION 32 cm. Large wader without distinctive colours, greenish-grey legs, long slightly upturned bill with greyer base. Whitish head with grey streaks, uniform face, pale eye-ring, indistinct supercilium and dark lores, streaked breast. In flight, white rump and back, pale grey tail, all-dark wings. **VOICE** Three loud notes of same length and strength *diu-diu-diu*. **HABITAT** Marshes, estuaries, lakes and fishponds, river banks.

Marsh Sandpiper *Tringa stagnatillis*

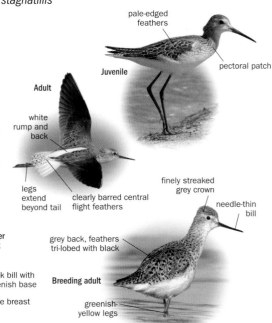

pale-edged feathers

Juvenile

pectoral patch

Adult

white rump and back

legs extend beyond tail

clearly barred central flight feathers

finely streaked grey crown

needle-thin bill

grey back, feathers tri-lobed with black

Breeding adult

greenish-yellow legs

IDENTIFICATION 24 cm. Similar to Greenshank but smaller, slimmer, has thinner and longer legs, and shorter, thinner, straighter bill. Very similar plumage with more marked head pattern, white breast without the streaks in winter. In flight, like Greenshank but with legs projecting further behind tail. **VOICE** Piping *pcheou* or trisyllabic call similar to that of Greenshank but quicker. **HABITAT** Marshes, wet meadows, fishponds.

grey mantle with pale-edged feathers

Winter adult

black bill with greenish base

white breast

dark
underwing-
coverts

dark axillaries
with white zebra
stripes

wide black bar

white
rump

dark above with
pale spots

white
eye-ring

yellow
legs

Adult

white belly
and flanks

Green Sandpiper *Tringa ochropus*

IDENTIFICATION
22 cm. Smallish
sandpiper with
dark plumage,
short straight
bill, extensive
white rump and dull black underwings. A
few small white markings on upperparts.
White spot above lores, dark breast with
abrupt lower edge, broad black bars on
tail. Dark greenish-grey legs. **VOICE** *tchuii-
tvi-tvi* with rising first notes followed by 1
or 2 rapid notes. **HABITAT** Marshes,
fishponds, wet meadows, canals.

pale grey
underwings

dark above with
rufous spots

Juvenile

diffuse
streaking
on breast

black-barred
tail

frosty dark
above

white
supercilium

Breeding adult

yellow legs

diffuse
streaking

Wood Sandpiper *Tringa glareola*

IDENTIFICATION
20 cm. Very
similar to Green
Sandpiper,
brown
upperparts with
more numerous pale spots, diffuse edge
to streaked breast, pronounced
supercilium behind eye, grey underside to
wings. Fine black bars on tail, white rump.
Greenish-yellow legs, more obviously
extending beyond tail in flight. **VOICE** Call
a shrill, rapid whistled *kif-kif-kif*. **HABITAT**
Marshes, fishponds, wet meadows.

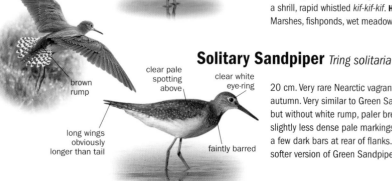

brown
rump

clear pale
spotting
above

clear white
eye-ring

long wings
obviously
longer than tail

faintly barred

Solitary Sandpiper *Tring solitaria*

20 cm. Very rare Nearctic vagrant, in
autumn. Very similar to Green Sandpiper
but without white rump, paler breast,
slightly less dense pale markings above,
a few dark bars at rear of flanks. Call:
softer version of Green Sandpiper's call.

Common Sandpiper *Actitis hypoleucos*

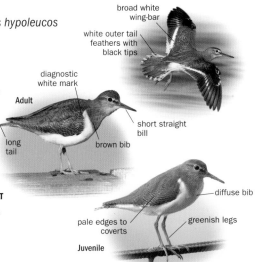

broad white wing-bar

white outer tail feathers with black tips

diagnostic white mark

Adult

short straight bill

long tail

brown bib

IDENTIFICATION
20 cm. Small, size of a Dunlin, often bent forwards, bobs tail. Long tail extends far beyond wings, short green legs, short straight bill. Clear-cut bib, white mark continues up to shoulder. Large white wing-bar in flight. Flight is a series of rapid wingbeats alternating with gliding on arched wings. **VOICE** Loud shrill trill, *hi-ti-ti-ti*... **HABITAT** Gravel pits, islands and banks of larger rivers, canals, rocky mudflats and coasts.

diffuse bib

greenish legs

pale edges to coverts

Juvenile

Spotted Sandpiper *Actitis macularius*

19 cm. Rare but annual Nearctic vagrant, very similar to Common Sandpiper; shorter tail hardly longer than wings, orange-yellow legs, bill with pale base appears slightly decurved, more well-defined supercilium. Juvenile: more scaly wing-coverts (more well-defined black than pale edges), uniform tertials. Breeding adult: round black spots on breast. Shorter wing-bar in flight. Voice sometimes different from that of Common Sandpiper with shriller mono- or disyllabic calls.

uniform fringes to tertials

pale greyish bill

Juvenile

short tail

brown above with dark stripes

yellow legs

black tip to bill

Breeding adult

black spots

Terek Sandpiper *Xenus cinereus*

24 cm. Rare but annual migrant, on mudflats. Looks like a small Greenshank with short legs. Long upturned bill, grey streaks on breast sides. Adult: dark 'wrists' on wing and black band on shoulder. In flight, grey rump, slender white trailing edge to wing. Call: whistled notes similar to those of Common Redshank.

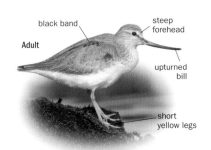

black band

steep forehead

Adult

upturned bill

short yellow legs

Lesser Yellowlegs *Tringa flavipes*

brownish-grey back

Winter adult

yellow legs

24 cm. Rare but annual vagrant. Similar to Common Redshank but longer legs, thinner more slender bill and long primary projection. Yellow legs, white bar on rump as in Wood Sandpiper. Diffuse streaks on breast. Call: a soft *tchu*, single or repeated. Larger pale markings on upperparts in breeding plumage.

long wings

short dark bill

diffuse streaking

brownish legs

Juvenile

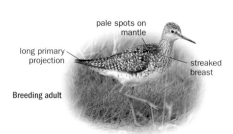

pale spots on mantle

long primary projection

streaked breast

Breeding adult

Greater Yellowlegs *Tringa melanoleuca*

cream indentations

First-winter

dark back

bill slightly upturned

barred tail

yellow legs

barred flanks

streaked breast and neck

Breeding adult

31 cm. Very rare Nearctic vagrant. Larger than Lesser Yellowlegs; resembles Greenshank but has yellow legs, long less-upturned bill; juvenile with cream indentations on back feathers. White rump and dark back. White breast with clear dark streaks, does not give appearance of a bib at distance. Trisyllabic call like that of Greenshank.

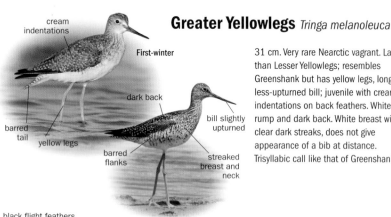

black flight feathers with white bar

white tail with grey band

legs extend beyond tail

grey legs

Winter adult

Willet *Tringa semipalmata*

grey with brown tint

grey bill with blunt tip

34 cm. Very rare Nearctic vagrant. Resembles Greenshank but more thickset, uniform grey in winter, white line above lores, black hand and underwing-coverts with broad white wing-bar, straight thick bill, yellow-grey legs. Call: repeated *kip kip*.

PHALAROPES Arctic breeders seen infrequently on migration, normally at coastal sites. Grey and white in winter, colourful in summer. Lobed toes. Swim with bobbing motion, moving head backwards and forwards. See p. 186 for breeding plumages.

Red-necked Phalarope *Phalaropus lobatus*

IDENTIFICATION 18 cm. All-black, thin bill. Winter: scaly grey above, feathers with dark centres, white 'braces'. Immature: black above with broad yellow 'braces', black crown, black eye-stripe behind eye. In flight, white sides to rump and narrow white wing-bar. **VOICE** Call: a short, nasal *tchep*. **HABITAT** Breeds on tundra ponds; on migration saltpans, shallow lagoons and other coastal sites.

Juvenile

black crown
black mask behind eye
golden-yellow line
thin black bill

Grey Phalarope *Phalaropus fulicarius*

IDENTIFICATION 21 cm. Thicker bill than Red-necked Phalarope, small amount of yellow at base of lower mandible. Winter: more uniform pale grey above, similar head pattern to that of Red-necked. Immature: grey with moulted scapulars. In flight, has broader white wing-bar and looks very like Sanderling. **VOICE** Loud *kitt* reminiscent of Coot's call. **HABITAT** Maritime, rarely near the coast. Very uncommon in winter but occurs near coast after storms or on lagoons. Rare inland.

black crown
black mask behind eye
uniform grey back
Winter adult

grey scapulars
dark coverts with pale edges
thick black bill
lobed toes
First-winter

Wilson's Phalarope *Phalaropus tricolor*

23 cm. Nearctic vagrant, slimmer than the other phalaropes but larger, with long slender neck; resembles Marsh Sandpiper. Long needle-like bill, yellow legs with short tibiae. Winter: uniform pale grey above, white below, long white supercilium extends onto neck. First-winter: black wing-coverts, scapulars and tertials with narrow well-defined white edges. In flight, grey upperparts with white rump; first-winter has black wings, no wing-bar.

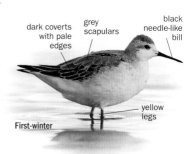

dark coverts with pale edges
grey scapulars
black needle-like bill
yellow legs
First-winter

PHALAROPES IN BREEDING PLUMAGE In spring a few migrant birds in breeding plumage are seen along the coast; small numbers of Red-necked Phalaropes breed in northern Scotland. Females are more colourful than males; the female chooses the more sober-coloured male who then incubates the eggs.

Red-necked Phalarope *Phalaropus lobatus*

faded red

Male

dark brown mantle with yellow line

lead-grey

lead-grey with yellow lines

deep red

white throat

ashy-grey upper breast

Female

Breeding: grey head, white throat, rufous collar, coal-coloured back with narrow golden 'braces'.

Grey Phalarope *Phalaropus fulicarius*

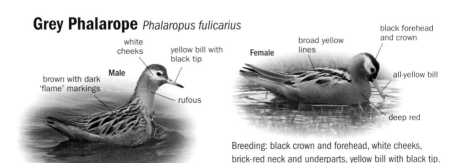

black forehead and crown

white cheeks

yellow bill with black tip

broad yellow lines

Female

brown with dark 'flame' markings

Male

all-yellow bill

rufous

deep red

Breeding: black crown and forehead, white cheeks, brick-red neck and underparts, yellow bill with black tip.

Wilson's Phalarope *Phalaropus tricolor*

black side to neck merging into red

white area

lead-grey back with dark red band

Male

reddish tint

white supercilium

white throat

reddish

black legs

Female

Breeding: black band through eye changing to rufous on neck, pale orange front to neck, small white supercilium above eye.

SKUAS (JAEGERS) Closely related to gulls, more decisive direct flight with quicker more regular wingbeats. Pointed outer wings, plumage dark at a distance. Most observations are of birds on active migration over the sea: breed on Arctic tundra (two species breed in northern Scotland) and winter at sea off the West African coast. Most birds seen on autumn migration with very few inland records. Chase terns and small gulls, and even sometimes Gannets, to rob their prey. The three smaller species are very similar, and can be identified by closely observing silhouette, bill, rump and underwing pattern. Summer adults have elongated central tail feathers, each species a different shape. Several different colour morphs, from pale to dark; uniform underwings in adults, barred in immature. Silent at sea.

Pomarine Skua *Stercorarius pomarinus*

46 cm. The biggest of the small skuas. Strong breast, thick bill with outer third dark. Breeding adult: long spoon-shaped central tail feathers, black crown circles bill on face, dark breast-band. Immature and winter: barred rump, undertail-coverts and axillaries, even in dark form. On underwing, pale bases to primaries and greater coverts form 2 distinctive white commas.

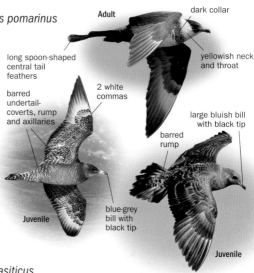

Adult

dark collar

long spoon-shaped central tail feathers

yellowish neck and throat

barred undertail-coverts, rump and axillaries

2 white commas

large bluish bill with black tip

barred rump

blue-grey bill with black tip

Juvenile

Juvenile

Arctic Skua *Stercorarius parasiticus*

41 cm. Smaller than Pomarine Skua, less prominent breast, smaller head, quite slim bill with outer third black. Breeding adult: pale around base of bill, long pointed central tail feathers. Immature and winter: barred undertail-coverts and axillaries but not on white background, rump more or less spotted; dark morph without barring, uniform blackish-brown. No double pale comma on underwing.

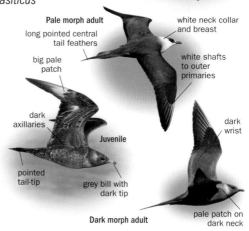

Pale morph adult

white neck collar and breast

long pointed central tail feathers

white shafts to outer primaries

big pale patch

dark axillaries

Juvenile

dark wrist

pointed tail-tip

grey bill with dark tip

Dark morph adult

pale patch on dark neck

Long-tailed Skua *Stercorarius longicaudus*

Juvenile

longer central tail feathers

barred rump

small bicoloured bill

pale round head

Juvenile

obviously barred

2 primaries with white shafts

long tail-streamers

yellowish neck collar and cheeks

small black bill

Breeding adult

38 cm. The smallest and slimmest of the skuas, slim bill half black at tip, cold-coloured plumage, narrower wings appear very long; white shafts to 2 outer primaries; flight often buoyant, the body appears to move up and down with the wingbeats. Breeding adult: streamers twice the length of tail; dark crown stops just below the eye and includes the forehead; white breast and grey belly without obvious separation, uniform dark grey undersides to wing. Immature and winter: pronounced white barring on rump, undertail-coverts and axillaries; no double pale commas on underwings.

Great Skua *Stercorarius skua*

54 cm. Size of a Herring Gull, entirely dark plumage except for white primary bases; energetic direct flight. Adult: black crown, dark brown body mottled below and with buff streaks above, even the underwing-coverts; thick black bill, black legs. Immature: rufous body with dark head, grey base to bill, pale grey on tarsus and webs of feet. More thickset than dark morph Pomarine Skua, tail shorter and squarer, and more extensive white on primaries.

dark brown breast

blackish-brown underwing-coverts

big white patch

dark but with beige streaks above and below

massive head

thick black bill

black tail

streaked brown mantle

white patch at primary bases

Subantarctic Skua *Stercorarius antarcticus lonnbergi*

52 cm. Breeds on subantarctic islands and the Antarctic peninsula; exceptional vagrant to N Atlantic waters. More thickset and compact than South Polar Skua, bill shorter and thicker than that of Great Skua, brown head without darker crown, buff fringes on mantle, more uniform underwing-coverts. Immature very difficult to separate from other 2 species of great skua; note the precise moult stage of primaries, leg colour (trace of pale blue in immature); dull plumage without obvious rufous colouring.

spotted mantle

uniform brown

uniform wing

uniform head

2 or 3 primaries in active moult in summer

South Polar Skua *Stercorarius maccormicki*

53 cm. Breeds in Antarctic, migrates as far as N Atlantic during southern winter; very rare. Very similar to Great Skua but slimmer, less massive bill, more uniform dull brown plumage (never rufous), darker underwing-coverts, crown no darker than head. Immature in active moult during our summer, often second, third and above flight feathers in simultaneous active moult (first and second in other 2 great skuas). Some individuals have paler bodies.

slimmer bill

4 primaries in active moult

Immature

Immature

pale body

Pale morph adult

contrast with underwing-coverts

pale head and neck

pointed tail feathers   First-winter

Immature

3 or more primaries simultaneously in moult in summer

GULLS Species of very variable size, occupying marine or freshwater habitats. The larger gulls have a yellow bill with terminal red spot (a few exceptions) when adult, which takes from three to five years according to species with many intermediate immature plumages (but also variable within a species). The smaller gulls attain adult plumage when two years old. They breed in colonies on cliffs, on inland lakes and even on flat roofs.

Black-headed Gull *Chroicocephalus ridibundus*

Winter adult
white head
red bill with black tip
dark spot
white flight feathers with black borders

chocolate hood
pale grey above
red bill
Breeding adult
red legs
dark spot
grey mantle with rufous feathers
brownish bill with dark tip
Juvenile

IDENTIFICATION
37 cm. Dark brown hood, pale grey mantle, slim dark red bill, red legs, white outer flight feathers bordered with black, black median flight feathers on underwing. Winter adult: orange bill with black tip, black spot behind eye. First-winter: narrow black bar to tail, black-brown secondaries and median coverts, black tips to all primaries, orange legs. **VOICE** Sarcastic laugh *crraaaaaaa*. **HABITAT** Large lakes, marshes for breeding. In winter, wetlands, coasts, fields, lakes.

Slender-billed Gull *Chroicocephalus genei*

Adult
black bill
pale grey mantle
black flight feathers
dark red legs
Adult
white primaries with black tips
dark iris
red bill
Winter adult
brownish mantle and coverts
brownish-pink bill
red legs
black tip to tail
Juvenile

IDENTIFICATION
40 cm. Plumage as in Black-headed Gull but more slender, long neck tinted pink; long thin bill, dark red to black when breeding, orange with black tip in winter; adult has dark iris. Juvenile has less pronounced wing pattern than that of Black-headed Gull, dark cheek spot, pale iris. Legs red (adult) or pale orange (juvenile). **VOICE** As Black-headed Gull but lower, dry and grating, *kreerr*. **HABITAT** Saltpans, brackish lagoons.

(Black-legged) Kittiwake *Rissa tridactyla*

IDENTIFICATION
40 cm. Medium-sized gull with long pointed wings, slightly forked tail, short black legs and small yellow bill. Similar to Common Gull in breeding plumage. Wings with pale grey hands and small terminal black triangle. Winter adult: diffuse grey patch at rear of cheek and grey on back of neck. First-winter: black W on upperside of white wings, narrow black bar on tail, black collar on back of neck, black patch on rear of cheek.
VOICE Very noisy at colony, *kitivek*, hence the name: nasal *kial* in flight. **HABITAT** Maritime, breeds on sea cliffs, winters at sea; very rare inland after storms.

First-winter
white tail with black band
black rear collar
black bill
dark spot on cheek
black W on wings
Winter adult
white tail
grey rear neck
dark patch
black eye with red eye-ring
yellow bill
grey above
black wing-tips
Adult
black legs

Little Gull *Hydrocoloeus minutus*

IDENTIFICATION
26 cm. Small, rounded wings with blackish undersides and white tip below, short thin black bill. Breeding adult: very black hood covering all the nape, no white crescent around eye, dark pink legs; in winter, dark spot at rear of cheek and rear crown. First-winter: black W above, grey secondaries (white in Kittiwake), narrow black bar on square tail, white underwings, greyish back of neck, pale pink legs. **VOICE** Nasal *kek*, often repeated rapidly.
HABITAT Breeds in freshwater marshes; on migration or in winter, on coasts or at sea, occasionally inland.

Juvenile
black bar
black underwings
Winter adult
black bar on tail
narrow white edges
matt black hood
dark above with pale feather edges
black patch
black crown
Breeding adult
white flight feathers
dark crown
small black bill
grey bar on secondaries
Juvenile
Winter adult

Mediterranean Gull *Larus melanocephalus*

dark band behind eye

black subterminal spots

incomplete white eye-ring

matt black head

pale grey mantle

red bill

red bill

Second-winter

white wings

scaly pattern above

black bar on tail

black bill

Adult

Juvenile

brown legs

IDENTIFICATION
39 cm. Black hood and blood-red legs, white-tipped wings. Adult: pale grey mantle, all-white primaries. First-winter: fine black bar on tail, black legs, black bill with grey base, dark mask behind eye. Second-winter: small black subterminal spots on outer primaries. Often accompanies Black-headed Gulls.
VOICE Call: short barked distinctive *ghia*.
HABITAT Breeds mainly on the coast, winters on fishponds and larger lakes, bays and estuaries, extensive mudflats.

Audouin's Gull *Larus audouinii*

Adult

red bill with black band and pale tip

dark iris

dull grey mantle

Adult

black primaries with small white spots

greenish-grey legs

greenish-grey bill with black tip

Second-year

grey wings with brown mottling

IDENTIFICATION
48 cm. Largish gull with dull grey mantle. Greenish-grey legs, red bill with black subterminal band and yellow tip, dark iris, almost no white trailing edge to tertials; extensive black wing-tips. Adult's dark bill unique in European gulls. Juvenile: all-black tail, white V on rump, uniform black tertials and mantle feathers with narrow cream edges, looking very scaly, moulted scapulars uniform mouse-grey (first-winter), grey bill with black tip. Second-summer: narrow black bar on tail and on secondaries, black hand to wing, red bill with black tip. **VOICE** Silent away from colonies. **HABITAT** Coasts, lagoons; feeds at sea, nests on small islands. Once very rare but has increased.

Common Gull *Larus canus*

IDENTIFICATION
43 cm. Medium-sized slender gull with round head, short slim bill; grey mantle
darker than that of Black-headed Gull, long wings. Breeding adult: greenish-yellow legs, yellow bill, black iris, big white mirrors on primaries, well-defined white crescent on tertials. Winter: hood of grey streaks, ill-defined black bar on bill. First-winter: well-defined black bar on tail, uniform wing-coverts, black tertials with large white borders, pink bill with black tip, pink legs. Second-winter: grey bill with black terminal band, small white tips to primaries, often some black on tail feathers or secondaries. **VOICE** Call: characteristic high-pitched *keeaa*. **HABITAT** Breeds on coast or inland in north, winters on lakes, lagoons, bays and estuaries.

large white spots on primaries
Winter adult
darkish hood
black iris
crescent on tertials
yellow bill with indistinct black bar
dark grey mantle
Breeding adult

dark grey mantle
First-winter
grey mantle, brown wings and tertials
First-winter
bicoloured bill
clear black bar
uniform greater coverts
pinkish legs

Ring-billed Gull *Larus delawarensis*

45 cm. Nearctic species; rare but regular in winter to the Atlantic coast of Europe. Very similar to Common Gull but has thicker bill, squarer head. Adult: yellow bill with well-defined black subterminal bar, pale iris, lighter grey mantle, smaller less well-defined white crescent on tertials, small white mirror at wing-tip. First-winter: diagnostic narrow pale fringes to tertials, broad black bar to tail is less clear-cut, thick pink bill with black tip, pink legs, scaly black marks on breast. Second-winter: traces of black on tail, entirely grey tertials.

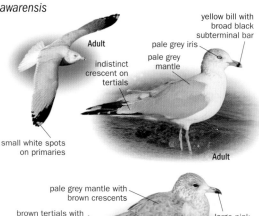

Adult
indistinct crescent on tertials
yellow bill with broad black subterminal bar
pale grey iris
pale grey mantle
small white spots on primaries
Adult

pale grey mantle with brown crescents
brown tertials with narrow pale edges
large pink bill with black tip
First-winter

Sabine's Gull *Xema sabini*

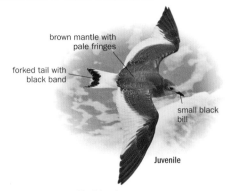

brown mantle with pale fringes

forked tail with black band

small black bill

Juvenile

IDENTIFICATION 33 cm. Characteristic tricoloured (black, white and grey) wings, forked tail. Breeding: sooty-grey hood bordered by black line, black bill with yellow tip. Juvenile: grey-brown with scaly white markings above, brown-grey back of neck and head; closely resembles immature Kittiwake, even when close. **VOICE** Silent at sea. **HABITAT** Oceanic. Rare migrant, passage birds off west coast in late summer. Comes closer to the coast during storms, very rare inland.

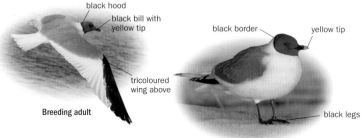

black hood

black bill with yellow tip

black border

yellow tip

tricoloured wing above

Breeding adult

black legs

Bonaparte's Gull *Chroicocephalus philadelphia*

black trailing edge

First-winter

white primaries

grey collar

pink legs

Winter adult

white primaries

clear black edge

black spot

small black spots

slim short black bill

Winter adult

pink legs

33 cm. Rare Nearctic vagrant; closely resembles Black-headed Gull but is smaller, slim short black bill, pink (neither orange or red) legs in winter, black on underwing limited to primary tips. First-winter has well-defined black line along trailing edge of wing.

Laughing Gull *Larus atricilla*

39 cm. Rare vagrant, medium-sized Nearctic gull, with sooty-grey mantle and black legs. Long black bill, reddish in summer. Adult has black triangle on tip of wing, extensive black hood when breeding. First-winter: dark tail with black band, brown-grey breast and flanks, brown-grey mask covers cheek and nape.

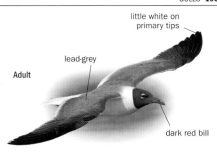

little white on primary tips

lead-grey

Adult

dark red bill

dark grey mantle

black bill

Winter adult

small white spots

brownish wings and tertials

dark grey mantle

blackish band behind eye

long black bill

First-winter

Franklin's Gull *Larus pipixcan*

34 cm. Rare Nearctic vagrant; resembles Laughing Gull but is smaller, rounder with shorter bill and legs. Adult has large white spots on primaries and white line along edge of black wing-tip in flight; dark red bill when breeding. First-winter: clear black bar on tail, white breast and flanks, solid black crown from eye to nape.

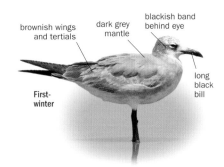

dark wings with white tips to black primaries

Juvenile

white band

partial black hood

Winter adult

black bill with red tip

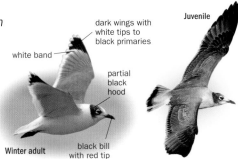

white eye-ring

small black bill

dark mantle

First-winter

brownish wings

blackish-red bill

medium grey

Breeding adult

big white spots on primaries

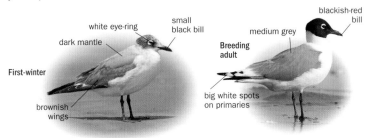

Ivory Gull *Pagophila eburnea*

Juvenile

black tips to tail and flight feathers

grey face

44 cm. Rare Arctic vagrant; occurs most years particularly in N Europe. Size of Common Gull with short black legs and short grey bill with yellow tip. Adult entirely white; immature has 'dirty' grey face and small black spots on wing-coverts, flight feathers and tail.

white body with black spots

'dirty' face

all white

grey bill with orange tip

white flight feathers with black tips

short grey bill with pale tip

First-winter

Adult

black legs

Ross's Gull *Rhodostethia rosea*

Winter adult

grey rear to neck, pinkish breast

small black bill

black eye with dark surround

black W

wedge-shaped tail with black band

white secondaries

tricoloured wing

very long wings

short bill

First-winter

short pink legs

31 cm. Very rare Arctic vagrant. Small, slender gull with short legs and long wedge-shaped tail. Somewhat similar to Little Gull but shorter black bill, pale undersides to wings, longer tail, broader white trailing edge to wing. Adult: pale grey above, including flight feathers, white below often with pink wash on breast; thin black collar in breeding plumage. Juvenile: black bar on wing, white secondaries, black tip to tail, pink legs.

Grey-headed Gull *Chroicocephalus cirrocephalus*

41 cm. Medium-sized African gull; rare vagrant recorded in
Spain and Italy. Resembles Black-headed Gull but larger,
stronger bill, black tip to wing with 2 subterminal white mirrors,
darker grey mantle, dark underwing; grey hood and white iris
with red eye-ring. Juvenile has black wing-tips, greyish nape,
sides of black terminal band on tail narrower.

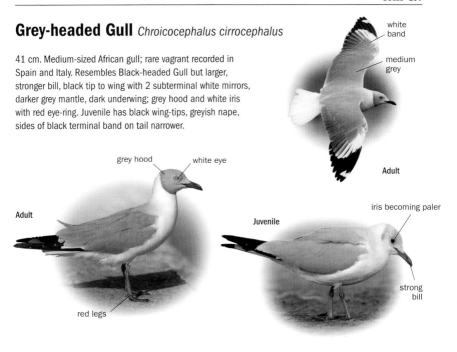

white band

medium grey

Adult

grey hood

white eye

Adult

Juvenile

iris becoming paler

strong bill

red legs

White-eyed Gull *Larus leucophthalmus*

41 cm. Breeds in the Red Sea; a few
vagrant records from Aegean and Adriatic
seas. Elongated body, long yellow legs,
long downturned bill, white crescent
above and below eye. Adult has
extensive black hood, greyish breast,
white trailing edge to dark wing; red base
to bill. Juvenile has black tail and white
rump, dark breast, finely streaked head
and neck, black bill.

dark grey

Adult

yellow legs

very long bill

streaked face

Winter adult

LARGE GULLS Adults may be identified from mantle and leg colour, structure and extent of black on primaries. Immatures are more complex and can be identified from a combination of criteria including structure, pattern of greater coverts, tertials, tail and scapulars. Adult plumage acquired after 4 or 5 years. Males are bigger and more thickset than females.

Herring Gull *Larus argentatus*

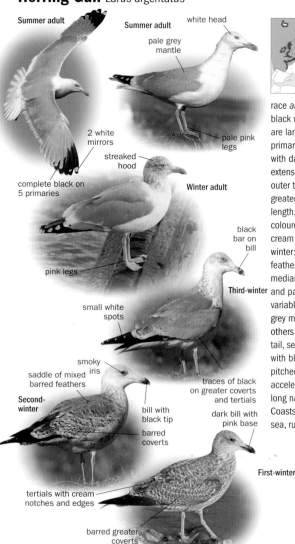

Summer adult

Summer adult

white head

pale grey mantle

2 white mirrors

pale pink legs

streaked hood

complete black on 5 primaries

Winter adult

pink legs

black bar on bill

small white spots

Third-winter

smoky iris

saddle of mixed barred feathers

Second-winter

traces of black on greater coverts and tertials

bill with black tip

dark bill with pink base

barred coverts

First-winter

tertials with cream notches and edges

barred greater coverts

IDENTIFICATION 54–60 cm. Adult: silvery mantle and pale pink legs; northern birds of race *argentatus* have less extensive black wing-tip, darker grey mantle and are larger with more white on outer primaries. In winter quite well marked with dark streaks. First-winter: not very extensive dark bar to tail, barred ends to outer tail feathers, pale inner primaries, greater wing-coverts barred along whole length. Often warm cream-and-brown coloured plumage. Tertials with large cream 'notches'. Pink legs. Second-winter: mantle mixed with some grey feathers, well-barred wing-coverts, median coverts greyish. Moult progress and pattern of new feathers very variable. Bill with pink base. Third-winter: grey mantle, greyish median coverts, the others slightly barred, traces of black on tail, secondaries and tertials; yellow bill with black tip. **VOICE** Varied, a high-pitched *gja gja gjagjagja...* in accelerating series, like a laugh. Also a long nasal drawn-out *oaaiaiaiai*. **HABITAT** Coasts, ports, cultivated fields near the sea, rubbish tips in winter.

Yellow-legged Gull *Larus michahellis*

IDENTIFICATION
52–58 cm. Adult has lead-grey mantle and yellow legs, more black on wing-tip than Herring Gull (fifth primary with wide black band), darker grey above. Generally more thickset. Head mainly white in winter with fine streaks restricted to back of crown. First-winter: very similar to Herring Gull but has darker inner primaries, inner greater coverts without bars forming a short wing-bar, narrow white edges to tertials without 'notches', whiter sides to tail. Generally duller in plumage, often appearing blackish-brown and white. Greyish scapulars with central black 'anchor'. Pink legs, scales in front washed brown in Atlantic Islands (Canaries, Madeira) birds. Second-winter: well-defined black bar to tail, dark inner primaries, dark wing-bar (greater coverts), many grey feathers on mantle, pale iris and pink legs. Third-winter: grey above, a few feathers vermiculated with black, pale yellow legs, bill with black tip. **VOICE** Deeper than that of Herring Gull. **HABITAT** Coasts, ports, cultivated fields, saltpans, large lakes and rivers.

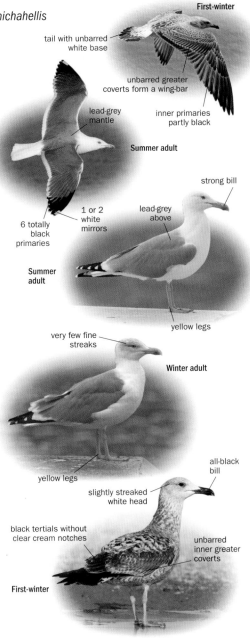

First-winter

tail with unbarred white base

unbarred greater coverts form a wing-bar

lead-grey mantle

inner primaries partly black

Summer adult

strong bill

lead-grey above

1 or 2 white mirrors

6 totally black primaries

Summer adult

yellow legs

very few fine streaks

Winter adult

yellow legs

all-black bill

slightly streaked white head

black tertials without clear cream notches

unbarred inner greater coverts

First-winter

Caspian Gull *Larus cachinnans*

big white mirrors

white crescents

pale grey above

Winter adult

dark iris

pale pink legs

pronounced white base to tail

pale grey mantle

white head

Second-winter

unbarred uniform greater coverts

wide bar on very white tail

First-winter

white head

streaked collar

ashy-grey scapulars

axillaries barred brown and white

First-winter

unbarred greater coverts with broad white edges

black tertials with narrow white edges and no notches

long slim bill

long wings

First-winter

IDENTIFICATION
55–60 cm. Adult has ash-grey mantle as Herring Gull, pinkish- or greyish-yellow legs, black reduced to inner web of outer primaries with white above; often long white spot on longest primary. Different structure, flat forehead, longer more slender bill apparently drooping, fuller chest. All-white head, even in winter, small dark eye. First-winter: elongated structure, flat forehead and long black bill; very pale; white head, half-collar of streaks on back of neck, moulted scapulars uniform ash-grey with central black line either thin or wider in centre; black greater upperwing-coverts with white tips forming a definite wing-bar in flight; white underwing-coverts and axillaries with small dark tip (underwing dark in Yellow-legged Gull); black tertials with thin white edges. Pink legs. Second-winter: many coverts and mantle feathers ash-grey, white scapulars with black anchor-marks, black streaks on hindneck. White underwings. Third-winter: white already present between black and grey at tip of central primaries. Band of streaks on hindneck, white head. **VOICE** More nasal than that of Yellow-legged Gull. Calls with upstretched neck and outspread wings. **HABITAT** Large rivers and coasts.

Lesser Black-backed Gull *Larus fuscus*

IDENTIFICATION
48–56 cm.
Smaller and
slimmer than
Herring Gull,
dark grey to
black mantle, yellow legs; long wings,
extensive black tips with 1 or 2
small white mirrors. Three distinct
subspecies: ssp. *graellsii* of W Europe
has slate-grey mantle, darker than that
of Yellow-legged Gull; ssp. *intermedius*
of Norway and Sweden with blackish-
grey mantle; ssp. *fuscus* of the Baltic
(see p. 208) has black mantle and
slender silhouette. Birds of intermediate
appearance between *graellsii* and
intermedius breed on the continent
between N France and the Netherlands.
First-winter: dark plumage, uniformly
dark primaries, unbarred greater coverts
form a long wing-bar, other coverts as
dark with little barring, dark tertials with
narrow pale edges at tips. Wide black
bar to tail with reduced white corners;
very streaked body. Pink legs washed
with brown in front. Second-winter: grey
feathers in mantle, paler than adult
feathers, streaked head and neck, bill
still dark. Upperparts more uniform
than those of Herring Gull. Pink legs.
Third-winter: quite uniform dark grey
upperparts, black bill with yellow tip,
pale yellow legs. **VOICE** Like that of
Yellow-legged Gull, deeper than that
of Herring Gull. **HABITAT** Coasts,
coastal marshes, large rivers and
extensive lakes.

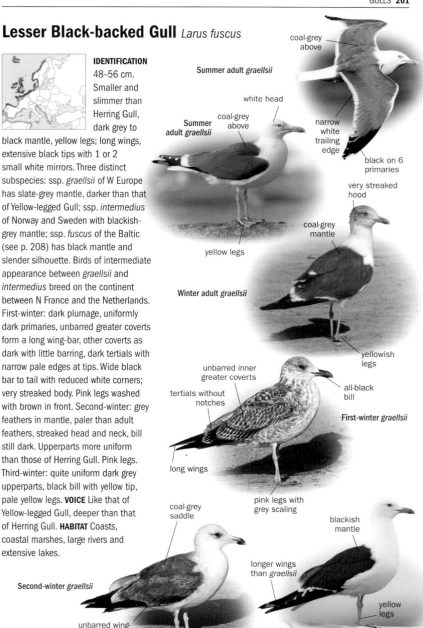

coal-grey
above

Summer adult *graellsii*

white head

Summer
adult *graellsii*

coal-grey
above

narrow
white
trailing
edge

black on 6
primaries

very streaked
hood

coal-grey
mantle

yellow legs

Winter adult *graellsii*

yellowish
legs

unbarred inner
greater coverts

tertials without
notches

all-black
bill

First-winter *graellsii*

long wings

coal-grey
saddle

pink legs with
grey scaling

longer wings
than *graellsii*

blackish
mantle

Second-winter *graellsii*

yellow
legs

unbarred wing-
coverts

pink legs

Summer adult
intermedius

Great Black-backed Gull *Larus marinus*

Second-winter

blackish-grey mantle

white tail

wings with pale brown and dark grey bands

Adult

intermediate white crescents

little contrast with black of wing-tips

large white tips

IDENTIFICATION
61–74 cm. Our largest gull, black mantle and pink legs, thickset with heavy bill, big round head, large white spots on primary tips; very long white spot on the outer primary, white 'pearls' between the black and edge of median flight feathers. First-winter: pale and cold plumage, narrow black terminal bar to tail, very white rump, white greater coverts with black indentations, pale inner primaries, broad white tips to tertials. All-black bill, pale pink legs. Second-winter: bill with pink base, pale grey feathers with black centres on mantle, very white body, tail with diffuse dark bar. Third-winter: black saddle, black median coverts, black band on yellow bill. **VOICE** Deeper and more raucous than that of other gulls. **HABITAT** Coasts, ports, typically maritime.

slightly streaked head

massive bill

First-winter

black-and-white plumage

narrow black bar on tail

dark iris

very thick bill

black mantle

Winter adult

pink legs

Glaucous Gull *Larus hyperboreus*

IDENTIFICATION
63–68 cm.
Large thickset
gull, white tips
to wings; short
wings, primary
projection shorter than in Iceland Gull,
longer and thicker bill. Plump body
appears front-heavy. First-winter: finely
barred beige to pale brown plumage,
primaries always paler, pink bill with
sharp black tip, black iris; worn plumage
whiter; barred tail feathers, primaries
sometimes have subterminal black
chevrons. Second-winter: more mottled
plumage, small pale tip to bill, pale iris.
Third-winter: resembles adult with less
uniform plumage, brown feathers here
and there, trace of black on bill. Winter
adult: pale grey above, large grey spots
on head, neck and breast. Pale grey
primaries with white tips. **VOICE** As
Herring Gull. **HABITAT** Maritime coasts,
fishing ports.

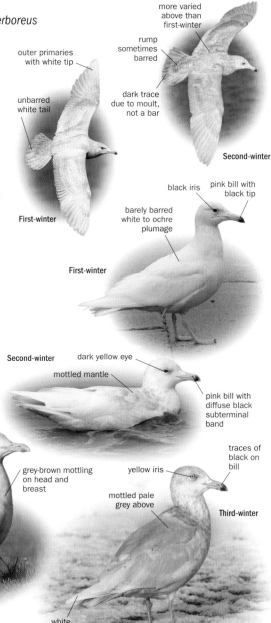

more varied
above than
first-winter

rump
sometimes
barred

outer primaries
with white tip

dark trace
due to moult,
not a bar

unbarred
white tail

Second-winter

black iris

pink bill with
black tip

barely barred
white to ochre
plumage

First-winter

First-winter

dark yellow eye

Second-winter

mottled mantle

pink bill with
diffuse black
subterminal
band

pale grey
above

traces of
black on
bill

Winter adult

grey-brown mottling
on head and
breast

yellow iris

mottled pale
grey above

Third-winter

white
primaries

pink legs

white
primaries

Iceland Gull *Larus glaucoides*

Winter adult

Third-winter

white tips to primaries

head and breast more or less streaked

all-white primaries

altogether very pale

yellow iris

primaries grade paler towards exterior

First-winter

brown bars under tail

body smoky to white depending on wear

IDENTIFICATION
52–60 cm. Small, slender gull, long white-tipped wings. Resembles Glaucous Gull but longer wings with longer primary projection, less heavy body, shorter and slimmer bill, shorter legs, less angular head. First-winter: like Glaucous Gull but bill with large diffuse black tip, rarely all dark. Variable plumage, some birds nearly white, others dark with dark subterminal chevrons on primaries. Second-winter: pale iris, grey bill with black subterminal bar and grey tip, plumage often whiter than in first-winter birds, grey-and-white mottled mantle. Third-winter: brown mottling on mantle and wing-coverts, bill with dark marks. Winter adult: pale grey above, white-tipped primaries, more or less obvious streaks on head and breast.
VOICE Shriller than that of Herring Gull.
HABITAT Oceanic, along coasts and in fishing ports. Breeds in Greenland.

white scapulars with fine brown bars

black bill with pinkish base

white primaries

narrow brown bars

First-winter

dense brown spotting

greenish bill

Third-winter

white primaries

RARE ARCTIC GULLS A few Nearctic or Arctic species that have already occurred in Europe. All are possible in winter especially since the retreat of the Arctic ice cap, allowing birds to disperse from the Pacific into the Atlantic.

Kumlien's Gull *Larus glaucoides kumlieni*

56 cm. Rare vagrant (treated as race of Iceland Gull); breeds in central Canadian Arctic, winters on the north-east coast of N America. Like Iceland Gull but with diffuse dark markings on primary tips, darker than the inner third and becoming darker towards wing-tip. Also a uniform dark bar on tail, easily visible in first- and second-winter birds. Bill often stouter, all dark in first-winter. Adult has variable amount of dark grey on tips of outer primaries, reminiscent of the pattern on wings of gulls with black tips but reduced, sometimes a mere hint of a grey pattern darker than the mantle.

Winter adult

brown bar on tail

black-tipped bill

more or less dark yellow iris

dense brown spotting

dark grey markings on a few outer primaries

Second-winter

brown chevrons on scapulars

black bill with pinkish-grey base

First-winter

diffuse brown on primary tips

uniform brown primary tips

Thayer's Gull *Larus thayeri*

58 cm. Very rare Nearctic vagrant; breeds in the W Canadian Arctic, winters in California. A few birds recorded in Europe (Britain, Denmark, Iceland and Spain). Similar to Kumlien's Gull (that may be a variable hybrid between Iceland and Thayer's Gulls), but adult has narrow black patterning on primaries separated from the grey by some white, only slightly marked on inner webs, dark iris and bright pink legs. More thickset with longer bill. First-winter: all-black bill, uniform brown body, small pale collar; juvenile scapulars kept throughout winter are dark without bars; tertials without bars but with small cream indentations; broad dark bar on tail; pale fringes to primaries.

uniform sooty head and neck

black bill

uniform greater coverts form a wing-bar

juvenile scapulars with extensive dark centres

First-winter

clear broad brown bar

First-winter

keyboard pattern on flight feathers

dark brown primaries with diffuse pale fringes

reduced amount of black

dark iris

Winter adult

long slim bill

more slender than Kumlien's Gull

American Herring Gull *Larus smithsonianus*

collar of brown spots

Second-winter

same grey as Herring Gull

Winter adult

all-black tail

strong bill

wing-bar

black marks continue on shaft forming a W

sometimes grey continues far along the shafts

white face

variable number of white mirrors

characteristic bill with black edges to base

greater coverts sometimes completely barred

First-winter

worn juvenile scapulars with large dark centres

First-winter

quite uniform sooty plumage

Second-winter

almost completely black tail feathers

52–58 cm. Very rare Nearctic vagrant. Replaces Herring Gull in N America, which it resembles, but more thickset. First-winter: very dark, all-black flight feathers, heavily barred rump, undertail-coverts densely barred or with large black chevrons, small cream indentations on tertials often worn in winter. Juvenile scapulars even in winter, some having been moulted, grey with black lozenges at base. Quite dark inner primaries, uniform bases to greater coverts form a wing-bar; very dark underwings; body often dark brown with pale collar. Second-winter: pale iris, very dark head and breast, all-black tail, undertail-coverts densely barred or with large black chevrons; ash-grey feathers with diffuse black shafts on mantle. Adult: distinctive black pattern on primaries: little black on inner webs, black continuing along shafts, thus forming a W; often has semi-circular white marks between black and grey on central primaries. Extensive area of dense streaks from head to breast in winter.

Glaucous × Herring Gull hybrids
Larus hyperboreus × argentatus

brown primaries becoming darker towards exterior

bill clearly bicoloured

First-winter

intact tertials

large brown bar on tail

as Glaucous Gull but brown primaries

Hybrids between the 2 species are frequent in Iceland, and are occasionally observed on our coasts in winter. Most resemble Glaucous Gull; young have pink bill with well-defined black tip but outer wing feathers darker than inner ones, becoming grey in subadults. Adults have very little black on primaries and pale grey mantle.

Slaty-backed Gull *Larus schistisagus*

55–68 cm. From the N Pacific; a few vagrant records in Europe (Britain, Iceland). Thickset, broad wings, adult with bright pink legs and slate-grey mantle, typically obvious white semicircles separate the black markings on outer primaries from the grey.

First-winter

black bill

large black bar on tail

slate-coloured back

unbarred greater coverts

black scales on legs

large white borders

Winter adult

bright pink legs

dark iris

Glaucous-winged Gull *Larus glaucescens*

brown spots

lead-grey above

dark grey tips

dark grey tips

Subadult

Winter adult

dark grey on primaries

just 1 white mirror

dirty pink legs

First-winter

black bill

brown primaries

50–68 cm. From the N Pacific; a few vagrant records in Europe (Britain, Norway). Thickset, heavy, with broad, short wings, dark pink legs. Pale lead-grey mantle, adults have coal-grey markings on primaries, like washed-out pattern of Herring Gull. Juvenile very uniform, looks smoky, dark brown primaries and uniform brown tail, entirely dark bill.

barred coverts

uniform sooty body

RARE EUROPEAN GULLS Two subspecies of European gulls that occur on the edge of the species' range (Azores and Finland); very rare vagrants on migration or in winter. Both may be more common than thought, but probably go undetected.

Baltic Gull *Larus fuscus fuscus*

a single white mirror

yellow legs

black mantle

very long wings

Adult

little colour on bill

primaries without white tips

pale head

slim black bill

dark scapulars with white edges

Second-winter

dull yellow legs

black tertials with narrow white border

Juvenile

long wings

50–65 cm. Subspecies of Lesser Black-backed Gull, a long-distance migrant that breeds around the Baltic Sea (Finland and further east) and winters in W Africa. Vagrant in W Europe, a few confirmed records involving birds ringed in the nest. Slender shape, long wings and thin bill. Slower moult than in other Lesser Black-backed Gulls. Adult has black mantle, a single small white mirror on the longest primary and white head in winter.

Azores Yellow-legged Gull *Larus michahellis atlantis*

small hood of very dense streaks

lead-grey mantle

Winter adult

generally a single white mirror

Winter adult

yellow legs

sooty-grey scapulars with anchor-shaped mark

First-winter

black bill

complete black bar on 6th primary

very uniform brown body

very streaked head

black bill

unbarred dark brown coverts

dark grey feathers

Second-winter

unbarred greater coverts

A subspecies of Yellow-legged Gull; adults have somewhat darker mantles, black on 6 outer primaries, hood of compact grey streaks in winter, sometimes almost absent. First-winter: uniform, or nearly so, brown upper- and underwing-coverts, narrow worn pale fringes to tertials, chocolate-brown body and mask, large black bar on white-based tail, front of tarsus dark brown, all-black bill, moulted scapulars of dark smoky colour. It is not unknown for birds to overwinter in W Europe.

OTHER RARE GULLS Four vagrant gulls: two with dark mantles, one with black hood in breeding plumage, the other a Nearctic subspecies of a common European gull.

Kelp Gull *Larus dominicanus vetula*

55–65 cm. Very rare vagrant from Africa; breeds in South Africa, Namibia and Senegal, vagrant to Morocco, Canaries and Portugal. Increasingly observed in Europe. Adult has black mantle and always an immaculate white head; resembles Great Black-backed Gull with thick-tipped bill but has pale yellow legs (greenish-grey in winter), very wide white trailing edge to wing, only outer primary with small white mirror, and no white between base of flight feathers and black tips to central primaries. Dark iris.

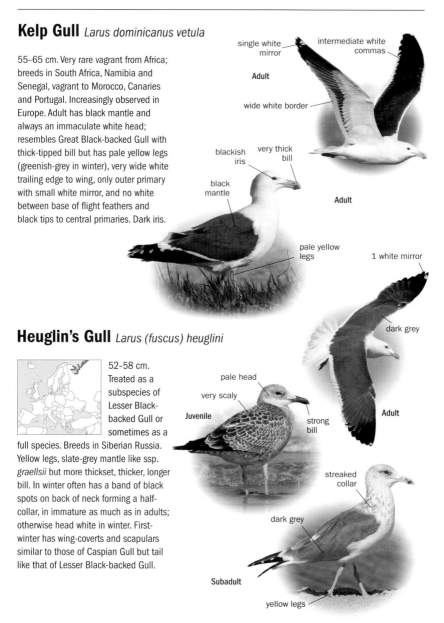

single white mirror

intermediate white commas

Adult

wide white border

blackish iris

very thick bill

black mantle

Adult

pale yellow legs

1 white mirror

dark grey

Heuglin's Gull *Larus (fuscus) heuglini*

52–58 cm. Treated as a subspecies of Lesser Black-backed Gull or sometimes as a full species. Breeds in Siberian Russia. Yellow legs, slate-grey mantle like ssp. *graellsii* but more thickset, thicker, longer bill. In winter often has a band of black spots on back of neck forming a half-collar, in immature as much as in adults; otherwise head white in winter. First-winter has wing-coverts and scapulars similar to those of Caspian Gull but tail like that of Lesser Black-backed Gull.

pale head

very scaly

Juvenile

strong bill

Adult

streaked collar

dark grey

Subadult

yellow legs

Pallas's (Great Black-headed) Gull *Larus ichthyaetus*

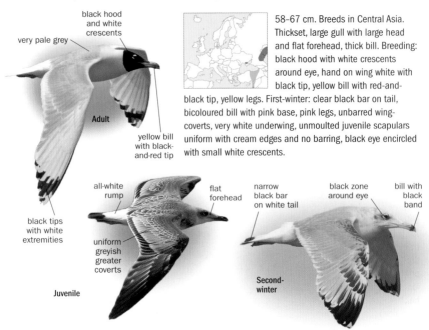

58–67 cm. Breeds in Central Asia. Thickset, large gull with large head and flat forehead, thick bill. Breeding: black hood with white crescents around eye, hand on wing white with black tip, yellow bill with red-and-black tip, yellow legs. First-winter: clear black bar on tail, bicoloured bill with pink base, pink legs, unbarred wing-coverts, very white underwing, unmoulted juvenile scapulars uniform with cream edges and no barring, black eye encircled with small white crescents.

black hood and white crescents

very pale grey

Adult

yellow bill with black-and-red tip

all-white rump

flat forehead

narrow black bar on white tail

black zone around eye

bill with black band

black tips with white extremities

uniform greyish greater coverts

Juvenile

Second-winter

Mew Gull *Larus canus brachyrhynchus*

43 cm. Nearctic form of Common Gull, sometimes treated as separate species; very rare vagrant to the Azores. Compared to Common Gull has shorter bill, pale brown iris, more white on primaries (outer primaries with big white spots and white band between the grey and black of inner primaries); in winter, smoky hood to head and neck; first-winter with totally dark brown tail, smoky-brown body.

large white spots

Adult

large white mirrors

all-dark tail

Juvenile

pale iris

much grey marking on neck

short bill

sooty body

Adult

TERNS Closely related to gulls, these mainly marine birds are smaller, very slim, have a thin pointed bill, short legs and long pointed wings. They breed in colonies on sandy or shingle islands, hunt fish by diving, bill first. All are migrants, wintering mainly in Africa; a few Sandwich Terns winter in southern Europe.

Common Tern *Sterna hirundo*

IDENTIFICATION
35 cm. Small tern with red legs, longish red bill with black tip, very forked tail but outer tail feathers shorter than wings when perched. Outer primaries have black trailing edge, above and below. Winter adult: black on crown behind eye, black bill. Juvenile: pale forehead, broad black leading edge to hand, black on secondaries forming a thin bar on wing, uniform dark grey primaries, grey rump, black tips to longest tail feathers. **VOICE** A slightly harsh repeated *kierri*. **HABITAT** Shingle river islands and banks, fishponds, lakes, gravel pits.

distinct black trailing edge

diffuse black trailing edge

black leading edge

dark outer tail feathers

Breeding adult

Juvenile

pale forehead

brown-and-ochre barring

orange base to bill

bill sometimes all red

Juvenile

Breeding adult

long orange-brown legs

long red bill with black tip

wings longer than tail streamers

long legs

Arctic Tern *Sterna paradisaea*

IDENTIFICATION
36 cm. Like Common Tern but more compact, short bill, very short legs, longer tail streamers. Adult: tail much longer than wings when at rest, shorter all-red bill when breeding, greyish underparts with white band on cheeks, all primaries translucent. Juvenile: large dark leading edge to wing, white secondaries, white rump. **VOICE** *krierr* as Common Tern, but harsher. Common migrant along the Atlantic coast, breeds in N Europe.

all-black bill

dark outer tail feathers

white trailing edge

angled behind cheek

Breeding adult

dark leading edge

Juvenile

very long streamers

pale trailing edge

slim dark red bill

streamers at least as long as wings

very short legs

Roseate Tern *Sterna dougallii*

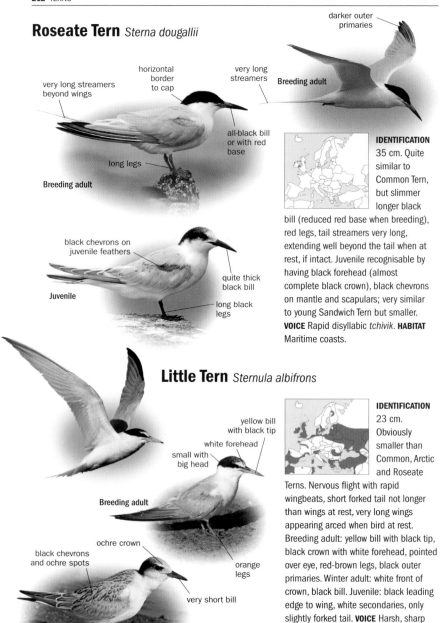

darker outer primaries

very long streamers beyond wings

horizontal border to cap

very long streamers

Breeding adult

all-black bill or with red base

long legs

Breeding adult

black chevrons on juvenile feathers

quite thick black bill

Juvenile

long black legs

IDENTIFICATION
35 cm. Quite similar to Common Tern, but slimmer longer black bill (reduced red base when breeding), red legs, tail streamers very long, extending well beyond the tail when at rest, if intact. Juvenile recognisable by having black forehead (almost complete black crown), black chevrons on mantle and scapulars; very similar to young Sandwich Tern but smaller. **VOICE** Rapid disyllabic *tchivik*. **HABITAT** Maritime coasts.

Little Tern *Sternula albifrons*

yellow bill with black tip

white forehead

small with big head

Breeding adult

ochre crown

black chevrons and ochre spots

orange legs

very short bill

Juvenile

IDENTIFICATION
23 cm. Obviously smaller than Common, Arctic and Roseate Terns. Nervous flight with rapid wingbeats, short forked tail not longer than wings at rest, very long wings appearing arced when bird at rest. Breeding adult: yellow bill with black tip, black crown with white forehead, pointed over eye, red-brown legs, black outer primaries. Winter adult: white front of crown, black bill. Juvenile: black leading edge to wing, white secondaries, only slightly forked tail. **VOICE** Harsh, sharp *kriitt*. **HABITAT** Large rivers, estuaries, shingle beaches.

Sandwich Tern *Thalasseus sandvicensis*

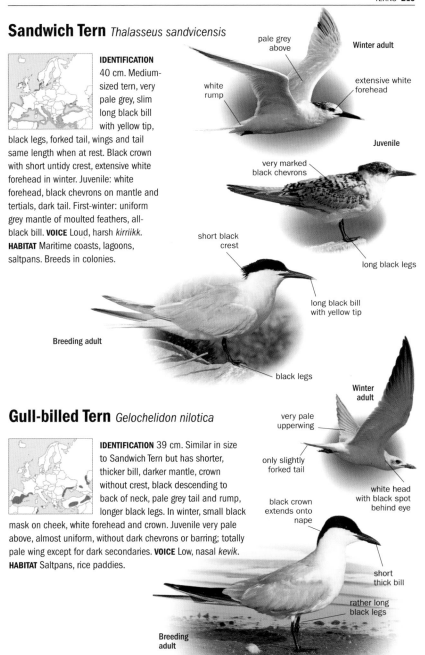

IDENTIFICATION
40 cm. Medium-sized tern, very pale grey, slim long black bill with yellow tip, black legs, forked tail, wings and tail same length when at rest. Black crown with short untidy crest, extensive white forehead in winter. Juvenile: white forehead, black chevrons on mantle and tertials, dark tail. First-winter: uniform grey mantle of moulted feathers, all-black bill. **VOICE** Loud, harsh *kirriikk*.
HABITAT Maritime coasts, lagoons, saltpans. Breeds in colonies.

pale grey above

Winter adult

white rump

extensive white forehead

Juvenile

very marked black chevrons

short black crest

long black legs

long black bill with yellow tip

Breeding adult

black legs

Gull-billed Tern *Gelochelidon nilotica*

IDENTIFICATION 39 cm. Similar in size to Sandwich Tern but has shorter, thicker bill, darker mantle, crown without crest, black descending to back of neck, pale grey tail and rump, longer black legs. In winter, small black mask on cheek, white forehead and crown. Juvenile very pale above, almost uniform, without dark chevrons or barring; totally pale wing except for dark secondaries. **VOICE** Low, nasal *kevik*.
HABITAT Saltpans, rice paddies.

very pale upperwing

only slightly forked tail

Winter adult

white head with black spot behind eye

black crown extends onto nape

short thick bill

rather long black legs

Breeding adult

Caspian Tern *Hydroprogne caspia*

IDENTIFICATION
53 cm. Large thickset tern, massive red bill with small black tip, flat crown, black legs. Black underside to outer primaries forming a triangle. Breeding adult: wide black crown and square nape without obvious crest. Winter adult: black forehead finely streaked with white. Juvenile: black forehead and crown, thin black chevrons on mantle, dark tail, primaries darker towards tips. **VOICE** Loud raucous *krai-ak*, recalling call of Grey Heron. **HABITAT** Lagoons, estuaries, bays.

very slightly forked tail

Breeding adult

dark tips to primaries

black triangle on underwing

Breeding adult

black crown

thick red bill with black tip

black legs

very black worn primaries

Winter

fine white streaking on crown

white forehead

MARSH TERNS Small terns with slightly forked tails, more hesitant flight, feed by snatching insects (or other small animals) from water surface. They breed in colonies on large well-vegetated freshwater lakes or flooded meadows. All are migrants, wintering in Africa.

Black Tern *Chlidonias niger*

IDENTIFICATION
24 cm. Small, slender marsh tern. Breeding adult: blackish body with darker head and greyer breast, uniform mouse-grey upperparts (nape, mantle, rump, tail and upperwings); grey underwings. Winter adult: white forehead, black crown, black pectoral patch on each side of the breast. Juvenile: slightly darker grey saddle and tail, mantle with black-and-cream barred feathers, pectoral patches present. The Nearctic subspecies *surinamensis* is a rare vagrant in Europe; smaller with grey flanks and more intense black crown. **VOICE** Harsh *kchlet*, similar to Little Tern's call. **HABITAT** Marshes, fishponds, flooded meadows.

Breeding adult

grey underwings

slightly forked tail

uniform mouse-grey above

Adult

thin black bill

black head

coal-grey body

Breeding adult

grey tail   white lower belly

intensive colour on crown

grey flanks

Juvenile ssp. *surinamensis*

Juvenile

well-defined black crown

grey tail

black patch

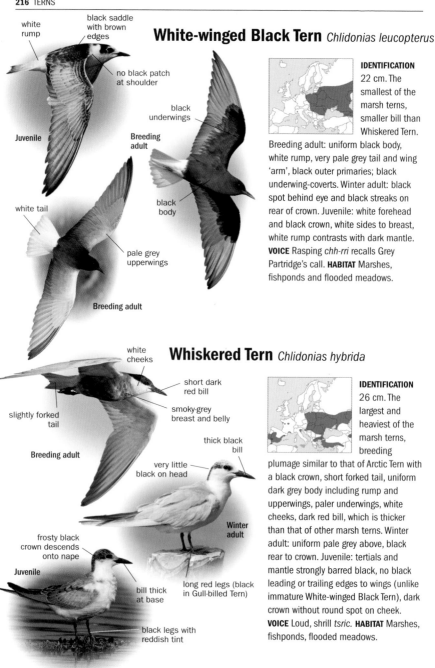

White-winged Black Tern *Chlidonias leucopterus*

white rump

black saddle with brown edges

no black patch at shoulder

black underwings

Juvenile

Breeding adult

white tail

black body

pale grey upperwings

Breeding adult

IDENTIFICATION
22 cm. The smallest of the marsh terns, smaller bill than Whiskered Tern.

Breeding adult: uniform black body, white rump, very pale grey tail and wing 'arm', black outer primaries; black underwing-coverts. Winter adult: black spot behind eye and black streaks on rear of crown. Juvenile: white forehead and black crown, white sides to breast, white rump contrasts with dark mantle. **VOICE** Rasping *chh-rri* recalls Grey Partridge's call. **HABITAT** Marshes, fishponds and flooded meadows.

Whiskered Tern *Chlidonias hybrida*

white cheeks

short dark red bill

smoky-grey breast and belly

slightly forked tail

thick black bill

Breeding adult

very little black on head

Winter adult

frosty black crown descends onto nape

Juvenile

bill thick at base

long red legs (black in Gull-billed Tern)

black legs with reddish tint

IDENTIFICATION
26 cm. The largest and heaviest of the marsh terns, breeding plumage similar to that of Arctic Tern with a black crown, short forked tail, uniform dark grey body including rump and upperwings, paler underwings, white cheeks, dark red bill, which is thicker than that of other marsh terns. Winter adult: uniform pale grey above, black rear to crown. Juvenile: tertials and mantle strongly barred black, no black leading or trailing edges to wings (unlike immature White-winged Black Tern), dark crown without round spot on cheek. **VOICE** Loud, shrill *tsric*. **HABITAT** Marshes, fishponds, flooded meadows.

RARE TERNS All species have already been observed in Europe; some have been found in Sandwich Tern roosts or colonies and can be identified by their size, bill shape, and mantle and rump colour.

Elegant Tern *Sterna elegans*

40 cm. Very rare vagrant, originating from the Pacific coast of America (California). Adult similar to Lesser Crested Tern but pale grey above (like Sandwich Tern), white rump and tail, long and slender bill looks downcurved with orange-red base; long shaggy crest. Has bred in Europe; hybrid offspring still occur, some of which are identical in appearance to pure Elegant Terns.

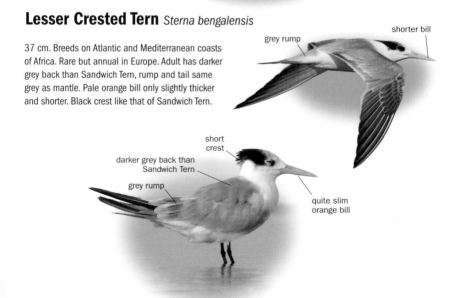

long shaggy crest

very long downcurved orange bill, sometimes red at base

pale grey above

white rump

long downcurved bill

Lesser Crested Tern *Sterna bengalensis*

37 cm. Breeds on Atlantic and Mediterranean coasts of Africa. Rare but annual in Europe. Adult has darker grey back than Sandwich Tern, rump and tail same grey as mantle. Pale orange bill only slightly thicker and shorter. Black crest like that of Sandwich Tern.

grey rump

shorter bill

short crest

darker grey back than Sandwich Tern

grey rump

quite slim orange bill

Royal Tern *Sterna maxima*

white rump

thick bill

46 cm. Breeds on coast of Mauritania and in Caribbean. Very rare vagrant. Larger than Sandwich Tern, smaller than Caspian Tern. Uniform orange, heavy thick bill; white rump and tail, white undersides of primaries with black tips forming a narrow trailing edge to wings. The forehead becomes rapidly white in summer.

pale grey above

extensive white forehead early in season

white primaries with black tips

thick-based orange bill

Cabot's Tern *Thalasseus (sandvicensis) acuflavidus*

thick bill

thick-based bill

white border to trailing edge narrower in fresh plumage

40 cm. Nearctic form of Sandwich Tern, genetically different; an exceptional vagrant to Atlantic coast of Europe. Very similar but larger, stronger bill, new flight feathers with narrower white inner borders. Juvenile has fewer dark markings, sometimes very pale and uniform black tertials with large white tips, but much overlap with Sandwich Tern.

Forster's Tern *Sterna forsteri*

35 cm. Winter vagrant from N America of near-annual occurrence. Very similar to Common Tern, but all-black bill in winter, black mask only on cheek, very pale underwings, especially inner primaries. Juvenile does not have darker wing-coverts in winter. Sandwich Tern is the only other tern likely along the Atlantic coast in winter.

black mask

strongly forked tail

pale grey primaries

large, well-defined black mask

thick black bill

very pale primaries

long red legs

Least Tern *Sternula antillarum*

23 cm. Nearctic species; an adult in England in the summers of 1983 to 1992 (same bird). Like Little Tern, but more uniform grey above, including tail and rump. Different call, squeakier. Juvenile only lightly marked above, but variable.

few black worn primaries

lightly marked above

thick bill

grey rump

Adult

Juvenile

pale orange legs

pale grey

white forehead

Adult

Sooty Tern *Onychoprion fuscatus*

short supercilium ending in open angle before eye

44 cm. Of tropical origin, a few pairs breed in the Azores; very rare on the Atlantic coast of Europe, normally in Sandwich Tern colonies. Large dark slender tern with tail as long as wings when at rest. Adult has uniform black upperparts with white sides to tail; white underparts; flight feathers blackish, even on primary bases of underwing (pale in Bridled Tern). Broad white forehead patch ends in front of eye.

short supercilium

blackish upperparts

dark primary bases

Bridled Tern *Onychoprion anaethetus*

long supercilium ending in a point

40 cm. Of tropical origin; nearest breeding sites are in Mauritania and the Red Sea; rare summer vagrant. Very similar to Sooty Tern but dark brown-grey upperparts, including rump and tail, contrast with blackish flight feathers. Underparts as in Sooty Tern but has pale primary bases coming to a point on underwing. Black crown, white supercilium finishes in a point above or behind eye.

dark brown upperparts

pale primary bases

long white supercilium

dark brown upperparts

Aleutian Tern *Onychoprion aleuticus*

33 cm. Breeds in the Bering Sea (N Pacific), 1 record from Britain, May 1979. Head like that of Bridled Tern with white supercilium coming to a point above eye, greyish body, lead-grey upperparts, white rump and tail, inner primaries with pale tips. At rest, tail as long as wings, short black legs.

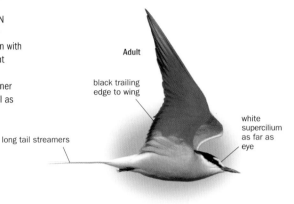

Adult

black trailing edge to wing

white supercilium as far as eye

long tail streamers

lead-grey upperparts

small bill

Adult

pale grey underparts

Brown Noddy *Anous stolidus*

42 cm. From the Caribbean and Persian Gulf; 1 record from Germany, October 1912. Sooty-brown body, wings and tail, white forehead and crown grading into grey hindcrown. In flight, pointed wings and long tail, long black bill.

white crown

black lores

sooty body

forked tail

AUKS Marine birds, black or dark brown above and white below; breed colonially on sea cliffs or in burrows (Puffin and Little Auk); they are expert divers, catching fish at sea, offshore or sometimes near coast, and fly just above the surface with fast uninterrupted wingbeats. Often gregarious in winter; silent at sea.

Razorbill *Alca torda*

Winter

white extends onto the nape

thick bill

unstreaked white flanks

thin white line

Summer

white tips to secondaries

big black head

thick bill

totally white underwings

Summer

unstreaked white flanks

IDENTIFICATION
41 cm. Stout black bill with thin vertical white line, often difficult to see.
In summer, black upperparts, head and breast with unstreaked white belly. In winter, head pattern very like that of Common Guillemot but has shorter black half-collar. White underwings and axillaries. Legs under the tail in flight.
HABITAT Breeds in colonies on sea cliffs.

Common Guillemot *Uria aalge*

underwings with thin black streaking

thin streaks on flanks

Summer

thin black eye-stripe

Winter

blackish-brown head

narrow bill

black streaks

white spots on secondaries

black streaks on flanks

Summer

IDENTIFICATION
41 cm. In summer has black-brown upperparts including head and breast; white breast with black streaks on flanks. In winter, white cheek with black line starting at eye. In flight, black collar often appears complete and black legs protrude beyond tail; greyish underwings, black streaks on flanks (more marked in N European race *aalge*, less so in *albionis* of S Europe including much of Britain). Bridled form has white eye-ring continuing into a white line above cheek. **HABITAT** Breeds in colonies on sea cliffs.

Brünnich's Guillemot *Uria lomvia*

Summer

long white line along gape

thicker bill

42 cm. An Arctic species, some breeding birds in very north of Europe; rare vagrant to Britain. Very difficult to safely separate from Common Guillemot but has thicker bill with white line at its base, uniform unstreaked flanks and white underwings, difficult to see in flight. The whole cheek is blackish in winter.

Summer

white line

unstreaked white flanks

white tips to secondaries

Winter

long white line on gape

pale throat

Atlantic Puffin *Fratercula arctica*

IDENTIFICATION 31 cm. Smaller than Razorbill with a large head. Breeding: very big red, yellow-and-blue bill; black head and neck with large pale grey cheek, dark triangle around eye; dark thighs, no white trailing edge to wing. Orange legs. Winter: boney plates on bill duller and darker, dark grey face, head appears entirely dark. Juvenile: slimmer black bill. **HABITAT** Colonial breeder, nesting in burrows in grassy slopes at top of sea cliffs.

thickset head and no obvious neck

blackish underwings

Summer adult

large white cheek

entirely black upperparts

enormous tricoloured triangular bill

Summer adult

Winter

blackish face

smaller, duller bill

Black Guillemot *Cepphus grylle*

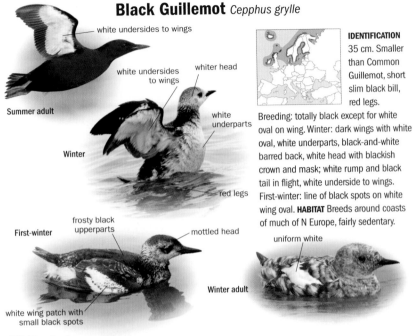

white undersides to wings

Summer adult

white undersides to wings

whiter head

Winter

white underparts

red legs

frosty black upperparts

First-winter

mottled head

white wing patch with small black spots

IDENTIFICATION
35 cm. Smaller than Common Guillemot, short slim black bill, red legs.

Breeding: totally black except for white oval on wing. Winter: dark wings with white oval, white underparts, black-and-white barred back, white head with blackish crown and mask; white rump and black tail in flight, white underside to wings. First-winter: line of black spots on white wing oval. **HABITAT** Breeds around coasts of much of N Europe, fairly sedentary.

uniform white

Winter adult

Little Auk *Alle alle*

white stripes

white collar

rounded wings

20 cm. Breeds from Arctic Canada to Spitsbergen. More numerous in Europe in some hard winters and during gales. Very small, plump body, large head and no obvious neck, short bill.
Appears miniscule at sea compared to other auks. Winter: black cheek with white border at rear, white trailing edge to wing, diagnostic white zigzag on scapulars. Breeding: all-black head.

small conical bill

all-black head

Summer

very short tail

white tips to secondaries

white stripes

thickset head

has look of a floating cork

Winter

black cheeks

VAGRANT AUKS Five species from the Pacific, which are very rare vagrants to Western Europe; only very few records for each species.

Tufted Puffin *Fratercula cirrhata*

38 cm. A Pacific auk, single records from Britain and Sweden. A large all-black puffin with white face and big red bill, long straw-coloured neck plumes, orange legs. In winter has black face and black base to bill, very visible white iris.

white face

enormous red bill

long yellow crest

completely black

orange legs

Parakeet Auklet *Aethia psittacula*

27 cm. A small Bering Sea auk, just 1 European record from Sweden in 1860. Thick upturned red bill, grey legs, white iris, long thin white line behind eye. Blackish-grey above, white below with grey band along flanks. Entirely dark wings. Totally black head in summer, pale throat in winter.

no crest

white line

white rear

white belly

Crested Auklet *Aethia cristatella*

24 cm. Another small Bering Sea auk with 1 record, Iceland in August 1912. Small but larger than Little Auk. Entirely blackish-grey throughout the year, curved crest feathers on the forehead; thick red bill, grey legs, white iris; thin white line behind eye.

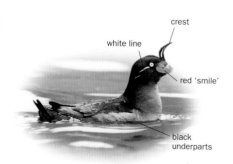

crest

white line

red 'smile'

black underparts

Ancient Murrelet *Synthliboramphus antiquus*

dark grey above

black head

25 cm. Small Pacific auk, 1 bird in Britain from 1990 to 1992. Black-and-white plumage, noticeably small bill black with pink tip, dark grey upperparts, white underparts, black head with white patches on sides of neck (like Stonechat). White throat in winter. A few white feathers behind the eyes on side of nape in summer. White undersides to wings, black band along flanks.

black bill with pink tip

white nick behind cheek

Long-billed Murrelet *Brachyramphus perdix*

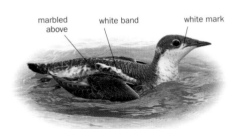

marbled above

white band

white mark

25 cm. Small Pacific auk. Three European records, all in 2006, in Britain, Romania and Switzerland. Black-and-white plumage in winter with white band on scapulars, white lores highlight the black around eye, thin white eye-ring, barred or streaked flanks. Shorter bill than that of Common Guillemot. Breeding: marbled brown underparts.

SANDGROUSE Closely related to pigeons. Medium-sized with round heads, short bills and short legs; rapid flight on pointed wings. Usually found in dry open habitats in south of Europe.

Pin-tailed Sandgrouse *Pterocles alchata*

IDENTIFICATION
28–32 cm. Looks like a cross between a partridge and a pigeon with short thick bill, slender body and elongated central tail feathers. Cryptic plumage. Orange head with black eye-stripe. Male: black throat, olive neck, wide rufous bib with fine black upper and lower edges; olive mantle with round yellowish spots, olive wing-coverts with black terminal bar. Female: white throat, 3 narrow black lines on orange breast, heavily barred wing-coverts, mantle vermiculated with black. In flight, white below, pointed wings with black undersides to flight feathers, long slender central tail feathers. **VOICE** In flight, repeated nasal *hin-han*, similar to call of Mediterranean Gull. **HABITAT** Arid steppes, dry stony grassland, with standing water visited in early morning.

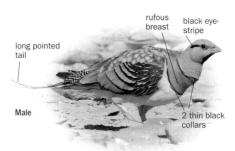

rufous breast
black eye-stripe
long pointed tail
Male
2 thin black collars

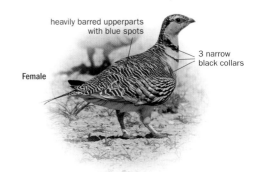

heavily barred upperparts with blue spots
3 narrow black collars
Female

Pallas's Sandgrouse *Syrrhaptes paradoxus*

30–40 cm. Very rare vagrant originating from Central Asian steppes. Some breeding records in Europe during 19th century following invasions, at a period when the species was much more abundant. Like Pin-tailed Sandgrouse but longer tail streamers, needle-like filament at tip of longest primary, black band on belly, black spots on axillaries, pale upperwings; greyish breast, orange head. Flight call: repeated dull *cou-ki-ric*.

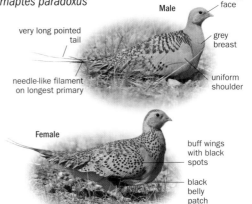

orange face
Male
very long pointed tail
grey breast
needle-like filament on longest primary
uniform shoulder
Female
buff wings with black spots
black belly patch

Black-bellied Sandgrouse *Pterocles orientalis*

orange cheeks

pale orange wings

black throat

black belly

Male

IDENTIFICATION 30–35 cm. Larger and heavier than Pin-tailed Sandgrouse with a short tail, extensive black on belly, a cream-coloured pectoral band with narrow black line at upper edge. Grey head and neck with orange throat underlined in black (male) or with creamy spots (female). Black uppersides to primaries in flight. **VOICE** A rolling *tcheurr* or *tchurrrrai-ka*. **HABITAT** Steppe with short vegetation; visits water to drink in morning.

Female

black belly

Male (left) and female in flight

tail streamer

brown belly

Chestnut-bellied Sandgrouse
Pterocles exustus

orange head

Male

Female

28–32 cm. Breeds in the Middle East and the African Sahel; 1 record from Hungary in August 1863. Resembles Black-bellied Sandgrouse with its blackish-brown belly but is smaller, has tail streamers, totally black underwings, and characteristic white spots on inner primaries visible in flight. Call: *vitt-car-a*.

tan wings   dark belly

Spotted Sandgrouse *Pterocles senegallus*

bicoloured underwing

tail streamer

black stripe on belly

Female

orange throat

Male in flight

29–33 cm. Breeds on fringes of Sahara; a record from Sicily in April 1909. Pale grey head and neck with wide orange throat patch, no pectoral band. Long pointed tail as Pin-tailed Sandgrouse, wings with prominent cream fringes. Distinctive black stripe down centre of belly visible in flight; pale underwings with black primaries.

black spots

PIGEONS AND DOVES Medium-sized birds with small heads and rounded muscular breasts. Some species have a very wide distribution, being common and familiar in much of Europe, others are restricted to islands.

Rock Dove (Feral Pigeon)
Columba livia

IDENTIFICATION 32 cm. White skin at base of black bill, orange eye, pink legs. The original wild form, the **ROCK DOVE**, is grey with 2 black wing-bars, black band at tip of tail, white lower back (often concealed), dark head and iridescent green and violet patches on neck. The domestic **FERAL PIGEON** has very variable plumage. Male displays by puffing out neck feathers, walking in circles and following the female. Juvenile: brown iris, soft thin bill without white skin at base, plumage entirely fresh. Walks rapidly on ground, sleeps with head tucked into neck; flight swift. **VOICE** Repeated monotone ascending cooing. **HABITAT** Originally nested on cliffs along steep-sided valleys and on the coast. Feral populations near human dwellings, in towns and villages, but not at high elevations. Breeds throughout the year, even in winter.

Wild form

orange iris

2 black bars

white back

uniform grey

brown iris

Juvenile

grey-and-black wing markings

Dark form

wings almost entirely black

random white patches

grey belly

Pied form

white flight feathers

buff coverts; some have entirely rufous wings

reddish-brown replaces black

Male rufous form

whitish head

very visible iridescence

dirty white wing-coverts

Pale form

Wood Pigeon *Columba palumbus*

no white patch on neck

slender bill

Juvenile

white leading edge

white iris

white patch

no white on back

pinkish neck

wide black bar

Adult

white leading edge

IDENTIFICATION
40 cm. Large pigeon with white patch on neck and white band on wing. Yellow bill with red base, white iris. Broad black band on tail, pinkish breast. Juvenile: darker bill and iris, no white patch on neck but has diagnostic white band on wing. **VOICE** Male's cooing has different tones, firstly rising then descending *rou-ru-rou-roro*. Claps wings on taking flight and in display. **HABITAT** All areas with trees, from lowland forests to town centres, near crops.

Stock Dove *Columba oenas*

black iris

2 narrow black lines

no white on back

white-tipped bill

Adult

black iris

black spots on wing

Juvenile

pinkish-grey underparts

IDENTIFICATION
30 cm. Slightly smaller than the Feral Pigeon. Has pink bill with white tip, black iris, pale pink legs, back and rump same grey as head, pinkish breast. Line of black spots on greater coverts and tertials; in flight, pale grey patch bordering black-tipped flight feathers. **VOICE** Long, rising, disyllabic dull cooing, repeated every second. Sings from cavity entrance or nearby branch. **HABITAT** Tree-dwelling, comes to ground to feed. Nests in a cavity in forests or large parks (e.g. disused chimney, avenue trees). In winter, feeds in stubble, often in flocks.

Laurel Pigeon *Columba junoniae*

IDENTIFICATION 40 cm. Distinguished from Bolle's Pigeon by having pale terminal band to tail, diffuse above but well marked below. Upperparts are more vinous, orange eye and long bill with white tip. More intense pink underparts, head with green sheen. **VOICE** Repeated trisyllabic cooing. **HABITAT** Endemic to the Canaries, in montane laurel and tree-heather forests.

more vinous above

white tip to bill

pale tip

Bolle's Pigeon *Columba bollii*

bright yellow tip to bill

IDENTIFICATION 37 cm. Small pigeon reminiscent of Stock Dove with green spots on neck, extensive pink flush on breast, wide indistinct grey band on black tail. Yellow tip to bill, yellow iris. **VOICE** Dull, hoarse, low cooing of 4 notes. **HABITAT** Endemic to the Canaries, in montane laurel and tree-heather forests.

more bluish above

bars on tail

Trocaz Pigeon *Columba trocaz*

IDENTIFICATION 43 cm. Similar to and replaces Wood Pigeon on Madeira, where it is endemic, but has red bill. Resembles Bolle's Pigeon but has less extensive pink on breast, silver-grey spot on neck, distinct grey band on tail. **VOICE** Cooing like Wood Pigeon but deeper and weaker, in 6 syllables. **HABITAT** Natural forests in rocky mountains with laurel and tree heather.

white eye

pinkish-red bill

Adult

grey eye

dark grey bill

Juvenile

well-defined band on tail

Collared Dove *Streptopelia decaocto*

red iris
black half-collar
buff
Adult

pale fringes to feathers
no collar

Juvenile

IDENTIFICATION
32 cm. Almost pigeon-sized but slimmer with a long tail. Grey-buff plumage, white under the tail. Narrow black collar bordered with white on hindneck. Dark flight feathers; black tail-base only visible underneath and when in flight; white undersides to wings. Adult has red iris. Juvenile: darker iris, no black collar.
VOICE Prolonged hissed call given when landing. A 3-note song with emphasis on the third, *ou-ou-hou*. **HABITAT** Often near dwellings in towns and villages, also in farmland with crops. More abundant in warmer climates. Gregarious in winter. Colonised Europe from Central Asia during latter part of 20th century.

(European) Turtle Dove *Streptopelia turtur*

black-and-white patch (3 or 4 black lines)
grey head
grey rump
Adult
white corners to tail
clear rufous scaling
no patch
diffuse scaling

Juvenile

IDENTIFICATION
27 cm. Scaly mantle and wings, black feathers with prominent large rufous fringes; outer wing-coverts uniform ashy-grey. Grey head, pinkish breast, white belly; a patch of small black-and-white lines on side of neck, which is absent in duller juvenile birds. Black tail with white tip, dark underwings. **VOICE** Song a long dull cooing, a long rising *rrouou-rrouou-rrrrroooouuuu...* **HABITAT** Open deciduous woodland, copses, hedgerows, forest clearings and edges.

VAGRANT DOVES The following three species have been recorded in Europe, although there is always a risk that the latter two in particular could be escapes from captivity. Similar to other European doves; check wing, neck and tail patterns.

Oriental Turtle Dove *Streptopelia orientalis*

32 cm. Like European Turtle Dove but stockier, thick neck and large head, thickset body, similar to a pigeon. Often no visible skin between eye and thick bill. Adults have diffuse dark rufous fringes to wing-coverts, outer coverts ashy-grey with dark centres; neck 'grille' on grey background; grey corners to tail in Siberian race *orientalis*, with dark grey belly; darker than Central Asian race *meena*, which has white tail corners and white belly. Dark grey rump, brown not grey nape. A few European records in autumn and winter, often in company of Collared Doves.

reduced pink skin

more marked scales but always diffuse fringes

black-and-white 'grille' (4–5 black lines)

white corners to tail

Ssp. *meena*

brown nape

grey-and-white 'grille' (4 or 5 black lines)

dark grey centres and diffuse pale rufous fringes

Ssp. *orientalis*

grey corners to tail

greyish undertail-coverts

Laughing Dove *Streptopelia senegalensis*

25 cm. Small, slender, longer tail and shorter wings compared to Turtle Dove; diagnostic small necklace of black spots. Uniform back and rufous inner wing-coverts. In flight, very dark underwings. A few spring records from the Mediterranean coast may concern wild birds originating from North Africa, where the species is increasing.

uniform vinous-red

Adult

long tail

pectoral band of black flecks

dark grey band

Juvenile

no black markings

large white corners to tail

Mourning Dove *Zenaida macroura*

30 cm. A Nearctic migrant; very rare autumn vagrant recorded in the Azores, Britain, Denmark, Germany and Iceland. Slender with long pointed tail, quite uniform reddish-grey plumage, black spots on wings, blue eye-ring and thin bill. Large white spot with black margin on outer tail feathers. Adults have a black spot at base of cheek.

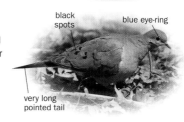

black spots

blue eye-ring

very long pointed tail

PARAKEETS Escaped exotic species that have established breeding populations in certain towns and cities. Brightly coloured; note size, head colour and tail length.

Rose-ringed (Ring-necked) Parakeet *Psittacula krameri*

blue-and-pink band

green plumage

red bill

Female

black chin and collar

Male

bluish tail

very long tail

40 cm of which half is the tail. Large slender parakeet with elongated tail. Small eye, red bill, female with uniform head; male has black throat with a black line continuing to behind cheek and finishing with a blue collar underlined with pink; blue central tail feathers. Very vocal, gives loud *kya-kya-kya* in series. Originating from the Indian subcontinent and Africa, escapes have established viable colonies in many urban areas.

Fischer's Lovebird *Agapornis fischeri*

white eye-ring

smoky rear head

red face

15 cm. Very small parrot with short tail, of E African origin; birds escaped from captivity have formed viable feral populations (a few tens of pairs) in S France. Red bill, white circle around eye, orange-red face, dark olive cap behind eye, yellow nape and breast, green belly; wings and upperparts grass-green, dark blue uppertail-coverts.

very short tail

Monk Parakeet *Myiopsitta monachus*

white face

blue-and-green wings

quite long tail

pale pink bill

30 cm. Introduced in Belgium, the Canaries and Spain. Small green parrot with grey face and blue wings, small pale orange bill, long green tail but not as long as that of Rose-ringed Parakeet. Colonial nests built on tree branches.

CUCKOOS Parasitic species that lay in other birds' nests. Shy and difficult to observe, they are more easily located from their calls.

Common Cuckoo *Cuculus canorus*

ash-grey above **Male**

long tail often raised

fine black barring on belly

reddish-brown barred black

fine black barring on head and breast

Female, rufous morph

reddish tail with larger black terminal band

dark iris

brown-and-white barring above

fine black barring

Juvenile

IDENTIFICATION 34 cm. May resemble a Sparrowhawk but has long tail, long pointed wings and slim unhooked bill. Ash-grey above, white underparts barred with black. Male has uniform grey head and breast, which are barred and have buff wash in female. The rufous morph (only females) has black barring on upperparts and more uniform rump. Young birds are darker, upperwing-coverts with dark-rufous, black-and-white barring. **VOICE** Well-known two-toned song *cu-cou*, the second syllable lower. It has a preceding higher note when excited, *ki-cu-cou*. The female's call is totally different, a rapid bubbling. **HABITAT** Parasitises the nests of other species (Robin, Wren, pipits, wagtails, reed warblers); forests, bushes, hedgerows, heath, wetlands, but absent from built-up areas.

Oriental Cuckoo *Cuculus optatus*

very wide black bars

Rufous female

widely separated black bars

large black bars

Male

32 cm. Breeds in taiga in the Urals. Very difficult to separate from Common Cuckoo, some males have more pronounced and more spaced barring on breast, yellowish undertail-coverts with larger bars, uniform white underwing primary coverts; rufous female with wider, denser bars, particularly on tail and tertials. **VOICE** A series of *pou* notes of the same tone, recalling Hoopoe's song.

Great Spotted Cuckoo *Clamator glandarius*

black flight feathers

ash-grey head

Adult in flight

lines of white spots

IDENTIFICATION
37 cm. Large, crested cuckoo with ash-grey crown, white underparts, white-spotted grey upperwings and mantle. Dark grey tail feathers with white tips. Juvenile: black crown, darker mantle and reddish bases to primaries that are kept into first summer. **VOICE** Noisy song, repeated loud *kliai*. Call: loud jerky chatter of varying speed: *ki-ki-ki-li-kiai kiai kiai kiai...* **HABITAT** Parasitises magpies, which rear the young cuckoos along with their own young. Heathland with trees, open and semi-open environments.

black head

red eye-ring

white-tipped black coverts

rufous base to flight feathers

very long tail

Juvenile

very long tail

short crest

dark grey crown

First-year

rufous bases

lines of white spots

Diederik Cuckoo *Chrysococcyx caprius*

white supercilium

metallic green

red bill

19 cm. Small cuckoo from Africa; 1 European record from Cyprus, April 1982. Short tail, red bill, clear white supercilium, prominent black-and-white barring on flanks. Male metallic green above with red iris; juvenile rufous with green barring.

Yellow-billed Cuckoo *Coccyzus americanus*

30 cm. Nearctic species; vagrant migrants occur in autumn, especially in September and October. Small, slender, long downcurved bill, yellow lower mandible with black tip. Grey crown and cheeks, pale eye-ring; brown-grey upperparts, rufous patch on primaries, tail feathers black with large white tips; white underparts.

yellow eye-ring

yellow lower mandible

reddish primaries

Juvenile

yellow base to bill

Adult

white tips to tail feathers

Black-billed Cuckoo *Coccyzus erythropthalmus*

30 cm. Nearctic species; a few European records. Very similar to Yellow-billed Cuckoo but grey lower mandible, red eye-ring, small white tips on tail feathers preceded by a black bar.

red eye-ring

grey base

Adult

black-and-white tips

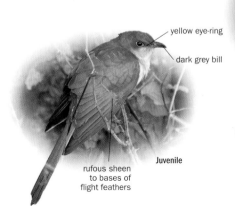

yellow eye-ring

dark grey bill

Juvenile

rufous sheen to bases of flight feathers

OWLS Nocturnal raptors with forward facing eyes in a flat face; they therefore have to turn their heads to see to the side. Facial disc guides sound towards ears; some species have erect feathers on head ('ears'); in others they are absent. Very soft plumage allows for silent flight, which is necessary to approach rodents at night. Some species also hunt during the day. They breed very early in the year, often starting to call in February, or even earlier.

'ears' sometimes flattened

heavily streaked breast

orange eyes

barred 'trousers'

(Eurasian) Eagle Owl *Bubo bubo*

IDENTIFICATION 60–75 cm. Larger than a buzzard, thickset, short tail and large head with prominent 'ears', dark orange eyes. Vermiculated brown-and-black upperparts, buff underparts with fine streaking, heavier streaks on breast. Black bill. **VOICE** Song: deep *hou-ou* with sharper first note, the second lower; male and female call to each other at twilight before leaving to hunt. **HABITAT** Undisturbed areas away from human dwellings, mountain ranges, gorges, foothills with cliffs. Breeds on escarpment, rarely on the ground.

long black 'ears'

dark back

short 'ears'

Pharaoh Eagle Owl *Bubo ascalaphus*

streaked breast

finely barred flanks

40–50 cm. Smaller and paler than European Eagle Owl, occurring in N Africa and Middle East; could potentially colonise southern Spain. Black border to facial discs, short 'ears', discreetly barred rufous belly, not striped. Higher-pitched song almost monosyllabic.

Snowy Owl *Bubo scandiacus*

white face

sometimes nearly all-white

Male

flight feathers less barred

yellow eyes

Female

white face

all-white face

finely barred below

black bars

Immature male

53–65 cm. Closely related to Eagle Owl, breeds in Arctic Scandinavia and Canada. Rare vagrant farther south in winter; ship-assisted birds occasionally cross the Atlantic to arrive on west coast of Europe. Male has almost uniform white plumage, barred with black above and below in female and young male. Totally white face with golden-yellow eyes, black bill, a trace of black 'ears' in young female. Small influx to W Europe in some winters.

narrow bars on tertials

Great Grey Owl *Strix nebulosa*

concentric circles

black 'goatee'

diffuse stripes

IDENTIFICATION 60–70 cm. Large, with a big head, all grey with a white 'X' between the eyes, yellow bill and black 'bib', long tail with black terminal band. Facial discs with faint concentric circles; piercing yellow eyes. **VOICE** Slow and very deep hooting, of about 10 notes. **HABITAT** Boreal forests, clearings, taiga.

big head

small yellow eyes

vermiculated below

Ural Owl *Strix uralensis*

markedly striped below

Adult small black eyes

uniform face

Juvenile

markedly striped below

obvious striping

IDENTIFICATION 50–60 cm. Large owl similar to Tawny Owl, but slimmer and bigger. Uniform facial disc with small black eyes and yellow bill, brown stripes on underparts, long tail with regular barring. **VOICE** Deep hooting in 7 syllables, slow and cooing, repeated. **HABITAT** Taiga with marshes, beech woods in mountainous central Europe.

Tawny Owl *Strix aluco*

IDENTIFICATION
37–43 cm.
Braces of
white droplet-
shaped spots
on shoulders.
Different plumage forms: grey, rufous
(reddish facial disc and mantle) and
intermediates. Black eyes, pale bands
on forehead, pale yellow bill. When
perched, wings longer than tail.
VOICE Different hooting phrases,
with first sound descending,
followed by quavering hoots
hou-ou... hou ou-ou-ou-ou-ou-
ou-ou. Call a strident repeated
ké-vit, hoarser and more strident
in young. **HABITAT** Forests,
woodland, even urban parks, and
mountains. The commonest owl
in Europe.

large head   black eyes

white 'braces'

white spots

large black
eyes

reddish-brown
above

round facial
disc

black 'conifer tree'
markings on underparts

no warm
colouring

pale
bill

Rufous morph

Grey morph

white spots

Barn Owl *Tyto alba*

IDENTIFICATION 33–39 cm. Pale
rufous, slightly silver above, white
heart-shaped face, small black eyes,
grey bill. White-bellied race (ssp.
alba) breeds in W Europe; the form
(ssp. *guttata*) with rufous, black-
spotted belly breeds in central Europe and may be seen in
W Europe in winter. Looks entirely white in flight from below.
Often hunts by watching from a roadside post. **VOICE** Long
and sinister hisses. **HABITAT** Open agricultural areas, villages.
Nests in old barns, steeples.

all white
below

black eyes with
brown 'tears'

white heart-
shaped face

silver
beading

Long-eared Owl *Asio otus*

cream X on face
orange eyes
black bill
strongly barred tan underparts
black-barred tan breast

pronounced black comma

orange area
several black bars

long erect 'ears'

erect slim posture

Roosting during day

IDENTIFICATION
34 cm. Slim body, long black 'ears', buff facial disc and orange eyes. Upperparts vermiculated with grey and black, diffuse white 'braces'. Strongly striped black below, narrowly barred tail. During the day perches erect with erected 'ears'. **VOICE** Song: dull, muffled *hou*, every 2 seconds. Juvenile's call is high-pitched, prolonged *tiii-u*. **HABITAT** Hedgerows, forests, parks. Breeds in abandoned corvid nest.

Short-eared Owl *Asio flammeus*

black spots
black 'comma'

short 'ears' often flattened
yellow eyes surrounded with black

very white

finely streaked breast

very dark black feathers with cream edges

black bill

IDENTIFICATION
36 cm. Very similar to Long-eared Owl, but upperparts mottled with pale yellow and black, only lightly streaked pale belly, cream facial disc, short 'ears' often folded. Yellow eyes with dark surroundings ('black-eyes'). In flight, white underwings with black comma at wrist and black spots on primaries; prominently barred tail. **VOICE** Call: raucous loud rasping 'bark'. Song: *pou-pou-pou...* in series of 10 to 20 notes, often given in high flight. **HABITAT** Open areas, meadows, scrub, marshes, agricultural plains, moors. Frequently hunts during daylight.

Hawk Owl *Surnia ulula*

IDENTIFICATION 40 cm. Medium-sized diurnal owl, slim with long tail, yellow eyes, vertical black bars on sides of face, underside barred grey as in Sparrowhawk. **VOICE** Song: long rapid bubbling. Alarm call *ki-ki-ki*. **HABITAT** Conifer forests, taiga, woodland edge.

white braces

black bars

often hovers

long tail

black streak

small yellow eyes

spotted white

barred belly

long tail

Marsh Owl *Asio capensis*

35 cm. Occurs in African marshes (including Morocco), very rare vagrant to Spain. Similar to Short-eared Owl but rounder wings, upperparts uniform earth-brown, pale face with black eyes and black 'tears', uniform brown breast, discreet brown barring on belly. Orange base to primaries visible in flight.

orange on primaries

black eyes

black 'mascara'

quite uniform earth-brown

Tengmalm's Owl (Boreal Owl) *Aegolius funereus*

big head

facial disc gives surprised expression

yellow eyes

uniform brown-grey with round white spots

yellow bill

breast mottled with brown

IDENTIFICATION 25 cm. Small owl with large square head, golden-yellow eyes. Dark brown plumage marked with round white spots above, especially on shoulders. Brown-and-white mottled underparts. Pale yellow bill. Juvenile: uniform chocolate-brown on fledging with yellow eyes and white supercilium. **VOICE** Song: rapid series of 5 to 10 melodious notes *tu-tu-tu-tu-tu-tu-tu...* becoming slightly higher-pitched. Alarm call; an explosive *gjeck*. **HABITAT** Conifer and mixed forest in mountains; beech and fir, spruce or pine; not necessarily ancient but must have Black Woodpecker holes for nesting.

(Eurasian) Pygmy Owl *Glaucidium passerinum*

head entirely beaded with white spots

small white supercilium

small yellow eyes

fine white bars

pale bill

IDENTIFICATION 17 cm. Small, size of a Hawfinch, short tail. Diurnal, often harassed by passerines. Big head, yellow eyes, white supercilium on brown face, pale yellow bill. White speckles on crown (not in young) and mantle. Flanks either barred (adult) or uniform brownish-grey (young), brown streaks on breast. **VOICE** Song: a soft but far-carrying *piu* repeated every 2 seconds, associated with a muffled phrase when excited, *piu tututu piu tu-tu-tu*. **HABITAT** Ancient forest in cold climates, thus in mountainous areas.

(Eurasian) Scops Owl *Otus scops*

IDENTIFICATION
20 cm. Small, ash-grey, big head, 2 wide, short 'ears', erected when asleep. Upperparts vermiculated grey and black, sometimes with a brown tint. Below, black streaks with black horizontal crossbars and diffuse pale bars. Grey face with yellow eyes. Wings as long as tail. **VOICE** Song: loud whistled *tiou* repeated every 2 or 3 seconds. **HABITAT** Forests, woodland, maquis, hedgerows. Breeds in tree cavity.

big grey 'ears'

big grey V between eyes

finely marked with black lines

yellow eyes

facial disc bordered black

black bill

Little Owl *Athene noctua*

IDENTIFICATION
23–27 cm. Grey-brown upperparts with sparse round white spots. Underparts brown with large white spots. Brown-grey facial disc, almost horizontal white supercilium gives appearance of being annoyed. Similar pattern on nape. Juvenile: uniform brown breast. Yellow eyes, pale yellow bill. Wings shorter than tail, very rotund when seen in undulating flight. **VOICE** Whistled song, drawn-out note finishing with an upward inflection. Call: descending *kiou*. **HABITAT** Farmland, hedgerows, orchards, meadows with pollarded trees. Nests in tree cavity, pile of stones, ruins. Also hunts during day.

long white supercilium

big round head

brown above with round white spots

yellow eyes

yellow bill

striped below

long legs

short tail

NIGHTJARS Nocturnal, insectivorous, hunting in flight with open mouth, long gliding flights with wings raised; long tail; their cryptic plumage allows them to remain unseen during the day, lying on woodland floor or a branch. Migrants.

European Nightjar *Caprimulgus europeaus*

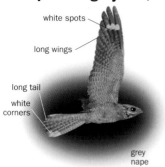

white spots
long wings
long tail
white corners

IDENTIFICATION 26 cm. Greyish plumage without warm hue. Uniform grey nape, pale line on shoulder, white line on closed wing. White corners to tail; male has white marks on primaries, absent in female. Elastic flight. **VOICE** Song: rapid, long, sometimes never-ending churring, *rururururururururur...* Call: loud mounting *kruii.* **HABITAT** Open woodland, clearings, woodland edge, maquis, heath.

grey nape
grey scapulars
Male
white band

cream band

At rest during day

Common Nighthawk *Chordeiles minor*

24 cm. A very rare Nearctic vagrant in autumn. A small nightjar with dark plumage (blackish-grey), pointed wings in flight, black flight feathers contrast with pale wing-coverts, slightly forked tail. White bar in middle of primaries. May fly during daylight. When perched, wings longer than tail.

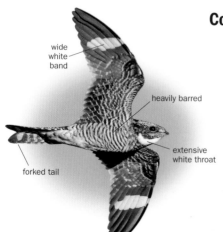

wide white band
heavily barred
extensive white throat
forked tail

grey wing-coverts contrast with black flight feathers
no white band

Red-necked Nightjar *Caprimulgus ruficollis*

IDENTIFICATION
32 cm. Breeds in Spain and N Africa, recently heard singing in the Alpilles, southern France. A little bigger than European Nightjar, similar plumage but has rufous collar and tan-coloured spots on all wing-coverts. Both male and female with white on primaries and tail corners. **VOICE** Song: a repeated, continuous *co-pok co-pok...* **HABITAT** Sandy heaths with scattered trees and stone-pine forest.

rufous collar

line of pale spots

rufous collar

tan spots

Egyptian Nightjar *Caprimulgus aegyptius*

25 cm. Small nightjar of the Sahara and Arabian deserts; migrant, very rare vagrant in the past, particularly in Italy and Malta. Short tail, very pale plumage, predominately buff and grey with barred black primaries above, whitish with black tips below.

sandy-grey

very uniform wings

uniform sandy plumage

SWIFTS Resemble swallows but most are larger with long, pointed scythe-shaped wings. Insectivorous, they swallow insects in flight, sometimes high in the sky and often in groups. Only perch in order to nest, even sleeping in flight. The different species can be identified by their size, silhouette and colour of rump and belly.

Common Swift *Apus apus*

white throat

uniform black above

forked tail

pale throat

pale throat

scythe-shaped wings

IDENTIFICATION 18 cm. Blackish plumage with pale throat; juveniles have slightly scaly plumage. Forked tail, slim wings. Gregarious, flying in groups, very noisy as they fly at high speed almost touching the rooftops, in the morning and evening. **VOICE** High-pitched call, long and piercing, *sriiiiii...*, given by groups in chorus. **HABITAT** Anywhere as long as it can nest: towns and villages, cliffs and gorges in valleys and mountains; readily breeds under roofs. A migrant that arrives in early May and leaves in August.

Pallid Swift *Apus pallidus*

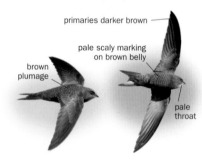

primaries darker brown

pale scaly marking on brown belly

brown plumage

pale throat

IDENTIFICATION 17 cm. Like Common Swift but dark brown plumage with contrasting dark back, extensive pale throat and slightly different silhouette. In flight, impression of wider hand amplified by the contrast between dark of dark outer primaries and paler inner primaries. At close range, body feathers with narrow cream borders give scaly appearance. **VOICE** Quite similar to Common Swift. **HABITAT** Nests in cavities, in buildings or cliffs.

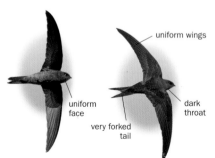

uniform wings

uniform face

dark throat

very forked tail

Plain Swift *Apus unicolor*

IDENTIFICATION 15 cm. Small brown-black swift with deeply forked tail, dark throat, agile flight with rapid wingbeats. **VOICE** Like Common Swift. **HABITAT** Endemic to Madeira and Canaries, a few recent winter records from Morocco. Very difficult to identify away from breeding sites.

Alpine Swift *Apus melba*

IDENTIFICATION 22 cm. Like a giant brown-and-white Common Swift. Underparts, including throat, white with brown collar, lower belly and undertail-coverts; underwings blackish-brown. Adults and juveniles identical. **VOICE** Strident, musical, rapid trill, *ti-ti-ti-ti-ti...*, unlike calls of other breeding swifts. **HABITAT** Nests in crevices in mountain and coastal cliffs. Uncommon migrant, present from April to September.

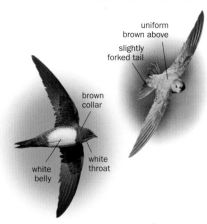

uniform brown above

slightly forked tail

brown collar

white throat

white belly

Little Swift *Apus affinis*

13 cm. Small swift with square tail, short wings with wide hand, distinct white throat and broad white rump patch extending around sides, sometimes visible from below. Less rapid flight than that of Common Swift. Call a high-pitched twitter.

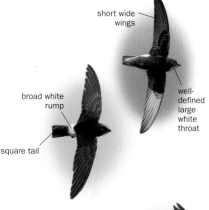

short wide wings

broad white rump

square tail

well-defined large white throat

White-rumped Swift *Apus caffer*

15 cm. Slim swift, smaller than Common Swift, long deeply-forked tail often held closed in flight, thus appearing long and slim; small white rump does not extend to sides, secondaries with narrow white trailing edge, distinct white throat. Narrower hand to wing than in Little Swift. A few breed in the very south of Spain, often laying in disused Red-rumped Swallow's nest.

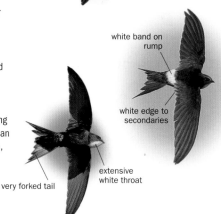

white band on rump

white edge to secondaries

extensive white throat

very forked tail

RARE SWIFTS Three species (two Asian and one Nearctic) are vagrants to Europe; they can be identified by their structure, and rump and throat colour.

Pacific Swift *Apus pacificus*

forked tail

rectangular white rump

no white on secondaries

scaly below

extensive pale throat

19 cm. Large Siberian swift, rare vagrant to N Europe. Resembles White-rumped Swift but larger, underparts with scaly pale markings. White throat, deeply forked tail, white band on rump. Descending, rough call, similar to that of Pallid Swift.

White-throated Needletail *Hirundapus caudacutus*

dark brown

cigar-shaped body

diffuse whitish mantle

white V below

white throat and forehead

20 cm. Large Asian swift, rare vagrant to N Europe. Like a giant Chimney Swift, cigar-shaped (short narrow tail, no visible neck) with white forehead, throat and undertail-coverts; pale mantle, the rest dark and contrasting.

Chimney Swift *Chaetura pelagica*

cigar-shaped body

brown plumage

pale throat

very short spiny tail

13 cm. Nearctic migrant, very rare autumn vagrant to Europe. Small brown swift with broad wings, looking almost spoon-shaped. Small, square tail without any white. Brown rump is paler than wings; pale throat, dark mask through eye.

KINGFISHERS Small to medium-sized birds, often colourful. They dive either into water or onto the ground to catch their vertebrate prey.

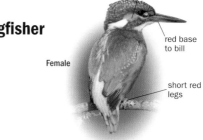

fine black bars

red base to bill

Female

short red legs

Common Kingfisher
Alcedo atthis

IDENTIFICATION
18 cm. Long bill, large head and very short tail. Metallic blue above, orange below. Darker blue wings, fine black bars on crown. Orange cheeks, broad blue moustache. All-black bill (male) or with a red base (female). Often perched low over water, on the lookout for small fish; low, direct, rapid flight. **VOICE** High-pitched piercing call, a long *tsiiiiiii*. **HABITAT** Rivers, estuaries and lakes with banks for excavating its nesting tunnel.

brilliant blue back

long all-black bill

orange belly

Male

White-throated Kingfisher *Halcyon smyrnensis*

IDENTIFICATION
28 cm. Big with large red bill, body dark brick-red with extensive white 'bib', turquoise upperparts, pale blue wings with black tips. **VOICE** Loud whistled trills. **HABITAT** Open areas but not necessarily near water. Widespread from Turkey eastwards; a few records from Greece.

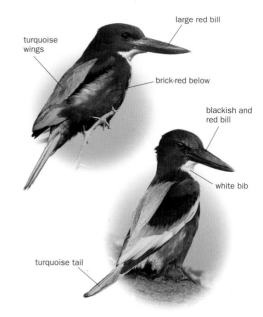

large red bill

turquoise wings

brick-red below

blackish and red bill

white bib

turquoise tail

Pied Kingfisher *Ceryle rudis*

pied plumage

black bill

long white supercilium

broad black band

Male

black collar

Female

IDENTIFICATION
26 cm. Big, black and white, with white collar and 1 (female) or 2 (male) black chest-bands. Long black bill. Often hovers when looking for fish. **VOICE** Calls piercing, metallic whistles. **HABITAT** Wetlands, coasts, mangroves. Widespread from Turkey eastwards and in Africa; rare vagrant recorded in Poland and Greece.

Belted Kingfisher *Megaceryle alcyon*

shaggy crest

blue collar

large grey bill

Female

white collar

rufous flanks and breast-band

Female

32 cm. Nearctic species; very rare vagrant to Iceland, the Azores, Britain and Spain. Blue-grey above with a white collar, and blue-grey pectoral band (male), doubled with an orange band descending onto the flanks (female). In flight, prominent white bases to black primaries.

ROLLERS, BEE-EATERS AND HOOPOE Medium-sized colourful migrants; rollers perch in the open looking for prey; bee-eaters catch insects in flight; hoopoes use their long bills to probe the ground.

European Roller
Coracias garrulus

blue head

big black bill

blue hand on wing

rufous mantle

black flight feathers

IDENTIFICATION 31 cm. Size of a Jackdaw, blue with black lores and rufous mantle. Black flight feathers, extensive blue corners to tail. Large, thick black bill. Immature paler than adult with streaked breast. Short legs; often seen perched on wire or bare branch. Butterfly-like flight. **VOICE** Raucous caw, *rak-ac*. **HABITAT** Open areas with a quantity of large insects and large trees with cavities for nesting.

Abyssinian Roller *Coracias abyssinicus*

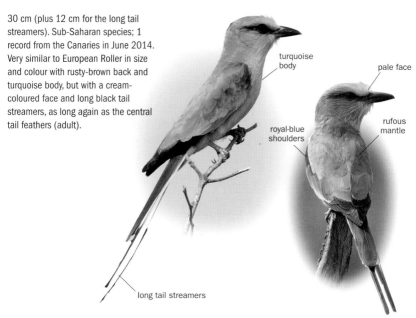

30 cm (plus 12 cm for the long tail streamers). Sub-Saharan species; 1 record from the Canaries in June 2014. Very similar to European Roller in size and colour with rusty-brown back and turquoise body, but with a cream-coloured face and long black tail streamers, as long again as the central tail feathers (adult).

turquoise body

pale face

rufous mantle

royal-blue shoulders

long tail streamers

European Bee-eater *Merops apiaster*

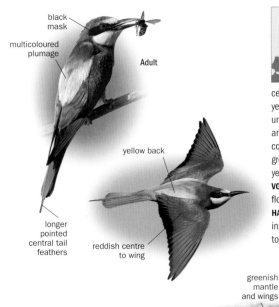

black mask

multicoloured plumage

Adult

yellow back

longer pointed central tail feathers

reddish centre to wing

IDENTIFICATION
27 cm. Slender, slightly decurved long bill, adult has elongated central tail feathers. Very colourful: yellow throat, black mask, turquoise underparts, rusty wing-coverts, crown and mantle. Adult: tail longer and colours more intense. Juvenile: duller, greenish above with pale shoulders, yellow throat. Often perches in the open.
VOICE Call: a rolling *prruuu*, given by flocks in flight, even high in the sky.
HABITAT Open areas with plentiful insects, open perches and sandy banks to excavate their nesting burrows.

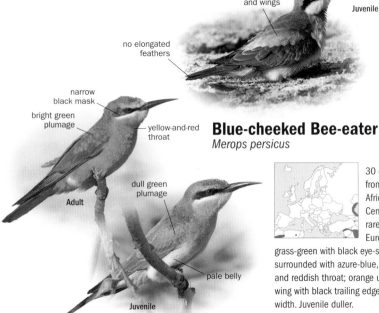

greenish mantle and wings

Juvenile

no elongated feathers

narrow black mask

bright green plumage

yellow-and-red throat

Blue-cheeked Bee-eater
Merops persicus

Adult

dull green plumage

30 cm. Migrant from North Africa and Central Asia; rare vagrant to Europe. Adult is grass-green with black eye-stripe surrounded with azure-blue, yellow chin and reddish throat; orange undersides of wing with black trailing edge of even width. Juvenile duller.

pale belly

Juvenile

Hoopoe *Upupa epops*

black-and-white barred back

pale orange head

streaked flanks

IDENTIFICATION
27 cm. Size of Blackbird, buff-orange body, wide black-and-white bands on back and wings, black tail with white bars. Long feathers on crown, with black tips, form a long crest, which is erected when bird is nervous. Long decurved bill. Terrestrial, hunts on the ground whilst walking, flies to perch at slightest disturbance. Flight undulating and butterfly-like, with very rounded wings. **VOICE** Song: fluty *oup-oup-oup*, lasting 1 second, repeated frequently. **HABITAT** Countryside with hedgerows, farmland, in warm climates. Feeds by probing ground with long bill.

round, pied wings

black tail with white base

raised crown-shaped crest

long decurved bill

black-and-white striped head

orange nape

White-throated Bee-eater *Merops albicollis*

green and turquoise above

20 cm. Very rare vagrant from sub-Saharan Africa; 1 record from Morocco, could occur in the Canaries. Small bee-eater, male with long central tail feathers; green mantle, blue wings and tail, black crown and eye-stripe on white face, black collar under white throat. Orange underwings with broad black trailing edge.

very long streamers

WOODPECKERS Arboreal, nesting in tree cavity excavated using their long dagger-shaped bills. Long sticky tongue, folded when not feeding, allows them to capture insects and larvae in wood, and also ants. They climb along tree trunks using their rigid tails as support. Undulating flight with alternating flaps and glides. Sedentary, except Wryneck, which winters in Africa.

(Eurasian) Wryneck *Jynx torquilla*

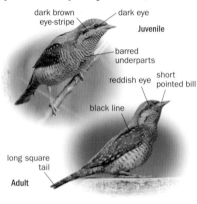

dark brown eye-stripe
dark eye
Juvenile
barred underparts
reddish eye
short pointed bill
black line
long square tail
Adult

IDENTIFICATION 17 cm. Member of woodpecker family; vermiculated plumage recalls that of owls. Long-tailed with widely-spaced bars. Grey back with large black central band extending onto crown, and narrow black 'braces'. Dark brown eye-stripe, buff with narrow black barring below. Short pointed bill. Often on the ground or on a branch; does not climb trunks like woodpeckers. **VOICE** Song: a series of 10 to 20 nasal notes, *ouin-ouin-ouin...* lasting 3 or 4 seconds. **HABITAT** Orchards, hedgerows, clearings. Feeds on ants and their larvae. Migrant, present in Europe from May to September.

Black Woodpecker *Dryocopus martius*

white eye
black crown
red nape
red crown
ivory-coloured bill
Female
Male

IDENTIFICATION 43 cm. Large, all black, resembles a Carrion Crow but has long neck, pointed tail, direct but irregular flight, which is somewhat fluttering, ivory-coloured bill. All-red crown (male) or hindcrown (female), even in juveniles. **VOICE** Call when perched: *kluuu-i*; in flight a rolled *krukrukrukrukru*. Song: monotone and regular *klui-klui-klui-klui...* **HABITAT** Mature deciduous, coniferous or mixed forests; fond of beeches for excavating nesting hole.

CONFUSION SPECIES

Carrion Crow
(p. 374)

Green Woodpecker *Picus viridis*

IDENTIFICATION
33 cm. Green above, yellowish rump, red crown, black face and white eye-ring.
Red moustache with black border (male) or totally black (female). Barred undertail-coverts and sides of tail. Juvenile: spotted black underparts, mottled pale upperparts. Often feeds on the ground. Strong, undulating flight.
VOICE Song: a monotone or descending series of whistled notes, sometimes appears almost shouted. Call similar to song but shorter and hoarser. Rarely drums, only for 1 or 2 seconds. **HABITAT** Forests, woodland, hedgerows and parks.

Juvenile
striped cheek
red crown
black face
barred underparts
red moustache
green back
black moustache
Female
yellowish rump
Male

'Iberian' Green Woodpecker
Picus viridis sharpei

Replaces Green Woodpecker in Iberia and the south of France, where hybrids occur. Identical to Green Woopecker but for grey face without obvious black coloration around eye, and undertail-coverts without bars. Song much more fluty and less 'shouted'.

grey face
Male
red moustache with narrow black border

Grey-headed Woodpecker
Picus canus

IDENTIFICATION
29 cm. Very similar to Green Woodpecker, but a little smaller and a shorter bill. Grey head with black lores, thin black moustache and grey crown; male with red patch on forehead. Duller rump and uniform tail in flight. Dark yellow iris. Arboreal and does not visit the ground.
VOICE Song: descending series of soft fluty notes. Often drums, for a duration of 1 second. **HABITAT** Lowland hedgerows and forests.

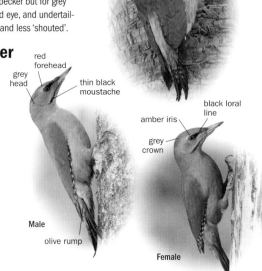

red forehead
grey head
thin black moustache
black loral line
amber iris
grey crown
Male
olive rump
Female

Great Spotted Woodpecker *Dendrocopos major*

red crown

black line almost joins on nape

unstriped flanks

black line joins bill and nape

red nape

Male

Juvenile

bright red undertail-coverts

black nape

black back

white 'braces'

Female

IDENTIFICATION 25 cm. Pied plumage with large white 'braces' on shoulders. Broad black moustache reaches bill and nape, isolating white cheek and a white patch on side of neck. Black crown and white forehead in adult; in juvenile red bordered with black. Male has red patch on nape. Red undertail-coverts, unstreaked flanks. **VOICE** Call: brief, isolated *kik*. Rapid drumming lasts less than 1 second; stops abruptly. **HABITAT** Forests, woodland, parks and gardens, in the countryside or urban areas; also at altitude.

Middle Spotted Woodpecker *Dendrocopos medius*

red crown

white 'braces'

pale red undertail-coverts

moustache reaches neither bill nor nape

fine black streaks

IDENTIFICATION 21 cm. Smaller than Great Spotted Woodpecker, shorter bill, entirely red crown bordered with white, pink undertail-coverts, black-striped flanks, black moustache does not reach bill or nape. Male, female and juvenile almost identical. **VOICE** Song: a series of plaintive nasal calls, *gvek*. Call: *kik-kik-kik...* in series. Does not drum. **HABITAT** Mature deciduous forests, particularly ancient oak forests.

Lesser Spotted Woodpecker *Dendrocopos minor*

IDENTIFICATION
15 cm. Very small, size of a House Sparrow, very small bill, red crown underlined with black (male and juvenile) or entirely black (female); finely streaked flanks, no red on undertail-coverts. Back finely barred black and white, no white 'braces' on shoulders. **VOICE** Song a rapid, high-pitched rattle, *kikikikiikikikikiki*. Drums for 1–2 seconds. **HABITAT** Deciduous woodland, parks and gardens.

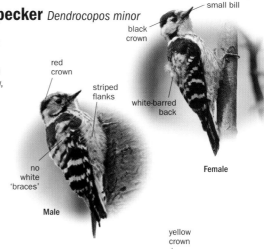

small bill

black crown

red crown

striped flanks

white-barred back

no white 'braces'

Male

Female

Three-toed Woodpecker *Picoides tridactylus*

IDENTIFICATION
23 cm. Small dark woodpecker without any red and different head pattern; black cheeks bordered by 2 thin white lines; yellow crown (male) or white mixed with black (female). Finely barred black-and-white mantle and back in birds from Alps and E Europe (ssp. *alpinus*) or totally white in northern birds (ssp. *tridactylus*). Dense black barring on flanks, black wings with lines of small white spots. **VOICE** Call: lower-pitched and softer than that of Great Spotted Woodpecker. Drums for 1–1.5 seconds. **HABITAT** Ancient conifer (fir and spruce) forests at altitude.

yellow crown

Male ssp. *alpinus*

black-and-white barred back

no yellow on crown

no white 'braces'

barred flanks

totally white back

Female ssp. *alpinus*

Male ssp. *tridactylus*

'Northern' White-backed Woodpecker *Dendrocopos leucotos leucotos*

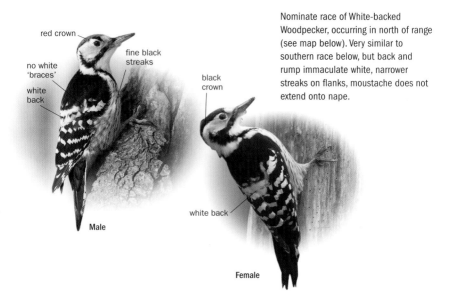

red crown

fine black
streaks

no white
'braces'

white
back

black
crown

white back

Male

Female

Nominate race of White-backed
Woodpecker, occurring in north of range
(see map below). Very similar to
southern race below, but back and
rump immaculate white, narrower
streaks on flanks, moustache does not
extend onto nape.

'Southern' White-backed Woodpecker *Dendrocopos leucotos lilfordi*

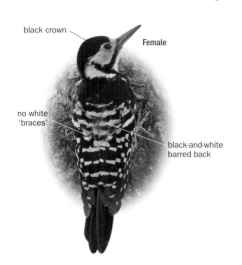

black crown

Female

no white
'braces'

black-and-white
barred back

IDENTIFICATION
27 cm. Pied
woodpecker with
large black
moustache reaching
the bill, the nape and
extending onto breast; flanks heavily streaked
black, barred axillaries, pinkish undertail-
coverts. Rump and back finely barred black
and white, no white 'braces' on shoulders but
black wings have thin white lines. Crown red
(male) or black (female). **VOICE** Call lower-
pitched and less sharp than that of Great
Spotted Woodpecker. Drumming lasts 2
seconds. **HABITAT** Mixed forests with much
larvae-infested wood. Also feeds at base of
dead trees. Occurs in southern part of range.

Syrian Woodpecker *Dendrocopos syriacus*

red nape

moustache joins bill but not nape

broad moustache

red crown

Adult male

streaked flanks

Female

Juvenile

IDENTIFICATION
24 cm. Pied woodpecker similar to Great Spotted, with similar head pattern but black comma does not reach nape, white (not black) feathers on nostrils, diffuse pink undertail-coverts; a little streaking on flanks is more obvious in juvenile, which has red crown with black edges. **VOICE** Softer call than that of Great Spotted Woodpecker; drumming longer (1–2 seconds). **HABITAT** Orchards, parks and gardens, hedgerows.

Yellow-bellied Sapsucker
Sphyrapicus varius

red

white bar

white supercilium

yellowish below

20 cm. Rare Nearctic vagrant recorded in Iceland, Ireland, Britain and the Azores. Head pattern very similar to that of Three-toed Woodpecker; crown and throat are speckled with black and white in juvenile, with some red in male. Black-and-white striped back, white bar on wing, white underparts sometimes with yellowish belly, black streaks on flanks.

Northern Flicker *Colaptes auratus*

red nape

buff face

black moustache

black spots

buff-barred black upperparts

long black tail

31 cm. Nearctic migrant; rare vagrant recorded in Iceland, Scotland, Denmark and the Azores. Large woodpecker, body mottled black, grey crown, red patch on nape, broad black moustache, buff face and breast, black pectoral crescent. Black bill and iris. Call: loud *wek wek wek*. Slender in flight; often on the ground.

LARKS Streaked brown-and-white terrestrial passerines. Male often sings in flight. Legs adapted for frequent walking, with long hind claw. Occurs in open, often cultivated habitats.

flattened crest
sandy colour
bill appears downcurved
long raised crest
buff edges to tail
streaked above
long bill
no primary projection

Crested Lark *Galerida cristata*

IDENTIFICATION
17 cm. White supercilium, long bill, obvious crest, streaked breast. Lower mandible with straight edge. In flight, orangey underwing-coverts, no contrast between uppertail-coverts and buff rump. Buff outer tail feathers. **VOICE** Short fluty song, with quavering, twisted notes, including imitations of other species. Normal call: fluty and melodious *tu-tli-tou* or *tu tli-ti tou*. **HABITAT** Open, stony environments. Garrigue, scrub, vineyards, waste ground, gravel pits, roadsides and along railway lines.

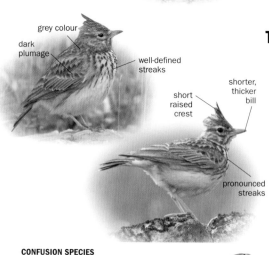

grey colour
dark plumage
well-defined streaks
shorter, thicker bill
short raised crest
pronounced streaks

Thekla Lark *Galerida theklae*

IDENTIFICATION
17 cm. Very similar to Crested Lark but has shorter, thicker bill, convex lower edge to lower mandible, short crest, more markedly streaked breast, generally darker more streaked mantle; grey underwing-coverts, rufous uppertail-coverts contrasting with dull rump. Buff outer tail feathers. **VOICE** Song less varied than that of Crested Lark. Call: *dou-di* or *dou-di-dou-dii,* a little deeper, louder last note. **HABITAT** Usually more broken ground than Crested Lark, often with bushes, garrigue, calcareous hillsides and dry rocky plateaus.

CONFUSION SPECIES

Skylark (p. 263)

Corn Bunting (p. 404)

(Eurasian) Skylark *Alauda arvensis*

IDENTIFICATION 18 cm. Large streaked lark, buff and brown, finely streaked breast, short primary projection. Short crest visible when erected. Bill shorter than Crested or Thekla Larks, slimmer than that of Calandra Lark. White trailing edge to wing visible in flight, white outer tail feathers (buff in Crested and Thekla Larks). **VOICE** Usually sings very high in the sky, hovering facing the wind; long, warbled, shrill phrases with repeated sounds *ti-ti-ti-ti-ti* or *tiu-tiu-tiu-tiu*. **HABITAT** Open agricultural areas, crops, meadows, scrub, set-aside, dunes, alpine meadows in summer. Ploughed fields, stubble and meadows in winter.

white trailing edge

streaked bib

white sides to tail

short crest rarely raised

pale supercilium and uniform buff face

white sides to tail

short bill

streaked buff bib

long primary projection

Woodlark *Lullula arborea*

IDENTIFICATION 15 cm. Small, compact lark, short tail and patterned head; pronounced white supercilium especially behind eye, rufous cheek with white spot on the malar area. Streaks on breast extend onto flanks. Pink legs. **VOICE** Plaintive song given from a high perch (dead branch, telephone pole), *tilu tilu tilu tilu tilu...* descending and accelerating. Variable rolled call, *li tou it* or *dlu it.* **HABITAT** Sparsely wooded open environments: hillsides, woodland edge, forest clearings, bushy scrub.

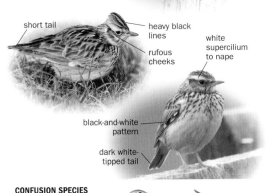

short tail

heavy black lines

rufous cheeks

white supercilium to nape

black-and-white pattern

dark white-tipped tail

CONFUSION SPECIES

Pipits
(pp. 274–278)

Crested and Thekla Larks
(p. 262)

Shore Lark (Horned Lark) *Eremophila alpestris*

black 'horns'
buff nape
broad black bib
Male
yellow face
black mask
small black bib
Winter

IDENTIFICATION
16 cm. Large-headed sandy-coloured lark. Yellow face, black lores extending into a moustache, small black 'horns' join together at front of crown, black breast-band. Yellowish-brown nape, slightly streaked sandy-grey back. Brown wash to finely streaked flanks. White sides to tail. Black legs. **VOICE** Call: *tsiip* similar to Meadow Pipit's call, or *tsii-sirp*. **HABITAT** Breeds in mountains above treeline in south, and on tundra in north. In winter, on the tide line and edge of mudflats, or saltmarshes; always near the sea.

Calandra Lark *Melanocorypha calandra*

black collar
black underwings
thick yellowish bill
white trailing edge
white spectacles
large black patch
short tail

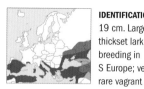

IDENTIFICATION
19 cm. Large thickset lark, breeding in S Europe; very rare vagrant elsewhere. Large head and thick bill. Black patch on side of neck. Uniform face with cream lores and streaked crown. Short tail, white outer tail feathers. Black underwing-coverts, large white tips to secondaries. **VOICE** Song: like that of Skylark but more fluty and varied, continuous flow of short phrases or single notes with imitations. Call: nasal, buzzing *kiltra* included in the song. **HABITAT** Dry, calcareous steppe and plains.

(Greater) Short-toed Lark *Calandrella brachydactyla*

cream supercilium

crown often reddish

Spring (worn)

strong pointed bill

IDENTIFICATION
14 cm.
Resembles a
small, slim
Calandra Lark.
Pale lores, white
supercilium continuing around the
reddish-brown cheek. Buff wash to top of
flanks with streaks or small black patch
on side of neck. Primaries covered
entirely by tertials. Very dark median
coverts with cream fringes. Juvenile has
streaked upper breast similar to Lesser
Short-toed Lark. **VOICE** Song: unending
repeated short phrases given in flight,
with imitations. Call: chirping *chup* or
chirrup. **HABITAT** Steppe-like areas,
showing preference for short, sparse, dry
grassland on sandy or stony soils.

small black patch

no primary projection

slightly streaked breast

Autumn

Lesser Short-toed Lark *Calandrella rufescens*

IDENTIFICATION
14 cm. Similar
to Short-toed
Lark but has
shorter bill, well-
defined streaks
covering whole breast, finely streaked
nape, no black patch on neck; short
(0.5 cm) primary projection. **VOICE** Call:
a buzzing *prrt*. **HABITAT** Steppe, saltpans.

short, thick bill

obvious primary projection

uniform face

heavily streaked crown

streaked bib

Dupont's Lark *Chersophilus duponti*

no crest

primary projection

pink legs

scaly upperparts

long downcurved bill

densely streaked

IDENTIFICATION 17 cm. Short-tailed lark with long slim downcurved bill, heavily streaked breast, pronounced supercilium. **VOICE** Song: repeated melancholic phrases with miaowing sounds. **HABITAT** Sandy steppe and semi-deserts with grassy tufts.

Bimaculated Lark *Melanocorypha bimaculata*

pale underwing-coverts

white tip to tail

very obvious white supercilium

long bill

short tail with white tip

17 cm. Rare vagrant to W Europe from Central Asia. Very similar to Calandra Lark but has longer bill, more marked head pattern with black lores, shorter tail with white tip, no white trailing edge to wings, grey not black underwings. Call: short *drip* similar to that of Short-toed Lark.

VAGRANT LARKS Asian or African species, rare vagrants to Western Europe; sometimes similar to European breeding larks.

(Greater) Hoopoe Lark
Alaemon alaudipes

uniform sandy above

long downcurved bill

21 cm. Large, slim lark of sandy Sahara and Arabian deserts; vagrant to Greece, Italy and Malta. Long legs and tail, long downcurved bill, white supercilium underlined with black, uniform sandy above, unique black-and-white patterned wings visible in flight. Flight call: deep, rolled *gruit*.

very long tail

uniform underparts

Bar-tailed Lark *Ammomanes cinctura*

short pink bill

14 cm. Small lark of sandy Sahara and Arabian deserts; vagrant to Italy and Malta. Short pinkish bill, uniform sandy mantle, rufous edges to wing feathers, sandy wash on breast, cream spectacles, tail all reddish with distinctive well-defined dark terminal bar. Call: short *tcherr* or dry nasal piping.

no streaks

Desert Lark *Ammomanes deserti*

long yellowish bill

16 cm. Similar to Bar-tailed Lark, prefers stony deserts; so far unrecorded in Europe. Larger with longer bill, orange-yellow with dark edges, diffuse broad terminal tail-band, dull edges to tertials. Call: rolling *tcheurr*.

streaked breast

long tail

White-winged Lark *Alauda leucoptera*

rufous crown

pale spectacles

white inner secondaries

rufous shoulder

IDENTIFICATION
18 cm. Resembles a large Short-toed Lark, with pale bill and pink legs, rufous crown and cheeks (male), rufous lesser and median coverts, white secondaries with black bases form a distinctive wing pattern in flight. **VOICE** Song like that of Skylark but rougher and more hesitant. **HABITAT** Dry steppe. Very rare vagrant to N Europe.

Black Lark *Melanocorypha yeltoniensis*

thick bill

very streaked

IDENTIFICATION 19 cm. Pale bill, grey legs, compact body with large head. Male: black with creamy chevrons, especially on upperparts, scapulars and flanks; chevrons very broad in winter. Female: buff, spotted on mantle and breast, uniform face, dark flight feathers, cream fringes underlined with fine black line on wing-coverts, blackish underwings. **VOICE** Song similar to that of Skylark, but higher-pitched and quicker. **HABITAT** Steppe, often near water. Very rare vagrant to N Europe.

Female

all black

ivory bill

cream chevrons

Male

very scaly

Juvenile

SWALLOWS AND MARTINS Slender with long pointed wings and forked tails, sometimes with long streamers. They hunt in flight by snapping-up insects with their thin, broad-based bills and breed in colonies; most species build mud nests above a void, on rock faces or buildings; Sand Martin digs a tunnel into a sandy bank. All are migrants, wintering in Africa.

Barn Swallow *Hirundo rustica*

IDENTIFICATION
17–19 cm, of which 2–7 cm are long tail streamers (longer in male). Black upperparts with a blue sheen, including rump, brick-red forehead; white underparts, brick-red throat with wide black band below, round white spot towards tip of each tail feather. Juvenile: pale throat and short streamers. Often perches on wires. **VOICE** Call: *vit* or *vit-vit*. Song: very rapid twitter, incorporating call notes. **HABITAT** Especially agricultural and rural areas but does occur in towns. Builds nest in an open building, a stable, hen shed; against a beam under the ceiling; half-cup of mud open at the top.

House Martin *Delichon urbicum*

IDENTIFICATION
14 cm. Smaller and without tail streamers of Barn Swallow. Black above with less blue sheen, white rump, white underparts right up to chin; all-black forked tail; white feathers on tarsus; grey underwing-coverts. Young are duller, with greyish underparts. **VOICE** Call: liquid *chirrrp*, twittering song incorporating call. **HABITAT** Breeds in colonies in towns and villages, also on cliffs. May hunt at a distance from colony. Nests on building, under an overhang, eaves of house or corner of a window, or overhang on cliff; nest is a closed half-ball of mud with small round entrance at top.

Sand Martin *Riparia riparia*

IDENTIFICATION
12 cm. Small, uniform brown above, white below with brown collar below a white throat (forming a slight downward point in its middle). Slightly forked brown tail. Juvenile: pale fringes to mantle and wing-coverts. In flight, brown underwing-coverts. **VOICE** Call: scratchy *tchrr*, shorter and less harsh than that of House Martin. **HABITAT** Breeds in large colonies in sandy banks of quarries, gravel pits, river banks; digs tunnel into the bank and nests in chamber at the end.

Crag Martin *Ptyonoprogne rupestris*

IDENTIFICATION
14 cm. Large, brown above with darker wings and tail, slightly forked tail, each tail feather with round white subterminal spot visible when tail is spread. Buff underparts with dark brown undertail-coverts, brown streaking on throat. In flight, thickset, with dark brown underwing-coverts. **VOICE** Call: *priit* or *chouit*. **HABITAT** Gorges and other craggy areas with cliffs for nesting; nest is a half-ball of mud under an overhang.

Red-rumped Swallow *Cecropis daurica*

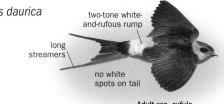

two-tone white-and-rufous rump

long streamers

no white spots on tail

Adult ssp. *rufula*

IDENTIFICATION
16–17 cm of which 5–6 cm are tail streamers, longer in male. Resembles Barn Swallow but has orangey rump, white throat finely streaked black, rufous nape and sides to neck encircling a small black crown; white undersides, buff wash to finely striped flanks. In flight, black undertail-coverts, no white spots on tail. Juvenile duller with pale fringes to wing feathers. The nominate Asian race, ssp. *daurica* (very rare vagrant to Europe): dense streaks on throat, breast and flanks, grey cheeks. **VOICE** Chirped *djuit* like a sparrow. **HABITAT** Mediterranean hillsides and foothills. Nests on cliffs or buildings, sometimes under a bridge; half-ball of mud with short access tunnel.

Adult ssp. *daurica*

black nape

streaked grey cheeks

fine but dense black streaks

black undertail-coverts

rufous nape

reddish rump

white throat

lightly streaked flanks

Adult ssp. *rufula*

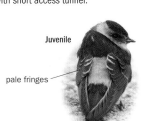

Juvenile

pale fringes

'American' Barn Swallow *Hirundo rustica erythrogaster*

17–19 cm. Nearctic race of Barn Swallow; as European race (p. 269) but juvenile has pale orange throat without black band below, just 2 dark patches on side of breast more or less touching, well-defined pale fringes on greater coverts and tertials, and underparts tinged rufous. Very rare vagrant to Europe (the Azores) in autumn.

Juvenile

orange throat without black border

black spot on side

Cliff Swallow *Petrochelidon pyrrhonota*

13 cm. Very rare Nearctic vagrant. Resembles House Martin but has rufous rump, whitish forehead, dark reddish throat and cheeks, grey collar; yellowish flanks and black undertail-coverts with white fringes.

buff collar

orange rump

dark brick-red throat

black underwing

orange rump

white forehead

rounded tail

dark throat

short tail

Brown-throated Martin *Riparia paludicola*

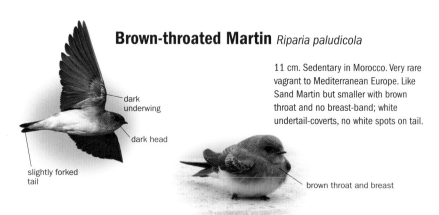

11 cm. Sedentary in Morocco. Very rare vagrant to Mediterranean Europe. Like Sand Martin but smaller with brown throat and no breast-band; white undertail-coverts, no white spots on tail.

dark underwing

dark head

slightly forked tail

brown throat and breast

Tree Swallow *Tachycineta bicolor*

15 cm. Nearctic hirundine, recorded in the Azores and Britain. Adult: bluish-black above and white below. Juvenile: blackish-brown above with smoky breast. Very similar to House Martin but has dark rump and small white crescents continue onto sides of base of rump. Dark grey underwing-coverts.

bluish-black above

white throat

white extends up onto sides

rump same as back

Purple Martin *Progne subis*

18 cm. Very large Nearctic swallow, vagrant to the Azores and Britain. Thickset, large dark head (including throat), broad wings with blackish undertail-coverts, finely streaked breast, slightly forked tail. Adult male has whole body bluish-black. Call: rolled *chairr*.

dark underwings

Immature

dark cheeks

scaly below

large bill

blackish-brown above

Juvenile

PIPITS Small, streaked terrestrial birds that walk on ground, with thin bills (slimmer than those of larks), and streaked breast and flanks. Often gregarious in winter and on migration. Species are very similar and are distinguished by intensity and amount of streaking above and below, head pattern, and amount of white in tail.

Tree Pipit *Anthus trivialis*

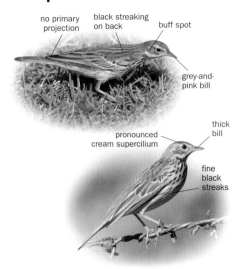

no primary projection — black streaking on back — buff spot — grey-and-pink bill — thick bill — pronounced cream supercilium — fine black streaks

IDENTIFICATION
15 cm. Very similar to Meadow Pipit but a little larger, more contrasting head pattern with buff supercilium, pale spot at back of cheeks, fine streaks on rear of flanks; pink base to bill; short rear claw. White outer tail feathers. **VOICE** Call: prolonged *tsii*, longer than call of Meadow Pipit. Sings from top of a tree, with repeated notes rising in intensity then flies up whilst singing to parachute downwards whilst giving repeated shrill notes. **HABITAT** Forest edges, clearings, meadows in wooded areas with isolated trees; open areas on migration.

Meadow Pipit *Anthus pratensis*

white sides — uniformly streaked mantle — pale lores — indistinct supercilium — grey-and-orange bill — broad black streaks — some birds are greyer

IDENTIFICATION
14.5 cm. Very similar to Tree Pipit but slightly smaller, more compact, broad streaks on rear of flanks, breast often more marked, more uniform head pattern, orangey base to bill. White outer tail feathers. Pale lores. Rear claw longer than that of Tree Pipit. **VOICE** Call: *tsui* or rolled *plit*. Song similar to that of Tree Pipit but less varied. **HABITAT** Moorland and wet meadows when breeding, often perching on fences; gregarious in pastures and coastal marshes in winter.

CONFUSION SPECIES

Corn Bunting (p. 404)

Skylark (p. 263)

Water Pipit *Anthus spinoletta*

IDENTIFICATION 17 cm. Summer: dark, only slightly streaked mantle, grey head, dark lores, white super–cilium, pinkish breast almost unstreaked. Winter: dark lores, well-defined white supercilium, only slightly streaked mantle, whitish and streaked below. White outer tail feathers. **VOICE** Call: *tsiip*, more scratchy than call of Meadow Pipit. Song: a long descending series of repeated notes given in song flight. **HABITAT** Alpine meadows in summer; rivers, wetlands and meadows in winter.

white supercilium
dark lores
grey head
pinkish breast
Breeding adult
slightly streaked mantle
dark lores
diffuse brown streaks
Winter
white edges to outer feathers

Rock Pipit *Anthus petrosus*

IDENTIFICATION 17 cm. Very similar to Water Pipit but darker. Dark lores, diffuse supercilium, streaked mantle, buff or greyish underparts with diffuse, dense streaking. Grey tips to outer tail feathers. Scandinavian race (ssp. *littoralis*) greyer with white tips to outer tail feathers, similar to Water Pipit but less well-defined supercilium, more streaked mantle and underparts. **VOICE** Call: soft, smothered *viisp*. **HABITAT** Rocky coasts, high tide line, sea wrack.

diffusely streaked brown mantle
dark face
diffuse black streaks
dark lores
diffuse broad streaks
buff edges to outer feathers
Ssp. *littoralis*

Red-throated Pipit *Anthus cervinus*

IDENTIFICATION 15 cm. Migrant, breeding in N Europe; rare spring and autumn passage migrant. Breeding: uniform orange or rufous face, female with black moustache. Autumn: like Meadow Pipit but more pronounced black stripes on mantle with obvious cream 'braces', more densely streaked breast and very heavy streaks on rear flanks, streaked rump; pale lores, yellow base to bill. **VOICE** Call: long *tsiiii*, more drawn-out than that of Tree Pipit. **HABITAT** Marshes, tundra.

heavily streaked back with pale 'braces'
pale lores
thick black malar-stripe
uniform orange face
Winter
Breeding adult
large black streaks
large black streaks
streaked rump
no primary projection

Tawny Pipit *Anthus campestris*

mantle hardly streaked

black lores

Adult

long tail

short claws

more obvious supercilium

streaked crown

more streaked mantle

Juvenile

IDENTIFICATION
16.5 cm. Long tail, pale colour with only slightly streaked sandy mantle; pronounced white supercilium, dark lores, very thin black malar-stripe, only slightly streaked breast. White outer tail feathers. Juveniles more streaked above and scaly on the wings. **VOICE** Call: chirped *chaip*, *tzip*. Song: fluty *tsi-lui*, slowly repeated. **HABITAT** Dunes, dry meadows, steppe with isolated bushes.

Berthelot's Pipit *Anthus berthelotii*

grey-brown and streaked

clear streaks

obvious supercilium

slightly streaked mantle

Worn plumage

Fresh plumage

IDENTIFICATION 14 cm. The smallest European pipit, with pronounced white supercilium and dark eye-stripe, bill with pink base, dull greyish-brown plumage, mantle hardly streaked (adult), or streaked with warmer colours (juvenile); white breast with short blackish-brown streaks. **VOICE** Call as that of Yellow Wagtail, song given in flight is a lively *chilp* repeated 5 to 7 times. **HABITAT** Open, stony or sandy environments with low vegetation. Endemic to the Canaries and Madeira.

Richard's Pipit *Anthus richardi*

18 cm. Siberian vagrant, a rare and localised migrant mainly found along coasts; gregarious and may overwinter. Large, thickset pipit, long legs, often stands upright. Rear claw longer than toe. Thick bill, marked head pattern, black streaking on breast, rufous wash on flanks. Dark pointed centres to median wing-coverts (not juveniles). Call: loud, explosive *pscheoo* given when taking flight or in flight.

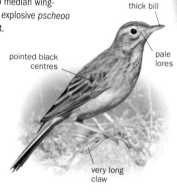

streaked mantle

thick bill

pointed black centres

pale lores

very long claws

very long claw

Blyth's Pipit *Anthus godlewskii*

17 cm. Siberian vagrant. Very difficult to separate from Richard's Pipit; a little smaller and more thickset, with short tail, shorter bill, shorter rear claw (same length as toe), more white in outer tail feathers, breast with bib of fine black streaks, more streaked mantle and crown, more contrasting head pattern with cheeks often reddish. In autumn, moulted median wing-coverts (not in juvenile) have a square anchor mark, less triangular than in Richard's Pipit. Two calls: a less explosive *pscheo* and chirped *chep* similar to that of Tawny Pipit.

pale lores

short bill

'bib' of thin short streaks

more streaked crown

black anchor-shaped centre

thinner bill

'bib' of small black streaks

black-and-white mantle

pink base

short primary projection

Pechora Pipit *Anthus gustavi*

thin black loral line

14 cm. Very rare Siberian vagrant. Resembles Red-throated Pipit but even more streaked above, black spot before eye, white supercilium indistinct behind eye, heavily streaked crown. Back striped black with very obvious white 'braces'. Two white wing-bars, short primary projection. Moves on the ground like a mouse. Call: *puit* or *pit* similar to call of Fan-tailed Warbler.

black-and-white patch

very obvious white supercilium

fine streaks on flanks

Olive-backed Pipit *Anthus hodgsoni*

only slightly streaked olive mantle

14.5 cm. Siberian vagrant, rare in autumn, exceptional in winter. Resembles a small Tree Pipit but has more contrasting head pattern with white supercilium behind eye (buff in front) underlined with black, black-and-white spots at rear of cheek, olive-brown lightly streaked back. Call: *tsiii*, a little longer than that of Tree Pipit.

mantle hardly streaked

Ssp. *rubescens*

pale lores

tawny wash to breast

more marked streaks

pale lores

white sides to outer tail feathers

greyer plumage

Ssp. *japonicus*

Buff-bellied Pipit *Anthus rubescens*

17 cm. Nominate race (ssp. *rubescens*) is a very rare Nearctic vagrant. Very similar to Rock and Water Pipits in winter, but lores pale like supercilium, less grey-olive, more diffuse streaks on underparts, fine streaks on buff-washed flanks, more streaked mantle but less than Meadow Pipit; white outer tail feathers. The Siberian race (ssp. *japonicus*) is similar but more olive-brown above, white underparts; winters in small numbers in Middle East. Call: a rapid, metallic *psipp* repeated several times on taking flight.

WAGTAILS Closely related to pipits but no streaking on mantle or underparts and a long black tail with white sides that is often wagged (hence the name). Spend much time on ground walking, undulating flight. Form roosts on migration and in winter.

Yellow Wagtail *Motacilla flava*

grey head

white supercilium

brown-grey mantle

spots on breast

lemon-yellow throat

Juvenile

often little yellow below

Male ssp. *flava*

olive-grey back

Female ssp. *flava*

whitish throat

pale yellow below

yellow head

olive cheek and crown

Male ssp. *flavissima*

pale bluish-grey head

Hybrid male *flava × flavissima*

white cheek

IDENTIFICATION 17 cm. Male bright yellow below, female pale yellow with white belly. Olive-green back, black wings with broad white or cream fringes to tertials and greater coverts. Different head pattern according to race, that of female recalling that of male. Juvenile is duller, sometime very grey, has buff wash to black-spotted breast; undertail-coverts more or less yellow. **VOICE** Call: rising, liquid *tsuip*. Song: slow indecisive repetition of notes similar to call, given from a perch, fence or tall plant. **HABITAT** Wetlands, along ditches of water meadows, reedbeds and also farmland, rape fields and pastures. Migrant, wintering in Africa.

GEOGRAPHIC VARIATION Separated by hybridisation zones where intermediates are frequent. Ssp. *flava* common on continent (ash-grey head, white supercilium, yellow throat); ssp. *flavissima* in Britain and near-continent (olive-green crown and cheeks, yellow

continued overleaf

Male ssp. *cinereocapilla*

dark grey head

no supercilium

white throat

supercilium and throat, head sometimes nearly all-yellow; **ssp. *cinereocapilla*** in SE Europe (dark grey head, white throat); **ssp. *iberiae*** in Iberia and N Africa (dark grey head, white supercilium and throat): **ssp. *thunbergi*** in Scandinavia (very dark uniform grey head, yellow throat, rolled call); **ssp. *feldegg***, from E Europe, a rare migrant to west (dark black crown extending onto nape, yellow throat, well marked wing-bars, call a very rolled *prriiai*). Intermediates occur that have short supercilium, white moustache, etc. Other eastern subspecies: ssp. *lutea* with lemon-yellow head and yellow wing-

Male ssp. *iberiae*

dark grey head

narrow white supercilium

white throat

dark blue-grey crown extends to nape

no supercilium

yellow throat

Male ssp. *thunbergi*

narrow white supercilium

dark grey head

yellow throat

Male hybrid *iberiae* × *flava*

white to very pale grey head

Male ssp. *leucocephala*

yellow throat

intense black crown

yellow throat

Male ssp. *feldegg*

bars; ssp. *leucocephala* with white head (often has trace of grey patterning); black-headed forms close to or intermediate with *feldegg*: *superciliaris* (white supercilium), *melanogrisea* (white moustache), *xanthophrys* (yellow supercilium). Asian subspecies, possible vagrants that have harsher call; juveniles without yellow in autumn resemble Citrine Wagtail: ssp. *tschutschensis* (resembles *flava*, very harsh call), *taivana* (black cheeks, green head, yellow throat and supercilium), *macronyx* (similar to *thunbergi*), *plexa* (similar to *cinereocapilla*).

green crown

green cheek with yellow centre

Hybrid male *lutea* × *beema*

all-yellow head

black head

white supercilium

'*superciliaris*' form

Male ssp. *lutea*

yellow supercilium

darker cheeks

Male ssp. *talvana*

black head

narrow yellow supercilium

'*xanthophrys*' form

dark edges

very similar to *flava*

mouse-grey above

Male ssp. *tschutschensis*

dark mottling

Juvenile of *tschutschensis* type

often no yellow or olive tint

White Wagtail *Motacilla alba alba*

black crown — white face

grey mantle

Breeding male

big black 'bib'

grey on crown

Breeding female

obvious white wing-bars

white throat

long black tail with white sides

Winter adult

pale grey head

Juvenile — whitish head

white flanks

different black-and-white head pattern

no yellow

Male ssp. *subpersonata*

white mask on black face

Male ssp. *personata* — much white

white face

black collar

much white

Female ssp. *leucopsis*

IDENTIFICATION
18 cm. Long tail, tricoloured plumage, grey, black and white. White head with black crown from above eye to nape, grey mantle, well-defined border with nape (male) or diffuse (female); black throat and bib reduced to a black band in winter. Grey mantle, black wings with white fringes to wing-coverts and tertials. Black bill and legs. Flanks white or washed pale grey, dark grey uppertail-coverts. Female with grey crown in winter, like juvenile. **VOICE** Call: soft *chilip*. Song: short phrase, sometimes babbled, incorporating call. **HABITAT** Breeds in rural environments, near farms, around buildings. Winters in fields, near water, even in towns.

MOROCCAN WAGTAIL *M. a. subpersonata* (N Africa): 1 record from Corsica. Head has different black-and-white pattern, with much black, white moustache and forehead, white crescent below eye, white spot on side of neck, grey mantle. Two Asian subspecies occur as rare vagrants. **MASKED WAGTAIL** *M. a. personata* (Central Asia): black head and breast, small white mask, dark grey mantle, white greater coverts; **AMUR WAGTAIL** *M. a. leucopsis* (China): male has white face, black mantle (grey in female), black crescent on breast, white greater coverts contrast with the rest, which are black.

Pied Wagtail *Motacilla alba yarrellii*

18 cm. British race of White Wagtail. Male has black mantle, back and uppertail-coverts. Female has coal-grey mantle. In winter, dark grey flanks, black or blackish uppertail-coverts, darker mantle. Call harsher and more rolling than White Wagtail, *chirrup*. Hybrids possible.

mix of dark grey and black on mantle

Winter female

black mantle

Winter male

blackish-grey rump

charcoal flanks

very broad white edges

blackish-grey flanks

Grey Wagtail *Motacilla cinerea*

IDENTIFICATION 18 cm. Grey mantle and head, white moustache and supercilium; black (male) or white (female and winter) throat. Lemon-yellow underparts, limited to lower belly and undertail-coverts in juvenile. Black wings with white edges to tertials. Longer tail than Yellow Wagtail, no olive tone to mantle. **VOICE** Call: loud *tii* or *tliii*. Song: the same notes in series, *tii-tii-tii...* **HABITAT** Banks of rivers and streams and mountain torrents in summer. Near water, even in towns, in winter.

ash-grey upperparts and head

white supercilium

black throat

very long tail

bright yellow

ash-grey mantle

bright yellow

Breeding male

pink legs

white throat

Female

Juvenile

bright yellow only under tail

cream breast

Citrine Wagtail *Motacilla citreola*

IDENTIFICATION 17 cm. Male: lemon-yellow head with black nape, grey mantle (ssp. *citreola*), black wings with broad white fringes to coverts and tertials. Female: face washed yellow, grey crown and cheeks, white belly and undertail-coverts, pale surrounds to cheeks. Juvenile in autumn: broad white supercilium extends to encircle cheek, dark line over supercilium above eye, broad white fringes to wing-coverts. **VOICE** Loud, rolled *tzrri*. **HABITAT** Marshes.

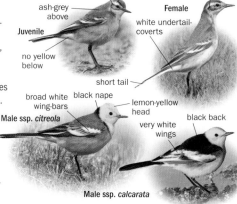

white supercilium underlined with black

cheek surrounded by white

cheek surrounded with yellow

ash-grey above

Juvenile

Female

white undertail-coverts

no yellow below

short tail

broad white wing-bars

black nape

lemon-yellow head

Male ssp. *citreola*

very white wings

black back

Male ssp. *calcarata*

ACCENTORS, WREN AND DIPPER Small insectivorous passerines with thin bills, usually seen on the ground. Wren is a widespread resident and Dipper is the only aquatic passerine in the region.

Alpine Accentor *Prunella collaris*

white spots

black-and-white speckled throat

pointed rufous streaks

Winter

yellow base to bill

little streaking on rump

heavy reddish-brown streaks

Summer

orange-pink legs

IDENTIFICATION
18 cm. Larger and more thickset than Dunnock, also has ashy-grey head and neck, but black-and-white mottled throat, broad reddish streaks on flanks and belly, grey mantle streaked black. Diagnostic black upper mandible with yellow base, yellow lower mandible with black tip. **VOICE** Song: muffled and ill-defined, reminiscent of that of Skylark as much as Dunnock. Call: *truiririp* or *tchurp*. **HABITAT** High mountains, scree and alpine meadows; descends even into villages in winter, often seen around ski resort restaurants. Occurs over 2,000 m when breeding; disperses in winter often far and at low altitude, sometimes in small flocks.

Black-throated Accentor *Prunella atrogularis*

black crown and cheeks

orange supercilium

traces of black on throat

orange wash to breast

Juvenile

15 cm. Rare Siberian vagrant. Habits and silhouette like those of Dunnock but has buff supercilium and moustache, blackish crown and cheeks, dark throat with pale speckles, warm brown mantle streaked black, buff breast and flanks with diffuse streaks.

Dunnock *Prunella modularis*

IDENTIFICATION
14.5 cm. Rather nondescript and unassuming; few characteristic features. Ashy-grey head with browner crown and cheeks, especially in female. Brown mantle streaked black, streaked buff flanks; reddish iris. Juvenile duller and streaked below, brown iris. **VOICE** Song: rapid bursts of shrill notes that may recall Wren, but shorter. **HABITAT** All environments with bushes, forests, farmland, urban areas, alpine meadows.

grey head
red iris
slim bill
reddish-brown mantle strongly streaked black
streaked brown flanks

Adult

dark brown iris

Juvenile

Siberian Accentor *Prunella montanella*

14 cm. Very rare Siberian vagrant, in winter. Very similar to Black-throated Accentor but warmer brown mantle, distinctively orange supercilium, uniform buff throat with no trace of black, black cheek with buff spot at rear. Call as that of Dunnock.

orange supercilium
black cheek
rufous above
uniform orange throat

(Eurasian) **Wren** *Troglodytes troglodytes*

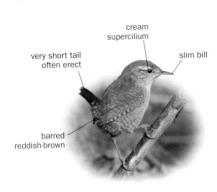

cream
supercilium

very short tail
often erect

slim bill

barred
reddish-brown

IDENTIFICATION 9.5 cm. Very small, entirely reddish-brown finely barred with black on wings and tail, with a short tail often held vertical. Indistinct pale supercilium, paler underparts, thin bill, pink legs. Short, round wings with direct, rapid flight. **VOICE** Call: a rattle or shrill *tic*. Song: shrill and energetic, rapid succession of varied notes, very loud for such a small bird. **HABITAT** Undergrowth in woodlands, bushes in parks and gardens, hedgerows in more open environments.

(White-throated) **Dipper** *Cinclus cinclus*

bill slightly
upturned

extensive
white 'bib'

rufous
band

Ssp. *aquaticus*

Ssp. *cinclus*

all-black belly

IDENTIFICATION 18 cm. Round body, very short tail, big head; extensive white bib, chestnut belly (ssp. *aquaticus* in central Europe, Britain and Ireland) or totally blackish (ssp. *cinclus* in much of continent, winter vagrant to Britain). Rest of plumage brown. Thin black bill, reddish-brown iris. Juvenile mottled grey above and below. **VOICE** Call: sharp *zit*, often repeated 2–4 times. Babbling song, sharp notes often barely audible against background of running water. **HABITAT** Fast flowing rivers and streams, mountain torrents in summer, large rivers in winter. Hunts insect larvae underwater, walking on the riverbed against the current.

ROBINS AND CHATS Small insectivorous passerines with thin bills, usually seen on the ground.

European Robin
Erithacus rubecula

IDENTIFICATION 14 cm. Very common. Dull brown above, dark orange face and breast encircled with blue-grey on neck. Buff-washed flanks, white belly. Terminal spots on greater coverts and tertials; sometimes a few also in adults, pointed, of darker colour. Newly fledged juvenile has scaly plumage and no orange on face. **VOICE** Song: from exposed perch, cheerful warble of high-pitched notes, accelerating and decelerating. Call: sharp, piercing *tsii*, or short repeated crisp *pit*. **HABITAT** Forests, copses, hedgerows, parks and gardens, even in urban areas.

uniform brown

reddish spots decrease in size inwards

extensive orange 'bib'

Adult

very scaly

no orange

Juvenile

First-winter

same-sized ochre spots

'Canary Islands' Robin *Erithacus rubecula superbus*

13 cm. Endemic race of European Robin, restricted to Tenerife and Grand Canary; sometimes considered a separate species on the basis of genetic differences. Broader blue-grey surround to orange face, rounder wings and a different song.

clear eye-ring

very wide grey band

Common Nightingale *Luscinia megarhynchos*

warm brown above

dark rufous tail

uniform cream breast

pink legs

IDENTIFICATION
16.5 cm. Big and slim, long tail often cocked, stands upright, long legs. Warm brown mantle, reddish tail. Plain face with large black eye. Uniform breast and flanks washed buff. Seven primaries visible on closed wing; outer primary longer than primary coverts. **VOICE** Song: melodious, loud, fluid, often given at night, each phrase of notes lasting a few seconds and repeated louder and louder, followed by a cascade of notes. Call: muffled *trrr* or loud *huit*. **HABITAT** Bushes, hedgerows, dense coppice, forest edges. The eastern race (ssp. *golzii*) is slimmer and duller, with grey supercilium and pale edges to wing-coverts and flight feathers, resembling Rufous Bush Robin.

more pronounced supercilium

beige-grey colour

pale reddish tail

Ssp. *golzii*

clear pale edges

Thrush Nightingale *Luscinia luscinia*

earth-brown

sometimes slightly mottled

reddish dark brown tail

mottled breast

IDENTIFICATION
16.5 cm. Like Nightingale but duller; grey-brown mantle, less reddish, darker tail; bib of diffuse spots on breast, often joining a dark malar-stripe. Only 8 primaries visible on closed wing; outer primary shorter than primary coverts. **VOICE** Song: louder but less musical than Common Nightingale. Calls: identical. **HABITAT** Dense undergrowth, bushes.

Bluethroat *Luscinia svecica*

IDENTIFICATION
14 cm. Usually on the ground, often upright. Dark grey-brown above, black inverted T on tail as wheatear, except on rufous, not white, background. White supercilium, yellow base to bill, black legs. Male: extensive blue bib bordered with black and red bands; coloured spot in centre of bib, white in ssp. *cyanecula* and smaller in ssp. *namnetum* from central and W Europe, red in larger ssp. *svecica* from N Europe. Blue is a little darker in *namnetum,* white spot sometimes absent in *cyanecula*, very small black band in *svecica*. Females are duller with dark brown malar-stripe and breast-band, sometimes a few blue feathers on the throat, buff flanks. Juvenile: cream or rufous tips to greater coverts. In autumn plumage duller, but male always has at least a few blue feathers on bib. Moults in autumn before migrating. **VOICE** Song: short melodious phrases with imitations. Call: dry *tac tac* or sometimes *huit* like nightingale.
HABITAT Ancient or grazed reedbeds with bushes, rarely with standing water; ditches in saltmarshes, meadows, polders; occasionally rape fields and other cultivated areas.

Male ssp. *cyanecula*

white spot

extensive blue 'bib'

black band

orange band

Adult male

cream supercilium

orange base to tail

red spot

Male ssp. *svecica*

Male ssp. *namnetum*
smaller size

orange bar sometimes reduced

ochre spots on greater coverts

black malar-stripe

little or no blue

Juvenile

Rufous Bush Robin *Cercotrichas galactotes*

Ssp. *galactotes*

reddish mantle

very pronounced supercilium

long rufous tail with black-and-white tip, often raised

earth-brown above

rufous tail

Ssp. *syriacus*

15 cm. Reminiscent of Nightingale with its long tail often raised and terrestrial habits. Rufous tail with characteristic black-and-white tip, narrow black moustache; white undertail-coverts; long pink legs. Rufous upperparts in ssp. *galactotes* of SW Europe, brownish-grey upperparts in ssp. *syriacus* of SE Europe. Call: drawn out *siiip*.

White-throated Robin *Irania gutturalis*

white supercilium, black cheek and white throat

Male

black tail

orange underparts

bluish-grey above

Female

black tail

orange flanks

black legs

17 cm. Like a large, slim redstart; grey upperparts with blackish tail, with long black legs and bill. Male: long white supercilium, black face with white triangle on throat, orange underparts. Female: brownish-grey with pale throat, orange band along flanks. Breeds in the Caucasus, common migrant in Arabian Peninsula.

REDSTARTS Reddish tail with brown centre, often flicked when alert and upright. Males more colourful than females. Hybrids between two species possible; male has streaks at border between orange and black.

Black Redstart *Phoenicurus ochruros*

IDENTIFICATION
14.5 cm. Juvenile and female entirely coal-grey except for reddish tail and orange undertail-coverts. Male: European race (ssp. *gibraltariensis*) blackish with grey upperparts, paler belly, white edges to secondaries forming a white panel. Turkey to Iran race (ssp. *ochruros*): black breast grading to rufous belly. Middle Eastern race (ssp. *semirufus*): bright orange belly, sharply defined from black breast; blackish above. Central Asian race (ssp. *phoenicuroides*): grey above, orange belly, long wings, resembles Common Redstart. **VOICE** Call: *hit* and *tac*. Song: begins with a few rising sharp notes followed by a sound like rustling paper and a short whistled phrase. **HABITAT** Scree, cliffs, towns and villages.

dark grey

grey underparts

Female
ssp. *gibraltariensis*

grey crown

white panel

black face

Male
ssp. *gibraltariensis*

Juvenile

orange tail

hardly any tail

Male ssp. *semirufus*

extensive black breast

grey crown

black throat

First-winter ssp. *phoenicuroides*

orange undertail-coverts

reduced white forehead

ash-grey mantle

Male ssp. *phoenicuroides*

black breast

Male ssp. *ochruros*

orange belly

orange lower belly

Common Redstart *Phoenicurus phoenicurus*

pure white edges form a large panel

ash-grey above

white forehead

black throat

Male ssp. *samamisicus*

Male

cream fringes

dark throat

orange breast

pale face

orange-cream underparts

Autumn juvenile male

orange tail

Female

IDENTIFICATION
14 cm. Female like female Black Redstart but paler underparts, beige with buff flanks, upperparts more sandy. Male has black face and throat, white forehead, grey upperparts, orange-red breast and belly, uniform wings. Black bill and legs. Buff fringes to wing feathers in autumn, cream fringes to face and throat in male. Eastern ssp. *samamisicus* has prominent white edges to secondaries and tertials forming a wing panel. **VOICE** Call: *huit* or *hi-tuc-tuc*. Song: short, starting with a few repeated notes *hi-hu-hu* followed by a rapid trill. **HABITAT** Open environments with trees, clearings, open forest, parks.

Red-flanked Bluetail *Tarsiger cyanurus*

bluish rump and tail

orange flanks

white throat surrounded by brown

blue above

white supercilium

orange flanks

blue tail

Breeding male

IDENTIFICATION
14 cm. Resembles a small thicket Robin. Male is dark blue above, with white supercilium and orange flanks. Female is earth-brown above with bluish rump and tail, orange flanks and white throat encircled by brown bib. Black bill and legs. Juvenile male has bluish wing-coverts, brownish-grey in juvenile female. **VOICE** Call: *tek-tek*. **HABITAT** Taiga forest.

VAGRANT REDSTARTS Three species; one African, the other two Asian, very rare in Europe; females difficult to identify.

Moussier's Redstart *Phoenicurus moussieri*

12 cm. Small redstart. Male: black above, orange-red below, long white supercilium from forehead to nape, large white wing patch. Female: as female Common Redstart but bright orange belly. Breeds in N Africa, rare vagrant to France, Malta, Spain and Britain.

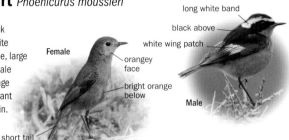

long white band
black above
white wing patch
orangey face
bright orange below
Female
Male
short tail

Eversmann's Redstart *Phoenicurus erythronotus*

15 cm. A Central Asian redstart; possible winter vagrant (2 old Russian records). Male: grey crown, black mask, orange back, white bar on shoulder, white spot at base of primaries. Female: orangey below. First-winter has white fringes to wing-coverts and tertials.

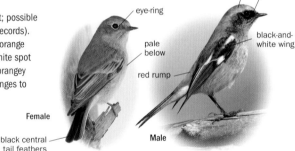

grey crown
black mask
eye-ring
pale below
red rump
black-and-white wing
Female
Male
black central tail feathers

Güldenstädt's Redstart *Phoenicurus erythrogaster*

16 cm. Large redstart from the Caucasus mountains; a few European records (possibly escapes). Male tricoloured with white crown and base of flight feathers, black breast, cheeks and mantle, rest of underparts and tail rufous-red. Female like Common Redstart, pale below but with thicker bill and uniform red tail.

brown-grey above
white crown
black above
pale below
red belly
Female
Male

VAGRANT CHATS Three Asian species closely related to the nightingales, already recorded in Europe in autumn.

Siberian Rubythroat *Luscinia calliope*

black lores

Male

dull greyish-brown above

red 'bib'

15 cm. Uniform brown chat with narrow white supercilium and black lores, warm brown below with pale moustache; male has bright red bib with a black border. Breeds in the Urals and further east; very rare vagrant to Europe.

narrow white supercilium

Female

black lores

pink legs

Female

uniform face

delicate scaly 'bib'

Siberian Blue Robin *Luscinia cyane*

12.5 cm. Small, short tail, pale pink legs. The blue-and-white male cannot be confused; female rather dull, all-brown with black eye on uniform face and blue tint to tail. Very shy and unconfiding, spends most of time on the ground. A few records from Britain and Spain.

pale pink legs

dark blue above

short tail

black face

black flanks

Male

cream spectacles

short reddish tail

breast heavily scaled with brown

Rufous-tailed Robin *Luscinia sibilans*

14 cm. Similar to Thrush Nightingale but smaller, has short rufous tail, underparts marked with brown chevrons, appearing scaly on breast, and pink legs. A few recent records from Britain and Poland.

pale pink legs

STONECHATS Small chats, closely related to wheatears. Often perch on tall plants or bushes, nervous, with short tail. Tricoloured plumage with black or brown, white and orange. Females browner.

Whinchat *Saxicola rubetra*

IDENTIFICATION
12.5 cm. Male: black head with white supercilium, white moustache and orange underparts; blackish mantle and rump with brown feather fringes, white sides to base of tail similar to wheatears. Female browner.
VOICE Call: *tic-tic*. Song: short babbled phrase similar to that of Common Stonechat. **HABITAT** Meadows in river valleys, alpine meadows.

white supercilium
black cheek
orange breast
brown cheek
Male
orangey breast
Female
short tail with white base

Common Stonechat *Saxicola rubicola*

IDENTIFICATION
12.5 cm. Male: black head, mantle and tail; white spot on each side of neck, white rump, black centres to uppertail-coverts; orange breast. Female: less contrasting, dark brown head and underparts, dark throat. The ssp. *rubicola* occurs in continental Europe; ssp. *hibernans* of Britain and NW Europe is darker on the rump.
VOICE Call: plaintive *uit* and dry *tac*. Song: short babbled phrase similar to that of Common Whitethroat. **HABITAT** Open environments, meadows with bushes, heathlands.

brown cheek
white half-collar
Male
black tail
white wing patch
dark throat
Female
black head
orange breast
Winter male
streaked uppertail-coverts
Breeding male

Siberian Stonechat *Saxicola maurus*

pronounced cream supercilium

very pale

white throat

unstreaked cream or rufous rump

Female ssp. *maurus*

black cheek and brown crown

pale brown-streaked back

Winter male ssp. *hemprichii*

white base to tail feathers, reduced here

almost complete white collar

all-black tail

Male ssp. *maurus*

reduced orange breast

thick bill

First-winter ssp. *stejnegeri*

rufous rump

possibly black shafts

white base to tail feathers, extensive here

Male ssp. *hemprichii*

12.5 cm. Replaces Common Stonechat in Siberia and the Orient. Male of Siberian ssp. *maurus* has a very wide white collar reaching the nape; reduced orange on breast, long wings, extensive pale rump, uniform pale uppertail-coverts without central black line. Female: very pale, uniform pale uppertail-coverts, cream throat. Central Asian ssp. *hemprichii* has white at base of outer tail feathers, especially on inner webs. The Caucasus ssp. *variegatus* has a little white at base of outer tail feathers (less than *hemprichii*, under the uppertail-coverts, mainly visible in the hand). East Asian ssp. *stejnegeri* has wholly black tail feathers, dark rufous rump, sometimes black central streaks on some larger uppertail-coverts.

Male ssp. *variegatus*

black coverts

Male ssp. *variegatus*

a little white

white hardly visible

Male ssp. *maurus*

much white, especially on inner webs

Male ssp. *hemprichii*

no white on tail feathers

pale supercilium

long bill

Female

Fuerteventura Stonechat *Saxicola dacotiae*

IDENTIFICATION 12 cm. Small stonechat with long bill giving a slender appearance. Male: black head, white throat, short narrow white supercilium, brown rump streaked black. Female: buff-brown finely streaked above, streaked rump, cream underparts. **VOICE** As Common Stonechat. **HABITAT** Endemic to Fuerteventura (Canary Islands); rocky hillsides with sparse trees or bushes.

white supercilium

Male

orange breast

Pied Bush Chat *Saxicola caprata*

14 cm. Rare vagrant from Central Asia, recorded in Cyprus. A little larger than Common Stonechat, male all-black with white rump and vent, white patch on shoulders. Female brownish-grey, paler below, white lower belly, rufous rump.

all black

white shoulder

white rump

WHEATEARS Terrestrial, often perching on the ground, or low rock or boulder. Most are easily recognised by their white tail marked with a black inverted T, the shape of the terminal bar helping to identify each species. Migratory.

Northern Wheatear *Oenanthe oenanthe*

black eye-stripe
ash-grey mantle
orangish throat
black wings
narrow brown eye-stripe
large white supercilium

Male

white sides to tail

Female

long cream supercilium

cream-and-rufous fringes on wing

orangish underparts

Juvenile

IDENTIFICATION
15 cm. Male: ash-grey above, white below, yellow wash on breast, slender black line through eye; white tail with big black T, terminal bar of constant width; white rump visible in flight. Female: browner, less contrasting plumage. In autumn, brown-grey mantle, orange to rufous fringes on wing. Some large migrants with brighter orange underparts are from Greenland (ssp. *leucorhoa*).
VOICE Call: grating dry *tac*, often repeated. Song: melodious short babble.
HABITAT Short grassland, on the coast or in mountainous areas; steppe, short chalk grasslands, dunes. Any open habitat on migration.

Seebohm's Wheatear *Oenanthe seebohmi*

white supercilium
Male
black throat and mask
black lores

Female

15 cm. Replaces Northern Wheatear in N Africa, recently observed in Iberia. Formerly considered to be a subspecies of Northern. Male has black throat (sometimes joining wing), black underwings, narrow tail bar, orange wash on undertail-coverts. Female has dark lores and sometimes throat.

Black-eared Wheatear *Oenanthe hispanica*

IDENTIFICATION
14.5 cm.
Breeding: tan
with black mask
and cheek
extending onto
throat in some males (dark-throated
form). Black wings isolated from black
throat. White tail with variable, irregular
terminal bar, wider on outer part than
centre. Orangish breast. In autumn,
broad rufous fringes on wing, pale
brown mantle without pale edges. **VOICE**
Call: *tac* or an alarm call *iiit*. Song:
Rasping dry babble, with imitations.
HABITAT Short limestone grassland on
rocky hillsides.

black mask

tan mantle

black
wing

Male ssp. *hispanica*

large white
base to tail

black throat

Male ssp. *hispanica*
(black-throated form)

faint supercilium

brown-grey above

orangish
breast

Female

much white
in tail

'Eastern' Black-eared Wheatear *Oenanthe (hispanica) melanoleuca*

14.5 cm. Eastern European race (from
Italy eastwards), sometimes considered
a separate species. As Iberian race but
male whiter, with black mask extending
above the bill on forehead. No orange
coloration, crown often grey.

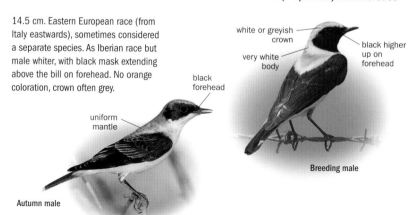

white or greyish
crown

black higher
up on
forehead

very white
body

black
forehead

uniform
mantle

Breeding male

Autumn male

Isabelline Wheatear *Oenanthe isabellina*

short supercilium
black lores
grey lores
Male
sandy mantle
buff breast
Female
often very upright posture
contrasting black alula
little white at tail base
short tail

IDENTIFICATION
16.5 cm. Similar to female Northern Wheatear but longer legs, shorter tail with broader black terminal band, black lores and pronounced white supercilium especially in front of eye, diffuse behind. Sandy colour above without grey tones; underparts washed buff. Blackish alula contrasts with the cream-coloured edges of the wing-coverts. Sexes similar but male has blacker lores. **VOICE** Call a loud *tchip*. **HABITAT** Steppe and rocky hillsides.

Pied Wheatear *Oenanthe pleschanka*

Var. *vittata*
white throat
white crown
black throat
Breeding male
mottled brownish-grey mantle
indistinct supercilium
mottled breast
Female
mottled mantle
dark throat
a lot of white in tail
scaly mantle
Winter male
black T extends along sides
Female

IDENTIFICATION
14.5 cm. Male black and white with greyish-white cap. In autumn, similar to Black-eared Wheatear but dull grey-brown mantle with scaly pale feather edgings. Female and first-winter like Black-eared but greyer and darker. **VOICE** Much like Black-eared Wheatear. **HABITAT** Open dry areas with some vegetation.

Cyprus Wheatear *Oenanthe cypriaca*

IDENTIFICATION
14.5 cm. Sexes similar; very similar to male Pied Wheatear but shorter primary projection; black extends farther down the back, grey centre of crown and nape, orange wash on breast. In winter, dark grey crown and nape, cream supercilium extends to nape, dark orange breast and belly, black mantle with pale scaly edgings. **VOICE** Song: hard *biz-biz-biz...* **HABITAT** Barren rocky habitats with bushes. Endemic to Cyprus, migrant.

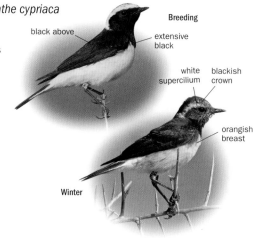

Breeding

black above

extensive black

white supercilium

blackish crown

orangish breast

Winter

Finsch's Wheatear *Oenanthe finschii*

15.5 cm. Breeds in rocky habitats with low sparse scrub, particularly in Turkey; migrant, possible vagrant to shores of Black and Aegean Seas. Black terminal tail-band of constant width; male similar to Pied Wheatear but white back. Female grey with reddish-brown cheeks.

white crown and mantle

black head

even black band

Desert Wheatear *Oenanthe deserti*

14.5 cm. Breeds in N Africa and Central Asia; rare spring and autumn vagrant to European coasts; rocky habitats, dunes and steppe. Sandy colour, tail entirely black. Male: black cheek and throat joins black shoulder and wing. Female: broad diffuse supercilium, pale cheeks and throat in autumn, greyish in summer. Large white rump.

white band

tail appears entirely black

black throat

indistinct supercilium

brownish-grey mantle

Male

white at very base of outer tail feathers

Female

Black Wheatear *Oenanthe leucura*

black crown

tail with broad
regular black
terminal band

plump
body

IDENTIFICATION
18 cm. Sedentary.
Large; entirely
black plumage
except for white
rump and tail-
coverts; white-based tail with black T, with
wide marginal band of constant width.
Female similar but duller. **VOICE** Song is a
muted twittering sometimes given in flight.
HABITAT Dry, rocky, sloping ground and cliffs.

White-crowned Wheatear *Oenanthe leucopyga*

white crown
in adult

Adult

slim
silhouette

18 cm. Breeds in stony desert around the Sahara and in the
Middle East; very rare vagrant. Large, black plumage, large white
rump, white tail with black centre and a few irregular black
spots. Immature has black crown, becoming white after a year.

black crown

First-year

outer tail feathers
almost completely white

slightly reddish
cheek

Kurdish Wheatear *Oenanthe xanthoprymna*

Female

greyish
neck

brownish-
grey back

white supercilium

Male

black
throat

black-and-
rufous tail

reddish rump
and tail base

15 cm. Breeds in Kurdistan, winters
around the Red Sea in rocky habitats.
One European record, from France in
May 2015. White sides to tail, reddish in
first-winter birds. Male: grey mantle,
black throat, white supercilium, rufous
undertail-coverts. Female: quite uniform
brown-grey, pale lores, throat sometimes
dark, white supercilium in front of eye.

ROCK THRUSHES Close relatives of wheatears, but larger, resembling small, short-tailed thrushes. Males very colourful, females and young duller with scaly plumage. They are migratory, occupying rocky habitats.

(Common) Rock Thrush *Monticola saxatilis*

IDENTIFICATION
19 cm. Male: tricoloured, slate-blue head, neck, mantle and rump, white back, orange-red breast, belly and tail-coverts; reddish tail with dark centre. Female: brown above with cream fringes, cream and orange below, reddish tail. As from July male moults and resembles female. Wings almost as long as tail. **VOICE** Call: *tak*, sometimes in series. Short song, fluty and melodious sometimes includes imitations. **HABITAT** Mountainous scree.

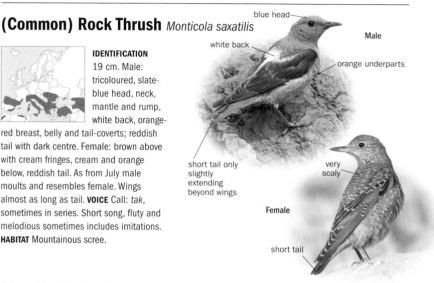

blue head

Male

white back

orange underparts

short tail only slightly extending beyond wings

very scaly

Female

short tail

Blue Rock Thrush *Monticola solitarius*

IDENTIFICATION 20 cm. Male: dark blue, black wings and tail; tail very much longer than wings; appears all black at a distance. Female: slightly bluish-grey, scaly black markings above, much black and cream barring on underparts. Young similar to female. Long black bill, black legs. **VOICE** Call: *tchuc tchuc* or *piip*. Song: similar to Mistle Thrush but shorter. **HABITAT** Rocky hillsides, scree, cliffs in gorges or plateaus, in warm climates.

Female

scaly underparts with buff-and-black markings

long tail

long bill

Male

dark blue body

black wings

CONFUSION SPECIES

Blackbird
(p. 304)

Northern
Wheatear
(p. 298)

THRUSHES Large passerines with melodious fluty songs; feed on the ground on woodland floor or in meadows, especially on worms, snails and fruit. Migrate or disperse for the winter.

Male
yellow eye-ring
orange-yellow bill
all black
yellow-and-brown bill
quite uniform brown plumage
breast often mottled
tail already black in young males
Female
rufous mottled breast
reddish spots on coverts
Juvenile
Male ssp. *torquatus*
nearly uniform underparts
brown-and-yellow bill
dark brown plumage
white fringes
yellow bill
dirty white crescent
white 'bib'
belly with white scales
Male ssp. *alpestris*
Female
pale fringes
yellow-based bill
hint of a 'bib'
Juvenile
scaly belly

Blackbird *Turdus merula*

IDENTIFICATION
24 cm. Male: totally black with orange-yellow bill and eye-ring. First-year male with more or less black bill. Female: brown, uniform or mottled below, sometimes slightly reddish. Juvenile: spotted, young males with darker wings and tail. **VOICE** Melodious song, long fluty phrases of mellow notes given from a prominent perch. Various calls: deep *chock*, loud nervous *chink*, *tritritritritrii* on taking flight. **HABITAT** Almost everywhere, from forests to city centres, throughout the year.

Ring Ouzel *Turdus torquatus*

IDENTIFICATION
23 cm. Similar to Blackbird but with pale fringes below; pale crescent on breast, white (male) or buff and barred (female); white edges to flight feathers and coverts. Prominent pale wing edges and well-marked scales in ssp. *alpestris* (S Europe), not so well marked in ssp. *torquatus* (N Europe). Male black with yellow eye-ring and bill; female brown. **VOICE** Song: different, repetition of a few babbled notes; various calls: *tcho tcho*, alarm call a rapid, metallic, muffled *tac-tac-tac-tac*... **HABITAT** Nests in open mountain conifer forests in south, upland moors with gullies in north; meadows and orchards on migration.

Song Thrush *Turdus philomelos*

orange underwing

uniform face

warm brown upperparts

inversed heart-shaped spots

IDENTIFICATION
23 cm. Small slim thrush, pale brown above, buff-washed white underparts with dark heart-shaped spots on flanks; wing-coverts edged buff. Uniform brown tail without white corners. Direct flight, not undulating, revealing orange underwing-coverts. **VOICE** Loud song, a series of repeated themes composed of 1–3 notes. Call: thin *sic*, also given in flight. **HABITAT** All habitats with trees, forests, woodland rides, hedgerows, parks and gardens, even in cities and mountainous areas. Feeds on worms and snails, the latter broken apart on favourite rocks ('anvils').

Mistle Thrush *Turdus viscivorus*

white underwing

contrasting cheek

grey-brown above

thickset body

round spots

IDENTIFICATION
27 cm. Large thrush recalling Song Thrush, but flank spots round (not upside-down hearts), generally greyer colour (less buff), clear cream fringes to wing feathers, white tail corners in flight, white underwing. **VOICE** Slow, very fluty song, shorter more melancholic phrases than Blackbird. Rattling, loud call *trrrrrr*, particularly given in flight. **HABITAT** Dense or open, coniferous or deciduous forests and hedgerows in summer, meadows and woodland edge in winter.

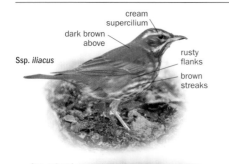

cream supercilium

dark brown above

Ssp. *iliacus*

rusty flanks

brown streaks

Ssp. *coburni*

large dense streaks

Redwing *Turdus iliacus*

IDENTIFICATION
21 cm. Small thrush, dark grey-brown above, well-defined white supercilium, brick-red flanks, underparts with blackish-brown streaks (Scandinavian race *iliacus*), larger and more numerous streaks (Icelandic race *coburni*). More compact and shorter tail than Song Thrush. **VOICE** Call: *tsiii*, louder and longer than Song Thrush's. **HABITAT** Meadows, woods, hedgerows, gardens in winter, often with Fieldfares. Northern breeder, common in winter in south.

Fieldfare *Turdus pilaris*

IDENTIFICATION
25 cm. Large thrush with dark brown mantle, ash-grey head and rump, black arrow-head shaped spots below forming a patch on each side of breast; yellow wash on breast and flanks; black tail; yellow bill with black tip. First-winter birds have juvenile outer greater coverts with fine white (not brown) fringes. **VOICE** Call a short, rough rattle in series, *trtt-trrt...* **HABITAT** As Redwing, often seen together.

white underwings

striped tan bib

grey head

chestnut mantle

black tail

large grey rump

black 'arrow-heads' on flanks

yellow bill with black tip

RARE SIBERIAN THRUSHES Various Asian species are rare visitors to Europe during the autumn migration; Black-throated Thrush is the least rare, and may overwinter.

Black-throated Thrush
Turdus atrogularis

25 cm. Grey above without any brown hue. Adult male: uniform black throat and bib, streaked with white in winter, yellow base to bill, legs black. Female: diffuse grey streaks on pale grey breast. Black tail without rufous sides, black flight feathers with grey edges, juvenile has white edges to wing-coverts; orangish underwing. Call when perched is softer than that of Blackbird; call in flight recalls that of Redwing.

uniform black head

yellow base to bill

broad black 'bib'

uniform grey above

dark lores

diffuse streaks

Male winter

Female

pinkish-brown legs

Red-throated Thrush *Turdus ruficollis*

25 cm. As Black-throated Thrush but face washed with orange, blackish malar bar, reddish feathers on breast; male has complete reddish bib and supercilium. Dull birds very similar to Black-throated Thrush but all have rufous fringes to outer tail feathers.

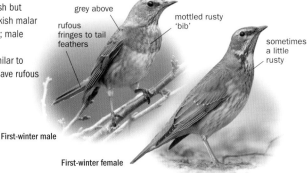

grey above

rufous fringes to tail feathers

mottled rusty 'bib'

sometimes a little rusty

First-winter male

First-winter female

Dusky Thrush *Turdus eunomus*

23 cm. Similar to Redwing in size and silhouette but blackish head with white supercilium, black 'arrowheads' below on flanks and often forming gorget across breast, blackish-brown mantle, extensive rufous margins on wings, and reddish rump. Yellow bill with black tip, black legs; white supercilium and throat.

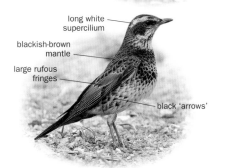

long white supercilium

blackish-brown mantle

large rufous fringes

black 'arrows'

cream supercilium

brownish-grey above

black malar-stripe

orange arrows

Naumann's Thrush *Turdus naumanni*

23 cm. As Dusky Thrush but brownish-grey above, underparts with reddish (not black) arrows, uppertail-coverts orangish with orange fringes to tail feathers; orange face with fine black malar bar and dark cheeks. First-winter birds have creamy face and supercilium, and buff-fringed feathers on wings. Hybrids with Dusky Thrush are intermediate between the 2, with both black and reddish arrow markings.

pronounced white supercilium

ash-grey head

grey-brown above

black lores

salmon-pink flanks

Eyebrowed Thrush *Turdus obscurus*

23 cm. Ash-grey head, white supercilium, black lores, white line under eye, salmon-pink breast and flanks, brownish-grey uniform upperparts. Yellow legs, black bill with orange base. Juvenile: yellow tips to tertials and greater coverts. Resembles a very pale Redwing, but no streaking on underparts.

speckled head

golden above with black scales

very scaly black below

White's Thrush *Zoothera dauma*

27 cm. Large scaly thrush. Feathers barred white, golden-yellow and black below. Pale golden-brown black-tipped feathers above. White corners to tail, median underwing-coverts black, lesser and greater coverts white. Underwing pattern of black band framed with 2 white bars is characteristic. Very shy, always hidden on ground. Closest breeding birds are in the Urals. Silent, rarely gives a *tsi* call, only audible at a few metres.

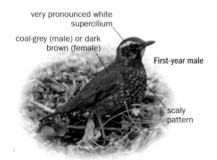

very pronounced white supercilium

coal-grey (male) or dark brown (female)

First-year male

scaly pattern

Siberian Thrush *Geokichla sibirica*

22 cm. Small thrush with pronounced white supercilium; dark blue-grey above and on breast, with dark arrowmarks on belly and undertail-coverts (male). Brown above and white with brown scaly markings below (female). White corners to tail, dark median underwing-coverts, lesser and greater coverts white, giving characteristic underwing pattern of black bar framed by 2 white bars.

RARE NEARCTIC THRUSHES Small terrestrial brown thrushes, rotund, only slightly larger than nightingales; the head and underpart plumage and contrast between back and tail are important in identification. Very rare vagrants to the Atlantic coast. Underwing white with central brown bar formed by the median coverts.

Swainson's Thrush *Catharus ustulatus*

18 cm. Reminiscent of a small Song Thrush. Pale lores join obvious cream eye-ring; buff wash to lores, face and throat; warm olive-brown above, pale fringes to greater coverts and tertials. Call: a soft *houit*.

prominent eye-ring and buff lores

diffuse spots

grey flanks

Grey-cheeked Thrush *Catharus minimus*

18 cm. Similar to Swainson's Thrush but duller; best separated by face pattern. Indistinct eye-ring, present particularly behind eye, indistinct lores, grey face and throat, brownish-grey flanks; upperparts duller than in Swainson's Thrush. Call: *vii-a*, different from monosyllabic call of Swainson's Thrush.

grey-brown tail and rump

uniform face without pronounced eye-ring

diffuse spots on white background

Hermit Thrush *Catharus guttatus*

17 cm. Differs from previous 2 species by reddish tail and undertail-coverts, tail sometimes cocked; warmer brown above (strong contrast with tail), prominent pale eye-ring, and more heavily marked breast spots. Call: soft *chuk*.

narrow pale eye-ring

well-marked large spots

reddish tail and rump

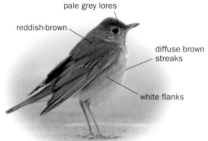

pale grey lores

reddish-brown

diffuse brown
streaks

white flanks

Veery *Catharus fuscescens*

17 cm. Long tail, upperparts and tail
bright reddish-brown, no contrast
between mantle and tail, tan face and
breast, latter with diffuse dark spots
(less distinct than other species in
genus). Call: descending *viou*,
sometimes disyllabic.

striped face

reddish above

black
spots on
flanks

long tail

Wood Thrush *Hylocichla mustelina*

20 cm. Larger than the 4 *Catharus*
species. Reddish upperparts, underparts
with large round black spots, cheeks
streaked with black, white eye-ring, pale
pink legs. Call: thin repeated *pit*. Very
rare vagrant recorded in Iceland, the
Azores and Britain.

white crescents

black head

slate-grey above

yellow bill with
black tip

brick-
orange
below

American Robin
Turdus migratorius

24 cm. Resembles Blackbird in size and
shape but has blackish head with white
spectacles, grey upperparts, black tail
with white corners visible in flight, white
throat with black streaking, and orange
breast. First-winter birds have pale
fringes on underparts giving scaly
appearance. Rare vagrant to Europe.

bluish above

orange wing-bars

orange
throat and
supercilium

black collar

Varied Thrush *Ixoreus naevius*

25 cm. Very colourful, mainly orange and
black. Adult has black pectoral band,
long orange supercilium, black-and-
orange wings, blue-grey mantle, dark
arrowmarks on rear flanks. First-winter
duller, with speckled breast-band. Very
rare vagrant to Europe, with records from
Iceland and Britain.

BUSH WARBLERS AND CISTICOLAS Insectivorous warblers of temporary or permanent wetlands. The bush warblers (*Cettia*) are of Asian origin and cisticolas (*Cisticola*) African, each with just one representative in Europe; both are sedentary and susceptible to hard winters.

Cetti's Warbler *Cettia cetti*

grey superucilium

uniform reddish-brown above

grey underparts

round tail

short round wings

pale pink legs

IDENTIFICATION 13.5 cm. Recalls an *Acrocephalus* but colour more reddish-brown, pronounced grey supercilium, long, rounder tail (10 broad tail feathers, not 12); undertail-coverts shorter than those of *Locustella* warblers and brown with pale tips, short rounded wings. Pink legs, pink base to lower mandible. Rarely comes into the open, often near ground. **VOICE** Very vocal. Call: a loud explosive *chip*. Song also explosive, rhythmic and characteristic, first few notes slightly hesitant followed by a slight pause then rapid series of similar notes. **HABITAT** Dense vegetation in wet habitats, reedbeds, edges of marshes, bramble thickets. Very sensitive to extreme cold and snow cover.

Fan-tailed Warbler (Zitting Cisticola) *Cisticola juncidis*

pale brown iris

striped crown

pale uniform face

heavily striped mantle

short tail

tail feathers tipped black and white

IDENTIFICATION 10 cm. Tiny; short rounded wings and tail. Uniform face with whitish lores, crown striped black; back striped buff and black, uniform rufous rump, buff-washed flanks. Tail feathers have black subterminal spots and white tips. Acrobatic, perches on the tops of vegetation and sings in characteristic long undulating flight. **VOICE** Very rhythmic song: metallic *tziks* given in series, 1 per second. Call: *zip* or *chip*. **HABITAT** Wetlands with short vegetation, wet meadows, edges of reedbeds and saltmarshes, as well as agricultural scrub.

CONFUSION SPECIES

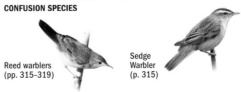

Reed warblers (pp. 315–319)

Sedge Warbler (p. 315)

GRASSHOPPER WARBLERS Warblers of damp brush, marshes and reedbeds, more or less terrestrial and often near the ground, including for nesting. Rounded wings; broad, rounded tail, long undertail-coverts nearly reaching tip of tail. Continuous stridulating songs recall those of crickets, given from a prominent position, with bill wide open. Migrants.

striped mantle

black-spotted breast

flanks slightly or not marked

diffuse edges to brown fringes

rounded tail

(Common) Grasshopper Warbler *Locustella naevia*

IDENTIFICATION
13 cm. Quite variable plumage; streaked crown and mantle. Buff breast marked with dark stripes or spots, sometimes plain. Tertials with diffuse brown borders, larger at base. Diffuse black streaks on the undertail-coverts, often reaching tip. **VOICE** Sometimes sings at night; long stridulating, high pitched and mechanical, the notes separable to the human ear. Can last for several minutes, with short gaps to take a breath. Call: *tic* similar to Robin. **HABITAT** Bushes, scrub, clearings, hedgerows, bramble thickets as well as marshes and wet meadows.

Savi's Warbler *Locustella luscinioides*

cream supercilium

rusty-buff undertail-coverts

rounded tail

diffuse white tips to undertail-coverts

rusty-buff flanks

rounded wings

warm brown above

IDENTIFICATION
14 cm. Plumage uniform warm-brown, reddish, indistinct supercilium, long rounded tail, bill with dark tip. Distinguished from reed warblers by darker colour, pink legs, very rounded wings, darker undertail-coverts with buff tips and more terrestrial habits. **VOICE** Long stridulating rattling song that can last for more than 30 seconds, higher-pitched and more rapid than that of Grasshopper Warbler, similar to that of Mole Cricket. Call: high-pitched *pit*, sometimes in series. **HABITAT** Ancient reedbeds, normally with a few bushes and usually in warm climates.

River Warbler *Locustella fluviatilis*

IDENTIFICATION
13 cm. Breeds
in Fenno-
Scandia and
E Europe.
Singing males
occur only rarely outside this range,
usually in dry bushy habitats. Resembles
Savi's Warbler but duller brown, diffuse
streaks on breast, dark undertail-coverts
with prominent white tips. **VOICE** Rapid
rhythmic song; each rattled note
separable to the human ear. **HABITAT**
Bushes, not necessarily on wet ground.

streaked
'bib'

clean white tips to
undertail-coverts

indistinct
supercilium

dull brown-
grey above

streaked
'bib'

Gray's Grasshopper Warbler *Locustella fasciolata*

15 cm. Asian migrant; very rare vagrant to W Europe.
Large *Locustella* warbler with large bill and uniform
unstreaked plumage. Dark brown above with reddish-
brown rump and tail. Whitish supercilium, dark eye-
stripe, greyish-white underparts with sides of breast
and flanks washed brownish. First-winter is more
yellowish below. Undertail-coverts shorter than in
other *Locustella* warblers. Primary projection
much shorter than that of Great Reed Warbler.
Contact call: *cherr cherr...*

grey supercilium

long bill

dark lores

brown wash
to breast
and flanks

Lanceolated Warbler *Locustella lanceolata*

black lines on mantle

black tertials with pale brown fringes

black streaks on flanks

12 cm. Rare Siberian warbler; vagrants occur in autumn. Very small, compact, with short tail; moves around on the ground like a mouse. Pronounced fine black streaks on breast and flanks. Undertail-coverts with prominent black centres. Narrow, well-defined brown fringes to tertials of constant width. Black streaks on mantle form unbroken lines. Call on migration: *tchurr tchurr...*

black and brown stripes

short tail

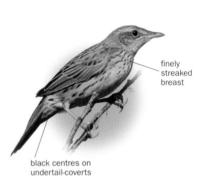

finely streaked breast

black centres on undertail-coverts

Pallas's Grasshopper Warbler *Locustella certhiola*

white fringes

rufous-brown mantle

creamy supercilium

rufous-brown flanks

uniform buff breast

13 cm. Rare Siberian warbler; vagrants occur in autumn. Very much like Grasshopper Warbler but dark tail feathers have diffuse white tips, small cream spots to tips of inner webs of tertials, more streaked crown showing marked contrast with cream supercilium, uniform rufous unstreaked rump. Contact call: *chir-chir.*

REED WARBLERS The members of this genus of warblers occur in wetlands, principally reedbeds. A few species have streaked plumage but most are unstreaked and careful observation is required to differentiate some of them. All are migratory.

Sedge Warbler *Acrocephalus schoenobaenus*

IDENTIFICATION 13 cm. Dark brown crown without central pale line, dark brown lores and eye-stripe, pronounced cream supercilium. Streaked back, plain rump. Tan wash to breast and flanks that are unmarked (adult) or spotted with black (juvenile). Differs from Aquatic Warbler in having dark lores and black spotting on breast. Lower mandible orange with black tip. **VOICE** Call: a dry *tec* or *churr*. Varied song a mix of grating notes and others more musical. **HABITAT** Reedbeds, meadows and other wet habitats with bushes, sometimes in scrub.

dark crown

white supercilium

streaked mantle

Adult

sometimes a pale central stripe

reddish rump

black lores

spotted with black

Juvenile

Aquatic Warbler *Acrocephalus paludicola*

IDENTIFICATION 13 cm. Very similar to Sedge Warbler, but paler and more contrasting plumage. Pale lores, broad cream supercilium, central cream stripe on crown. Mantle with blackish-brown stripes, 2 pronounced buff 'braces'. Finely streaked reddish rump; tan-washed breast, adult with fine black streaks on flanks. First-winter birds more colourful. **VOICE** Calls: soft *tak*, *tuc-tuc*, grating *churr*. **HABITAT** Wet meadows, edges of reedbeds.

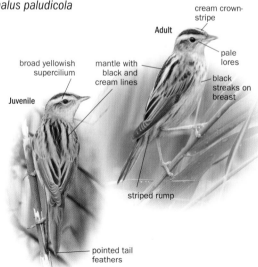

cream crown-stripe

Adult

pale lores

broad yellowish supercilium

mantle with black and cream lines

black streaks on breast

Juvenile

striped rump

pointed tail feathers

Moustached Warbler *Acrocephalus melanopogon*

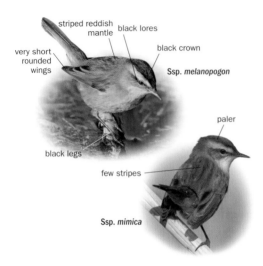

striped reddish mantle · black lores · black crown

very short rounded wings

Ssp. *melanopogon*

paler

black legs

few stripes

Ssp. *mimica*

IDENTIFICATION
12.5 cm.
Resembles
Sedge Warbler
but darker and
more

contrasting plumage. Black crown, white supercilium wider behind eye, black lores, eye-stripe and moustache. Reddish-brown mantle striped black, uniform reddish rump, rufous-washed flanks. Black bill, including lower mandible. Short, rounded wings; short primary projection. **VOICE** Song composed of long phrases that include loud *tututututu* phrases similar to those of Common Nightingale. Call: *tac* or *trrt*. **HABITAT** Reedbeds, particularly areas of reeds with bushes.

Great Reed Warbler *Acrocephalus arundinaceus*

pronounced white supercilium

massive silhouette

large bill with dark tip

very long wings

graduated tail

grey legs

IDENTIFICATION
19 cm. Large,
obvious
supercilium,
dark lores, long
thick bill, lower

mandible tipped black. White throat, buff washed flanks. Long primary projection, equivalent to length of tertials. Long rounded tail. Often perched at top of reed when singing. **VOICE** Call a low *tcheuk*. Song slower and lower-pitched than that of other *Acrocephalus* warblers, with loud far-carrying croaking notes. **HABITAT** Ancient reedbeds with water, mature stands of reeds bordering open water.

(European) Reed Warbler *Acrocephalus scirpaceus*

diffuse rufous fringes

indistinct tan supercilium

IDENTIFICATION
13 cm. Rounded tail, reddish-brown plumage with a more colourful rump, buff wash on flanks. Flattened forehead, pale supercilium in front of eye. Primary projection: two-thirds or three-quarters of length of tertials. Entirely pale lower mandible. Orange-brown feet with yellow soles. Reddish iris (adult) or dull brown (juvenile). **VOICE** Call: subdued *cherr*. Song composed of repeated, metallic, grating or melodious rhythmic sounds, *ker-ker-ker chiruc-chiruc-chiruc...*, without imitations. **HABITAT** Reedbeds with water; bushes also on migration.

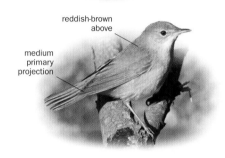

reddish-brown above

medium primary projection

Marsh Warbler *Acrocephalus palustris*

IDENTIFICATION
13 cm. Very similar to Reed Warbler but plumage with less rufous tones, longer wings, primary projection equivalent to the length of the tertials; bill a little stouter. Pale fringes to the flight feathers, well-defined on tertials. Pale legs and dull rump. **VOICE** Call: a rolled *chirr* or dry *tak*. Song has recurring *zi-chay* theme and many imitations. **HABITAT** Wet marshes with bushes, willow carr, brambles and nettles, but not flooded reedbeds.

long primary projection

strong bill

dull olive-brown above

cream fringes to flight feathers

'Ambiguous' Reed Warbler *Acrocephalus scirpaceus ambiguus*

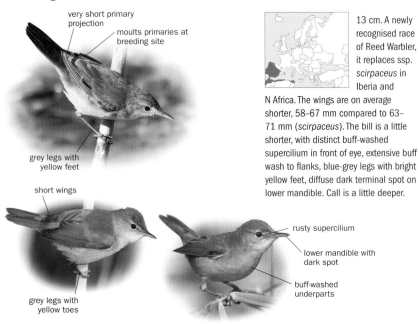

very short primary projection

moults primaries at breeding site

grey legs with yellow feet

short wings

grey legs with yellow toes

rusty supercilium

lower mandible with dark spot

buff-washed underparts

13 cm. A newly recognised race of Reed Warbler, it replaces ssp. *scirpaceus* in Iberia and N Africa. The wings are on average shorter, 58–67 mm compared to 63–71 mm (*scirpaceus*). The bill is a little shorter, with distinct buff-washed supercilium in front of eye, extensive buff wash to flanks, blue-grey legs with bright yellow feet, diffuse dark terminal spot on lower mandible. Call is a little deeper.

Paddyfield Warbler *Acrocephalus agricola*

black above pronounced white supercilium

rufous fringes to tertials

very white below

short primary projection

supercilium wide behind eye

rounded wings very short

13 cm. Plumage warm brown above, rump tinged rufous, brighter than back and mantle; whitish below. Very pronounced white supercilium, distinct behind eye, lined below by dark lores and above by dark edges to crown. Lower mandible has long black tip, as in Great Reed Warbler; legs orangish. Wings short, primary projection one-third of tertial length.

Blyth's Reed Warbler *Acrocephalus dumetorum*

IDENTIFICATION
13 cm. A migrant that breeds from Scandinavia to central Asia, vagrants occur elsewhere in late summer and autumn. Very similar to European Reed and Marsh Warblers but duller plumage, very wide cream supercilium in front of eye, but little behind, no or only slight pale fringes to secondaries and tertials. Short wings, reduced primary projection. More or less grey legs, lower mandible with dark spot as in 'Ambiguous' Reed Warbler. **VOICE** Calm song with repeated imitations. **HABITAT** Bushes, clearings, dense vegetation.

pronounced wide supercilium in front of eye

dull brown-grey above

no pale fringes to flight feathers

very short primary projection

pronounced supercilium in front of eye

uniform wing

Thick-billed Warbler *Acrocephalus (Iduna) aedon*

18 cm. A large Siberian warbler; its relationship with other species is at present uncertain. It has recently been placed in a new genus *Iduna*, that includes a few other renamed warblers. Vagrant, recorded a few times in Scotland. Long tail, long silhouette with large head, thick yellow and black bill, uniform pale face with pale lores and striking large round eye, no supercilium, more reddish crown, sometimes ruffled; very short primary projection. Call: *tchac* in series.

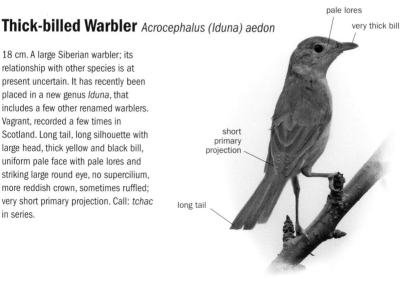

pale lores

very thick bill

short primary projection

long tail

TREE WARBLERS Insectivorous warblers with broad-based bill, square tail and short undertail-coverts. Four species in the *Hippolais* genus; others, brown and buff without any yellow, have recently been placed in a separate genus, *Iduna*. Wing length and pattern, behaviour (flicking tail) and calls allow species separation.

Icterine Warbler *Hippolais icterina*

pale lores

pale fringes to secondaries

blue-grey legs

long primary projection

IDENTIFICATION 13.5 cm. Very similar to Melodious Warbler. Olive above, pale yellow below, including lores that are only slightly extended as a supercilium over eye. Long wings, primary projection equal to tertial length. Very visible pale wing panel, formed by pale fringes to all the flight feathers. Orange bill with dark ridge, blue-grey legs, including soles. Juvenile: yellow only on face and breast. **VOICE** Call: *tchaitaivoui* with more attenuated second syllable, as well as *tec*, sometimes in series. Song: more musical and elaborate than that of Melodious Warbler; long, less strident musical phrases with more varied imitations. **HABITAT** Bushes, scrub and hedgerows.

Melodious Warbler *Hippolais polyglotta*

shorter primary projection

poorly marked pale fringes

Adult

brown legs

sometimes grey above

short primary projection

sometimes very little yellow

Juvenile

IDENTIFICATION 13 cm. Very similar to Icterine Warbler but wings shorter, primary projection two-thirds of tertial length. Cream to olive primary fringes that may form a pale panel, never white. Juvenile less yellow with white belly and undertail-coverts; rare individuals without yellow pigmentation are brown above and cream below, looking like species of *Iduna* genus, but do not flick the tail and have a simple call. **VOICE** Call: *kerr* similar to sparrow's chirp, brief *tac* or repeated *taitaitai*... Song in 2 phases, first short with repeated notes, often including imitations, followed by rapid warble. **HABITAT** Bushes, scrub, re-growth and hedgerows.

CONFUSION SPECIES

Reed warblers (pp. 315–319)

Willow Warbler (p. 333)

Wood Warbler (p. 335)

Olive-tree Warbler *Hippolais olivetorum*

IDENTIFICATION
17 cm. Large, grey *Hippolais* with pale bulbous spot on lores, white wing panel and white edges to greater coverts, long thick bill, long primary projection; sometimes breast washed with grey and dark centres to undertail-coverts. **VOICE** Call: deep *tchac*. **HABITAT** Open woodland, maquis, orchards; leaves in August.

white supercilium in front of eye

beige below

mouse-grey

white fringes

long primary projection

Upcher's Warbler *Hippolais languida*

IDENTIFICATION
14.5 cm. Very similar to Olivaceous Warbler, thicker bill, longer tail, which is darker than body; often swings tail, longer primary projection (three-quarters of tertial length); pale edges to secondaries and pale fringes to greater coverts in fresh plumage. **VOICE** Call: clear dry *zac*. **HABITAT** Bushes and orchards on dry hillsides.

brown-grey above

very long dark tail

pale fringes in autumn

long bill

Eastern Olivaceous Warbler *Iduna pallida*

brown-grey above

sooty tail

IDENTIFICATION
13 cm. Breeds in SE Europe and Central Asia, occurs rarely in W Europe, mainly on Mediterranean coast. Dull plumage with uniform pale area in front of eye and short supercilium behind eye. Long, square-ended tail, often flicked downwards when nervous. Cream fringes to secondaries and tertials. **VOICE** Call: dry *tek* or *tchec*, or a nasal series *taitaitaita...* Song: *Hippolais*-like song of short repeated phrases. **HABITAT** Bushes, shrubs, orchards.

short cream supercilium

straight bill

olive-grey

often flicks tail downwards

short primary projection

Western Olivaceous Warbler *Iduna opaca*

larger and thicker bill

sandy-brown

paler lores

13 cm. Very similar to Eastern Olivaceous Warbler, bill larger at base with concave sides and no downward flicking of tail, a diagnostic behavioural difference requiring much observation time. Primary projection a little longer. Song less repetitive than that of Eastern Olivaceous Warbler.

long bill

uniform wing

flicks tail very little

short primary projection

Booted Warbler *Iduna caligata*

clear pale fringes

short bill, dark tip to lower mandible

silhouette similar to leaf warbler

IDENTIFICATION
11.5 cm. Breeds from extreme SE Finland to Central Asia. Small with relatively short tail, wide supercilium continues behind eye, underlined with diffuse black line. Well-marked pale fringes to flight feathers and greater coverts, contrasting with dark centres to tertials. Buff wash to flanks. Orange-brown legs, lower mandible orange with dark tip. Often nervously flicks wings and tail. **VOICE** Call: a slightly liquid *trec*. **HABITAT** Low scrub and bushes.

pronounced pale supercilium, dark above

white-sided tail

Sykes's Warbler *Iduna rama*

12 cm. Rare autumn vagrant from steppes of Central Asia. Very similar to Booted Warbler but ill-defined fringes on wings, almost uniform tertials; shorter primary projection, no dark line under supercilium, white flanks and longer bill with orange tip to lower mandible. Resembles Olivaceous Warbler but is smaller, has more obvious supercilium, short primary projection, uniform wings. Call on migration: *tec*, often doubled. Flicks its tail in all directions, including upwards.

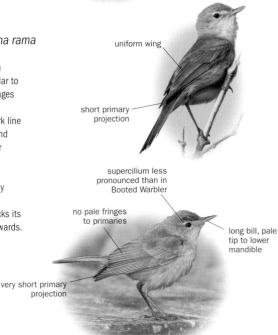

uniform wing

short primary projection

supercilium less pronounced than in Booted Warbler

no pale fringes to primaries

long bill, pale tip to lower mandible

very short primary projection

SYLVIA WARBLERS Small passerines, normally insectivorous but feed on berries in autumn. Most species are migrants that winter in the Sahel; many are particularly associated with the Mediterranean area when breeding. They inhabit woodlands and bushes, maquis and garrigue.

Blackcap *Sylvia atricapilla*

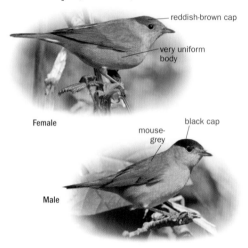

reddish-brown cap

very uniform body

Female

mouse-grey

black cap

Male

IDENTIFICATION 14 cm. Grey-brown plumage, male with black crown, the female's is rufous and juvenile's dull brown; forehead always grey. Paler underparts, pale grey with brown flush to flanks. Grey legs, grey bill with black tip. **VOICE** Song: fluty and rhythmic of short melodious phrases. Call: slightly liquid *tac*. **HABITAT** Undergrowth and bushes in woodland, woods, parks and gardens.

Sardinian Warbler *Sylvia melanocephala*

dull brown above   grey head

tertials with brown fringes

Female

brownish-grey flanks

red eye-ring   black head

Male

white throat

dark grey body

IDENTIFICATION 13.5 cm. Crown and cheeks totally black in male, grey in female. Adults have red eye-ring, immature white. Grey flanks often separate the white throat. **VOICE** Call: very loud *tratratratra...* or *kraikraikraikai*. Song more melodious, phrases include rattles similar to call. **HABITAT** Undergrowth, bushes, gardens.

Rüppell's Warbler *Sylvia rueppelli*

IDENTIFICATION
13 cm. Similar
to Sardinian
Warbler but
more slender,
stronger slightly
downcurved bill; male has black bib and
white moustache; undertail-coverts
marked with black chevrons, white
fringes to tertials. **VOICE** Call: *zac*. Song:
calmer than that of Sardinian Warbler.
HABITAT Dense thorny bushes.

white fringes to tertials

long downcurved bill

Male

grey chevrons under tail

black throat and white moustache

dark grey head

Female

chevrons under tail

white moustache

black spotting on throat

Cyprus Warbler *Sylvia melanothorax*

IDENTIFICATION
13 cm. Similar
to Sardinian
Warbler but with
black chevrons
under tail, white
fringes to greater coverts and tertials,
white eye-ring, yellowish base to bill (grey
in Rüppell's Warbler). Male: black head,
underparts including throat with large
black spots, white moustache. Female:
grey head, black marks on underparts.
VOICE Call: guttural *zrec*. Song: calm,
jerky, monotonous warbling. **HABITAT**
Bushes, scrub. Breeds exclusively in
Cyprus, winters around the Red Sea.

white eye-ring

Male

short bill

blackish below

broad white moustache

Female

black chevrons below

Lesser Whitethroat *Sylvia curruca*

Ssp. *curruca* — grey-brown mantle — dark cheek — ash-grey head

Ssp. *curruca/blythi* — brown cheek

sandy above

Ssp. *minula/halimodendri*

IDENTIFICATION
13 cm. Dark grey crown, darker cheeks, white throat. Dull brown-grey mantle, wings similar, black tail with white sides. Whitish underparts. Grey base to bill, dark grey legs. **VOICE** Short song, a few warbled notes followed by a rapid, fluty trill *tiaitiaitiait...* or *chica-chica-chica...* Call: dry *tak*, sometimes in series, especially in eastern races. **HABITAT** Cool undergrowth, bushes. **GEOGRAPHIC VARIATION** Ssp. *curruca* (Europe) sometimes shows a diffuse white supercilium in autumn; ssp. *blythi* (Siberia) has buffish breast, brownish wash to cheeks and nape, rounder wings, all-white tips to outer tail feathers; ssp. *minula/halimodendri* (Central Asia) has a paler sandy mantle, often shorter bill, entirely white tips to outer tail feathers (no brown around shaft), angular white spot at top of outer tail feather; ssp. *althaea* (Iran) has dull grey head, dark greyish-brown mantle showing no contrast with crown, shorter wings, much white on 3 outer tail feathers.

head and mantle same colour

Ssp. *althaea*

sandy above

Ssp. *minula/halimodendri*

much white on tail

round head and short bill

Ssp. *minula/halimodendri*

Western Orphean Warbler
Sylvia hortensis

grey mantle — black head

pale iris

Male

dark grey head

dark iris

grey-brown mantle

Female

IDENTIFICATION
15 cm. Large, thickset, dull black crown in male, coal-grey in female. Ashy-grey mantle (browner in female), white tips to some tail feathers. Buff wash to flanks, uniform undertail-coverts. Thick bill with grey base. Pale yellow iris in adult, dark in juvenile. **VOICE** Song: short, loud, melancholy phrases finishing with *tiro tiro tiro*. **HABITAT** Steppe and dry meadows with trees, open orchards.

juvenile male has smoky iris

Eastern Orphean Warbler *Sylvia crassirostris*

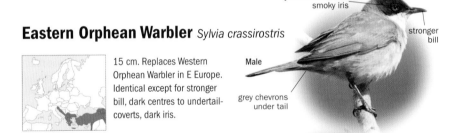

Male

stronger bill

15 cm. Replaces Western Orphean Warbler in E Europe. Identical except for stronger bill, dark centres to undertail-coverts, dark iris.

grey chevrons under tail

black tail feathers

Ménétriés's Warbler *Sylvia mystacea*

head and mantle same colour

Female

white eye-ring

Male ssp. *mystacea*

12.5 cm. Very rare vagrant from Middle East; 1 bird trapped in Portugal, September 1967. Slender, long black tail contrasts with sandy mantle, diffuse edges to tertials, yellowish base to bill, white eye-ring. Male: Front of head black grading into grey on nape, indistinct white moustache, Middle Eastern race (ssp. *rubescens*) has greyish-white throat and breast, which are pale pink in Caucasus race (ssp. *mystacea*). Female: uniformly coloured head and back, pale buff underparts. Call: explosive *tsec* like that of Sardinian Warbler.

diffuse nape

grey breast

pinkish breast

Male ssp. *rubescens*

Garden Warbler *Sylvia borin*

no white fringes · grey patch · uniform face

IDENTIFICATION 14 cm. Uniform brown-grey plumage, greyer sides to neck; quite plain face with a hint of a supercilium in front of the eye. Thick grey bill, robust grey legs. No white in tail feathers. **VOICE** Song: like that of Blackcap but louder with longer phrases, without last fluty notes. Call: *tec*, often in series. **HABITAT** Undergrowth, bushes, parks and gardens.

Barred Warbler *Sylvia nisoria*

white wing-bars · orange eye

Adult male

barred below

dark iris

clear cream fringes

Juvenile

black chevrons · pink base

IDENTIFICATION 15 cm. Large mouse-grey warbler, uniform upperparts, pale fringes to crown, rump and scapulars giving a scaly look; whitish underparts barred grey. Pale fringes to wing-coverts and tertials. Black bill, pink base to lower mandible. Yellow iris in adult, dark in juvenile. Juvenile plumage uniform with obvious pale fringes to wing feathers; sometimes has dark marks on flanks, always has grey chevrons on undertail-coverts. **VOICE** Call: long, harsh *tsssrt*, also dry *tac*. **HABITAT** Bushes, open environments with thickets.

Asian Desert Warbler *Sylvia nana*
African Desert Warbler *Sylvia deserti*

pale centres · orange-ochre

bright yellow bill

dull brown-grey

dark centres

yellow eye

African Desert Warbler

Asian Desert Warbler

rufous rump

11 cm. Two very similar species. Asian Desert Warbler is a rare vagrant from Central Asia, wintering in the Arabian Peninsula. Small, very pale, sandy-grey plumage, reddish tail with white edges; yellow iris, pale face with white eye-ring. African Desert Warbler is resident in N Africa and is paler and more ochre; tertials have pale centres.

Common Whitethroat *Sylvia communis*

IDENTIFICATION
14 cm. Male: ash-grey head, white eye-ring and throat, brown back, rufous edges to tertials and greater coverts, black tail with white sides; pink wash to the breast. Female: duller, brown head. Juvenile: less marked rufous edges to wing feathers. **VOICE** Short song, fluty phrase starting with *tilu tilou* followed by a rising and falling warble. Call: *tac*, sometimes doubled.
HABITAT Thick or scattered bushes, areas of regrowth, coppice, hedgerows in agricultural areas, scrub.

grey head

rufous fringes

white throat

pink breast

Male

brown head

less marked rufous fringes

Female

Spectacled Warbler *Sylvia conspicillata*

IDENTIFICATION
12.5 cm. Very similar to Common Whitethroat but smaller, more colourful; darker head with dark lores, more pronounced white eye-ring, very broad rufous fringes on wings, pink breast. Juvenile: pale and uniform; rufous wings are only noticeable difference from Whitethroat except size.
VOICE Call: sharp *tsit* or harsh rattle. Song: similar to Whitethroat, short phrase starting with a few repeated fluty notes *tititutou*, followed by a varying warble. **HABITAT** Dry saltmarsh with samphire, low bushes in garrigue, lavender fields.

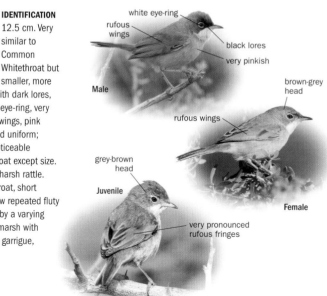

white eye-ring

rufous wings

Male

black lores

very pinkish

brown-grey head

rufous wings

grey-brown head

Juvenile

Female

very pronounced rufous fringes

Dartford Warbler *Sylvia undata*

intense grey

red eye-ring

white spots

Male ssp. *undata*

wine-red as far as undertail-coverts

Juvenile

orange or reddish-grey underparts

very long tail

brown fringes

white centre to belly

Male ssp. *dartfordiensis*

IDENTIFICATION
12.5 cm. Dark warbler with a long tail. Male: coal-grey above, wine-red below, white speckles on throat. Female: brown-grey above, less colourful underparts, more extensive pale lower belly. Short round wings, red eye-ring. Tail often raised. Juvenile: paler below, buff, sometimes pinkish-grey. The Atlantic race (ssp. *dartfordiensis*) is browner above, Mediterranean race (ssp. *undata*) is greyer. Often stays hidden in thick bushes. **VOICE** Call: characteristic descending *tchurr*. Song: grating, short, rapid warbling phrases. **HABITAT** Heaths, patches of heather, garrigue, open maquis and burnt forest.

Marmora's Warbler *Sylvia sarda*

pink eye-ring

pink base to bill

grey underparts without pink tint

brown fringes

Juvenile

Male

pink base to bill

grey throat

IDENTIFICATION
12 cm. Similar to Dartford Warbler but less colourful. Male: entirely coal-grey, red eye-ring, pink base to bill. Female: duller, pale throat and pale grey underparts. Juvenile: pale underparts, buff-grey with brown wash above, very similar to juvenile Dartford Warbler. **VOICE** Call: short dry *trec* or *tzek,* very different to longer plaintive call of Dartford Warbler. Melodious song, short phrase finishing with a rapid trill *tiaitiaitiaiatiaitiai*. **HABITAT** Low garrigue and maquis; more open, shorter vegetation than Dartford Warbler.

Balearic Warbler *Sylvia balearica*

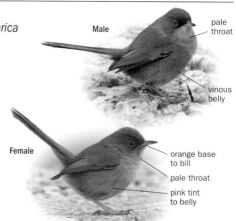

Male

pale throat

vinous belly

Female

orange base to bill

pale throat

pink tint to belly

12 cm. Once considered conspecific with Marmora's Warbler, which it resembles. A Balearic Islands endemic, resident. Male as Marmora's Warbler but with paler throat, orange base to bill; shorter bill and different song. Call: a grating *tchairr*.

Moltoni's Warbler *Sylvia subalpina*

IDENTIFICATION 12 cm. Very similar to the Subalpine Warblers but male has pink tint to underparts, wine-red down to belly; however, there is much individual variation and call is the best means of identifying birds away from their breeding grounds. Juvenile: sandy; male with grey nape and cheeks isolating the more orange-tinted crown. **VOICE** Call: characteristic, a slightly muffled rolling *krrrrrrr*, reminiscent of a short phrase of Wren or Mistle Thrush. **HABITAT** Breeds on Corsica, Sardinia and the Balearic Islands and a few sites on the nearby Italian coast. Rare vagrant elsewhere.

narrow white moustache

wine-red below

coloured flanks

Male

white eye-ring

pinkish below

Female

white eye-ring

Juvenile

male with reddish forehead

cream to pale rufous fringes

Western Subalpine Warbler *Sylvia inornata*

fine
moustache

orange-red
bib

orange flanks
and belly

Male

Female

bluish-grey
above

white eye-ring

sometimes
hint of
moustache

pale orange
colour below

IDENTIFICATION
12 cm. Small,
bluish-grey
upperparts,
reddish throat
and breast with
thin white moustachial-stripe. Beige
fringes to tertials. Black tail with white
sides. Male: red eye-ring, orange-red
throat, breast and much of flanks.
Female: duller, white eye-ring, brown-
grey above, slightly pinkish throat,
moustache only slightly visible or not at
all. Juvenile: nondescript, sandy-grey,
beige fringes on wings (rufous in very
similar Spectacled Warbler). **VOICE** Call:
dry *taic*. Song: softer and more musical
than that of Common Whitethroat, short
babbled phrases. **HABITAT** Low bushes,
thick or sparse, garrigue, maquis,
coppices, hedgerows.

Eastern Subalpine Warbler *Sylvia cantillans*

pinkish flanks

Male

brick-red
throat

Male

bluish-grey
above

drab flanks

broad white
moustache

short brick-
red bib

IDENTIFICATION
12 cm. Eastern
form that breeds
in the Balkans
and Turkey. Ssp.
cantillans
breeds in Italy, ssp. *albistriata* further
east. Like Western Subalpine Warbler but
male has brighter red throat and breast,
contrasting sharply with white flanks and
belly; broad white moustache. **VOICE**
Call: short *trek*, often doubled or tripled.
HABITAT As Western Subalpine Warbler.

LEAF WARBLERS Insectivorous, migrant warblers with rotund bodies and marked supercilium. Brown or olive plumage, often with some yellowish colouring. Leg and wing colour important in identification, especially presence or absence of wing-bars. Calls vary according to species. Many European species winter in the Sahel.

Common Chiffchaff *Phylloscopus collybita*

no wing-bar

Breeding adult

thin white crescent under eye

black legs

IDENTIFICATION
10.5 cm. Small, quite rotund, short wings, olive-brown plumage, pronounced supercilium before eye, dark legs.

Buff wash on flanks. Often has yellow colour on face, supercilium and underwing. Very similar to Willow Warbler. The Scandinavian race (ssp. *abietinus*) is similar but bigger. **VOICE** Call: plaintive, rising *hui*, less disyllabic than that of Willow Warbler. Song: rhythmic, series of alternating notes on 2 tones, *chiff chaff...* (hence its name). **HABITAT** Forests, woodland, bushes, coppice, hedgerows, scrub; all environments with a dense bushy strata.

Juvenile

short primary projection

buff wash

dark legs

Willow Warbler *Phylloscopus trochilus*

pronounced supercilium

Breeding adult

greyish mantle

pure yellow wash on face

brown legs

IDENTIFICATION 11 cm. Brown above, greyish in spring adults. Long obvious supercilium with yellow wash. In autumn, the plumage is browner above, the underparts sometimes have entire yellow wash. Long primary projection, about two-thirds the length of the tertials. Orange-brown legs. Very similar to Common Chiffchaff but has longer wings, lighter coloured legs, obvious supercilium, yellowish colouring on face, less brown underparts and different voice. The Siberian race (ssp. *acredula*) is bigger and paler with grey underparts. **VOICE** Call: soft, disyllabic *hu-i*. Song: a succession of notes repeated 2–5 times, often with descending tone at start, *tsitsitsi tsaitsaitsai tututu tvaitvaitvaik-tu*. **HABITAT** Areas with bushes and shrubs, young forestry plantations.

pronounced supercilium

lemon-yellow wash

long primary projection

Juvenile

brown legs with orangish feet

Iberian Chiffchaff *Phylloscopus ibericus*

yellow undertail-coverts

pale lower mandible

bright yellow supercilium

pale legs

long primary projection

IDENTIFICATION 10.5 cm. Very similar to Common Chiffchaff; differs in having white underparts and yellow wash on face and breast, with longer wings and different wing formula. **VOICE** Song starts like that of Chiffchaff but finishes quickly with characteristic accelerating trill, *tietietietietietietie...* Call: *huit* similar to call of Willow Warbler. **HABITAT** Much as Common Chiffchaff: mainly deciduous or coniferous forest on sloping ground.

Siberian Chiffchaff *Phylloscopus collybita tristis*

sandy plumage without any yellow

black bill with pale edges

diffuse narrow wing-bar

black legs

11.5 cm. Rare Siberian vagrant, treated as race of Common Chiffchaff. Like Common Chiffchaff but with greyer coloration, yellow only on wing and tail feathers. Cream tips to greater coverts form a diffuse wing-bar. No yellow on head, supercilium or underparts, except for wrist on underwing. Black bill with pale edges to mandibles, characteristic. Dark legs, often blackish. Oscillating, descending, melancholy call *hii*. In spring, song like that of Common Chiffchaff but less orderly.

Canary Islands Chiffchaff *Phylloscopus canariensis*

olive-brown above

long supercilium

long bill

buff breast

IDENTIFICATION 12 cm. Recently treated as a separate species. Like Common Chiffchaff but has longer bill and shorter primary projection; pronounced long supercilium, olive-brown mantle, yellow underwings, brown legs. **VOICE** Song as Common Chiffchaff but a little more irregular and explosive, reminiscent of Cetti's Warbler. **HABITAT** Endemic and sedentary on Canaries, in bushes and undergrowth.

Western Bonelli's Warbler *Phylloscopus bonelli*

olive-brown above

pronounced
yellow fringes

pale
lores

yellowish-olive
rump

IDENTIFICATION 11.5 cm. Very uniform face, indistinct cream supercilium, white eye-ring; brown-grey crown and mantle, very pronounced yellow fringes to wing and tail feathers; yellowish rump and uppertail-coverts. **VOICE** Call: rising *dju-i*, clearly disyllabic. Song: a monotone trill lasting about 1 second, sometimes with a different tone between phrases, *tiaitiaitiaitiaitiaitiaitiai...*, *tiutiutiutiutiutiutui...* **HABITAT** Deciduous woodland, pine plantations, coppice, thickets.

Eastern Bonelli's Warbler
Phylloscopus orientalis

grey above

pale
lores

olive
rump

grey above

olive fringes
to wing and
tail feathers

11.5 cm. Formerly conspecific with Western Bonelli's Warbler. Similar to Western Bonelli's but has greyer mantle and head without olive tint, and very contrasting yellow rump. The best feature is the distinctive call, a monosyllabic abrupt *djip*, similar to Crossbill's call.

Wood Warbler *Phylloscopus sibilatrix*

yellow fringes on wing

very long
primary
projection

olive-green mantle

some individuals
without bright yellow

broad supercilium
underlined with dark
eye-stripe

bright
yellow
face

IDENTIFICATION 12 cm. Large, brightly coloured, long wings, long primary projection. Olive-green above, lemon yellow throat and breast (variable), white belly. Long and well marked yellow supercilium, underlined with black. Greenish-yellow fringes to wing feathers, white on tertials. **VOICE** Call: loud monosyllabic *tju*. Song: accelerating acute trill, changing rhythm in the middle; *tyi tyi tyi-tyi-tyi-ti...* *titititititititititi...* alternating with slower notes in series *tieu-tieu-tieu*. **HABITAT** Ancient, mature deciduous woodland, particularly with oaks.

RARE MIGRANT LEAF WARBLERS In autumn, a few vagrant oriental leaf warblers arrive in Europe, often detected by their different calls. They occur in bushes and shrubs, moving through the foliage or on the ground; most frequently found on the coast, and coastal islands.

Yellow-browed Warbler *Phylloscopus inornatus*

white on tertials

long supercilium

bill quite orange

dark bar

2 whitish or yellowish wing-bars

supercilium sometimes yellow

orange toes

10 cm. A small Siberian leaf warbler with olive back and white underparts, long white supercilium sometimes washed yellow, underlined with black as far as the nape. Two whitish or yellowish wing-bars, the inner one underlined with black. Lower mandible pale with dark tip. Lively and difficult to observe well in the tops of trees or shrubs. As soon as winter plumage is attained, birds are less green and less yellow. Obviously disyllabic call, *psi-huit*. Rare but annual migrant, mainly in October.

Hume's Leaf Warbler *Phylloscopus humei*

beige supercilium

brown-grey mantle

dark bill

a single distinct wing-bar

black legs

no dark line under wing-bar

indistinct second wing-bar

10 cm. Very similar to Yellow-browed Warbler but has dull grey-brown plumage, beige supercilium, a single obvious buffish wing-bar, and a second indistinct, cream-coloured one on the median coverts. Sometimes has yellow fringes to flight feathers but always a grey-brown and beige appearance overall, without any yellow or olive. Dark lower mandible sometimes with pale base. Variable call: *huit* or *hui*, or a *tsi-uit* similar to that of Yellow-browed Warbler but with different tone. Very rare migrant usually arriving in November.

Pallas's Leaf Warbler *Phylloscopus proregulus*

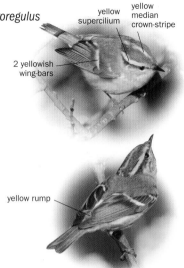

yellow supercilium

yellow median crown-stripe

2 yellowish wing-bars

9 cm. Very small, round with large head and short tail. Broad yellow supercilium, yellow median crown-stripe, olive-green upperparts with lemon-yellow rump visible in flight. Two yellow wing-bars. White underparts washed with yellow on the flanks. Very active, moves in cover of leaves, sometimes hovers in the open. Call: *djui,* sometimes nasal, similar to Willow Warbler's call, with finch-like quality.

yellow rump

Caucasian Mountain Chiffchaff *Phylloscopus lorenzii*

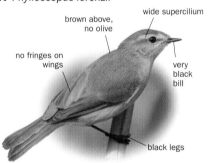

wide supercilium

brown above, no olive

no fringes on wings

very black bill

black legs

11 cm. Similar to Common Chiffchaff but has dark lores and eye-stripe underlining pronounced white supercilium, black bill with yellowish base to lower mandible, no green or yellow fringes on wings or tail, earth-brown underparts, brown wash to flanks. No olive coloration in plumage; blackish legs. Call: plaintive *tuu* like that of Siberian Chiffchaff. Breeds in the Caucasus, wintering to the south; potential vagrant to W Europe.

Plain Leaf Warbler *Phylloscopus neglectus*

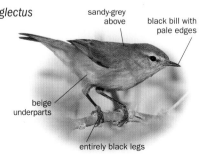

sandy-grey above

black bill with pale edges

beige underparts

entirely black legs

9.5 cm. Very small, black bill with pale edges to mandibles, black legs (toes included), sandy colour above and cream below, no yellow or olive coloration; long cream supercilium from bill. Short rounded wings. Smaller than Caucasian Mountain Chiffchaff, more sandy and less pronounced supercilium. Breeds in Central Asia, winters in Arabian Peninsula. One documented record: a bird caught in Sweden in October 1991.

Dusky Warbler *Phylloscopus fuscatus*

supercilium white in front of eye

earth-brown above

black lores

pinkish or orange legs

thin bill

small eye

sometimes flicks wings

11 cm. Normally terrestrial, dark brown, pale orangey legs, well-defined supercilium, white in front of eye, buff behind. Thinner bill than Radde's Warbler, but variable. Quite rounded wings. Call: a dry *tek*, sometimes given in series, often the best way of finding a bird hidden in dense bushes or brambles. Sometimes climbs into shrubs. A rare vagrant occurring in October and November, sometimes wintering.

Radde's Warbler *Phylloscopus schwarzi*

supercilium buff in front of eye

brown lores

rear of supercilium often sweeps upward

orange legs

supercilium yellow in front of eye

thick bill

sometimes yellowish

orange legs

12 cm. Very similar to Dusky Warbler but more thickset, thicker bill (variable), warmer and browner coloration, especially below, and different supercilium: buff and less pronounced in front of eye, whiter behind. Pale orangey legs, long supercilium often finishing in upward sweep on nape. Call: liquid *tchek* or *dzoui*. Often remains hidden near ground, rarely coming out of cover but may climb into shrubs. Very rare vagrant, in October.

Greenish Warbler *Phylloscopus trochiloides*

IDENTIFICATION 10 cm. Olive-green, well-defined supercilium joins above bill; cream wing-bar on greater coverts; dark brown legs, orangey lower mandible.
VOICE Call: a near-disyllabic *tislee*, similar to that of Pied Wagtail. Song: a high-pitched series of notes, sometimes ending with a trill. **HABITAT** Breeds in northern mixed and conifer forest and scrub. Breeds in E Europe; winters in Asia.

Two-barred Greenish Warbler *Phylloscopus plumbeitarsus*

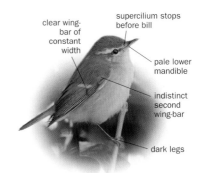

10 cm. Asiatic counterpart of Greenish Warbler; a very rare vagrant to Europe. Less olive, browner above, whiter below, legs just a little darker, supercilium stops before the bill, so does not join above the bill (as Arctic Warbler). Distinguished from latter species by shorter wings, different call, structure, an obvious wing-bar of even width on the greater coverts, a second wing-bar on the median coverts, no dark tip to lower mandible.

Green Warbler *Phylloscopus nitidus*

10 cm. Breeds in the Caucasus; very rare vagrant to Europe. Very similar to Greenish Warbler (and sometimes considered conspecific) but brighter green above and has yellow wash on underparts including supercilium; often has 2 yellow wing-bars.

Arctic Warbler *Phylloscopus borealis*

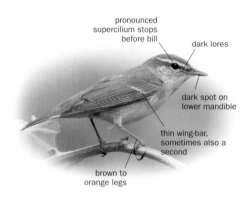

pronounced supercilium stops before bill

dark lores

dark spot on lower mandible

thin wing-bar, sometimes also a second

brown to orange legs

IDENTIFICATION
11 cm. Olive-brown above, cream below, long white supercilium stops before forehead and thus does not join over bill. Long primary projection, narrow wing-bar on greater coverts that becomes thinner towards mantle, rarely a second pale wing-bar on median coverts. Pinkish-brown legs, thicker bill than Greenish Warbler, dark spot on lower mandible. **VOICE** Call: hard, dry *dzic*. Song: a monotone trill like that of Bonelli's or Wood Warblers. **HABITAT** Boreal forests, winters in Asia.

Eastern Crowned Warbler *Phylloscopus coronatus*

long white supercilium underlined with black

pale median crown-stripe

all-orange lower mandible

pale yellow undertail-coverts

11 cm. Breeds in E Siberia; recently recorded in Europe (Britain, Germany and the Netherlands). Resembles Arctic Warbler but crown darker than back, indistinct pale median crown-stripe, yellow undertail-coverts, totally orange lower mandible without dark tip.

Pale-legged Leaf Warbler *Phylloscopus tenellipes*

pronounced white supercilium

2 buffish-white wing-bars

dark tip to lower mandible with pale base

pink legs

10.5 cm. Originates from E Asia; very rare vagrant, observed once in England in October 2012. Olive-brown plumage, darker crown, olive fringes to flight feathers, 2 buffish-white wing-bars, pink legs, long white supercilium stops at bill, half of lower mandible is dark. White undertail-coverts.

CRESTS Very small passerines with rounded shape, a yellow crown-stripe, black-and-white markings on the wings, and very high-pitched songs and calls. Often associated with roaming tit flocks in winter.

Goldcrest *Regulus regulus*

IDENTIFICATION
9 cm. Olive mantle, uniform face, black eye with pale surround, dark malar-stripe, golden-yellow band along top of crown edged black; male has bright orange-tipped crest, raised when excited. Short, barred wings, white wing-bar bordered with black square, white tips to tertials. Juvenile has uniform head. Canaries race (ssp. *teneriffae*) has black band across forecrown and richer buff underparts. **VOICE** Very shrill call, *tsi, tii*, often quavering; shrill song, repeated rapid 3-note phrase, *ti-tsue-ti ti-tsue-ti...* **HABITAT** Mixed and conifer woodland.

olive mantle

all-yellow

Female

uniform face

orange tips

black-and-white wing pattern

yellow crest with black sides

Male

black joins in front of eyes

Ssp. *teneriffae*

long bill

Ruby-crowned Kinglet *Regulus calendula*

10 cm. Vagrant Nearctic crest, observed in the Azores, Iceland (November 1987, October 1998) and Ireland (October 2013). Grey plumage, incomplete broad white eye-ring in front of and behind eye, olive edges to flight feathers, large olive rump. Male has bright red crest without black sides.

no black on crown

olive-grey

white half-spectacles

Firecrest *Regulus ignicapilla*

black-and-white wing pattern

black lores

orange patch

IDENTIFICATION
9 cm. Olive mantle; broad white supercilium and yellow crest, separated by broad black coronal stripe. Thin black eye-stripe and white patch below eye. Pale orange patch on sides of neck. Wings as those of Goldcrest. **VOICE** Call: very high-pitched *tsi*, less quavering than that of Goldcrest. Song: accelerating and repeated very high-pitched note *tsitsitsitsitsitsi...* **HABITAT** Mature deciduous or mixed forests, parks and gardens.

long white supercilium

yellow crest with black sides

slim bill

round body

olive mantle

pale forehead

Madeiran Firecrest *Regulus madeirensis*

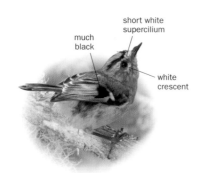

much black

short white supercilium

white crescent

IDENTIFICATION 9.5 cm. Like Firecrest but supercilium reduced to a large crescent above eye, which, with the crescent below eye, gives an appearance of spectacles; black lores, more black on wing and longer bill. **VOICE** Call: like that of other crests, plus a piercing *ouizz* and one like that of Siberian Chiffchaff. **HABITAT** Endemic to forests on Madeira.

OLD WORLD FLYCATCHERS Migrants that feed on insects captured in flight or on the ground, searched for from a perch. Classically, they sit upright on a bare branch and then fly out to catch prey before returning to the same or another open perch. They have slim bills, wide at the base, and the gape is equipped with bristles that help guide prey into the mouth. They nest in cavities. Spotted and Pied-type flycatchers winter in Africa, Red-breasted winters in the Indian subcontinent. Five species breed in Europe, most of the others occur as rare vagrants.

Spotted Flycatcher *Musicapa striata*

Juvenile

autumn juveniles have white fringes

some individuals less streaked below

streaked crown

dull grey above

very long wings

Adult

brown streaks below continue onto flanks

few streaks on crown

greyish-brown above

almost uniform breast

black bill

scaly juvenile feathers

Adult ssp. *tyrrhenica*

reddish tint to rump

Juvenile ssp. *tyrrhenica*

IDENTIFICATION 14 cm. Large dull flycatcher, brown-grey above with a long tail; uniform mantle, dark streaks on crown; dark grey streaks on breast up to chin; white underparts, buff wash on flanks; cream fringes to secondaries, tertials and greater coverts. Juvenile: plumage has pale spots on fledging, resembles adult after rapid moult but pale fringes to all coverts. Black bill and legs. **VOICE** Call: piercing, high-pitched *zi* or *zit*, difficult to hear. Song: barely audible twitter given from exposed perch, incorporating call notes. **HABITAT** Forest edges, clearings, parks and gardens with large trees and open spaces.

GEOGRAPHIC VARIATION In Corsica and Sardinia the race *tyrrhenica* is more uniform, browner above, has fewer streaks on crown, diffuse pale grey markings on breast rarely as high as sides of throat. In spring, individuals of the pale race *balearica* (endemic to the Balearics) could occur elsewhere in Europe, especially on Mediterranean coasts.

CONFUSION SPECIES

Garden Warbler (p. 328)

Other flycatchers (pp. 344–347)

PIED FLYCATCHERS Males have black-and-white plumage, females are brown and white. Juveniles in autumn are like females but white fringes to tertials end in a drop-shape on the shaft without continuing onto the inner web. Young males have black undertail-coverts, females brown. Migrants arrive in April and depart in August or September. Hybrids exist.

Pied Flycatcher *Ficedula hypoleuca*

black nape

small white patch

Male

small white patch
sometimes absent

brown
above

white fringe decreasing
in width

white sides
to tail

drop-shaped
white tip

Female

big white
patch

Juvenile

white in tail

all-black tail

Male ssp. *iberiae*

IDENTIFICATION
13 cm. Male: black above, small white forehead patch, white fringes to inner greater coverts and tertials, reduced white area at base of primaries. White on outer tail feathers. Female: brown (a few males are like females) with patch at base of primaries, less white on tertials. Male of Iberian race (ssp. *iberiae*) has much larger white forehead patch continuing higher over bill, more white in wings, little or no white in tail, particularly in first-summer. Juvenile in autumn: white fringes to tertials widen at tips. **VOICE** Call: loud *hui*, especially heard from migrants. Song: pleasant quite long rhythmic phrase of repeated notes with sudden changes of pitch. **HABITAT** Breeds in mature oak or mixed forests. On migration, in any open area with suitable perches.

Atlas Flycatcher *Ficedula speculigera*

extensive
white forehead

much
white

Male

little or
no white

big white
patch

13 cm. Very closely related to Pied Flycatcher; breeds in the Atlas mountains of N Africa, potential vagrant to Europe. Male: large white forehead patch, extensive white patch at base of primaries, totally white greater coverts, rarely has white on outer webs of outer tail feathers. First-year males difficult to separate from *iberiae* birds of same age.

Collared Flycatcher *Ficedula albicollis*

hint of pale grey collar

Female

paler grey rump

big white patch

IDENTIFICATION
13 cm. Male: black and white, continuous wide white collar, some first-year males have grey or black nape, much white at base of primaries, little or no white in tail (only on outer feather), extensive white patch on forehead, white rump. Female: as Pied Flycatcher but broad white patch at base of primaries, pale rump, plumage often paler. **VOICE** Call: plaintive, abrupt *hii*, less lively than that of Pied Flycatcher. Song: different from that of Pied Flycatcher, a series of quite slow, prolonged whistles with changes of pitch. **HABITAT** Mature deciduous forests.

big white patch

wide white collar

Male

white rump

no white on tail

big white patch

Semi-collared Flycatcher *Ficedula semitorquata*

13 cm. Male: pied plumage with white sides of neck forming a clear half-collar, extensive white at the base of the primaries, and on the greater and median coverts. Winter plumage: white fringes to tertials of constant width. Male has white on 2 or 3 outer tail feathers. Female: 2 wing-bars on greater and median coverts. Beware of Pied × Collared Flycatcher hybrids that can be very similar to Semi-collared but have less white on tail feathers.

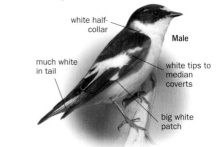

white half-collar

Male

much white in tail

white tips to median coverts

big white patch

narrow regular white fringes

white tips to median coverts

Female

big white patch

Red-breasted Flycatcher *Ficedula parva*

brown to blackish-brown uppertail-coverts

pale eye-ring

Juvenile

orange base to bill

narrow eye-ring

white on tail

Breeding male

orange bib

pale brown mantle

tail often raised

white on tail

Female

11 cm. Small and brown; tail with white base and inverted black T. Dull brown above, whitish below, buff wash on breast. Narrow pale eye-ring, uniform face. Nervous, perches in the open to hunt, flicks tail vertically. In spring, male has orange throat, grey head. **VOICE** Call: insistent *it*, rough *zrrt* or dry *zit*. Song similar to that of Willow Warbler. **HABITAT** Forests.

Taiga Flycatcher *Ficedula albicilla*

black uppertail-coverts

grey cheek

black base to bill

greyish breast

Female

orange throat underlined with grey

Adult male

11 cm. Asian counterpart of Red-breasted Flycatcher. Can be distinguished in autumn by blackish uppertail-coverts, darker than tail; fringes to tertials thinner and more clear-cut; very dark lower mandible; whiter underparts; pale face with indistinct eye-ring. Spring male differs from Red-breasted in smaller orange bib surrounded by grey, and browner crown. Very rare autumn vagrant to Europe. Call; a rattle *trrrrrr*, reminiscent of flight call of Mistle Thrush.

Brown Flycatcher *Musicapa daurica*

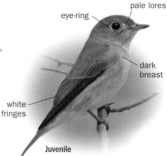

eye-ring
pale lores
dark breast
white fringes

Juvenile

12 cm. Asian vagrant with a few records from Britain, Denmark, Greece and Sweden. White eye-ring and pale lores form clear spectacles, large head with dark malar-stripe, smoky breast. Very broad bill with orange base. Pale fringes to wing feathers, no white on tail.

Mugimaki Flycatcher *Ficedula mugimaki*

white supercilium
white on wing

Adult male

14 cm. Very rare Asian vagrant, recorded in western Russia. Somewhat reminiscent of Red-breasted Flycatcher. Immature male brown-grey above, orangey breast and upper belly, narrow cream eye-ring, black tail and narrow white fringes to greater coverts and tertials. Adult male: black above, broad white supercilium behind eye, white band on shoulder, orange below.

dark grey
orange throat and breast
white wing-bars

Juvenile male

Narcissus Flycatcher *Ficedula narcissina*

yellow supercilium
yellow throat
Male
yellow rump

13 cm. Asian migrant; 1 bird caught in France in August 1942 is of doubtful origin. Immature dull, cream below, dull brown above, olive rump and reddish tail. Adult male: black with long lemon-yellow supercilium, large yellow rump, white band on shoulder, yellow underparts.

TYRANT FLYCATCHERS The *Empidonax* species of Nearctic flyctachers are very difficult to separate. Three migrant species have occurred in Europe as very rare vagrants; other species could also occur. Distinctive as a group, olive-brown above, two wide cream wing-bars, cream fringes to flight feathers stop before coverts, pale eye-ring, bill with very large base. Identification is very difficult and often requires the bird to be caught to obtain measurements and wing formula, as colour criteria are variable; for example, a Least Flycatcher caught in Iceland in 2003 had an orange lower mandible, an Alder Flycatcher also caught in Iceland just a few days later had a largely dark lower mandible (in disagreement with generally described bill colours).

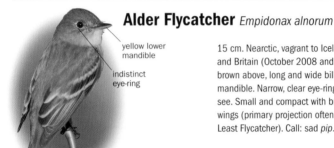

Alder Flycatcher *Empidonax alnorum*

yellow lower mandible

indistinct eye-ring

15 cm. Nearctic, vagrant to Iceland (October 2003) and Britain (October 2008 and October 2010). Olive-brown above, long and wide bill with all-yellow lower mandible. Narrow, clear eye-ring sometimes difficult to see. Small and compact with broad tail, quite long wings (primary projection often longer than that of Least Flycatcher). Call: sad *pip*.

Least Flycatcher *Empidonax minimus*

distinct eye-ring

dark tip to bill

14 cm. Nearctic, 1 bird recorded in Iceland (October 2003). Olive-brown above, lower mandible with dark tip (sometimes reduced). Clear eye-ring. Small and compact with narrow tail, short to medium length wings (primary projection usually shorter than that of Alder Flycatcher), bill generally shorter than that of Alder Flycatcher. Call: short, dry *pouit* or *pit*.

Acadian Flycatcher *Empidonax virescens*

pronounced eye-ring

long primary projection

yellowish below

15 cm. Nearctic, recorded in Iceland (October 1967) and Britain (October 2015). Greenish-olive above, bill with broad base, totally orange lower mandible, very clear cream eye-ring, very long primary projection; smoky breast, yellow wash on underparts. Call: hard *pouist* or sad-sounding *pic*.

OTHER TYRANT FLYCATCHERS Three other species have occurred as vagrants in Europe; they have characteristic structure and plumage making identification much less complicated than for members of the *Empidonax* genus.

Eastern Phoebe *Sayornis phoebe*

17 cm. Nearctic, vagrant to Britain (April 1987). Larger than *Empidonax* flycatchers. Black of large head grades into grey nape and mantle, long black tail (frequently wagged), all-black bill, and diffuse grey wing-bars. Underparts variable, whitish or pale yellowish. Juvenile has buffy wing-bars and stronger yellowish colour on underparts. Call: clear chirped *chip*.

blackish head and cheek

black bill

diffuse wing-bars

Eastern Kingbird *Tyrannus tyrannus*

21 cm. Nearctic, vagrant to Ireland (October 2012). Large flycatcher with big black head and white throat, characteristic black tail with white terminal bar, grey back, whitish fringes to all wing feathers, and white underparts. Juvenile is browner and has scalier wing-coverts.

blackish head

black tail with white tip

whitish fringes

Fork-tailed Flycatcher *Tyrannus savana*

20–35 cm. From Central and S America, vagrant to N America and Spain (1 record, October 2002). Confusion impossible due to very long black tail streamers. Black wings, tail and crown, ash-grey mantle and white underparts.

black cap

grey above

very long forked tail

PENDULINE TIT, LEIOTHRIX, REEDLING, PARROTBILL AND LONG-TAILED TIT The five species on pages 350–352 belong to five different families and are mainly of Asian or African (*Remiz*) origin. They have short, stout legs and are often acrobatic like the true tits. The Leiothrix and Parrotbill are introduced.

Penduline Tit *Remiz pendulinus*

dark rufous mantle

Male

black forehead

pointed grey bill

no black mask

grey forehead

duller mantle

Juvenile

reddish crown

extensive black mask

Female

Male ssp. *caspius*

IDENTIFICATION 11 cm. Pointed bill, brown back, grey head with black mask. Male has reddish forehead, obvious mask, rufous breast; female is duller and has less developed mask. Juvenile: uniform face without mask, beige back. Nest: ball of soft vegetation with access tunnel hanging from a branch. **VOICE** Call: very shrill, short or trailing and descending. Song: discreet and varied, with finch-like trill, high-pitched and plaintive notes. **HABITAT** Riparian forest and marshes in summer, reedbeds in winter. The darker-headed form in the Volga and Caspian areas (ssp. *caspius*) has prominent pale fringes on wing and tail feathers.

Red-billed Leiothrix *Leiothrix lutea*

red bill

short forked tail

yellow throat

IDENTIFICATION 14.5 cm. Introduced exotic species, originally from Asia. Thickset and colourful, very discreet in habits. Yellow throat and orange-red breast, large black eye and whitish lores forming a pale face mask, bordered below with a dark moustache. Grey mantle, and red-and-orange fringes to wing feathers. **VOICE** Simple fluty song, reminiscent of that of Blackcap but shorter and less melodious. **HABITAT** Forest environments and dense undergrowth. Populations established in parts of France and Spain.

Bearded Reedling *Panurus biarmicus*

IDENTIFICATION
12 cm. Inhabits wetlands. Both sexes have long graduated buff tail with white edges, and black-and-white pattern on otherwise rufous wing. Male has grey head with long moustache in front of eye and uniform black undertail-coverts. Female has plain buff upperparts, rarely with black streaking on crown and back. Orange bill, black legs, pale yellow iris. Juvenile: black back, dark lores and yellow bill (male), grey lores and dark bill (female). **VOICE** Call: bouncy *ping*, often given by flocks as a contact call. **HABITAT** Ancient reedbeds, nearly always flooded, sometimes drier habitats in winter.

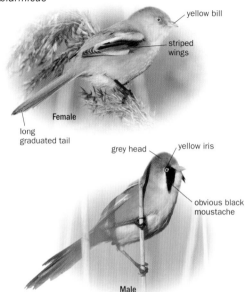

yellow bill

striped wings

Female

long graduated tail

grey head

yellow iris

obvious black moustache

Male

Vinous-throated Parrotbill *Paradoxornis webbianus*

IDENTIFICATION 12 cm. Small size, long rufous tail and large head, reminiscent of Long-tailed Tit with short, stubby bill. Rufous head with orange face, some individuals have grey face and pale throat. Gregarious in winter. **VOICE** Call a buzzing rapid series *tchai-tchai-tchai*, with repeated whistles *tu tu tu*. **HABITAT** Bushy reedbeds. Introduced to the Brabbia marshes in Milan, Italy.

large head

grey mantle

rufous crown

long tail

rufous wings

Long-tailed Tit *Aegithalos caudatus*

black mask
black mantle
very long tail

Ssp. *europaeus*

extensive white on tertials
clear border with black nape
all-white head

Ssp. *caudatus*

very wide black mask
grey mantle

Ssp. *irbii*

grey mantle
pale brown band

Ssp. *siculus*

IDENTIFICATION 14 cm, of which 9 cm is long, graduated tail, black with white sides. Black back with pink shoulders, white below sometimes flushed pink. Black wings with white fringes to secondaries and tertials. Mainly white head with broad black supercilium, widening at rear, very wide and covering sides of head in juvenile. Various races breed in Europe and differ in plumage colour and markings; hybrids occur. Some, but not all, subspecies are described here. The ssp. *rosaceus* occupies much of W Europe including Britain and Ireland and has a dark-spotted breast. Ssp. *europaeus* throughout much of central Europe has a slimmer black band on the head. Ssp. *caudatus* from N Europe has an entirely white head sharply demarcated from the black nape, and much white on tertials; it occasionally irrupts into more southern areas in winter. Ssp. *irbii* is found in southern Iberia and on Mediterranean islands. In all races, yellow (adult) or red (juvenile) eye-ring. Gregarious. **VOICE** Very vocal, members of a group stay in contact using a shrill *tsii tsii tsii* or rapid trill *ti-rrr ti-rrr* or *trrtrrtrrtrrtrr*. Song: a barely audible twitter. **HABITAT** Areas with bushes and trees, hedgerows, parks and gardens; in agricultural, forested or urban areas.

TITS Small, tree-dwelling passerines that breed in cavities, with strong thin bills and short sturdy legs. Acrobatic, they readily hang upside down on branches. Often in mixed flocks in winter. Until recently, all grouped in one genus *Parus*; they are now separated according to genetic relationships, with five different genera occurring in Europe: *Parus, Cyanistes, Lophophanes, Periparus* and *Poecile*.

Crested Tit *Lophophanes cristatus*

IDENTIFICATION 11.5 cm. Uniform brown above, cream below. Head with elegant black-and-white pattern; small black bib, black surround to white cheek, black collar bordering the brown neck. Long black crown feathers tipped white, raised as a crest when excited. Red (adult) or yellow (juvenile) iris. **VOICE** Song: a few shrill notes followed by rapid trill *titi tutututututu...* Call: a few simple high-pitched calls, on a single tone, sometimes incorporating the trill of the song. **HABITAT** Conifer forests and woods, parks and gardens mainly in winter. Will come to bird tables.

head pattern still obvious from behind

black-and-white crest

earth-brown mantle

black throat

Coal Tit *Periparus ater*

IDENTIFICATION 11.5 cm. Small, black-and-white; long white patch on nape, large black bib and white cheeks, coal-grey back, black wings with 2 white wing-bars. Buff wash to flanks. Juvenile: yellowish cheeks. Various races in Europe: British race (ssp. *vieirae*) is more olive on the back, the continental race (ssp. *ater*) occurring on much of the continent has bluer back. **VOICE** Song: monotonous rhythmic *ti-tue ti-tue ti-tue ti-tu*. Call: shrill, simple *tsi* or *tue*. **HABITAT** Occurs in conifers, from forest to copse; parks and gardens. Sometimes comes to bird tables in winter.

dark grey mantle

long white nape patch

white cheek

no yellow

CONFUSION SPECIES Marsh and Willow Tits (p. 356)

Great Tit (p. 354)

Crests (p. 341)

Great Tit *Parus major*

Female

wide black band reaches undertail-coverts

black line disappears between legs

Male

white cheek

olive mantle

yellow belly

IDENTIFICATION 14 cm. Large; green back, yellow below separated in 2 by a black vertical band, wide and continuing between the legs (male), narrower and finishing at the lower belly (female). Black head with white cheeks and yellow nape. Juvenile: yellowish cheeks and duller below. **VOICE** Various songs, a repeated *ti-tu ti-tu, u-ti u-ti* or *ti-ti-tou ti-ti-tou*, also tinkling twitters. Various calls, *pi-tchr-tchr-tchr, pi-trr* or *tchin* reminiscent of a Chaffinch. **HABITAT** All environments that have trees, even if isolated, from mountains to city centres. Nests in a cavity; readily adopts a nest box.

Blue Tit *Cyanistes caeruleus*

blue crown

greenish mantle

Adult

blue wings

yellow underparts

grey crown turning blue

yellow cheeks on fledging

Juvenile

IDENTIFICATION 12 cm. Small, blue and yellow, almond-green back. White head with blue crown, black eye-stripe becomes blue behind eye, to continue around cheek; black throat. Male brighter than female. Yellow breast with thin, short black central line. Juvenile: duller with yellowish cheeks. **VOICE** Song finishes with a rapid trill after a few insistent, separated notes, *ti ti ti taitutututututu*, or *tai-tai tutu*. Varied calls, *trrrtrrrtrr, titi trr-trr, trrtrr ai-tai*. **HABITAT** All environments with bushes or trees, from forests to parks and gardens, even in city centres.

Azure Tit *Cyanistes cyanus*

12 cm. Breeds in Siberia, very rarely winters in Europe. Absolutely no yellow coloration, white crown and belly, azure-blue back, long graduated tail with white sides and broad white edgings on wing. Pleske's Tit, a hybrid between Azure and Blue Tits, is very occasionally seen in Europe: very similar to Azure Tit but less white on wing, shorter tail, some blue on crown and some pale yellow on breast.

white crown
sky-blue mantle
extensive white in wing
no hint of yellow

African Blue Tit *Cyanistes teneriffae*

IDENTIFICATION 11.5 cm. Closely related to Blue Tit, which it replaces in N Africa and the Canary Islands. The ssp. *ultramarinus* of N Africa has blue mantle, broad white wing-bar and bluish-black crown. There are several subspecies in the Canary Islands with blue mantles and long, strong bills. Ssp. *teneriffae* (Tenerife, La Gomera) and ssp. *hedwigii* (Gran Canaria) have blue mantle and no wing-bar; ssp. *ombriosus* (El Hierro) has a narrow wing-bar and green tint to mantle; ssp. *degener* (Fuerteventura, Lanzarote) has large wing-bar; ssp. *palmensis* (La Palma) has narrow wing-bar and greyish mantle. **VOICE** Calls similar to those of other tits more than Blue Tit. **HABITAT** Forest, woods, parks and gardens.

no wing-bar
Ssp. *teneriffae*

thick bill
blue mantle
broad wing-bar
blackish-blue crown
Ssp. *degener*

blue mantle
wing-bar
Ssp. *ultramarinus*

Marsh Tit *Poecile palustris*

black bill with white base
'dirty' cheek
indistinct beige fringes
small black bib

IDENTIFICATION 11–12 cm. Pale brown above, whitish below, black crown and small black bib. Black bill thicker than that of Willow Tit with diagnostic white spot at base of upper mandible. Uniform dark brown wings, no distinct pale panel on secondaries. **VOICE** Varied songs, *pitchou* or *piti-tchou*, or series of shriller rapidly repeated nasal notes, *tchi-tchi-tchi*... Normal shrill call, *pit*, *pitye* and *chicabebebebe*. **HABITAT** Mature deciduous woodland, notably with oak or beech. Also parks and gardens with mature trees; comes to bird tables in winter.

Ssp. *rhenanus*
big 'bib'
pale panel
buff flanks

white cheeks
white fringes
all-black bill
less colour
Ssp. *montanus*

Willow Tit *Poecile montanus*

IDENTIFICATION 11–12 cm. Pale brown above, whitish below, black crown extends further onto nape and black bib larger than in Marsh Tit; thicker neck, shorter outer tail feathers, thinner entirely black bill and rear cheek is a cleaner white. Distinct whitish panel on secondaries (sometimes hint of one in Marsh Tit). Various races throughout Europe: British race (ssp. *kleinschmidti*) is darker than continental races with browner back, dirtier cheeks and buff flanks; N and E European races (ssp. *loennbergi* and ssp. *borealis*) are paler and greyer. **VOICE** Song: in a slow series *tiu tiu tiu tiu tiu*. Normal call: a series of nasal notes *ti-tchu tchu tchu*... **HABITAT** Cool forest, ancient riparian woodland in lowlands, conifer forest at altitude.

CONFUSION SPECIES

Blackcap (p. 324)

Bullfinch (p. 403)

Sombre Tit *Poecile lugubris*

IDENTIFICATION
13.5 cm. Grey tit with extensive dull black bib; brownish-black crown extends to behind the cheeks, which appear as a very white triangle. Quite long bill, no brown on flanks. **VOICE** Like Marsh Tit but grating. Call: shrill *si-si-si* or rolled *chrrrr*. **HABITAT** Forest, bushes, orchards.

triangular white cheek

thick bill

very big bib

Siberian Tit *Poecile cinctus*

IDENTIFICATION
13 cm. Round body with a large head, long tail. Warm-brown mantle, rufous flanks, dull brown-grey crown, big black bib, lores blacker than crown. **VOICE** Song: *tchi-uir tchi-uir...* or *tchai tchai tchai*. Call: *si-si-taitaitai* similar to that of Willow Tit. **HABITAT** Ancient taiga forest, conifer and birch forests.

brown crown

very white cheeks

chestnut mantle

big 'bib'

buff flanks

NUTHATCHES Small thickset birds with big head and short tail, blue-grey back and long, thick dagger-shaped bill. They climb up trunks and along branches using their short legs and strong toes, and can descend upside down. They nest in tree holes or rock crevices.

Eurasian Nuthatch *Sitta europaea*

Ssp. *caesia*
blue-grey
black mask
long pointed bill
orange underparts

IDENTIFICATION 14 cm. Blue-grey above, orange underparts with white throat and darker undertail-coverts, reddish with white spots. Black mask less visible in juveniles. Short, rounded wings, short tail has white corners. Scandinavian race (ssp. *europaea*) has white underparts, rufous restricted to under the tail. Siberian race (ssp. *asiatica*) is small and pale with white supercilium. **VOICE** Very noisy. Varied calls, often a repeated *tui*. Song: long rhythmic series of repeated note *tui tui tui* ... or rapid *tioutioutiout*... **HABITAT** Forests and woodlands, parks and gardens with trees, even in towns and cities.

orange limited to under tail

white breast

Ssp. *europaea*

Ssp. *asiatica*

white supercilium

white below

Western Rock Nuthatch *Sitta neumayer*

mask wide behind eye

orangey-cream underparts

thick legs

IDENTIFICATION 15 cm. Large grey-and-white nuthatch, long bill and robust legs, long black eye-stripe, cream wash to belly; often on ground or on rocks, rarely on trees. **VOICE** A series of accelerating, descending whistles. **HABITAT** Rocky and rugged environments with scattered trees or bushes, very different from that of Eurasian Nuthatch.

Corsican Nuthatch *Sitta whiteheadi*

IDENTIFICATION
12 cm. Blue-grey above, whitish with buff wash below. White supercilium, black eye-stripe, black crown (male) or grey with dark forehead (female). White cheeks. Smaller and more lively than Eurasian Nuthatch. Often in tit flocks in winter. **VOICE** Song: a long rapid trill *didididididi...* Normal call: hoarse repeated nasal trill. **HABITAT** Mature Corsican Pine forests, sometimes mixed with Maritime Pines. Occurs mainly at 1,000–1,500 m, sometimes lower in winter.

white supercilium

black crown

whitish underparts

Male

short tail

blue-grey crown

Female

Krüper's Nuthatch *Sitta krueperi*

12 cm. Breeds in pine forests of Turkey and Lesbos. Blue-grey above, whitish below with reddish breast-band and rufous undertail-coverts. Well-defined black cap (male) or less extensive (female). White supercilium and black eye-stripe. Song: a nasal *tuituituituitui*. Call: *djui*, similar to that of Greenfinch.

white supercilium and forehead

grey nape

reddish-brown breast

Male

reddish undertail-coverts

Red-breasted Nuthatch *Sitta canadensis*

10.5 cm. Small Nearctic arboreal nuthatch, rare vagrant to Iceland (May 1970) and Britain (October 1989 to May 1990). Resembles Corsican Nuthatch with black head and long white supercilium, white throat and cheeks, but dense orange (male) or washed orange (female) breast and belly. Call: slow, nasal *niac niac...* in series.

black crown

long white supercilium

orange below

TREECREEPERS Brown and white, elongated, climb trees in spiral fashion clinging close to trunk, using their rigid tail as a support. Rarely leaves bark on which it finds its insect food. Two very similar species.

Short-toed Treecreeper *Certhia brachydactyla*

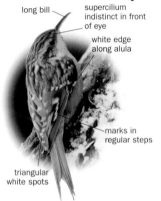

long bill

supercilium indistinct in front of eye

white edge along alula

marks in regular steps

triangular white spots

IDENTIFICATION 12 cm. Very similar to Eurasian Treecreeper; differs in voice, longer bill, supercilium ill-defined before eye but very visible and white behind eye, buff or dirty white flanks and yellow markings on wings arranged in regular steps, without a break. Triangular white spots on tips of flight feathers, 2 large separations between feathers on closed wing. White on alula extends onto outer feather edge.
VOICE Very shrill call, *tsiiii*, barely audible. Very high-pitched rising song, *tu toutai tutaitii*, sometimes preceded by the call.
HABITAT Woods and forest, parks and gardens.

Eurasian Treecreeper *Certhia familiaris*

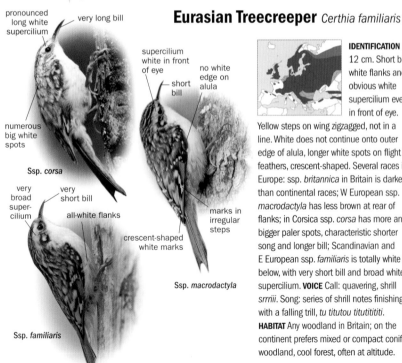

pronounced long white supercilium

very long bill

supercilium white in front of eye

short bill

no white edge on alula

numerous big white spots

Ssp. *corsa*

very broad supercilium

very short bill

all-white flanks

marks in irregular steps

crescent-shaped white marks

Ssp. *macrodactyla*

Ssp. *familiaris*

IDENTIFICATION 12 cm. Short bill, white flanks and obvious white supercilium even in front of eye.
Yellow steps on wing zigzagged, not in a line. White does not continue onto outer edge of alula, longer white spots on flight feathers, crescent-shaped. Several races in Europe: ssp. *britannica* in Britain is darker than continental races; W European ssp. *macrodactyla* has less brown at rear of flanks; in Corsica ssp. *corsa* has more and bigger paler spots, characteristic shorter song and longer bill; Scandinavian and E European ssp. *familiaris* is totally white below, with very short bill and broad white supercilium. **VOICE** Call: quavering, shrill *srrriii*. Song: series of shrill notes finishing with a falling trill, *tu titutou titutititi*.
HABITAT Any woodland in Britain; on the continent prefers mixed or compact conifer woodland, cool forest, often at altitude.

Wallcreeper *Tichodroma muraria*

IDENTIFICATION 16 cm. Reminiscent of a treecreeper with a short tail, very rounded wings, long downcurved bill. Bright red colour on wing-coverts and base of flight feathers, readily visible in flight. Grey body, male has black throat and breast in summer (white in male in winter and in female). Climbs on rock faces, or on stone buildings, sometimes with open wings; has butterfly-like flight. **VOICE** Call: *tui* and rolled notes. Song: a short twitter starting with 4 or 5 fluty notes, reminiscent of a finch. **HABITAT** Breeds at high altitude, on cliffs or rock faces; lower in winter, even on buildings.

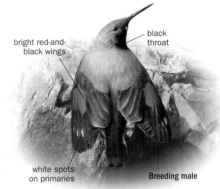

bright red-and-black wings

black throat

white spots on primaries

Breeding male

Female

white throat

grey

short tail

long downcurved bill

Winter

white spots

robust legs

Golden Oriole *Oriolus oriolus*

IDENTIFICATION 24 cm. Size of Blackbird but slimmer, discreet in tops of trees. Male: black wings, black tail with yellow corners, uniform golden-yellow body, black loral stripe and red bill. Female: green back, yellow rump and undertail-coverts, thin streaks on flanks, dark bill. Immature: as female but more strongly streaked below. **VOICE** Call: a rough *raaahh*. Song: a short, descending fluty phrase. **HABITAT** Mature deciduous woodland, riparian woodland.

greenish-yellow

black lores

Female

black streaks

black wings

reddish bill

golden-yellow body

yellow patch

Male

SHRIKES Medium-sized passerines with hooked bill and black mask. Hunt from a perch looking for insects or small invertebrates, sometimes other birds. Can store excess food on thorns or barbed-wire, termed 'larders'.

Red-backed Shrike *Lanius collurio*

ash-grey

chestnut

black mask

head sometimes grey

Male

white on tail

greyish nape

Female

more or less barred reddish-brown mantle

barred flanks

brown tail

Female

IDENTIFICATION
17 cm. Male: grey head and black mask, chestnut mantle, grey rump, pink-washed white underparts, black tail with white feather bases (black inverted T). Female: brown barred with black above, dark scaly marks below, brown mask, grey nape. Juvenile: very barred. **VOICE** Call: loud *cha*. Song: very quiet warble. **HABITAT** Open environments with bushes. Farmland with hedgerows, bushy alpine meadows.

Masked Shrike *Lanius nubicus*

finely barred crown

white shoulder

Juvenile

grey-black mantle

Female

long tail

long tail with much white

extensive white forehead

all-black above

white 'braces'

orange flanks

Male

IDENTIFICATION
17 cm. Slender with long tail. Resembles Woodchat Shrike with a large white forehead, white shoulders, but is more slender, has black crown and orangey breast and flanks. Male more colourful and contrasting than grey-mantled female. Juvenile like that of Woodchat Shrike but slimmer, longer and narrower black tail with white sides, slim bill, dark rump. **VOICE** Male's song is a quiet pleasant warble; alarm call is a dry rattle. **HABITAT** Dry semi-open environments, maquis, olive groves.

Woodchat Shrike *Lanius senator*

IDENTIFICATION
18 cm. Black-and-white plumage, white forehead, rufous crown extending to mantle, male more colourful. White below, black mantle with white scapulars forming 2 bands, white rump, white sides to tail. Black wings with white base to primaries visible on closed wing. The Corsican race (ssp. *badius*) lacks the white square at base of primaries. The eastern race (ssp. *niloticus*) has more white in wings and black on head. Juvenile is pale, scaly brown-grey above, scaly white below, black-fringed white scapulars contrast with mantle and wing-coverts; more slender than juvenile Red-backed Shrike. **VOICE** Call: varied, *kret* or *kiwit*. Song: muffled musical warble with rough notes and imitations. **HABITAT** Semi-open environments with bushes. Hedgerows, maquis and sparse garrique.

reddish crown

white forehead

broad uniform black mask

white 'braces'

white rump

Male ssp. *senator*

dull reddish crown

blackish-brown mask

pale lores

white patch

Female ssp. *senator*

Male ssp. *badius*

no white

very broad black mask

Male ssp. *niloticus*

big white patch

white band

no red

extensive white bases

pale crown

white scapulars with black edges

coloured greater coverts

white patch

Juvenile ssp. *senator*

Juvenile ssp. *niloticus*

Lesser Grey Shrike *Lanius minor*

grey forehead

barely scaled

white fringes

pale base

Juvenile

grey forehead

thick black bill

Young adult

white on tail

ash-grey

black forehead

Adult

pinkish underparts

big white patch

IDENTIFICATION 20 cm. Black mask across eye covers much of forehead (less in first-year birds); ashy-grey from crown to rump, white underparts with pinkish wash on breast. Black wings with white base to primaries, white sides to tail. Long primary projection. Juvenile: reduced black mask; dark barring above but not below and long primary projection. **VOICE** Call: hard, mono- or disyllabic. Song: long warbling with imitations. **HABITAT** Semi-open areas with trees.

Iberian Grey Shrike *Lanius meridionalis*

white forehead

Juvenile

slim bill

narrow white supercilium

lead-grey

small white patch

pinkish underparts

Adult

IDENTIFICATION 24 cm. Larger than Lesser Grey Shrike, darker grey mantle, black face mask limited to lores and cheek, with thin white line above only reaching to eye. White patch at base of primaries, white band on shoulder, pinkish wash to white breast. **VOICE** Call: hard *shaaa*. Song: very slow separated notes, often preceded by 2 metallic notes, *tu-tu...* **HABITAT** Open dry environments with isolated bushes or trees.

CONFUSION SPECIES

Northern Wheatear (p. 298)

Great Grey Shrike *Lanius excubitor*

IDENTIFICATION
24 cm. Very similar to Iberian Grey Shrike but lighter ash-grey, no clear supercilium, white bases to secondaries form a continuous white wing-bar in flight; slimmer black bill; large white corners to tail. Juvenile finely vermiculated on crown and underparts.

VOICE Call: nasal, drawn-out *schaiaiaiai* in series. Song: very slow, a few repeated notes often starting with a rapid *tlu-tlu*..., higher-pitched than that of Iberian Grey Shrike. **HABITAT** Hedgerows, meadows with bushes, thickets, with some large trees; also scrub in winter.

GEOGRAPHIC VARIATION Breeds in much of N and central Europe becoming scarcer in south of range; winters further south, a few birds coming to Britain. The ssp. *koenigi* in the Canaries is smaller, lead-grey above, with grey flanks, broad black mask and fine white line above eye. The N African ssp. *elegans* is a possible vagrant to Europe; it is paler grey, with white fringes to secondaries, wide white base to primaries, and pale flanks. See also Steppe Grey Shrike (p. 366).

Adult

white spot

ash-grey

white bases

white supercilium

narrow black mask

ash-grey

white underparts

Adult

little white

lead-grey

greyish flanks

Ssp. *koenigi*

little white

little white

strong bill

less white than *elegans*

Form '*dodsoni*'

pale grey

thick bill

much white

Ssp. *elegans*

Steppe Grey Shrike *Lanius (excubitor) pallidirostris*

pale lores

big white tips to secondaries

thick pale bill with dark tip

Juvenile

much white in tail

long bulbous bill

pale grey

much white

narrow but complete black mask

Adult

24 cm. Breeds in Central Asian steppes, winters in Iran and Arabian Peninsula; sometimes considered to be a separate species. Very rare vagrant to Europe. Very strong thick-based bill, very pale grey mantle. Adult: black lores, all-black bill. Juvenile in autumn: dark cheeks, pale lores, pink base to bill. Compared to Great Grey Shrike: more white on tail, on tertials and at base of primaries but black base to secondaries; tips to secondaries with large white tips giving impression of broad continuous wing-bar in flight, staggered between primary bases and tips of secondaries.

Northern Shrike *Lanius (excubitor) borealis*

white supercilium

Adults ssp. *borealis*

slim bill

finely barred

small white patch

brownish tint

pale lores

scaly below

Juvenile ssp. *borealis*

24 cm. Often considered races of Great Grey Shrike, but sometimes given specific status: Nearctic race (ssp. *borealis*) is a rare vagrant in the Azores; Siberian race (ssp. *sibiricus*) is rare winter visitor to Ukraine. Numerous fine black scaly markings below, little white at base of primaries, no white at base of secondaries, very pale grey upperparts. Narrow black mask stops in front of eye and does not continue to bill, with white line above. Juvenile very scaly below, pale base to bill, warm brown wash to crown, mantle and flanks.

Isabelline Shrike *Lanius isabellinus*

17 cm. From W Asia, rare vagrant in Europe. Uniform sandy-brown above (even juveniles), buff-washed flanks, brown scaly markings in autumn, brown mask but pale lores, white base to primaries, sometimes hardly visible. Rufous tail. Male has black mask. Same sandy-brown colour on crown, nape and mantle.

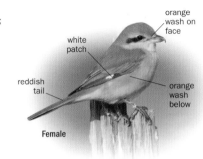

orange wash on face

white patch

reddish tail

orange wash below

Female

fairly uniform buff face

faint scaling

Juvenile

pale mask behind eye

buff wash and brown scales

Juvenile

pale lores

orange wash to flanks

Female

white supercilium

pale lores

orange wash to flanks

Female

sometimes no supercilium

black mask sometimes wide

orange tint to supercilium

sometimes grey above

rufous tail

Male

Male

Turkestan Shrike *Lanius phoenicuroides*

17 cm. From Central Asia, rare vagrant in W Europe. Very similar to Isabelline Shrike. Male white below and crown more rufous than mantle, well-marked black mask with white line above. The 'karelini' form has a grey crown. Juveniles have white underparts, and black scaly markings on white flanks.

reddish crown

wide black mask with white above

white patch

whitish underparts

rufous tail

Male

brown mask

black scaling on white underparts

Female

brown mantle

grey crown

Male

reddish tail

upperparts sometimes sandy-grey

grey crown

Form 'karelini'

black mask onto forehead

Male

rufous crown

pronounced scaling

Juvenile

white supercilium

black scaling

Female

Hybrid Red-backed × Isabelline/Turkestan Shrikes

Some individuals show characteristics intermediate between those of Isabelline and Turkestan Shrikes and Red-backed Shrike; hybridisation occurs where their distributions overlap. Note black markings on the tail, grey on crown or back more or less evident according to the parentage of the individual.

grey above

grey above

brown inverted T

reddish tail with black tip

orange flanks

Brown Shrike *Lanius cristatus*

18 cm. Vagrant from Asia that arrives late in autumn, sometimes November. No white patch on base of primaries. Reddish brown, graduated tail. Similar to Red-backed Shrike but no barring above, slightly barred buff-washed flanks. Brown mask with white line above.

white supercilium

no white

black ear-coverts

brown mantle

reddish-brown graduated tail

short primary projection

Male

Female

Long-tailed Shrike *Lanius schach*

23 cm. Asian species, very rare vagrant to N Europe and Middle East in autumn and winter. Large; long black rounded tail with cream sides; orangey rump, flanks and band on scapulars; grey crown and mantle; broad black mask covers part of forehead. Juvenile is similar but scalier and with narrower face mask.

black fore-head

Juvenile

extensive black forehead

grey crown

rufous-orange scapulars

white patch

graduated tail

Adult

very long tail

CROWS AND JAYS Opportunist large passerines, some with entirely black plumage, most species do not sing but have loud, simple call. Crows are able to learn by experience.

Eurasian Jay *Garrulus glandarius*

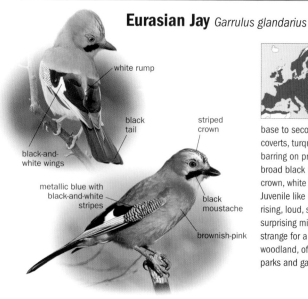

white rump

black tail

striped crown

black-and-white wings

metallic blue with black-and-white stripes

black moustache

brownish-pink

IDENTIFICATION
34 cm. Colourful woodland crow with pinkish-brown body, black tail, black wings with white base to secondaries, pinkish-brown wing-coverts, turquoise-blue, black-and-white barring on primary-coverts. White face with broad black moustache, black-streaked crown, white iris. White undertail-coverts. Juvenile like adult. **VOICE** Normal call: a rising, loud, screamed *schaaaa*. Song: surprising mixture of clicks and babbles, very strange for a crow. **HABITAT** Deciduous woodland, of oak but not exclusively, copses, parks and gardens, even in towns.

(Spotted) Nutcracker *Nucifraga caryocatactes*

long conical bill

speckled with white

dark brown crown

white spots

black wings

IDENTIFICATION
32 cm. Small brown crow, spotted white. Dark-brown crown, black flight feathers, black tail with white tips, white undertail-coverts. Long black bill, pale face. Fluttering, butterfly-like flight, from top of one conifer to another, where it freely perches in view. The Siberian race (ssp. *macrorhynchos*) is a rare vagrant to Europe; it has a longer and slimmer bill, bigger white spots on the body, and wider white bar on the tail. **VOICE** Call: a hissed, monotone, sad-sounding *cha-cha-cha-cha*. **HABITAT** Montane conifer forest, particularly pine, fir and larch.

Siberian Jay *Perisoreus infaustus*

IDENTIFICATION
28 cm. Smaller than Eurasian Jay, brownish-grey above with reddish rump and sides to tail. Head darker with small white spot on forehead, small black bill. Reddish bases to flight feathers and primary coverts visible in flight. **VOICE** Normally silent; sometimes gives mewed, whistled or croaking call. **HABITAT** Ancient conifer forests with lichens, taiga.

white forehead

tail with reddish sides

black head

orange 'wrists'

Azure-winged Magpie *Cyanopica cyanus*

IDENTIFICATION
33 cm. Small magpie with long tail, black cap, sky-blue wings and tail, sandy-brown mantle; very difficult to confuse with other species. Juvenile has scaly upperparts. Forms family groups; quite shy. **VOICE** Call: squeaky, nasal *vrruie*. Song: discreet twittering. **HABITAT** Pine and Holm Oak woodland.

frosted crown

Juvenile

black cap

beige underparts

blue wings

blue tail

Adult

graduated tail

white primaries

white 'braces'

iridescent blue and green

rounded wings

long tail

Common Magpie *Pica pica*

IDENTIFICATION
45 cm. Smaller and slimmer than the Carrion Crow. Pied plumage with green metallic sheen on tail and blue on wings. Long, rounded tail. White inner sides to primaries. **VOICE** Varied call, a guttural *cha-cha-cha-cha...* or *chra-cac*. Varied song, with some twittering, rattling and raucous notes. **HABITAT** Open areas with trees, agricultural land or urban zones; commoner near dwellings.

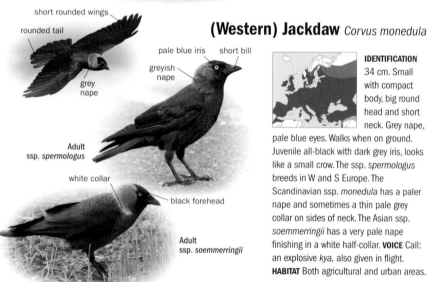

short rounded wings

rounded tail

grey nape

pale blue iris

short bill

greyish nape

Adult ssp. *spermologus*

white collar

black forehead

Adult ssp. *soemmerringii*

(Western) Jackdaw *Corvus monedula*

IDENTIFICATION
34 cm. Small with compact body, big round head and short neck. Grey nape, pale blue eyes. Walks when on ground. Juvenile all-black with dark grey iris, looks like a small crow. The ssp. *spermologus* breeds in W and S Europe. The Scandinavian ssp. *monedula* has a paler nape and sometimes a thin pale grey collar on sides of neck. The Asian ssp. *soemmerringii* has a very pale nape finishing in a white half-collar. **VOICE** Call: an explosive *kya*, also given in flight. **HABITAT** Both agricultural and urban areas.

Daurian Jackdaw *Corvus dauuricus*

32 cm. From Asia, very rare vagrant to various parts of W Europe. Some adults have whitish belly, breast and collar; other adults and juveniles are all-black. Dark iris.

grey

black belly

long wings

pointed bill

Adult bicoloured form

Alpine Chough *Pyrrhocorax graculus*

very rounded wings

tail often spread

yellow-brown bill

Adult

Juvenile

short yellow bill

long wings

red legs

Adult

IDENTIFICATION
38 cm. Small mountain crow with shortish yellow bill, red legs, tail longer than wings. All-black plumage without metallic sheen. Black soles to feet, only slightly decurved bill, black iris. In flight, rounded wings and tail, glides frequently, moving along ridges and cliffs in flocks. Walks when looking for food. Juvenile has yellowish bill and pale brown legs. **VOICE** Normal call a rolled trill, birds reply to each other. **HABITAT** Alpine meadows; descends to mountain villages in winter, sometimes as low as 1,000 m in bad weather; common around ski resorts and their restaurants.

Red-billed Chough *Pyrrhocorax pyrrhocorax*

short yellowish-brown bill

Juvenile

wings shorter than tail

long red decurved bill

red legs

Adult

IDENTIFICATION
39 cm. Like Alpine Chough but longer, downcurved, red bill. Longer red legs, more slender body, wings same length as tail. In flight wings rounded with obviously fingered tips. Juvenile has shorter yellowish-brown bill and duller pink legs. **VOICE** Call: long, nasal *chiaaahh*. **HABITAT** Dry, short calcareous grassland, alpine meadows or near the coast. Nests in pairs in cliff crevices or caves, forming flocks as soon as the young fledge.

CONFUSION SPECIES

Carrion Crow (p. 374)

Rook (p. 375)

Blackbird (p. 304)

brownish tint

sometimes scaly appearance

bill with rounded edges

glossy black

Adult

Worn plumage

Carrion Crow *Corvus corone*

IDENTIFICATION
46 cm. Completely black, black bill with convex edges, square-ended tail, feathered bill base; plumage sometimes iridescent. Juvenile very similar to adult. On occasions, some worn wing feathers have pale grey centres. **VOICE** Call: a caw, *crooa*, of variable tone. **HABITAT** Any open environment, in towns, in the country and at altitude up to alpine meadows. Sometimes occurs in groups in urban areas or fields.

Hooded Crow *Corvus cornix*

black head

pale grey body

bib of black streaks

IDENTIFICATION
46 cm. Identical to Carrion Crow except for ashy-grey body; head and neck black, black streaking on breast. Hybrids occur with black markings on darker grey body. **VOICE** As Carrion Crow. **HABITAT** All environments, rural or urban, but not in forests.

House Crow *Corvus splendens*

grey neck

slender silhouette

black face

39 cm. An Indian crow, introduced by ships from the Middle East, or by other means. Now breeding in the Netherlands. Slender with long heavy bill and steep forehead giving head a characteristic shape. Nape and neck variably grey, with contasting black face.

Rook *Corvus frugilegus*

IDENTIFICATION
45 cm. Totally
black like
Carrion Crow but
has longer,
straight-sided,
pointed bill and rounder tail. Adult has
characteristic bare grey skin at base of
bill; juvenile has feathered base to bill
as in Carrion Crow, and differs only in
shape. **VOICE** Call: a raucous, mournful,
long crowing *kraaaa*... **HABITAT** Nests
high in tall trees in noisy colonies. Feeds
in fields and meadows. May even inhabit
towns but never in forest.

long feathered
skin

Juvenile

long
straight bill

grey
skin

Adult

long tail

Common Raven *Corvus corax*

IDENTIFICATION
64 cm. The
biggest crow,
totally black,
heavy bill
feathered at
base, massive head, long graduated tail.
VOICE Call: a repeated guttural *raa-raa*...
or *rooo-roo*, with rattling sounds when
displaying. **HABITAT** Rough open terrain
with cliffs for nesting, often in
mountainous regions and foothills, along
the coast or in quarries; occasionally
builds nest in a tree or on a pylon.

quite long
neck

graduated
tail

very thick
bill

thick neck

Pied Crow *Corvus alba*

white breast

graduated tail

48 cm. A sub-Saharan crow occurring as a vagrant in N Africa, Spain and the Canaries (maybe ship-assisted). Has recently bred in NW Africa. Medium-sized black-and-white crow, size of Carrion Crow but with large bill like that of Raven. White breast and upper belly continues into a white collar on hindneck.

thick bill

white collar

wings as long
as tail

white breast

Brown-necked Raven *Corvus ruficollis*

brown head

tail shorter
than wings

52 cm. Small raven of arid steppes in Middle East and Sahara Desert; rare vagrant to Spain (April 2013), possibly ship-assisted. Resembles Common Raven but has less massive bill, brown sheen on nape and crown, and tail shorter than wings when perched.

STARLINGS AND ALLIES Generally dark plumage like that of Blackbird but smaller and more compact, shorter tail, and slimmer, more pointed bill. They mostly walk on the ground (do not hop).

Common Starling *Sturnus vulgaris*

IDENTIFICATION
22 cm. More compact than Blackbird. Metallic sheen on neck, white tips on upperparts, buff tips on underparts, body feathers more marked in winter. Male: a little more colourful with blue-based yellow bill. Female: duller, dark bill with pink base. Juvenile: pale brown on fledging with cream fringes to wing feathers. Adult male with worn plumage very like Spotless Starling but always has buff chevrons on undertail-coverts. **VOICE** Call: raucous *kerrr*. Song: mix of shrill, knocking and fluty notes given whilst vibrating wings. **HABITAT** Open countryside, forest edges, agricultural land, parks and gardens; nests in cavities. Comes together in large roosts in winter, often in town centres.

all-black iris

yellow with blue base

iridescent green and violet

Breeding adult

speckled with pale rufous

brown iris

dark bill

Winter female

speckled with white

dark brown

black lores

black bill

grey head

moulted body

pale reddish fringes

Juvenile

black iris

green-and-violet sheen

First-winter

CONFUSION SPECIES

Blackbird (p. 304)

Winter male

Spotless Starling *Sturnus unicolor*

Female
uniform black plumage
all-yellow bill
uniform oily-looking plumage
yellow bill with blue base
pale pink legs
Male
bright pink legs

IDENTIFICATION
22 cm. Like Common Starling but entirely uniform plumage in summer, violet sheen on neck, feathers appear oily. Male has yellow bill with blue base, female completely yellow bill. Pink legs. In winter the white feather tips are less numerous and less dense than in Common Starling. Juvenile: like Common Starling, but a little darker.
VOICE Song less stereotyped and more melodious than Common Starling.
HABITAT As Common Starling.

Rose-coloured Starling *Pastor roseus*

shaggy black crest
pink body
pink bill with black base
Adult male
yellow bill
pale rump
beige below
Juvenile
pink legs

22 cm. Vagrant to W Europe from breeding areas in E Europe and Central Asia, usually in late summer and autumn, occasionally in winter. Similar to Common Starling but has bicoloured body with black head, neck, wings and undertail-coverts, rest of body pink. Pink bill, pale pink legs, short crest. Male: has longer crest and black base to bill. Female: shorter crest and browner wings. Juvenile: beige plumage with paler rump, yellow bill and pale pink legs, pale edges to flight feathers; juvenile plumage lasts until late autumn, followed by moult into adult-like plumage but brown back and brown edges to head feathers.

(Bohemian) Waxwing *Bombycilla garrulus*

IDENTIFICATION
18 cm. In flight, size and silhouette similar to that of starling but differs in large crested head and pinkish-buff plumage. Thin black mask, small black bib on throat. Black tail with yellow terminal bar, black wings with white edges to primary coverts. Male: long crest, sharp lower limit to bib, waxy red spots on secondaries. Female: shorter crest, diffuse border to bottom of bib. Peculiar pattern on flight feathers varies according to age; yellow edges to primary tips, continuing as narrow white lines extending onto tips of inner feather shafts in adults, absent in juveniles. Gregarious in winter. **VOICE** Call: rapid, ringing trill *siirrrr*. **HABITAT** In winter, fruit or berry-bearing bushes and shrubs in open or semi-open environments, even coming to parks and gardens; can come to bird tables.

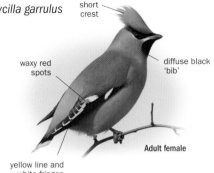

short crest

waxy red spots

diffuse black 'bib'

Adult female

yellow line and white fringes

long crest

yellow streaks

black bib with sharp border

reddish rear

Juvenile male

long crest

'bib' with sharp border

Adult male

short crest

diffuse border

white lines in ladder pattern

Juvenile female

no white lines

Cedar Waxwing *Bombycilla cedrorum*

short crest

Adult

short diffuse 'bib'

white undertail-coverts

white line on tertials

Juvenile

uniform wing

17 cm. Nearctic, vagrants have occurred in the Azores, Britain, Ireland and Iceland. A little smaller than Waxwing, diffuse black on chin, white undertail-coverts and yellowish belly, fine white line above and below black mask, uniform wings with white inner border to tertials; black tail with yellow tip. Juvenile: brownish-grey with short black mask on pale face. Call: vibrant *sriii*.

Daurian Starling *Agropsar sturninus*

grey head

pied above

short bill

short tail

18 cm. Small Asian starling; very rare vagrant to W Europe. Thickset with short tail and short, thick bill, face and underparts pale grey, small blackish crown, cinnamon undertail-coverts. Obvious black eye, black bill and legs, white wing-bar on median coverts, pale grey rump; black (male) or brown (female, juvenile) mantle.

Common Bulbul *Pycnonotus barbatus*

20 cm. From N Africa, has recently bred in the south of Spain. Size of a starling, more elongated with long brown tail, diffuse dark face, often has angular nape, white undertail-coverts. Brown above, buff below. Noisy, loud *tchar*, *tchui* or *tchuvi* calls. Butterfly-like flight, like that of alighting Blackbird.

blackish-brown head

brown above

long tail

Common Myna *Acridotheres tristis*

24 cm. An Asian bird introduced here and there: Canaries, Russia. Large wine-brown starling with black head, white-tipped black tail, white undertail-coverts, yellow legs and bill; white base to primaries very visible in flight. Very vocal.

yellow bill

yellow skin

black head

wine-red

white base to primaries

orange legs

Crested Myna *Acridotheres cristatellus*

25 cm. Another Asian species introduced in Europe, near Lisbon in Portugal. Similar to Common Myna but all-black with white primary bases forming a very visible white square in flight; spiky crest on forehead, white fringes to undertail-coverts, yellow bill, yellowish iris and pink legs.

short crest

pale yellow bill

white base to primaries

whitish scaling under tail

SPARROWS Species often associated with man, nesting under eaves, in cavities, or making a large round ball of grass in dense trees. Males separated by head and breast patterns; females vary little between species; juveniles as females until post-juvenile moult, which can be very rapid.

House Sparrow *Passer domesticus*

Juvenile male

uniform rump

black bib appearing

IDENTIFICATION 15 cm. Male: ash-grey crown, chestnut nape, white spot behind eye, black lores and bib, greyish cheeks, chestnut mantle with black streaks, grey rump and white wing-bars; pink legs; black bill in summer, yellow with black tip in winter when head feathers have pale edges. Female: beige and brown, streaked above, uniform below, beige supercilium wider behind eye. **VOICE** Call: chirps, *tchirp* or *tchurp*, and rapid rattle *chr-chr-chr...* Song: rhythmic series of chirpings. **HABITAT** Common near human dwellings, in towns or the countryside, next to the sea or in mountains.

chestnut band

grey crown

grey cheeks

chestnut with black streaks

black bib

pale supercilium

striped mantle

big yellow bill

Female

Male

brown mantle with black stripes

Italian Sparrow *Passer italiae*

chestnut crown

white supercilium

grey fringes

white supercilium

white cheek

Breeding male

IDENTIFICATION 15 cm. Like House Sparrow but male has entirely chestnut-brown crown in summer (feathers with grey fringes in winter), whiter cheeks, more contrast on mantle; female identical to House Sparrow. Hybrids are numerous where the 2 species overlap in alpine areas. Formerly considered a subspecies of House Sparrow, now recently separated. **VOICE** and **HABITAT** As House Sparrow.

Winter male

Tree Sparrow *Passer montanus*

IDENTIFICATION
14 cm. Small sparrow with black spot in centre of white cheek, rufous crown, white half-collar. Brown mantle streaked black, beige rump, black bill in summer, yellow with black tip in winter. Both sexes and all ages have same plumage. **VOICE** Call: liquid chirp, *tschirp*; *tec* in flight. Song: like that of House Sparrow but higher-pitched. **HABITAT** Villages, countryside with hedgerows, cultivated areas near houses. More rural than House Sparrow, often in mixed urban/cultivated areas; has disappeared from many towns where it once nested in parks. Comes to bird feeders.

chestnut crown

black spot on white cheek

black bill with yellow base

striped black

small black bib

Spanish Sparrow *Passer hispaniolensis*

IDENTIFICATION
15 cm. Male: chestnut crown, large black bib extends onto breast and flanks, black-and-buff streaking on mantle; thin white supercilium in front of eye and a little behind; finely streaked grey-brown rump. Broad white fringes on underparts in winter. Female: as House Sparrow but often has more contrasting braces on mantle and only slightly streaked breast; well-marked chevrons under the tail; thicker bill. **VOICE** Chirping calls of a sparrow, song more strident than that of House Sparrow. **HABITAT** In general more rural than House Sparrow.

chestnut crown

white supercilium

black-and-white striped mantle

white cheek

Breeding male

black-streaked upper breast

heavily striped mantle

Female

brown streaks

well-marked undertail-coverts

Rock Sparrow *Petronia petronia*

broad supercilium
white spots
Juvenile
pink legs
pale median crown-stripe
thick conical bill
discreet yellow spot
short tail
Adult
brown lines

IDENTIFICATION 14 cm. Size of House Sparrow, larger head, short tail, long wings. Similar to female House Sparrow but appears larger, heavily streaked underparts including flanks, dark chevrons on undertail-coverts, short tail feathers with white tips. Yellow spot on throat hardly visible, beige median crown-stripe, dark lateral crown-stripes and prominent buff supercilium behind eye. Large conical yellow bill with black tip. **VOICE** Call: *chi* or *duj* reminiscent of that of a finch; long, nasal, rising *pey-iii*. **HABITAT** Open rocky environments, short grassland.

White-winged Snowfinch
Montifringilla nivalis

black and white
yellow bill
grey head
black lores
black bill
white throat
Winter
Breeding male

broad white sides to tail

CONFUSION SPECIES

House Sparrow (p. 382)

Snow Bunting (p. 410)

IDENTIFICATION 17 cm. Large finch of mountaintops with grey head and brown mantle. Bicoloured wings, black primaries and primary coverts, secondaries and their coverts white; white tail but central feathers black and outer feathers with black tips. Male has small black bib, black lores and bill in summer; white chin and yellow bill in winter. Female has horn-coloured bill and paler throat. Pale brown iris, black legs with thick toes. **VOICE** Call: finch-like rising *titu*, *titititti...* **HABITAT** Short, rocky alpine grassland at very high altitude, above 2,000 m, even in winter when it occurs on windblown ridges; may visit restaurants at higher ski-resorts.

Dead Sea Sparrow *Passer moabiticus*

grey crown

Male

yellow spot

rufous coverts

IDENTIFICATION 12.5 cm. Small sparrow, male with distinctive head pattern and chestnut wing-coverts. Male: narrow black bib, cream moustache and supercilium, grey crown and cheeks, yellow patch on sides of neck; brown mantle with black streaking, grey rump. Female: small, with big head, cream below, small pale bill. **VOICE** Similar to House Sparrow but quieter. **HABITAT** Arid areas with bushes and tamarisk trees near water. In Europe, only breeds on Cyprus; a vagrant flock in Greece, October 1972.

Female

uniform cream

Pale Rock Sparrow (Pale Rockfinch)
Carpospiza brachydactyla

no streaks

strong bill

indistinct wing-bars

beige below

15 cm. Like Rock Sparrow with uniform sandy head and mantle, without streaks below, slightly slimmer bill; indistinct pale supercilium and white tips to tail feathers; no clear white wing-bar. Call: *djui* of Greenfinch. Arid areas with sparse bushes. A nomadic migrant species that breeds in Turkey; possible vagrant.

Yellow-throated Sparrow *Gymnoris xanthocollis*

14 cm. Quite similar to Pale Rock Sparrow but bill slimmer and more pointed, rufous lesser coverts, median coverts with large white tips, and an additional wing-bar on greater coverts; male has white chin and yellow throat; tail longer and totally brown. Call: piercing loud *tchiaa*. Breeds in Turkey, winters in India; potential vagrant.

pointed bill

clear wing-bar

Juvenile

rufous shoulder

black bill

Adult

yellow spot

INTRODUCED EXOTIC FINCHES Frequently observed escaped cagebirds that could form viable populations in the wild. Some are already established.

Indian Silverbill *Euodice malabarica*

uniform face

conical black-and-grey bill

white uppertail-coverts

pointed black tail

11 cm. Very small, pale brown above, whitish below, fulvous flanks; black wings and tail, white undertail-coverts. Very thick bill with grey lower mandible thicker than black upper mandible. Quite long, thin, graduated tail appears pointed. Call: a vibrant chirping. Often in flocks, in parks and gardens, feeds on the ground. Introduced population near Nice, SE France.

African Silverbill *Euodice cantans*

black uppertail-coverts

enormous bill

barred tertials

10 cm. Very similar to Indian Silverbill but has black rump and uppertail-coverts; discreet barring on mantle, tertials and flanks. From the Sahel region of Africa; escapes occur, sometimes in the company of Indian Silverbills.

Tricoloured Munia *Lonchura malacca*

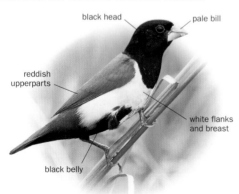

black head

pale bill

reddish upperparts

white flanks and breast

black belly

11 cm. From Sri Lanka and India, introduced in the Tagus estuary, Portugal. Black head, white flanks and upper belly, black lower belly and undertail-coverts, rufous above (wings, mantle, rump and tail). Blue-grey bill, greyish legs. Discreet, usually in bushes on the sides of crops.

Common Waxbill *Estrilda astrild*

11 cm. Escape from captivity. Brown
upperparts finely barred with black,
beige underparts finely vermiculated with
brown, black undertail-coverts. Slim red
mask under dark brown crown, small
conical bright red bill. Juvenile more
uniform. Gregarious. Call: buzzing *tzep* or
sharp *pi*. Established in Spain, in
agricultural areas, scrub and set-aside.

very finely barred

red mask

short red bill

very finely barred

Red Avadavat *Amandava amandava*

10 cm. Escape from captivity. Male red
with white spots on upperparts, black
tail, black wings with a few white spots,
red bill. Female olive-brown above,
cream below, red rump and bill. Call:
sharp *chit* similar to call of Penduline Tit.
Established in Spain, in scrub and
bushes on edges of wetlands.

unbarred

black mask

red bill

white droplets

Iago Sparrow *Passer iagoensis*

13 cm. Endemic to Cape Verde; has arrived in the Netherlands
on ships. Male: black crown, white supercilium in front of eye,
small black bib; rufous lesser coverts, reddish-brown scapulars
have broad black stripes. Female: plumage shows much
contrast, beige mantle streaked black, very pronounced
long supercilium.

dull greyish plumage

pronounced white supercilium

bright bill

black crown

rufous mask

rufous shoulder

Female

Male

Black-headed Weaver *Ploceus melanocephalus*

uniform mantle

extensive black face

orange wash to breast

Male

short tail

streaked mantle

white iris

bicoloured bill

Female

15 cm. African origin, introduced to the Tagus estuary, Portugal. Male: black head and neck, orange breast, yellow underparts and almost uniform olive mantle; black iris and black bill when breeding. Female: white iris, indistinct supercilium, yellow face, grey bill and more streaked mantle. Gourd-shaped nest weaved into a tree, often a tamarisk on the edge of a reedbed.

Yellow-crowned Bishop *Euplectes afer*

bright yellow above

black bib

yellow supercilium

black belly

Male

Female

very short tail

11 cm. African origin, introduced into Portugal, around Alcochete. Small passerine with very short tail and short conical bill. Male: yellow and black, lemon-yellow feathers on back and rump raised in display, black face and belly. Female and non-breeding: noticeable and very long yellowish supercilium, streaked mantle and flanks, pink-and-black bill.

FINCHES Colourful and closely related seed-eating passerines that occur in Europe throughout the year; many are frequent visitors to bird tables.

(Common) Chaffinch *Fringella coelebs*

IDENTIFICATION
14 cm. Two
white wing-bars,
black tail with
white sides.
Male: blue-grey
cap and nape, pinkish brick-red cheeks
and underparts, brown back and olive
rump. Pale brown fringes to feathers in
winter. Female: brown above, olive rump.
Juvenile: as female. **VOICE** Calls: various,
tchink, a rolling *ruuu* and brief *tiou* in
flight. Song: falling phrase of clear
notes finishing with a rising flourish.
HABITAT Wooded areas, forests,
hedgerows, parks and gardens; as much
at home in towns as at higher altitudes.
GEOGRAPHICAL VARIATION Ssp. *africana/
spodiogenys*, a vagrant from N Africa,
has blue head, big white crescents
above and below eye, olive back and
pale pink underparts; different call. The
5 subspecies from the Atlantic Islands
(Madeira, Canaries and Azores) have
blue or green mantles and are larger.

grey crown

black forehead

white wing-bars

diffuse broad pale supercilium

white wing-bars

Breeding male

Female

olive-green rump

white supercilium

blue cheeks

olive-green mantle

black face

pale pink

Male ssp. *spodiogenys* (N Africa)

pink face

olive mantle

very thick bill

Ssp. *moreletti* (Azores)

pink face

olive mantle

Ssp. *maderensis* (Madeira)

blue mantle

black forehead

orange face

Ssp. *canariensis* (Canaries)

Brambling *Fringilla montifringilla*

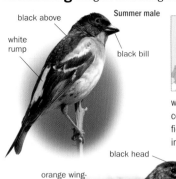

Summer male

black above
white rump
black bill

IDENTIFICATION 14 cm. Resembles Common Chaffinch but has orange wing-bars, orange breast, black ovals on flanks and white rump. Male: black head and back, feathers with buff edges in winter. Female: pale head with dark lateral lines; tricoloured wings with orange lesser coverts. **VOICE** Call: rising *djui*. **HABITAT** Crops, stubble, ploughed fields and wasteland near woods, in which it sometimes roosts in large numbers.

black head
orange wing-bars
Winter male
orange shoulders
white rump
brown spots

uniform buff head with lateral brown lines
Winter female
scaly mantle
less colourful breast

Blue Chaffinch *Fringilla teydea*

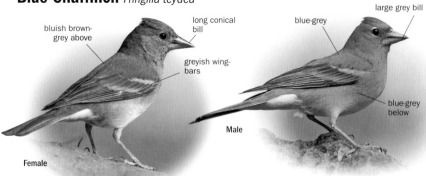

bluish brown-grey above
long conical bill
greyish wing-bars
Female

large grey bill
blue-grey
blue-grey below
Male

IDENTIFICATION 17 cm. Large; long strong conical bill, very uniform plumage both above and below. Male greyish-blue above, 2 indistinct greyish wing-bars, only the undertail-coverts are whiter. Female greyish above, grey-brown below, 2 cream wing-bars. **VOICE** Call: grating *tshrouit*, song shorter and slower than that of Chaffinch. **HABITAT** Montane pine forests; endemic to Tenerife and Gran Canaria (Canary Islands).

(European) Greenfinch *Carduelis chloris*

IDENTIFICATION
15 cm Large and thickset, pale thick conical bill, brownish in colour (female) or green and yellow (male). Bright yellow bases to flight feathers and outer tail. Male has greyish wing-coverts and uniform mantle. Female has slightly streaked brownish mantle and yellowish rump, duller than male. Young streaked above and below. There are many subspecies, each slightly different in plumage, some brighter than others. **VOICE** Call: nasal *djuai* and loud *tiu* repeated in series. Song: successive trills of repeated notes *tiaitiatiaitiaitiaitiai tututututututu...* **HABITAT** Hedgerows, copses, forest edges, parks and gardens; readily comes to bird tables in winter.

streaked crown

yellow fringes

Juvenile

greenish-brown with faint streaking

Female

strongly streaked

blackish-brown coverts

green strong face

pink bill

grey coverts

yellow rump

Male

yellow band

(European) Goldfinch *Carduelis carduelis*

IDENTIFICATION
12 cm. Multicoloured, broad bright yellow panel on black wing, black tail, white rump and uppertail-coverts; red face, black lores, white cheeks edged with black collar. Pale brown back, pale brown patches on sides of breast. Quite long pointed bill, pink with black tip. Red on face reaches to back of eye in male, stops before eye in female. Juvenile has uniform buff head. **VOICE** Call: ringing *tu-ti* or *ti-tu*, *ti-vit vit* or a hissing when alarmed. Song: repeated and linked chirping phrases of metallic notes, accelerating then slowing, slower than that of Serin. **HABITAT** Scrub, hedgerows, parks and gardens.

red face passes eye

bright yellow patch

white rump

black lores

conical pink bill with black tip

uniform beige face

white wing-bars

Male

Juvenile

a few black spots

black collar

red face stops before eye

hazel-coloured upper breast

Female

European Serin *Serinus serinus*

- lemon-yellow face
- **Male**
- very short bill
- bright yellow rump
- broad black streaks
- yellow wash to face
- heavily streaked with black
- forked tail

Female

IDENTIFICATION
11 cm. Small, chubby, no visible neck and small bill, short tail, male has bright yellow face. Striped mantle, black streaks on flanks, bright yellow rump evident in flight. Female duller than male with more streaked flanks. Two diffuse thin wing-bars, yellow in male, buff in female and young. **VOICE** Normal call: jingling *trilili*. Song: long very rapid jingling phrases, shrill and metallic, quicker than that of Goldfinch, given when easily visible at top of a tree. **HABITAT** Open environments with large trees, parks and gardens; typical of large trees in village squares.

(Eurasian) Siskin *Carduelis spinus*

- forked tail
- yellow rump
- yellow wing-bars
- yellow supercilium
- **Female**
- black cap
- black bib
- **Male**
- black streaks

CONFUSION SPECIES

Citril Finch (p. 395)   Yellowhammer (p. 405)

IDENTIFICATION
12 cm. Black wings with 2 yellow (adult) or white (juvenile) bars. Male: black crown and chin, black-streaked flanks; streaked olive mantle; bright yellow rump and outer tail feathers. Female: white throat, streaked crown, heavily streaked underparts; yellow colouring limited to face, rump and wing-bars. Often in flocks in winter. **VOICE** Call: metallic *tli-u* or *pli*. Song: repeated phrases, more reminiscent of an *Acrocephalus* warbler than a finch. **HABITAT** Mixed and coniferous forests, woods with silver birch and alder. May occur in gardens in winter.

(Common) Linnet *Carduelis cannabina*

IDENTIFICATION
14 cm. Male:
uniform
chestnut back,
grey head, pink
forehead, red
wash to breast, grey bill. Female:
streaked crown and back, pale area
around eye, diffusely streaked flanks.
White edges to tail and flight feathers,
diffuse buff edges to greater coverts.
Young: much more streaked. **VOICE** Call:
a trilling *tieu-tieu-tieu*... Sings from a
prominent perch, rapid babble
incorporating call notes. **HABITAT** Scrub,
hedgerows, gardens near fields, alpine
meadows. Gregarious in winter,
sometimes forming mixed flocks with
other finches.

black-and-pink speckles on forehead

chestnut mantle

pink breast

black-and-white tail

Male

streaked brown mantle

white fringes on primaries

streaked underparts

Juvenile

Twite *Carduelis flavirostris*

IDENTIFICATION
14 cm. Similar
to Common
Linnet but face
and underparts
with buff wash,
heavily streaked flanks, short yellow bill
and streaked back; male has streaked
pink rump. **VOICE** Call: shriller and more
metallic than that of Linnet. **HABITAT**
Breeds on moorland, winters in short
coastal vegetation, dunes, scrub.

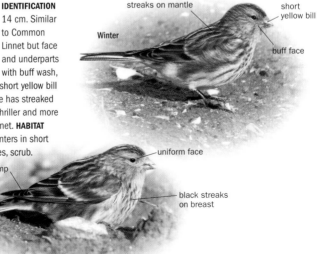

blackish-brown streaks on mantle

Winter

short yellow bill

buff face

uniform face

pink rump

Winter

black streaks on breast

Common Redpoll *Carduelis flammea*

Ssp. *cabaret*

red forehead

small black face

buff wash to face

striped flanks

no buff colour

raspberry-pink breast in male

Ssp. *flammea*

IDENTIFICATION
14 cm. Small finch streaked above and below (including flanks), with small black bib, red forehead, short yellow pointed bill and 2 white wing-bars; male has pinkish breast. Central black stripe on undertail-coverts, heavily streaked reddish rump. Lesser Redpoll (ssp. *cabaret*) has buff wash on face and flanks; Mealy Redpoll (ssp. *flammea*) is larger, without warm tones in plumage. Intermediate birds are numerous. **VOICE** Call: *cheu-cheu-cheu...*, more metallic than that of Linnet; very rapid trill, *trrrriiiii*. Song: rapid babble incorporating call notes. **HABITAT** Conifer forests in summer; scrub, birches and alders in winter, sometimes comes to bird tables.

Arctic Redpoll *Carduelis hornemanni*

Ssp. *hornemanni*

whitish face

buff face

streaked white mantle

white or streaked flanks

white undertail-coverts

Ssp. *exilipes*

immaculate white rump

buff face

immaculate white undertail-coverts

streaked white flanks

Ssp. *hornemanni*

IDENTIFICATION
14 cm. Paler than Common Redpoll, very little streaking on flanks, uniform white rump, all-white undertail-coverts or with a thin central line at most, white belly, barely streaked breast, buff cheeks. The Greenland race (ssp. *hornemanni*) is larger than the Scandinavian race (ssp. *exilipes*); Icelandic birds are intermediate. **VOICE** Call very similar to that of Common Redpoll. **HABITAT** Tundra, bushy scrub.

Citril Finch *Serinus citrinella*

IDENTIFICATION
12 cm. Yellow
underparts,
slightly streaked
olive mantle,
yellow rump.
Olive forehead, grey nape, yellow face
and throat. Black wings with 2 large
yellowish ill-defined wing-bars. Young:
streaked olive-brown above, streaked
yellowish below. **VOICE** Call: metallic *di*,
often given in series. Song similar to that
of Goldfinch but less metallic. **HABITAT**
Uncommon at altitude in conifer forests
and at the treeline, in bushy habitat
transitional with alpine meadows.

grey neck
uniform olive
mantle
Male
olive-yellow
face
lemon-yellow
below

greenish-yellow
wing-bars
Female
less bright
yellow

Corsican Finch *Serinus corsicanus*

IDENTIFICATION
12 cm.
Replaces Citril
Finch in Corsica.
Identical except
for chestnut
mantle with fine dark streaks, contrasting
more clearly with yellow rump; distinction
easiest in adult males. **VOICE** Very similar
to that of Citril Finch. **HABITAT** Uncommon
in all open and semi-open habitats,
scrub with bushes, garrigue, from the
coast to the mountains. Endemic to
Corsica and Sardinia.

extensive
yellow face
chestnut mantle
with black streaks

CONFUSION SPECIES

Siskin (p. 392)

Serin
(p. 392)

Linnet (p. 393)

(Atlantic) Canary *Serinus canaria*

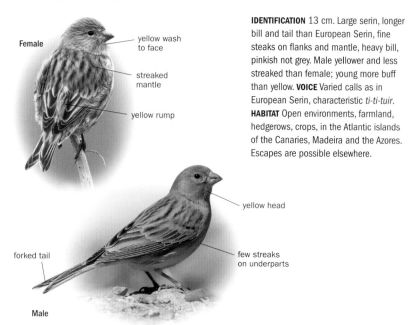

Female
yellow wash to face
streaked mantle
yellow rump
yellow head
forked tail
few streaks on underparts
Male

IDENTIFICATION 13 cm. Large serin, longer bill and tail than European Serin, fine steaks on flanks and mantle, heavy bill, pinkish not grey. Male yellower and less streaked than female; young more buff than yellow. **VOICE** Varied calls as in European Serin, characteristic *ti-ti-tuir*. **HABITAT** Open environments, farmland, hedgerows, crops, in the Atlantic islands of the Canaries, Madeira and the Azores. Escapes are possible elsewhere.

Red-fronted Serin *Serinus pusillus*

black head
red forehead
yellow fringes

12 cm. Occurs in mountains from Turkey to the Himalayas; very rare winter vagrant to Cyprus and Greece. Typical serin silhouette with small, short dark bill. Black head with red forehead (adult) or buff-streaked face (juvenile), black-and-brown streaked mantle, broad lines of black streaks on flanks. Call: a trilled *fiirrrr* or rising *doui*.

Common Crossbill *Loxia curvirostra*

IDENTIFICATION
16 cm. Thickset finch with long crossed mandibles allowing seeds to be extracted from conifer cones. Red head, breast and rump in male, olive in female, streaked undertail-coverts; black wings and tail. Juvenile: streaked crown and underparts, pale edges to wing-coverts. Bill size and call varies according to specialisation for one or another conifer. **VOICE** Call: between *tip* and *tup*, according to origin. Slow song of repeated notes, incorporating call notes. **HABITAT** Conifer forests. Gregarious, subject to irruptions. Breeds early, at end of winter.

Male — red body — crossed mandibles — orange coloration — white edges — slightly forked tail

Immature male

Juvenile — streaked mantle — streaked crown

green rump

Female — greenish-grey body — striped flanks

Scottish Crossbill *Loxia scotica*

IDENTIFICATION 16 cm. Bill intermediate in structure between that of Parrot Crossbill and Common Crossbill; however, the latter's bill size varies clinally, the largest near that of size of Scottish Crossbill (see photo). Probably impossible to identify away from breeding area. **VOICE** Tonality intermediate between the other 2 closely-related species. **HABITAT** Ancient pine forests, endemic to N Scotland.

thick bill

Male

Parrot Crossbill *Loxia pytyopsittacus*

big head

enormous bill

bulbous
lower
mandible

Male

IDENTIFICATION
17 cm. As
Common
Crossbill but
with larger bill,
cutting edges of
mandibles are parallel and often pale,
bill as tall as it is long; heavier head and
neck. **VOICE** Call: deeper *tup*. **HABITAT**
Prefers pines.

enormous
bill

yellow
rump

enormous
bill

pale edges

Juvenile female

Adult
female

Two-barred Crossbill *Loxia leucoptera*

quite slim
bill

2 broad white
wing-bars

raspberry-red

Male

IDENTIFICATION 15 cm. As
Common Crossbill but
smaller and slimmer, 2 broad
white wing-bars of inversed
graduated width (lower bar
widest on inner coverts,
upper bar widest on outer coverts); white spots on
tertials; male is raspberry-red. Slimmer bill. **VOICE**
Call: *tep*, but also characteristic nasal *ouin*. **HABITAT**
Prefers larches, taiga forests.

slim bill

streaked
below

narrower
wing-bars

greenish

Juvenile

Female

Pine Grosbeak *Pinicola enucleator*

IDENTIFICATION
19 cm. Very
large, big head,
long tail; similar
to crossbills but
only slightly
hooked grey bill (not crossed), dark
lores, white wing-bars. Raspberry-red
head, breast, mantle and rump in male;
olive-brown mottled with black in female;
grey flanks and vent in both sexes. **VOICE**
Call: rapid double or triple *tui*. **HABITAT**
Scandinavian and Siberian taiga.

white fringes
to tertials
and coverts

mix of scaly
red and grey

thick
uncrossed
bill

First-
winter
male

grey mantle

yellow to
orange head

Adult
female

scaly red-and-
black mantle

extended
orange
below

First-winter male

small black mask

raspberry-red

Adult
male

Common Rosefinch *Carpodacus erythrinus*

red face
brown lores
strong bill
Male
unstreaked below

IDENTIFICATION 15 cm. Medium-sized, with strong conical grey bill. Male: red head, breast and rump. Female: grey-brown, diffusely streaked breast, pale wing-bars; uniform white belly and undertail-coverts. Diffuse streaks on mantle. Autumn juvenile more streaked on flanks and mantle, better-defined wing-bars. Beady black eye on rather plain face. **VOICE** Call: *huit* similar to that of Chiffchaff. Song: characteristic *tsitsévitsa* (often translated as *pleased-to-meet-you*). **HABITAT** Areas with bushes and trees, often near dunes or wetlands.

olive fringes
diffuse streaks
narrow wing-bars

Female and juvenile

House Finch *Carpodacus mexicanus*

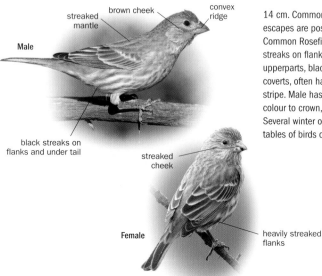

streaked mantle
brown cheek
convex ridge
Male

14 cm. Common Nearctic cagebird; escapes are possible. Similar to Common Rosefinch but has large black streaks on flanks, more striped upperparts, black centres to undertail-coverts, often has dark cheeks and eye-stripe. Male has red or orange-yellow colour to crown, throat and breast. Several winter observations at bird tables of birds of doubtful origin.

black streaks on flanks and under tail
streaked cheek

Female
heavily streaked flanks

Trumpeter Finch *Bucanetes githagineus*

grey head

pink rump

big red bill

Male

IDENTIFICATION
13 cm. Silhouette of a bullfinch with short tail and large red (male) or yellow bill; uniform pale grey and buff plumage, male has pink wash on face, pink (male) or buff (juvenile) fringes to tertials and greater coverts. **VOICE** Call: buzzing *chic* or *tset*. **HABITAT** Dry stony steppe, desert edges. A few pairs breed in S Spain.

small black eye, plain face

short thick red bill

pinkish-buff body

pink rump

Male

Desert Finch *Rhodospiza obsoleta*

13.5 cm. From Middle East and Central Asia; a few European observations are possible escapes. Resembles Trumpeter Finch but has uniform sandy body, pink, black-and-white pattern on wings, black tail with white edges, black (male) or pale (female and juvenile) lores. Black bill in summer, yellow in winter. Call: vibrant *tvoui* or *drrr*.

pale lores

Female

black lores

black bill

pink-and-white fringes

Male

much white in tail

Pallas's Rosefinch *Carpodacus roseus*

heavily streaked mantle

red face

fine streaks

Female

16 cm. Siberian species; 2 old records from Russia, escapes possible elsewhere. Male: raspberry-red throat and crown speckled with white, extensive red on underparts, narrow white wing-bars. Female: like Common Rosefinch but has reddish face, underparts well-marked with streaks until well behind flanks.

heavily streaked mantle

white spots on throat and forehead

Male

uniform red below

Long-tailed Rosefinch *Uragus sibiricus*

uniform face

very short bill

broad white wing-bars

white cheeks

broad white wing-bars

Female

very long tail

Male

14 cm. Breeds from the Urals to Japan; very rare vagrant or escape in Europe (Denmark and Finland). Small with small round head and short grey bill, white-sided long tail, 2 broad white wing-bars. Male: white speckling on cheeks and crown, pinkish-red breast and rump. Female: uniform face, pink rump, streaked breast and mantle. Call: metallic *pink*.

(Eurasian) Bullfinch *Pyrrhula pyrrhula*

black cap

white wing-bar

pinkish-red

bluish-black

short thick black bill

Male

white rump

greyish-pink below

Female

IDENTIFICATION
16 cm. Rotund silhouette, large head and thick neck, black cap continuing onto face; short thick black bill; grey mantle, broad dirty white wing-bar on black wing; all-black tail, black undertail-coverts with white rump very visible in flight. Underparts pinkish-red (male) or pinkish-buff (female and juvenile). Juvenile on fledging: uniform buff head, buff wing-bar. **VOICE** Call: falling plaintive *tiu*. Slow song incorporating the call on various tones. **HABITAT** Bushes and undergrowth, deciduous and conifer woods and forests, orchards; parks and gardens in winter; may come to bird tables.

Juvenile

Azores Bullfinch *Pyrrhula murina*

IDENTIFICATION 17 cm. Like a female Eurasian Bullfinch (and long thought to be a subspecies of this) but has greyish wing-bar, brownish-grey mantle, pale but not white rump, and larger bill. **VOICE** Call like that of Bullfinch. **HABITAT** Endemic to the indigenous wet forests of São Miguel island in the Azores. Locally called Priolo.

thick bill

grey wing-bar

beige rump

Hawfinch *Coccothraustes coccothraustes*

hazelnut head

black mask

black secondaries

Male

enormous pink bill

short tail with white tip

grey secondaries

grey neck

Female

IDENTIFICATION
18 cm. Large; big head and massive conical bill, short tail. Dark brown mantle, black wings with white greater coverts, white tips to tail feathers. Secondaries black (male) or grey (female); inner primaries and outer secondaries twisted at tip. Juvenile duller with black spots on breast and belly, pale throat. **VOICE** Call: shrill *sic*. Song very shrill, of similar tone to call. **HABITAT** Mature deciduous forest, particularly of oak or beech; parks and gardens in winter, will come to bird tables.

big yellowish bill

beige mantle streaked black

Corn Bunting *Emberiza calandra*

big head

heavily streaked below

pink legs

IDENTIFICATION
18 cm. Large, dull plumage without any hint of yellow, rather indistinct.
Brown, buff and white; striped above and streaked below. Big head, finely streaked throat and cheeks, diffuse pale supercilium. Yellowish bill with dark tip, pink legs. **VOICE** Call: high-pitched *pit*. Song: a rising, accelerating jingle (likened to jingling keys). Sings from a perch such as a bush or fence post. **HABITAT** Lowland agricultural areas; steppe, meadows, crops, scrub.

Yellowhammer *Emberiza citrinella*

IDENTIFICATION
16 cm. Yellowish
plumage and bright
rufous rump. Male:
yellow head, dark
edge to cheeks,
sometimes has reddish median crown-stripe
and malar-stripe. Dense rufous stripes on
olive breast, more sparse on yellow flanks.
Female: duller, striped head washed with
yellow, rufous rump (grey-brown in Cirl
Bunting). Black tail with white outer edges.
Juvenile is more streaked, yellowish below,
distinctive rufous rump. **VOICE** Call: *tzip*, *tiu*.
Song: phrase of rising notes, the last deeper
and longer, *ti-ti-ti-ti-ti-ti-ti-ti-ti tuuu* (rendered
as 'a-little-bit-of-bread-and-no-cheese').
HABITAT Sedentary in farmland (meadows or
crops) with hedgerows, alpine meadows,
other bushy environments.

Female
yellow wash
on face
striped flanks
yellow
head
streaked
rufous rump
rufous
breast
reddish rump
Male
white sides to tail

Cirl Bunting *Emberiza cirlus*

IDENTIFICATION
16 cm. Striking
yellow face pattern
and grey-brown
rump. Male: pale
yellow head marked
with blackish lines; black streaks on crown
and black bib. Olive upper breast, rufous
spots on upper flanks, lower flanks finely
streaked. Female: olive-brown mantle striped
with black, rufous shoulders but grey-brown
rump, very pale yellow face, olive-grey
cheeks and breast. Juvenile is buff-coloured,
heavily streaked below. **VOICE** Call: a short
tzip similar to call of Song Thrush. Song: a
monotone series of notes repeated for a few
seconds *zi-zi-zi-zi-zi-zi-zi-zi...* **HABITAT**
Sedentary in semi-open environments of
warmer climates, hedgerows, crops, parks
and gardens; may come to bird tables in
winter, especially in the north of its range.
Confined to the south-west in Britain.

Female
fairly uniform
yellowish face
streaked
olive rump
black-and-
yellow mask
olive
rump
olive
breast
Male

Ortolan Bunting *Emberiza hortulana*

olive-grey head

yellowish eye-ring

Male

yellow moustache

reddish-olive rump

pink bill

fine streaks

Juvenile

IDENTIFICATION 16 cm. Ash-grey head and breast with pale yellow throat and moustache. Orange-rufous belly; brown mantle streaked black, grey-brown rump; black tail with white outer edges. Narrow yellowish eye-ring, pink bill with small dark tip. Female a little duller with streaked crown and breast. Juvenile has cream-coloured more streaked underparts, particularly breast and flanks. **VOICE** Call: *tseu, tsip*. Song varies geographically; some birds give a repeated note for 1 or 2 seconds with or without a deeper terminal note, *ti-ti-ti-ti-ti-ti-ti-ti tu*. **HABITAT** Farmland, calcareous grasslands and steppe with bushes, sunny and dry foothills, vineyards and hedgerows in cultivated areas. A summer migrant to Europe.

beige crown

grey neck

rufous belly

black-and-white mask

Female

reddish rump

Male

Rock Bunting *Emberiza cia*

IDENTIFICATION 16 cm. Resembles Cirl Bunting but head grey with black mask, only slightly streaked rufous rump; grey lesser coverts, grey bill with black tip, pink legs; female duller than male; juvenile dull and streaked. White sides to tail. **VOICE** Call: sharp, dry *tic*. Song: chirping reminiscent of *Sylvia* warbler. **HABITAT** Bushy areas on calcareous soils with short vegetation and rocky outcrops; alpine meadows, limestone plateaus, sunny mountainsides.

(Common) Reed Bunting *Emberiza schoeniclus*

white moustache · slim black bill · white collar

rufous lesser coverts

Male

IDENTIFICATION 16 cm. Long white-sided tail, grey rump, brown mantle striped black. Male: extensive black crown and bib (with pale fringes in winter), white moustache and collar. Female: dark cheeks, buff supercilium, black malar-stripe, streaked breast; pale zone in centre of streaked crown; finely streaked flanks. All plumages have rufous lesser underwing-coverts; often has pale 'braces' on back. Dark legs, black bill, upper mandible has straight upper edge. **VOICE** Call: plaintive *tsili*. Song: short trill followed by 2 or 3 chirped notes, *tririri tsiai piu*. **HABITAT** Reedbeds particularly with *Phragmites*, with or without bushes; also stubble, ploughed fields, ditches and occasionally gardens in winter.

bigger rounded bill

Male ssp. *caspius*

black-and-cream stripes on mantle

cream moustache and supercilium

grey rump

Female

'Thick-billed' Reed Bunting
Emberiza schoeniclus witherbyi

Plumage identical to that of nominate race but this race differs in bill shape, which is larger with convex (not straight) ridge to upper mandible. **VOICE** Similar. **HABITAT** As Common Reed Bunting. A rare bird, supposedly sedentary, occurring in Mediterranean reedbeds in S France and Spain.

thick bill, convex ridge to upper mandible

Male ssp. *witherbyi*

Black-headed Bunting *Emberiza melanocephala*

diffuse streaks

slightly streaked

Female

black hood

reddish mantle

bright yellow

Male

no white on tail

IDENTIFICATION
17 cm. Large bunting with black hood, uniform chestnut mantle, bright yellow underparts including undertail-coverts. Rufous rump and long black tail without white sides. Female: uniform buff head, finely streaked crown, well-defined border between cheek and throat; diffusely streaked mantle; creamy to yellowish underparts, bright yellow undertail-coverts; pale eye-ring. Juvenile: as female. **VOICE** Call: nasal *dzit*, *tchuip*. Song: short plaintive, descending, fluty phrases. **HABITAT** Dry open environments, short calcareous grassland with a few bushes.

prominent streaking

streaks

Female

yellow collar

Male

reddish head and bib

yellow rump

Red-headed Bunting *Emberiza bruniceps*

16 cm. Rare vagrant from Central Asian steppes. Very similar to Black-headed Bunting but male has reddish head and thinner bill; female identical except for more clearly streaked mantle, less clearly streaked crown and diffuse border between cheek and throat. Call: as that of Black-headed Bunting.

Pallas's Reed Bunting *Emberiza pallasi*

thin
pointed bill

14 cm. Rare Siberian vagrant to Europe. Similar to Reed
Bunting but clearly smaller and slimmer, more pointed bill with
pink lower mandible, brown-grey and not reddish lesser wing-
coverts in first-winter. Malar-stripe does not reach bill, very
obvious pale 'braces' on back, flanks unstreaked or nearly so.
Pale rump. Call: *pseoo; tslip* on taking flight.

Male

straight ridge
to upper
mandible

Female

pale rump

pale lower
mandible

grey lesser
coverts

orange
bill with
black tip

First-winter

streaked
rump

streaked
flanks

Lapland Bunting *Calcarius lapponicus*

IDENTIFICATION
16 cm. In winter
has dull
streaked
plumage except
for broad rufous
fringes to greater coverts and tertials.
'Open' face, cream, with dark crown and
outline to rear cheek, male has rufous
nape, buff breast and flanks with diffuse
black streaking, black malar-stripe. Pale
brown mantle and rump streaked black.
Discreet on the ground, walks in grass.
VOICE Flight call: short trill, *prrrt,* and
more musical *chu.* **HABITAT** Short grass,
grassy saltmarsh, tidal wrack, grassy
dunes, coastal meadows. Breeds in
wet bushy upland areas and moors
and in tundra.

reddish nape

Breeding male

black
bib

reddish
nape

buff
cheeks and
supercilium

pale
lores

Winter

Snow Bunting *Plectrophenax nivalis*

chestnut cheek

streaked brown mantle

Male ssp. *insulae*

black-and-white wings

white face

short yellow bill

cream-and-black mantle

Male ssp. *nivalis*

black-and-white tail

brown mantle

broad reddish edges to scapulars

buff mantle

little white

Female ssp. *nivalis*

white head

black bill

white rump

Female ssp. *insulae*

Breeding male

IDENTIFICATION
17 cm. Brown and sandy-coloured body, black-and-white wings. Black tail with a white base. Plain whitish face, buff on rear-cheek, forehead and crown, duller colours in female. Short yellow bill, black eye. Wings differ according to sex: male has white inner primaries with black tips, totally white wing-coverts (adult) or with black tips (first-winter); female has black primaries and black base to greater coverts. Male is whiter than female, adults whiter than juveniles of same sex. **VOICE** Typical call: short musical trill *tiriri*; also *piu*. **HABITAT** Gregarious in winter; dunes, foreshore, areas of short maritime grass.

CONFUSION SPECIES

Snowfinch (p. 384)

Skylark (p. 263)

Rustic Bunting *Emberiza rustica*

IDENTIFICATION
15 cm. Short crest at top of white nape, sometimes erect. The chestnut bib extends to the flanks as spots. Black cheeks with white spot at rear, broad white supercilium behind eye, wide black bands on sides of crown. Striped chestnut mantle, rufous rump. Pointed bill with pink lower mandible, pink legs. **VOICE** Call: sharp *zit*. **HABITAT** Wet scrub and forests.

short crest
pale central crown-stripe
white rear-cheek spot
First-winter male
diffuse large reddish streaks

black-and-white head
Breeding male
large reddish arrowmarks

Little Bunting *Emberiza pusilla*

IDENTIFICATION
14 cm. Resembles a small Reed Bunting but has different head pattern. Reddish cheeks and lores, supercilium white behind eye, reddish in front of eye. Narrow white eye-ring. Black bill with straight culmen, pink legs. Thin black streaks on flanks. **VOICE** Call: short, very sharp *tic*. **HABITAT** Open forest, clearings, near water.

cream eye-ring
reddish face
black edge to cheek
streaked flanks

greyish rump
pale lores
reddish cheek

Yellow-breasted Bunting *Emberiza aureola*

yellow crown-stripe

yellow lores

black-streaked mantle

black streaks

Female

black head

Breeding male

black collar

bright yellow

IDENTIFICATION
15 cm. Yellow below, thin black streaks on flanks, brown mantle heavily streaked black, streaked reddish rump. Median and lesser wing-coverts whitish in juvenile male. Pale cheek with dark border and no malar-stripe. Pointed bill with straight culmen, pink legs. **VOICE** Call: very shrill short *pit.* **HABITAT** Bushes near water, marshes.

Pine Bunting *Emberiza leucocephalus*

Female

white rear-cheek patch

white fringes

reddish rump

reddish streaks

rufous head

white cheek bordered black

reddish rump

Breeding male

16 cm. Siberian counterpart of Yellowhammer but has no yellow in the plumage and bright rufous rump. Female very similar to that species but no hint of yellow, white primary fringes. Male: reddish throat and supercilium, white cheek with a black border, white crown with thin black borders; reddish bib continuous with reddish streaks of flanks. Call: as Yellowhammer. Very rare winter vagrant, in flocks of other buntings.

Cretzschmar's Bunting *Emberiza caesia*

IDENTIFICATION
15 cm. Very similar to Ortolan Bunting but reddish rump, male has rusty-orange not straw-coloured throat and moustache; bluer-grey on the head. Female duller than male, with streaked breast. Juvenile very difficult to separate from Ortolan but rump a warmer brown, fringes to wing feathers redder. **VOICE** Song and call similar to those of Ortolan. **HABITAT** Dry grassy, rocky areas with bushes.

bluish-grey head

reddish throat and moustache

Male

reddish rump

streaked crown

fine streaks **Female**

reddish rump

diffuse pattern

Juvenile

Cinereous Bunting *Emberiza cineracea*

IDENTIFICATION 16 cm. Recalls Ortolan Bunting but has grey bill, slightly streaked mantle, no brown coloration. Male: greenish-grey head, pale yellow throat and moustache, yellow wash on face, grey wash on breast and flanks and white belly (ssp. *cineracea*, Lesbos and W Turkey) or with pale yellow wash (ssp. *semenowi*, Middle East). Juvenile very uniform, grey bill. **VOICE** Clear *tchrip* or chirped *tchuilp*, as Cretzschmar's Bunting. **HABITAT** Poorly vegetated rocky hillsides.

grey bill

fine streaks

Juvenile ssp. *semenowi*

yellow head

Male ssp. *semenowi*

grey bill

yellow belly

Male ssp. *cineracea*

grey breast

VAGRANT BUNTINGS Asian species, and one African, that occur very rarely on migration, especially in autumn when they are difficult to identify, as they very much resemble European buntings in first-year plumage.

Chestnut Bunting *Emberiza rutila*

traces of red

bright reddish rump

First-winter male

pale face

yellow belly

reddish upperparts

yellow belly

Breeding male

streaked reddish rump

Juvenile

yellowish belly

heavily streaked

15 cm. Breeds in E Siberia. Male unmistakable. Female: brown upperparts streaked black, rufous rump, yellowish underparts with a white chin, black streaks on breast and flanks. First-year male with a few reddish feathers on crown, cheeks and breast. Pointed bill with pink base to lower mandible. Very little white in outer tail feathers. Call: sharp *zic* like Little Bunting's.

Black-faced Bunting *Emberiza spodocephala*

grey head

Male

blackish face

black streaks

heavily streaked mantle

Female

greyish head

black streaks

15 cm. Siberian species. Male: dark grey head and breast, diffuse black loral zone and chin, pale yellow belly with black streaks on flanks; brown mantle with black stripes. First-winter: yellowish face, dark malar-stripe and bib of dark stripes on breast. Dull brownish-grey rump. Pink base to bill. Call: sharp *zit*.

Yellow-browed Bunting *Emberiza chrysophrys*

15 cm. Siberian species. Recalls Rustic Bunting but has thin
black streaks on breast and flanks, and yellow supercilium.
Rufous rump, black crown with white nape, pale pink legs.
Female like male but browner cheek. Call: short *zit*. A few
European records (Britain, France, Sweden).

black cheek with
white spot
yellow
supercilium

Male

white spot on rear cheek

yellow
supercilium

Female

black
malar-
stripe

black streaks

Grey-necked Bunting *Emberiza buchanani*

15 cm. Migrant of Central Asian origin,
with records from Germany, Norway,
Sweden, Finland and the Netherlands.
Very similar to Cretzschmar's Bunting but
lacks grey breast-band; moustache and
chin yellowish (not rusty); long pointed
bill, reddish scapulars contrast with
greyish mantle, grey rump; tertials dark
with reddish-brown fringes of uniform
width, without the typical step of other
buntings. Female similar but duller.

tertials with
regular fringes

rufous
scapulars

long bright
pink bill

grey rump

Female

rufous
scapulars

pink bill

tertials with
regular fringes

Male

Chestnut-eared Bunting *Emberiza fucata*

Juvenile

buff supercilium

large black streaks

rufous cheeks

reddish
shoulders

bib of black
streaks

Male

streaked rump

15 cm. East Asian species; very rare vagrant with 1 autumn record in Scotland. Resembles Little Bunting but reddish-chestnut cheek (darker), buff supercilium and submoustachial-stripe, black malar line joins a 'bib' of black streaks, with a reddish wash below the pectoral band; larger bill with dark grey upper and pink lower mandibles; rufous lesser coverts, streaked rufous rump. Female similar but duller. Call: explosive *pzic*.

House Bunting *Emberiza sahari*

ill-defined
supercilium

grey head

dark lores

rufous
upperparts

Male

reddish belly

brown head

slightly streaked
mantle

bicoloured bill

rufous wings

Female

14 cm. A common species in North Africa, recently observed in the south of Spain. Grey head and neck with streaked 'bib', dark eye-stripe and streaked crown, almost uniform reddish-brown mantle and rusty-buff belly; pink lower mandible, pale grey moustache. Female duller and more uniform. Call: chirped *dvuit* or melancholic *djuou*.

VAGRANT NEARCTIC PASSERINES Many species of North American passerines have been recorded in Europe, mainly in the autumn, generally after strong Atlantic depressions that take them off their normal migration route. Very rare, most records are from western Europe, especially Britain and Ireland, with the majority in September and October; a few arrive in May and June. Many belong to the American wood-warbler family, the Parulidae. All species of American passerines that have occurred in Europe are included here.

Philadelphia Vireo *Vireo philadelphicus*

13.5 cm. Small grey-headed vireo with olive mantle and yellow underparts, black eye with narrow, dark eye-stripe and white supercilium, white crescent below eye; short bill. A few records from the Azores and Britain.

White-eyed Vireo *Vireo griseus*

13 cm. Black lores contrasting with yellow supercilium, yellow spectacles around grey (young) or white (adult) eye, grey neck and olive crown; olive back, yellow flanks and 2 narrow white wing-bars. Several autumn records from the Azores.

Yellow-throated Vireo *Vireo flavifrons*

14 cm. Bright, large-headed vireo. Bright yellow face and breast, black lores and yellow spectacles. Olive upperparts, grey wings with 2 white wing-bars. Call: descending trill. Recorded in Britain and Germany.

Blue-headed Vireo *Vireo solitarius*

14 cm. As Yellow-throated Vireo but dark grey head, white spectacles, grey back, yellowish flanks. Has a double white wing-bar. Call similar. Not as yet recorded in Europe, but possible.

Red-eyed Vireo *Vireo olivaceus*

15 cm. Recalls a *Sylvia* warbler. Ashy-grey
crown, white supercilium with black
margins. Olive-brown above, white below.
Thicker bill than that of a warbler, with
slightly hooked tip. Juvenile has brown
iris, adult red. Discreet, rarely leaving
cover, slow movements. Call: nasal trailing
craiai. The most frequent vireo in Europe.

Ovenbird *Seiurus aurocapilla*

15 cm. Small warbler, often on the
ground, unobtrusive. Brown above, white
below with black spots, uniform face
with narrow white eye-ring, orange
centre to crown with black borders. Call:
chip. Recorded in Britain, Ireland,
Norway and Azores.

Northern Waterthrush
Parkesia noveboracensis

15 cm. Dark brown above, very long
white supercilium, white underparts
striped black. Resembles a small thrush
but when near water can recall a small
dipper. Yellow wash to supercilium and
breast, black spots on throat. Often bobs
its short tail whilst walking upright like a
pipit. Call: *tzinc*. Recorded from Britain,
Ireland and Norway.

Louisiana Waterthrush
Parkesia motacilla

15 cm. Very similar to Northern
Waterthrush but plain throat, prominent
white supercilium and less dense, more
diffuse streaks on underparts; thicker
bill. One record from the Canaries.

Common Yellowthroat *Geothlypis trichas*

13 cm. Very discreet, rarely leaving low
dense cover. Uniform olive-brown above,
brown flanks, yellowish undertail-coverts,
yellow throat sharply bordered with
brown, trace of dark grey mask in young
male. Rounded tail, pale legs. Recorded
from Britain and Iceland.

Tennessee Warbler *Oreothlypis peregrina*

12 cm. Small warbler with pointed bill,
fairly nondescript. Dull grey plumage with
olive mantle and yellow undertail-
coverts, dark eye-stripe, slightly streaked
grey flanks. No white, either in tail or
wings. Call: single *chip*. Recorded in
Britain, Azores, Faeroes and Iceland.

Golden-winged Warbler *Vermivora chrysoptera*

12 cm. Small warbler with pointed bill,
ashy-grey with black cheek surrounded
with white, extensive black 'bib', bright
yellow crown and wing-coverts. White
corners to tail. Call: harsh *chic*. Recorded
in the Azores and Britain.

Blue-winged Warbler *Vermivora cyanoptera*

12 cm. Very similar to Golden-winged
Warbler but olive above, bright yellow
below except white under tail, blue-grey
wing-coverts with 2 white wing-bars,
narrow black eye-stripe. Recorded in the
Azores and Ireland.

Black-and-white Warbler *Mniotilta varia*

13 cm. Black-and-white striped, unmistakable. Moves along branches and twigs in similar way to nuthatch. Male more marked on face and flanks than female. Call: a dry *tik*. Recorded in Britain and Iceland; annual in the Azores.

Northern Parula *Setophaga americana*

11 cm. Small, reminiscent of *Phylloscopus* warbler; blue-grey head, greenish-brown mantle, grey wings with 2 white wing-bars, yellow throat and breast. Black lores, white line above and below eye. White belly, white corners to tail. Slim bill, black legs with yellow feet. Call: *chip*, sharp descending *tsiip* in flight.

Black-throated Blue Warbler *Setophaga caerulescens*

13.5 cm. Sexes different. Male: blue above including wings and tail, square white patch at base of primaries, black of face continues along flanks, white centre to breast, belly and undertail-coverts. Female: uniform olive-brown above, traces of cream supercilium and moustache almost encircling darker cheeks; uniform wings, dusky underparts. Call: harsh *stip*. Recorded in the Azores and Iceland.

Yellow Warbler *Setophaga petechia*

12 cm. *Sylvia* warbler silhouette but with
short tail. Yellow underparts including
undertail-coverts, olive-green above,
uniform face with contrasting black eye;
young females have paler underparts
and olive head. Black wings and tail with
yellow fringes. Dark bill with pink base to
lower mandible, pink legs. Call: soft *tsip*.

Hooded Warbler *Setophaga citrina*

13.5 cm. Uniform olive above, uniform
lemon-yellow below, olive head with yellow
face and cheeks, dark around lores, hints
of black surround to cheeks in young
male. Long tail with white outer edges.
Call: *tiip*. Recorded in Azores and Britain.

Wilson's Warbler *Cardellina pusilla*

12 cm. Small and rounded, totally lemon-
yellow below and olive above, small short
bill, no yellow or white in tail. Male has
small black cap, not reaching eye.
Uniform yellow face with olive cheeks.
Call: harsh *jimp*. Recorded twice in Britain
(October 1985 and October 2015).

Canada Warbler *Cardellina canadensis*

13.5 cm. Uniform blue-grey above,
lemon-yellow below, white eye-ring and
large yellow supercilium in front of eye.
Grey streaks on breast, white undertail-
coverts. Yellow legs, no wing-bar and no
white on tail. Call: short *tiup*. Records
from the Azores, Iceland and Ireland.

Blackpoll Warbler *Setophaga striata*

14 cm. Lightly streaked above and below, orangey legs. Juvenile: olive-green mantle finely streaked brown; yellow-washed breast with diffuse streaks; suggestion of yellowish supercilium, dark lores. Two slender white wing-bars, white spots towards tips of flight feathers. Call: harsh *tsip* and loud *smac*.

Cerulean Warbler *Setophaga cerulea*

12 cm. Male is blue and white, unmistakable. Short tail with small white subterminal spots in corners. Juvenile: bluish-olive above, without streaks (unique in the group); pale yellow supercilium, throat and breast, 2 white wing-bars. One record from Iceland, October 1997.

Bay-breasted Warbler *Setophaga castanea*

14 cm. Uniform yellow-olive mantle, dark lores and indistinct eye-ring. Two white wing-bars, small white corners to tail, yellowish undertail-coverts (white in Blackpoll Warbler), greenish sides to neck (grey in Blackpoll Warbler). Grey legs without any yellow. Call: clear *chip*. Recorded in Britain (October 1995).

Pine Warbler *Setophaga pinus*

14 cm. Juvenile is almost uniform mouse-grey. Uniform above, pale grey below, 2 narrow white wing-bars, thin white eye-ring. Large head with thick bill is reminiscent of Garden Warbler. White corners to the tail. Adult breeding: uniform olive above and yellow below with diffuse streaking on flanks. Call: dull, sharp *chip*. Not yet observed in Europe, but could occur.

Chestnut-sided Warbler *Setophaga pensylvanica*

13 cm. Juvenile: greenish-yellow above, slightly streaked on mantle; uniform pale grey lores and cheeks with thin white eye-ring; characteristic contrast between entirely greenish-yellow crown and grey cheeks. Black wings with 2 white wing-bars; white corners to tail. Winter adult male: chestnut flanks. Call: *chip* and buzzing *jrrt* in flight. Recorded twice in Britain (September 1985 and October 1995).

Black-throated Green Warbler *Setophaga virens*

13 cm. Green mantle, yellow on head surrounds dark cheek, white underparts with large diffuse black spots on flanks. Two white wing-bars. Often appears to have a large head. Call: a harsh *tsic*, as many Nearctic warblers. Records from Germany and Iceland; annual in the Azores.

Blackburnian Warbler *Setophaga fusca*

13 cm. Grey mantle streaked black with cream braces, grey head with pronounced yellowish supercilium, yellow crescent under eye, grey cheek surrounded with yellow; yellowish breast and belly, grey-striped flanks. White outer tail feathers and 2 white wing-bars. Similar to young Cerulean Warbler but has streaked back; and to young Blackpoll Warbler but has different head pattern. Call: a harsh *tsic*. Records from Britain and Iceland.

Magnolia Warbler *Setophaga magnolia*

13 cm. Juvenile has unique plumage combination: ash-grey head, olive-green mantle, yellow band on rump, lemon-yellow underparts with large diffuse spotting on flanks. Two thin white wing-bars, white vent, narrow white eye-ring. White in tail forms a subterminal transverse bar. Call: discreet *vint*. Records from the Azores, Britain and Iceland.

American Redstart *Setophaga ruticilla*

13.5 cm. Long tail is often lifted and flicked, marked with an inverted black T with yellow base, reminiscent of a wheatear. In autumn has ash-grey head, narrow white spectacles, greyish-olive mantle, white underparts, yellow patch on sides of breast at the 'shoulder'; adults have yellow base to secondaries. In breeding plumage male is black and dark orange.

Yellow-rumped Warbler *Setophaga coronata*

14 cm. Striped brown-grey above, heavily grey-streaked below with yellow mark under 'shoulders'. Well-defined supercilium and black legs. Large wide corners to tail and narrow yellow rump particularly evident in flight. Fond of junipers and conifers. Records from Britain and Iceland, annual in the Azores. Call: a harsh *tchic*.

Cape May Warbler *Setophaga tigrina*

13 cm. Uniform plumage, ill-defined pale supercilium, dark lores, uniform grey mantle and greenish rump, narrow diffuse wing-bars, diffuse grey streaking on breast and yellow spot on sides of neck. Two British records (June 1977 and October 2013).

Palm Warbler *Setophaga palmarum*

14 cm. Uniform plumage, long yellowish-grey supercilium and black lores, bright yellow undertail-coverts. Slightly streaked back, very uniform wings, yellow rump and white corners to tail visible in flight. Rufous streaks on flanks and rufous crown in breeding plumage. Recorded in Iceland (October 1997).

Prairie Warbler *Setophaga discolor*

12 cm. Yellow with greyish (female) or yellow (male) head with paler area around eye, diffuse black streaks on flanks, traces of orange on olive mantle. Two diffuse yellow wing-bars, white corners to the tail. One record from the Azores in October 2012.

Yellow-throated Warbler *Setophaga dominica*

14 cm. Grey, black and white with extensive lemon-yellow 'bib', long white supercilium, white crescent under eye, long slender bill. Two white wing-bars, large black streaks on flanks, grey mantle. White patch behind cheek on neck. One record from the Azores in October 2013.

Scarlet Tanager *Piranga olivacea*

17 cm. Unifrom olive above, yellow below, uniform face with round black eye and thick grey to yellow bill with dark culmen. Wings and tail darker than body, grey legs. Male has black wings in winter; bright red body in summer. Call: two-toned, *chic-brrr*. Recorded in Britain, France, Iceland and Ireland.

Summer Tanager *Piranga rubra*

19 cm. Larger than Scarlet Tanager, longer entirely pale bill, orangey-olive plumage in autumn, especially on tail and tertials. Adult male is all red. Call: *pitoc* in a falling series. Records from the Azores and Britain.

Bobolink *Dolichonyx oryzivorus*

18 cm. Like a large sparrow with pointed pink bill. Autumn: tawny head with lateral black lines on crown, pale lores, uniform nape; streaked mantle with pale braces, uniform buff rump obvious in flight. Tawny underparts with fine streaks on flanks. Short tail with narrow very pointed tail feathers. Pink legs. Call: soft *tcheuc*; musical *boinc* in flight.

Rose-breasted Grosbeak *Pheucticus ludovicianus*

20 cm. Big and thickset with large head and massive pink bill with grey tip. Black-brown cheeks and crown, large white supercilium and moustache, dark brown mantle striped black. Tawny below with thin brown streaks on flanks (male) or breast and flanks striped (female). Red (male) or yellow (female) underwing-coverts. Call: rising *iic*; a *ouic* in flight.

Brown-headed Cowbird *Molothrus ater*

19 cm. All-dark bird with finch-like conical bill. Adult male: black with brown head. Female: brown above, buff below, brown undertail-coverts. Black legs and grey bill. Young spotted on mantle and breast, like young Common Rosefinch. Call: when perched a harsh rising rattle, *siiititi* in flight. Recorded in Britain and Norway.

Evening Grosbeak *Hesperiphona vespertina*

17 cm. Large Nearctic grosbeak, with massive pale yellow bill. Male: brown head and mantle, yellow forehead, black-and-white wings with yellow scapulars, all-black tail. Female: sandy-grey head with thin black line around bill and eyes, less white in wings, white in tail. Varied calls including a shrill loud *tiu*. Very rare vagrant recorded in Norway and Scotland.

Male

Female

Yellow-headed Blackbird *Xanthocephalus xanthocephalus*

23 cm. New World icterid with thick black conical bill. Male: black with yellow head and breast, white primary coverts, black mask in front of eye. Female: brown with diffuse supercilium and dull yellow 'bib', entirely brown wings. Recorded in the Netherlands and Iceland; other records are possible escapes.

Male

Female

Grey Catbird *Dumetella carolinensis*

black cap

coal grey

rufous
undertail-
coverts

21 cm. Appears like a Nightingale in Blackcap's plumage. Dark grey plumage with black cap and rufous undertail-coverts. Slim, long black tail. Usually stays hidden in dense vegetation. A few records from Belgium, Britain, Germany and Ireland.

Northern Mockingbird *Mimus polyglottos*

21 cm. Smaller than Brown Thrasher; grey and white with black legs, dark eye (juvenile), 2 thin wing-bars, dark eye-stripe, mouse-grey upperparts and long black tail with white sides, sometimes raised when bird is on ground; white bases to primaries visible in flight. Recorded in Britain, the Canaries and the Netherlands.

Brown Thrasher *Toxostoma rufum*

24 cm. Large, with long reddish tail, long downcurved bill, rufous above, 2 black-and-white wing-bars. Well streaked with black below, yellow iris on pale face. Call: harsh *tchaik*. A bird overwintered in Britain during the 1966/67 winter, and a vagrant in Germany in 1836.

Baltimore Oriole *Icterus galbula*

22 cm. Can appear similar to Golden
Oriole, slim with pointed bill, yellow
colour on breast, long orange tail. Grey
head, streaked grey back, black wings
with double white wing-bars. Male totally
orangey-yellow below, orangey head.
Flight call: *vit*. Recorded from the Azores,
Britain and the Netherlands.

Lark Sparrow *Chondestes grammacus*

16 cm. Characteristic head pattern with
black-bordered chestnut cheeks, white
spot on rear cheek, white spectacles,
large white submoustachial-stripe, black
malar line, chestnut crown with black
median crown-stripe; black spot in
centre of otherwise uniform breast, long
black tail with brown centre and large
white corners. Two European records,
both from Britain (1981 and 1991).

Eastern Towhee *Pipilo erythrophthalmus*

20 cm. Often on the ground, long tail,
black conical bill, pink legs; Male: Black
head, breast and mantle, extensive
rufous on flanks; black wings with white
primary bases and edge to tertials.
Female: brown replaces black. Call:
harsh *tohi*. One record from Britain
(June 1966).

Indigo Bunting *Passerina cyanea*

13 cm. Small compact bird without distinctive markings when not a male in breeding plumage. Tawny-coloured with blue sheen on lesser coverts in juvenile male. Uniform face, grey bill, double rufous wing-bars, diffuse streaking on breast. Call: *tsic*. Occurs annually in the Azores.

Dark-eyed Junco *Junco hyemalis*

15 cm. Resembles a Chaffinch in shape but is entirely dark grey with white belly, face a little darker; female is browner above. Pink bill with black tip, white sides to tail. Call: *tik*.

Dickcissel *Spiza americana*

16 cm. Resembles a large elongated sparrow; striped mantle, yellow supercilium and breast, large pale bill, rufous shoulders; finely streaked on flanks. Call: dry *chaic*. Recorded in Norway (July) and the Azores (October).

White-throated Sparrow *Zonotrichia albicollis*

17 cm. Well-defined white throat above grey breast, broad white supercilium (bright yellow in front of eye), white median crown-stripe, black sides to crown. Some individuals have tawny stripes on head. Large grey bill, pink legs. Call: *chink*, a *siit* in flight. Habitually recorded in spring in Europe.

White-striped form

Tawny-striped form

White-crowned Sparrow *Zonotrichia leucophrys*

17 cm. Very similar to White-throated Sparrow but thinner, more pointed, orange-pink bill. Juvenile has grey supercilium and throat, brown stripes on head (black-and-white in adult). Call: *pink*, a *siip* in flight. Recorded in Britain, Ireland, France, the Netherlands and Iceland.

Adult

Juvenile

Fox Sparrow *Passerella iliaca*

18 cm. Large, very rufous sparrow with long tail. Bright rufous tail, wings, malar-stripe and heavy rufous streaks below; wide central rufous breast-patch of streaks, lower flanks with dark, fine inverted V markings. Ash-grey supercilium, neck sides and rump. Pink legs, grey-and-yellow bill. Call: loud *smac*. Records from Britain, Estonia, Finland and Iceland.

Song Sparrow *Melospiza melodia*

16 cm. Grey-and-rufous sparrow, broad reddish-brown streaks on breast and flanks, converging into a patch in centre of breast, wide malar bars, grey supercilium and median crown-stripe, rufous around cheek. Reddish fringes to wing and tail feathers, rounded tip to tail. Pink legs, grey bill. Call: *jimp*. Records from Belgium, Britain, the Netherlands and Norway.

Lincoln's Sparrow *Melospiza lincolnii*

14.5 cm. Similar to Song Sparrow but has large grey supercilium, dark rufous crown (which is sometimes erected into short crest) with grey median crown-stripe, finely streaked breast with buff wash, slimmer more pointed bill, Heavily striped rump, no red in grey tail. Call: short *chip*. Two autumn records from the Azores.

Savannah Sparrow *Passerculus sandwichensis*

14 cm. Small, heavily striped blackish-brown above and below, little red coloration, creamy-yellow supercilium in front of eye, creamy median crown-stripe, slightly forked tail. Pink legs, pink-and-grey pointed bill. Call: *stip*, shrill and strident. Recorded in Britain and the Azores.

NEW WORLD WARBLERS IN BREEDING PLUMAGE Very occasionally a vagrant American warbler survives the winter and is observed in the spring, in a plumage that is very rarely seen in Europe, even by the most ardent birdwatcher.

Blackpoll Warbler *Setophaga striata*

14 cm. White cheek with black crown, black streaks above and below, black malar line, double white wing-bar; the legs are the most colourful part of the bird.

Chestnut-sided Warbler *Setophaga pensylvanica*

13 cm. Narrow yellow crown patch, black mask and chestnut flank patch. Black-and-white striped mantle, obviously striped rump, dark legs.

Bay-breasted Warbler *Setophaga castanea*

14 cm. Black face, reddish crown and throat, pale yellow patch on side of neck, pink legs.

Cape May Warbler *Setophaga tigrina*

13 cm. Bright yellow head with orange cheeks and black crown, black eye-line. Yellow underparts streaked black, green mantle with black streaking and bright yellow rump.

Cerulean Warbler *Setophaga cerulea*

12 cm. Characteristic and unique, pale blue colour with black streaking on mantle, black pattern on face and black streaking on flanks. Blackish-grey legs.

Magnolia Warbler *Setophaga magnolia*

13 cm. Black mantle and cheeks, ash-grey crown, white supercilium behind eye. Underparts yellow with heavy black streaks on breast and flanks. Bright yellow rump contrasts with rest of upperparts. Blackish-brown legs.

Index

Photographic credits

t: top, b: bottom, m: middle, l: left, r: right, c: centre

Adam Juan C. 28 b, 49 m, 231 t & m, 276 br, 287 b, 334 bl, 355 m, 390 b. **Agami.nl © Guyt Marc** 75 b. **Al Dhaheri Khalifa Ahmed** 195 br, 212 tr, 254 tr, 337 br. **Alfrey Peter** 64 bl, 69 tg, 212 mr, 355 bl. **Al Hajji Rashed** 104 br, 121 tr, 160 br, 220 br, 291 br, 295 bl, 297 b & m, 303 m, 322 tr, 327 br, 362 br, 363 ml, 367 mr & b, 368 m, 369 t, 385 m. **Alshaheen Omar Khaled** 90 bl, 100 mr & b, 104 m, 128 tl & b, 220 bl, 238 b, 247 bl, 280 br, 291 ml, 292 tl, 297 tr, 318 br, 346 ml. **Al-Sirhan Abdulrahman** 120 ml, 266 br, 281 tr, & ml. **Arlow Steve** 54 ml, 100 ml, 103 ml, 104 bl, 136 tr, 161 tr, 175 tl, 209 m, 252 tr, 318 bl, 323 bl, 325 tl, 328 m, 335 m, 363 br, 379 tl, 413 tr. **Armada Rafael** 53 b, 67 b, 68 bl, 88 b, 116 bl, 122 m, 141 br, 302 mr, 319 m, 323 tl, 344 b, 380 m, 381 t, 385 tr, 389 m, 396 t & m, 401 bl, 416 b, 426 t. **Audevard Aurélien** 6, 7 bl, 8, 9, 10, 11, 12 ml & b, 13, 14 ml & b, 15 c & bl, 16 tr, 17 b, 18 mt, 19 t, 21 t & m, 22 t, mr & b, 23 mr, c & b, 24 m, 25 mr, 26 ml & b, 27 b, 28 t, 29 m & b, 30 mt, 31 tr, 33 t & bl, 37 tr & ml, 38 tm & b, 39 t & b, 40 mr, 43 tr, 44 t & b, 48 t, 49 t, 51 tr & m, 55 b, 58 t, 59 t & bl, 60 tl, 61 bl, 62 b, 65 tr, 66 m, 77 t & b, 79 tl, 81, 83 c & br, 84 tl, ml & b, 85 m & bl, 86 t & m, 87 t & ml, 89 b, 90 m & bl, 91 t, 93 t, 94 tl & b, 97, 98 tr, 104 tl, 106 tl & ml, 108 t, 109 bl & br, 110 t, 111 t, 113 b, 114 bl, 118 t & m, 120 bl, 126 t, 129 tr, & m, 131 mtr, 134 t, 137, 138 t, 139 t, 140 tl & mr, 141 tl, 143 m &b, 144 tl, 148 tl & b, 149, 153 l, 154, 155 m & bl, 156 m, bl & b, 157 m & br, 159 ml & b, 161 b, 162 tr & m, 163 tl & b, 164 tl & b, 165 m & br, 166 t & b, 167 b, 168 m & bl, 169 mr & b, 170 t, 171 m, 172 b, 173 b, 174 t, 175 ml, 176 tl, mr & b, 177 ml & b, 178 t & mr, 180 tr & bl, 181 tl, ml & br, 182 tm, m & br, 183 tl & b, 184 t, 185 t & m, 190 tl, m & b, 192 tl, 193 tr, mr & b, 195 tl, 196 tl, ml & br,198 t, mr bl, 199 br, 201 t, ml & bl, 202 t & m, 203 tr, m & b, 204 b, 205 ml, 206 mr, 207 m & b, 208 bl, 209 bl, 211 t & bl, 212 b & ml, 213 t & bl, 214 t & m, 216 t & bl, 217 b, 227 b, 229 tl, 230 tr & bl, 232 tl & br, 233 tr & ml, 235 tr & m, 236 m & b, 238 m, 242 tl, 246 m, 248 tr, 250 tr, 251 m, 253 t, 254 tl, m & b, 255 tl & m, 256 br, 258 m, 262 t & br, 263 bl, 264 br, 265 t l, 267 b, 269 tl & m, 270 b, 271 tl, 272 t & ml, 274 tr, mr & br, 275 t, mr and br, 276 t, 277 tl & b, 278 tr, m &b, 279 t, 280 t & bl, 281 br, 282 ml & b, 283 tr, m & bl, 285 t, 286 t & m, 287t & mr, 288 t & m, 289, 290 tr &bl, 291 tl & mr, 292 m & bl, 295 t & m, 298 t & m, 299 bl, 300 tr, c & bl, 301 br, 302 bl, 303 tr & b, 304 t, 305 tl, 306 tl & bl, 307 ml, 308 t & m, 311 t, 317 tr & b, 320 ml & bm, 321 b, 323 tr, 324 t & bl, 326, 327 tl & mr, 328 t, 330 m, 332 tl, 333, 334 m, 335 t, 336 tr & bl, 337 tl, 338 tl, 341 tl, 342 t, 343 t bl, 345 bl, 346 t, mr & bl, 347 m, 350 t, ml & ml & b, 353 m & bl, 354 m & b, 356 t, m & bl, 358 t, 362 tr & m, 363 t, mr & bl, 364 ml & br, 367 tr, 368 tl, & br, 369 m, 370 tr, 372 tr, 373 tl, m, bl & br, 374 tr, ml and b, 375 tr, & b, 377 tr, ml & bl, 378 bl, 379 tr & br, 381 b, 382 m, 383 t, 384 tr & bl, 385 tl, 389 t, 390 t & m, 391 t & bl, 392 mr & bl, 393 t, 39(t, bl & br, 396 b, 400 t, 401 tr, 404 tl & b, 406 tr & br, 408 tr & b, 409 t, m & br, 410 tl & m, 411 tl & b, 412 tl & br, 413 mr, 414 tl & bl, 415, 447 (cover). **Aussaguel Christian** 105 tr & bl, 107 mr, 114 tr & m, 117 b, 123 t, 132 bl, 133 mr, 142 tr, 151 tr, 245 bl, 252 tl, 382 bl. **Bacelli Franco** 316 tl. **Balestra Robert** 47 t, 84 tr, 257 tr, 282 tr, 351 bg, 362 tl, 382 br. **Bath Mike** 69 b, 130 br, 174 mr. **Belchev Boris** 261 t. **Berthemy Bruno** 108 b, 111 m, 117 mr, 364 bm. **Besseau Gérard** 223 bl. **Bisetti Jean** 7 t, 12 t, 29 ml, 33 m, 50 t, 60 tr, 99 tl & br, 106 br, 107 t, 113 tl, 115 t, 117 tr, 127 tl, 129 tl, 178 ml, 256 tl & bl, 257 tl, 287 ml , 311 ml, 361 mr, 392 br, 397 tl, 405 tl, 406 tl, 407 ml. **Bloch Cécile** 78 m, 96 mr, 182 tr, 243 b, 351 bm, 376 t. **Bonnet Romain** 50 bl. **Bonser Richard** 31 bl, 37 mr, 38 mg, 55 br, 60 b, 63 bl, 67 t & mr, 68 tl, 145 t, 148 tr, 156 tr, 176 tr, 178 bl, 194 br, 200 b, 205 bl, 206 ml, 216 br, 217 t, 239 tl, 307 tr, 332 bl, 351 tl, 370 b, 394 bl, 399 t. **Bougeard Bernard** 86 br, 96 b, 118 br, 126 mr, 161 tl, 167 tl, 189 tm, 209 t, 224 mr. **Boulanger Julien** 18 tr, 45 t, 47 br, 55 tr, 65 bl, 75 c, 77 ml, 109 tr, 136 br, 164 tr, 173 t, 187 ml & b, 188 bl, 194 t, 203 tl, 204 tl, 222 tr & br, 224 bl, 242 br, 262 bl, 263 tl, 264 tl, 265 tr, 275 ml, 336 tl, 364 mr, 372 ml, 394 tl, 410 bm. **Bouresli Hamad** 105 br, 120 bm, 123 b, 291m, 300 ml, 316 tr & br, 327 bl, 337 bl, 367 ml. **Brandt Thorkil** 331 tr. **Breton G** 225 b. **Buckx Lars** 128 br, 209 br, 322 br, 376 m. **Buysee Didier** 91 br, 112 bl, 272 br. **Cacopardi Saverio** 48 br, 119 tl & mr, 135 ml, 352 br. **Cain Cédric** 414 mr. **Caldas Armando** 311 mr. **Cat Jason Joey** 79 tr, 144 m & bl, 351 br. **Catley Graham** 19 mr, 83 tr, 101 ml & bl, 125 ml, 146 m, 180 tl, 215 tl, 239 tr, ml & b, 272 mr, 273 t & bl, 284 m, 300 br, 325 tr & br, 338 b, 357 br, 371 tr, 413 ml. **Champion Mikael** 70 tl, 237 bl. **Chardon Norbert** 240 br. **Cherrug Stefan** 62 t, 197 br, 221 t. **Collin Didier** 232 tr, 258 b, 360 ml. **Colon Alfredo** 92 t. **Cools Paul** 365 bl. Cordoba Alban 106 tr. **Croset Fabrice** 14 mr, 15 br, 58 b, 87 b, 93 b, 113 tr, 115 b, 133 ml & br, 238 t, 242 tm, 269 br, 270 tl, 311 br, 315 tl, 316 bl, 343 br, 344 tr & ml, 356 br, 365 tr, 403 tr, 405 bl. **D'Arpino Barbara** 366 br. **Dandois Philippe** 139 b, 152 b, 253 bl, 386 m. **Dansette Edouard** 24 t, 82 m, 101 br, 130 tr & mr, 138 bl, 145 bl, 211 br, 213 br, 222 tl & mr, 299 br, 305 bl, 393 br. **Das Deepankar** 386 b. **Daubignard Julien** 21 b, 87 mr, 119 ml, 141 tr, 142 bl, 146 br, 159 mr, 192 ml, 199 tl & m, 249 t, 251 tl, 263 c, 266 tl, 269 tr, 270 tr, 274 bl, 378

tr, 252 br, 257 bl, 278 tr, 307 tl & mr, 313 t, 319 b, 337 tr, 339 t, 340 t & m, 347 b, 357 bl, 369 bl, 400 br, 413 br, 430 m. **Poklen Jeff** 189 m & br, 217 ml, 225 t, 294 tl & b. **Port Christina** 189 tl. **Price Stuart** 226 t & m, 358 mr. **Price William** 136 c, 172 tl. **Pusch Bernhard** 64 tr, 134 bl, 151 tl, 155 tl, 265 br, 304 bl. **Quélennec Thierry** 50 m, 136 tl, 183 ml, 232 bl, 288 b, 290 br, 320 mr, 345 br, 361 t. **Rabby Jean-Marc** 91 bl, 95 ml, 105 tl, 107 bl, 158 bl, 294 tr, 314 ml, 324 br, 392 tl, 395 bm. **Read Marc** 125 mr. **Reeber Sébastien** 17 mr, 18 mb & b, 20 b, 30 br, 32 t, 41 t, 66 b, 86 br, 138 br, 188 tr. **Reed Tom** 189 bl, 215 mr, 401 tl. **Reigada Pepe** 125 b. **Reinink Earl** 366 bl. **Riall Steve** 251 bl, 271 mr, 357 t. **Riou Ghislain** 182 bl. **Rougeron Antoine** 64 br. **Royse Robert** 17 ml, 27 t, 32 b, 34 br, 37 br, 42 b, 46 tl, 54 t, 82 b, 89 t & m, 107 br, 142 br, 179 bl, 194 mr & bl, 195 t, 210 b, 215 ml, 218 tl & b, 221 m, 235 tl, 237 br, 261 bl, 310 tr & br, 348 349 t & m, 359 br, 380 t, 400 tl, 417 bl, 418 br, 419 b, 427, 428, 429 m & b. **Samwald Otto** 48 bl, 69 ml, 70tr, 123 ml, 140 tr, 245 tl, 291 bl, 301 m, 345 tr, 358b, 367 tl, 368 bl. **Sansault Eric** 174 ml. **Scheller Jensen Morten** 329 tl, 408 tl. **Seguin Jean–François** 360 ml. **Selmeczi Kovacs Adam** 240 bl & m, 260 br. **Shiff Yael** 295 br, 302 ml, 325 bl, 362 bl. **Sogaard Hansen Jens** 207 m, 218 tr, 294 ml, 308 b, 340 b, 347 t, 372 br, 418 bl. **Sorensen Helge** 14 t, 15 t & mb, 16, 18 tl, 19 ml & tl, 20 t, 23 ml, 25 t & b, 26 mr, 30 tr & bl, 31 mr, 33 tl & mb, 34 t, mr & bl, 35 m & b, 36 ml, 38 tl & mr, 39 m, 40 t & ml, 44 c, 55 bl, 56 br, 57 b & mr, 82 br, 83 tl, 84 mr, 85 t, 90 t, 93 ml, 99 tr, m & bl, 101 mr, 102 tl, tr & ml, 103 mr, 106 bl, 116 tm, 124 tm, 130 tl & ml, 131 tl, mbl & br, 132 tl, mr & br, 133 bl, 152 t & mr, 153 r, 155 tr & br, 156 br, 157 tr & br, 159 tr, 162 tl & b, 163 tr, 165 t, 166 m, 167 tr & m, 171 br, 177 tr & mr, 180 m & br, 181 bm, 182 tl & mr, 183 tr, 186 mr, 191 bm, 201 br, 219 t, 222 bl, 223 m, 224 b, 241 t, mr & b, 242 tr & bl, 243 tl, 244 t, 245 br, 248 tl & m, 259 t, 262 mr, 264 tr, 270 ml, 283 tm, 286 b, 290 tl, 292 tr, 294 mr, 299 m, 304 br, 305 tr & br, 306 m & br, 320 t, 345 tl, 358 ml, 360 b, 365 t, 366 mr, 371 tl, 372 tl, 373 bm, 375 tl, 381 m, 383 m, 387 tr, 393 bl, 394 tr, 397 tr & m, 398 tl, 399 ml & b, 404 bl, 409 bl, 410 br, 426 b. **Steen E. Jensen** 29 t. **Steffen Benjamin** 69 mr, 70 bl, 231 br, 389 br. **Tempier Jean-Claude CEN-PACA** 119 br. **Tenovuo Jorma** 70 m, 116 tr, 196 mr, 179 bl, 243 tr, 398 br, 411 tr. **Tenovuo Olli** 231 bl. **The Sound Approach © René Pop** 69 tl. **The Tubenoses Project © H. Shirihai** 61 tl, 63 ml, 70 bm & br. **Thonnerieux Yves** 255 b, 388 br. **Trévoux Yves** 339 m. **Tupman Kevin** 92 ml. **Van den Berg Arnoud** 311 bl, 318 t, 320 bl. **Vanhove Frédéric** 68 tr, 170 m, 361 bl. **Van Rossum Rene** 315 b, 342 b, 377 br, 398 mr. **Vaslin Matthieu** 15 mt, 55 c, 80 ml, 135 tl, 151 br, 195 ml, 210 tl, 314 b, 355 t, 372 bl. **Vèque Julien** 132 tr & ml. **Vollot Benjamin** 407 b. **Watson Mike** 424 tl. **Westerbjerg Andersen Michael** 268 bl, 283 br, 293 mr, 402 br. **Whitaker David** 397 b. **White Ian** 96 tr, 140 b, 158 m, 249 bl. **Williams John** 31 br, 246 bl. **Yap Francis** 69 hm. **Yeshwanth H. M.** 105 m. **Zufelt Kirk** 71 t & bl. **Zwiebel Brian** 225 m.